MAKING ORGANIZATIONS COMPETITIVE

RALPH H. KILMANN

INES KILMANN

AND ASSOCIATES

MAKING ORGANIZATIONS COMPETITIVE

ENHANCING NETWORKS AND RELATIONSHIPS ACROSS TRADITIONAL BOUNDARIES

Jossey-Bass Publishers
San Francisco   •   Oxford   •   1991

MAKING ORGANIZATIONS COMPETITIVE
Enhancing Networks and Relationships Across Traditional Boundaries
by Ralph H. Kilmann, Ines Kilmann, and Associates

Copyright © 1991 by: Jossey-Bass Inc., Publishers
350 Sansome Street
San Francisco, California 94104
&
Jossey-Bass Limited
Headington Hill Hall
Oxford OX3 0BW

Library of Congress Cataloging-in-Publication Data

Making organizations competitive : enhancing networks and
  relationships across traditional boundaries / [edited by] Ralph H.
  Kilmann, Ines Kilmann and associates. — 1st ed.
      p.   cm.
  Includes bibliographical references and index.
  ISBN 1-55542-285-3
    1. Competition.   2. Organizational effectiveness.   I. Kilmann,
  Ralph H.   II. Kilmann, Ines.
  HD41.M3   1991
  658.4′02—dc20   90-40516
                                                              CIP

Manufactured in the United States of America

The paper in this book meets the guidelines for
permanence and durability of the Committee on
Production Guidelines for Book Longevity of the
Council on Library Resources.

JACKET DESIGN BY WILLI BAUM

FIRST EDITION

Code 9083

THE JOSSEY-BASS MANAGEMENT SERIES

CONSULTING EDITORS
ORGANIZATIONS AND MANAGEMENT

WARREN BENNIS
UNIVERSITY OF SOUTHERN CALIFORNIA

RICHARD O. MASON
SOUTHERN METHODIST UNIVERSITY

IAN I. MITROFF
UNIVERSITY OF SOUTHERN CALIFORNIA

CONTENTS

ix

To Donald F. Fink and Benjamin C. Robertson,
whose manner of caring and giving
has no equal

PREFACE

Never before in the history of the world have so many organizations had to question their very purposes, strategies, structures, and cultures as have had to recently. Currently, one of the major responsibilities of senior executives is to revitalize their organizations for a competitive world. What made for success in yesterday's protected domestic marketplace will not lead to success in today's competitive global economy. In a regulated environment, organizations can live with inefficiency for some time; in a competitive environment, inefficient organizations die very quickly.

This book provides up-to-date, state-of-the-art knowledge on what makes an organization more competitive. By "competitive" we mean satisfying all internal and external stakeholders over an extended period of time. Included in this focus are all the traditional management levers *inside* the organization — such as revitalizing the culture, skills, teams, strategies, structures, and rewards that make up the organization's internal systems. Of particular interest are all the cooperative efforts that cut *across* the traditional boundaries of an organization — such as union–management, government–business, university–industry, and international experiments, along with mergers, acquisitions, and joint ventures to capture economies of scale and new technological advantages. These "outside" arrangements and relationships extend the reach of the organization around the globe. In essence, this book concerns *all* the processes and structures, both human and technological, both inside organizations and across organizational boundaries, that can make an organization more competitive.

Background of the Book

From October 19 to 22, 1988, the Program in Corporate Culture at the Joseph M. Katz Graduate School of Business at the University of Pittsburgh sponsored a conference on making organizations more competitive. The objective of the conference was to find the experts—across different disciplines and functional areas of specialization—who would be willing to contribute their latest thinking on this important topic. A summary of what transpired before, during, and after the conference illustrates how an orchestrated approach can produce a comprehensive volume of information on such a far-reaching subject.

The Program in Corporate Culture was founded in September 1983 to develop new knowledge on the impact of culture on organizational success and to disseminate this knowledge so that managers could make their organizations more competitive. The first major event sponsored by the program was a conference, held in 1984, on the topic of managing corporate culture, which resulted in a book, *Gaining Control of the Corporate Culture* (1985). The second conference, which took place in 1986 on the topic of managing organization-wide transformation, also resulted in a book, *Corporate Transformation: Revitalizing Organizations for a Competitive World* (1988). The first project focused primarily on the people aspects of the organization; the second expanded the scope by including the strategic and business aspects of managing large-scale systems change. This book, the third major project of the Program in Corporate Culture, further expands our efforts by examining anything and everything that can increase an organization's competitiveness in our global economy.

The experts represented here were chosen in either of two ways. First, we made a list of people who, in our view, had demonstrated a keen understanding of the topic through academic research or direct involvement in organizational efforts at increasing competitiveness. In this way, ten people were invited to present papers at the conference. Second, we mailed a conference announcement including a call for papers to more than thirty thousand members of professional organizations and corporations — including the Academy of Management, the American Psychological Association, the American Marketing Association, the Institute of Management Sciences, the American Society for Training and Development, and top executives of the thousand largest U.S. organizations — in an effort to uncover important research and reports not yet published. Our expectations were more than realized: Fifty papers covering a wide range of material on competitiveness were submitted.

The submitted papers were then subjected to a thorough review. Each paper received at least two independent reviews and was evaluated on the basis of four criteria: innovativeness in approach to the topic, quality in developing the approach, practical usefulness in guiding management action, and clarity of expression for a broad audience. In cases of disagreement, the papers were reviewed by a third person, and a discussion among the editors resolved any differences in opinion. (All the submitted papers were also reviewed and discussed over a one-month period in a seminar of fourteen doctoral students majoring in organizational studies, strategic management, management information systems, behavioral accounting, human resources, and marketing.) The entire review process allowed the editors to select the ten best papers from the total of fifty. Detailed editorial recommendations for revision were then sent to the authors. The invited papers were subjected to a similar review to help the authors fine-tune their ideas and improve their style as well.

The review process did not end with the editors, however. At the three-day conference, all authors delivered their papers to an audience of both academics and executives, with thirty minutes for presentation and twenty minutes for discussion. Thus the authors could clarify their thoughts for a broad audience and benefit from active debate and immediate comment. Moreover, since all the papers presented during the conference concerned the topic of competitiveness, there was ample opportunity for each author to learn from the presentation and discussion of other papers. As editors, we were delighted to see the thinking evolve as the conference progressed. In fact, in reviewing the revised papers, which were submitted *after* the conference, we were able to observe the impact of the conference experience on each paper. As a result of this comprehensive editorial and interactive review process, the chapters in this book offer original ideas whose arguments are clearly conceived and well developed.

Audience

Both academics and executives should find *Making Organizations Competitive* a valuable resource. The book may be of particular interest to chief executive officers; senior operating executives; vice-presidents of corporate organization, planning, and development; manufacturing executives; human resource managers; marketing managers; general managers; quality control managers; plant superintendents; management consultants; organizational development executives; management training and development executives; and administrators and directors of nonprofit organizations. As well, the book should be of interest to scholars specializing in organizational theory, behavior, and development; industrial psychology; strategic planning; management information systems; marketing; industrial engineering; education; and public administration.

Overview of the Contents

The twenty chapters in this volume are organized into three parts (plus an introductory and a concluding chapter by the editors): "Understanding and Managing Competitiveness," "Managing People and Processes Within Organizations," and "Managing Networks and Relationships Across Boundaries." Chapter One summarizes five recurring themes discussed throughout the three-day conference: creating new models of organizations and institutions, developing new linkages out of old categories, redefining the role of top management, developing global mindsets and competitive skills, and redefining organizational goals and performance assessments. These five themes, which are woven throughout the book, provide an overview of what we have learned about making organizations competitive.

Part One, "Understanding and Managing Competitiveness," comprises four chapters that provide a broad analysis of the topic — both historically and presently. Chapters Two, Three, and Four examine competitiveness from strategic, structural, and manufacturing viewpoints, respectively. These three approaches undoubtedly will remain key leverage points for enhancing competitiveness worldwide. Chapter Five summarizes the diverse literature on competitiveness by sorting the great variety of approaches according to human and technological factors both inside and outside the organization.

Part Two, "Managing People and Processes Within Organizations," consists of eight chapters — all addressing the human side of organizations. Chapter Six examines the central role a firm's human resource strategy and tactics play in gaining competitive advantage. Chapter Seven adds the important but elusive concept of organizational culture to discussions of managing human resources and suggests how a quality-conscious culture fosters competitiveness. Chapter Eight examines how organization-wide participation can be sustained by the appropriate executive behavior, structures, and processes — resulting in a high-involvement, competitive organization. Chapter Nine combines the topic of leadership with its flip side of followership and suggests how both roles (and skills) must work together in order to utilize all human resources effectively. Chapter Ten considers the challenge of educating people (leaders *and* followers) so they have the necessary experiences and skills to succeed in a competitive world. Chapters Eleven through Thirteen discuss the core processes that organizational members must perform successfully in order to foster competitiveness: establishing and maintaining clear strategic direction, defining and updating the organizational logic, ensuring compatibility of interests, and improving the fundamental processes of goal setting and decision making.

Part Three, "Managing Networks and Relationships

Across Boundaries," contains six chapters that show how an organization can extend its reach to resources around the world as well as integrate its efforts across its own functional boundaries. Chapter Fourteen considers the network of transnational relationships that are already occurring among different international institutions and the basis on which these arrangements will be established even more extensively in the future. Chapters Fifteen and Sixteen explain how more cooperative relationships can be formed between labor and management and between universities and industry, respectively. Chapters Seventeen through Nineteen suggests how more cooperative efforts across traditional boundaries—such as R & D, manufacturing, sales, and marketing—can also improve an organization's competitiveness.

Chapter Twenty, the concluding chapter, takes a look into the future to examine the network system that will shape our organizational experiences in a global economy. We propose the ingredients of the "perfectly competitive organization" and show how this ideal model can meet the demands of the twenty-first century. The ultimate challenge, however, is to *transform* traditional organizations that may have been successful in the past into elaborate networks of interpersonal and electronic relationships for success in the future.

Acknowledgments

Many people played key roles in making possible both the conference and this book. Dean H. J. Zoffer and former executive associate dean Andrew R. Blair at the Joseph M. Katz Graduate School of Business at the University of Pittsburgh provided the impetus to form the Program in Corporate Culture and embark on these major projects. Camille Burgess, administrative assistant to the Program in Corporate Culture, managed all the conference and book arrangements, including conference registration and all correspondence, efficiently and effectively. Jeanette Engel worked diligently with hotel personnel to ensure a smooth operation. Doctoral students Jeffrey Allenby, Denis Collins, Hyogun Kym, Lyman Reed, June Russell, and

Louise Serafin were invaluable in reviewing manuscripts, chairing sessions, and managing a variety of other important aspects of the conference.

We would like to express our appreciation to all the contributors to this book for their ideas and insights. And, certainly, their papers very much benefited from the active involvement of the hundred participants at the conference who asked probing questions at every session.

Finally, we wish to give special acknowledgment to some highly competitive organizations (and their quality-conscious members) that inspired us to examine the topic of competitiveness by their very example: Allstate (Phil Pechersky); Audio Arts (Dick Wright); Blackwood Gallery (Don Fink and Ben Robertson); David Israel (Bob Israel and Louise Weimer); Dobisky Associates (Frank Dobisky and John McLain); Horovitz, Rudoy & Roteman (Gordon Scherer); Jeff Linz Carpet; Management Centre Europe (Karen O'Donnell); Mellon Bank (Carol Kuszaj); Napoli Landscaping; Syntropy Audio Images (Cindy Spring); USAir (Dean Engel); Visual In-Seitz, Inc. (Kris Salvatore and Bob Seitz); Webb, Burden, Ziesenheim & Webb, P. C. (Russ Orkin); Wetzel (Mervis) Motors Works (Mitchell O'Kelly); and XICOM, Inc. (Noreen Fennell). While some of these firms are not large in size by most standards, all of them have touched our lives in a big way. They have demonstrated a consistent, sincere, and total-quality approach to satisfying all relevant stakeholders—particularly us.

Pittsburgh, Pennsylvania   Ralph H. Kilmann
September 1990   Ines Kilmann

THE AUTHORS

R alph H. Kilmann is professor of business administration and director of the Program in Corporate Culture at the Joseph M. Katz Graduate School of Business, University of Pittsburgh. He received both his B.S. and M.S. degrees from Carnegie Mellon University in industrial administration and his Ph.D. degree from the University of California, Los Angeles, in management. Since 1975 he has served as president of Organizational Design Consultants, a Pittsburgh-based firm specializing in the five tracks to organizational success. Kilmann has published more than one hundred articles and ten books on such topics as organizational design, strategy, and structure; problem management; and organizational change and development. He is the developer of the MAPS design technology and co-developer of several diagnostic instruments, including the Thomas-Kilmann Conflict Mode Instrument and the Kilmann-Saxton Culture-Gap Survey. One of his recent books, *Managing Beyond the Quick Fix: A Completely Integrated Program for Creating and Maintaining Organizational Success* (1989), describes his systematic approach to improving the competitiveness of all types of organizations. Kilmann has also written *Gaining Control of the Corporate Culture* (with M. J. Saxton, R. Serpa, and Associates, 1985), *Corporate Transformation: Revitalizing Organizations for a Competitive World* (with T. J. Covin and Associates, 1988), and *Escaping the Quick Fix Trap: How to Make Organizational Improvements That Really Last* (audio, 1989).

Ines Kilmann is vice-president of Organizational Design Consultants, a management consulting firm specializing in the five tracks to organizational success. She received her B.B.A. degree from Bernard M. Baruch College in management and her M.P.A. degree from the University of Pittsburgh in public administration. Prior to her consulting work, Kilmann spent fifteen years in various management positions with The Equitable in New York. Her current research interests include comparative cultural analysis of different industries in different nations. She is particularly concerned with studying the processes for overcoming resistance to change by examining the causes of cynical and depressed corporate cultures.

Riad Ajami is associate professor of international management and strategy and director of the international business program at Ohio State University. He received his Ph.D. degree from Pennsylvania State University. He has had appointments at the University of Pennsylvania; the University of California, Berkeley; the Harvard Center for International Affairs; and American University. Ajami's most recent research has focused on foreign investment in the United States, oil economics and the Middle East, U.S. economic competitiveness, and international debts and lending. He is the author of numerous books and articles, including *Arab Response to Multinationals* (1979) and *International Debts and Lending: Structure and Policy Response* (1986).

H. Igor Ansoff is professor of management at the United States International University and president of Ansoff Associates, a consulting firm specializing in strategic management. He received his B.S. degree from Stevens Institute of Technology and his Ph.D. degree from Brown University. He has held professorships at Carnegie Mellon University; Vanderbilt University; and the European Institute for Advanced Studies in Management, Belgium. He has held senior management positions with the Lockheed Aircraft Corporation and its subsidiaries and was employed by the Rand Corporation. Ansoff has been a leading pioneer in the development of long-range planning, strategic planning, strategic management, and strategic issue management. He is the author of more than ninety articles and books on planning, strategy, and management, including *Implanting Strategic Management* (1984) and *The New Corporate Strategy* (1987).

David E. Bowen is assistant professor of management and organization at the School of Business Administration, University of Southern California. He received his M.B.A. and Ph.D. degrees from Michigan State University. His present research interests focus on models of staff effectiveness and on the definition, measurement, and implementation of service quality. His recently published articles can be found in *Research in Organizational Behavior*, *Academy of Management Review*, and *Organizational Dynamics*.

Harriette L. Chandler is a principal with Adelie Corporation, Cambridge, Massachusetts. She received her B.A. degree from Wellesley College, her M.A. degree from Clark University in history, international relations, and government, her M.B.A. degree from Simmons Graduate School of Management, and her Ph.D. degree from Clark University in international relations and government. Chandler's other employment experiences with Adelie include manager of training and documentation, senior marketing strategist, and manager of marketing services.

Thomas G. Cummings is professor of management and organization at the Graduate School of Business Administration, University of Southern California. He received his B.S. and M.B.A. degrees from Cornell University and his Ph.D. degree from the University of California, Los Angeles, in sociotechnical systems. His major research and consulting interests include planned organization change, transorganizational systems, occupational stress, and designing high-performance organizations. Cummings has been involved in several large-scale organization design and quality-of-work-life projects in both union and nonunion settings. He has authored or coauthored over thirty scholarly articles and books, including *Industrial Relations: A Multidimensional View* (1985) and *Organizational Development and Change* (3rd ed., 1985).

Terrence E. Deal is professor of education at Peabody College, Vanderbilt University. He received his B.A. degree from Laverne College in history and physical education, his M.A. degree from California State University, Los Angeles, in educational administration, and his Ph.D. degree from Stanford University in educational administration and sociology. He has coauthored five books, including *Corporate Cultures: The Rites and Rituals of Corporate Life* (with A. Kennedy, 1983) and *Modern Approaches to Understanding and Managing Organizations* (with L. Bolman, 1984).

Jay R. Galbraith is professor of management and organization and a member of the Center for Effective Organizations at the University of Southern California (USC). He received his B.A. degree from the University of Cincinnati and his Ph.D. degree from Indiana University. He has taught at the University of Pennsylvania and Massachusetts Institute of Technology. Prior to joining the faculty at USC, he directed his own management consulting firm. Galbraith's principal area of specialization is organizational design, change, and development. Recently he has concentrated on major strategy and structure changes in organizations. He is the author or coauthor of numerous books and articles, including *Organization Design* (1977) and *Strategy Implementation: Structure, Systems and Process* (2nd ed., 1986).

Thomas G. Gunn is vice-president of procurement and distribution in product and technology operations at Unisys Corporation. He was previously a partner in and national director of Arthur Young's Manufacturing Consulting Group. Gunn coordinated Arthur Young's approach to manufacturing industries and assisted companies in creating manufacturing strategies and modernization programs that use world-class manufacturing technology and practices to further their competitive advantage. He is the author of two books, *Computer Applications in Manufacturing* (1981) and *Manufacturing for Competitive Advantage* (1987).

Kathleen Gurley is a Ph.D. candidate in the Department of Organizational Behavior at Case Western Reserve University. She received her B.A. degree from Hood College and her M.B.A. degree from Case Western Reserve University. Gurley was previously employed as organizational development administrator and manager with the Goodyear Tire and Rubber Company. Her research interests include cross-functional teams, team development, sociotechnical change processes, large-system change, and learning mechanisms in organizations.

Roy B. Helfgott is distinguished professor of economics at New Jersey Institute of Technology and a consultant with Organization Resources Counselors. He received his B.S. degree from City College, New York, his M.A. degree from Columbia University, and his Ph.D. degree from the New School of Social Research. He has taught at Bernard M. Baruch College, University of the City of New York, and Pennsylvania State University. Helfgott has served as industrial development officer with the United Nations and research director of the New York Coat Joint Board of the International Ladies' Garment Worker's Union. He is the author or coauthor of numerous books and articles, including the recently published *Computerized Manufacturing and Human Resources: Innovation Through Employee Involvement* (1988).

Peter Hess is associate professor and chair of the Department of Management at Western New England College. He received his B.A. degree from Georgetown University in psychology and his Ph.D. degree from the University of Massachusetts. He has held the position of visiting fellow at Yale University. Hess's research and consulting interests include leadership, planning, and organizational change. He has been involved in major change projects in industrial, educational, and health care organizations.

Robert E. Kelley is adjunct professor of business at Carnegie Mellon University and president of Consultants to Executives and Organizations, Ltd. He received his B.A. degree from Drake University and his Ph.D. degree from Colorado State University. He has been a senior management consultant with the Stanford Research Institute. Kelley has advised national and international clients on how to lead valuable employees and how to manage knowledge-intensive businesses. He is currently studying what separates star from average performers in brain-power-intensive settings, such as R & D and MIS, and how to improve the quality of service in American business. Kelley is the author or coauthor of numerous books and articles, including *The Gold-Collar Worker: Harnessing the Brainpower of the New Workforce* (1985) and *Consulting: The Complete Guide to a Profitable Career* (1986).

Charles A. Khuen is chairman of Adelie Corporation, a subsidiary of AT&T. He received his B.S. and M.S. degrees from the University of Michigan in engineering. His focus throughout his professional career has been sales and marketing management. Prior to becoming president of Adelie, Khuen directed the marketing and corporate sales support efforts for the office automation product line at Prime Computer and served as director of information systems at International Management Services, Ltd., of London.

Edward E. Lawler III is professor of management and organization and director of the Center for Effective Organizations at the University of Southern California. He received his B.A. degree from Brown University and his Ph.D. degree from the University of California, Berkeley. His areas of expertise include the changing work scene; unions and their power base; work motivation, pay systems, and organizational change; and participative management strategies. Lawler is the author or coauthor of more than 150 articles and 15 books, including *Pay and Organization Development* (1981), *Managing Creation* (1983), *High-Involvement Management: Participative Strategies for Improving Organizational Performance* (1986), and *Strategic Pay* (1990).

Kenneth D. Mackenzie is Edmund P. Learned Distinguished Professor at the University of Kansas School of Business and president of Mackenzie and Company, a consulting firm that specializes in organizational design and development. He received his B.A. degree and his Ph.D. degree from the University of California, Berkeley, in mathematics and business administration, respectively. He has concentrated his research work on developing a theory of how organizations work and then applying it to make them more productive and adaptable. Mackenzie is the author or coauthor of numerous books and articles on strategic assessment, organizational analysis, personal counseling, human resources, interpersonal conflict, and compensation systems. His most recent book is *Organizational Design: The Organizational Audit and Analysis Technology* (1986).

Maria L. Nathan is research scientist at the Center for Crisis Management and is currently working on a Ph.D. degree in management and organization at the University of Southern California. She received her B.A. and M.A. degrees from the University of Akron in psychology and a second M.A. degree from the University of Missouri in applied psychology. Nathan was formerly manager of employee relations for Transohio Savings Bank, Cleveland. Her research interests include interorganizational relations, the formation of transorganizational systems, managerial scanning of the business environment, and management succession.

William A. Pasmore is associate professor of organizational behavior at Case Western Reserve University. He received his B.S. and Ph.D. degrees from Purdue University in industrial management and administrative sciences, respectively. He is an active consultant specializing in the application of advanced sociotechnical systems to improve organizational effectiveness. His research interests include the study of global social innovation and the application of sociotechnical systems to research and development organizations. Pasmore is the author or coauthor of numerous books and articles, including *Designing*

Effective Organizations: The Sociotechnical System Perspective (1988) and *Research in Organizational Change and Development* (1988).

Carl A. Rodrigues is assistant professor of management and international business at Montclair State College, New Jersey. He received his B.B.A. and M.A. degrees from Florida International University and his Ph.D. degree from Nova University. His current research interests include improving organizational competitiveness in the global economy and an analysis of cross-cultural organization development efforts at an American Indian reservation. Rodrigues has published numerous articles and is founder and editor of *Issues in International Business,* a journal that covers international topics of current interest to managers and scholars. One of his most recent publications, "Five Organizational Typologies for Developed and Developing Nations," appeared in *International Strategic Management* (1989).

Benjamin Schneider is professor of psychology and business management at the University of Maryland and vice-president of Organizational and Personnel Research, Inc. He received his B.A. degree from Alfred University in psychology and business administration, his M.B.A. degree from the University of the City of New York, and his Ph.D. degree from the University of Maryland. His professional experience includes a position at Yale University, a Fulbright Award to Israel, and a chaired professorship at Michigan State University. Schneider's most recent research and consulting work has been on the assessment of service climate and culture, the design of human resources systems to enhance service organization effectiveness, and research on how "the people make the place." He is the author or coauthor of more than fifty articles and four books on these topics, including *Staffing Organizations* (2nd ed., with N. Schmitt, 1986) and *Facilitating Work Effectiveness: Concepts and Procedures* (with F. D. Schoorman, 1988).

Joyce Shelleman is a Ph.D. candidate and part-time instructor of organizational studies at the Joseph M. Katz Graduate School of Business, University of Pittsburgh. She received her B.A. degree in psychology and her M.P.A. degree with a concentration in health care management, both from Pennsylvania State University, Harrisburg. Prior to beginning her doctoral studies, she worked for five years implementing and managing strategic planning systems in hospitals. Shelleman is currently completing her dissertation on participants' attitudes toward strategic planning. Her current research interests include behavioral issues in strategic management and the management of adaptive processes, particularly in professional organizations.

Caren Siehl is assistant professor of management and organization at the School of Business Administration, University of Southern California. She received her Ph.D. degree from the Graduate School of Business, Stanford University, in organizational behavior. Siehl is currently conducting research on the impact of organizational culture on mergers and acquisitions and on the use of cultural artifacts to improve service. Among her published articles is "After the Founder: An Opportunity to Manage Culture," which appeared in *Organizational Culture* (1985).

Patrick A. Sullivan is assistant professor of strategic management at the United States International University. He received his B.S. degree from Marquette University in civil engineering, his M.B.A. degree from San Diego State University, and his Ph.D. degree from the United States International University. He was formerly senior manager with the U.S. Department of the Navy, Naval Facilities Engineering Command; he retired after thirty-three years of government service.

Dave Ulrich is on the faculty of the School of Business and faculty associate at the Institute of Social Research, University of Michigan. He is on the core faculty of the Michigan executive program and is director of advanced professional development for human resource professionals. He received his B.A. degree from Brigham Young University and his Ph.D. degree from the University of California, Los Angeles. He has consulted with many public and private organizations on strategic planning, implementing strategic plans, managing change, and using human resources for competitive advantage. Ulrich has published numerous articles in *Academy of Management Review, Human Relations, Human Resource Management, Human Resource Planning, Journal of Management, New Management, Planning Review,* and *Sloan Management Review.*

Brian Uzzi is a Ph.D. student in the department of sociology at the the State University of New York, Stony Brook. He received his B.B.A. degree from Hofstra University in accounting and his M.S. degree from Carnegie Mellon University in industrial administration. His research interests include the formation, duration, and dissolution of interorganizational relationships, individual mobility and achievement, and new organizational forms. He has recently coauthored an article, "A Framework for the Conceptualization, Design, and Strategic Management of Planned Change Systems," in *Knowledge and Society* (forthcoming).

H. J. Zoffer is dean of the Joseph M. Katz Graduate School of Business at the University of Pittsburgh. He received his B.B.A., M.A., and Ph.D. degrees from the University of Pittsburgh, where his major fields of interest were economics and corporation finance. He serves on the boards of directors of a number of industrial concerns. He is past president of the American Assembly of Collegiate Schools of Business (AACSB), past president of the American Association of University Administrators (AAUA), and current president of the AAUA Foundation. Zoffer is past chairman of the Accreditation Research Committee of the AACSB. He is the author of a number of articles and books on such subjects as individual and group decision making under risk, the social responsibility of business, continuing education for managers, corporate risk analysis, accounting education, and improving institutional credibility. Zoffer's articles have appeared in such journals as *Management Review, Academy of Management Review, Management Accounting,* and *Journal of General Management.*

MAKING ORGANIZATIONS COMPETITIVE

1

INTRODUCTION: KEY THEMES IN MAKING ORGANIZATIONS COMPETITIVE

RALPH H. KILMANN
INES KILMANN

Improving the functioning of an organization—so that it can satisfy all its diverse stakeholders over an extended period of time—has been the subject of both theoretical and practical interest for quite some time. But every few years the terminology changes. Just during the past decade, for example, many terms have been used to discuss "improving things": *productivity, efficiency, effectiveness, excellence, success,* and *total quality management.* Recently it seems that the term *competitiveness* has captured the spotlight.

We do not mean to suggest that all the diverse ways of talking about improving organizations are the same nor that their methods for bringing about improvements are identical. As new labels are coined, our understanding of the problem continues to evolve—especially since the context and nature of organizational problems keep changing. Improving efficiency for the regulated, domestic environment of the 1950s, for example, was done quite differently from the programs on quality improvement being conducted for the deregulated, global environment of the 1990s. The recent approach to quality is linked to external (as well as internal) customers and suppliers whereas previous efforts at efficiency were based mostly on internal considerations of material and labor costs. While cost efficiency remains a major concern in every competitive arena, most people now realize that cost control must be combined with other efforts at improvement, such as formulating and communicating a clear strategic vision, inspiring creativity and innovation, ensuring risk taking in decision making, keeping information technology up to date, constantly monitoring and adapting to customer needs, and developing cooperative programs with labor leaders, community representatives, and foreign governments (and other key stakeholders as well). A *combination* of improvement efforts is vital when competing in a global — multistakeholder — environment.

This book's focus on competitiveness accepts the most recent terminology as a basis for a thorough discussion of the complex topic of improving organizations in today's dynamic world. But this choice of language also recognizes that we know much more about organizational dynamics than we did just a few years ago. The term *competitiveness* is not just putting old wine into new bottles. In the past decade, in fact, most organizations have *had* to function in a competitive world — like it or not. In most cases, it was not a matter of choice but one of accepting the harsh reality that rapid technological change (including personal computers, fax machines, and telecommunication) and sweeping political change (including national and international deregulation of many industries) have combined to create a fast-paced, interconnected world. The topic of global competitiveness, like "future shock," is no longer just an academic concept. We have learned about competitive behavior and organizational survival the hard way.

As described in the preface, at the three-day conference on "Making Organizations More Competitive" there was considerable discussion about the topic that went beyond the strict contents of papers. While much of this discussion was certainly initiated by the presentations, the conference, as is usually the case, developed into an additional forum for testing ideas by a most experienced audience of a hundred academics and executives. In the very last session of the conference, we sought to integrate all the discussions that took place during the three-day experience. This final session was entitled "What have we learned about making organizations competitive?" As a way of introducing the subsequent chapters in this book, we now summarize five key themes that caught everyone's attention.

Creating New Models of Organizations and Institutions

At the conference, many authors presented their vision of what should guide our efforts at becoming more competitive. In session after session a conceptual framework was presented as representing the *ideal* for organizations or institutions to adopt. These speakers indicated that while no organization today possesses all the ideal attributes of their model, many organizations have already discovered the benefits derived from adopting a few of these special qualities. They then showed how an integrated approach could be developed by combining everything that has been learned piecemeal. The real power of the model, however, is directing an organization's attention to the *whole* package of attributes, processes, or ingredients — not just one or two. In a sense, then, the various models presented in this book are combinations of what is already being tried by one organization or another.

Ansoff and Sullivan (Chapter Two), for example, suggest that the firm's strategy must be congruent with the turbulence in the environment and the organization's ability to respond. They develop a number of equations that account for return on investment (ROI) according to multiplicative and additive properties of production efficiency, marketing effectiveness, market attractiveness, and product/service responsiveness. The authors then develop detailed frameworks to guide a firm in deciding how to maximize its ROI and, hence, its competitive position — depending on the environmental challenges in the marketplace. Their research data, which they summarize for the reader, support the basic theory of strategic responsiveness for a variety of industries and nations.

In a similar way, Galbraith (Chapter Three) considers the transition of environmental challenges over time and how the firm's strategic responses can best be managed by different organizational forms — such as matrix overlays, networks, neoconglomerates, and clean-sheet (new-business) start-ups. In each case, the issue is determining the key environmental challenges and then selecting matching — congruent — responses: a contingency approach to linking environmental flux to competitive strategy to organizational structure. A related approach is taken by Ajami (Chapter Fourteen) by linking contractual arrangements across transnational firms and institutions in which each entity can provide any one of three necessary ingredients for a successful joint venture: technological and managerial know-how, capital for financing, or local labor and raw materials for manufacture.

Gunn (Chapter Four) provides a systematic set of concepts and methods for developing a world-class manufacturing organization — starting from a traditional, functional operation. He shows the critical interplay among business strategy, information-technology strategy, manufacturing strategy, and, at the core, the people of the organization (including the human resources strategy). He suggests that no company to date has integrated its planning and activities to keep all these elements in a dynamic alignment, but we have seen what the various parts of the model contribute to the ultimate goal: globally competitive manufacturing for old-time U.S. industries. One message is clear: Just following one or two guidelines of the whole model, while well intentioned, is likely to stir up more difficulties than it solves. Similarly, applying the whole model to only a piece of the organization (such as a single business unit) might very well create a mess, since resource support and strategic relationships must be aligned with policies of corporate headquarters. Manufacturing, therefore, should no longer be treated as an isolated function that can be improved without regard to all the other — interdependent — parts of the organization, let alone the changing nature of the external environment. It seems that strategy, structure, *and* manufacturing are all converging into an integrated approach for competitive success.

Lawler (Chapter Eight) reflects on his twenty-five years of experience in developing high-involvement organizations through all the combined methods of participative management. His ideal model is organization-wide participation, a flattening of the traditional management hierarchy, an extensive use of task forces that cut across hierarchical lines and functional areas, and an interchangeable team of executives that includes representatives from both inside and outside the organization. While there are examples of one department or division of a firm adopting such a high-involvement model, it is difficult to cite a large established organization that has implemented such a transformation from its original, traditional approach. It seems that newer firms, not burdened by past assumptions and ingrained habits, have a much easier time establishing an organization-wide participative approach from the start. Lawler suggests, as does Gunn, that applying the model piecemeal to interdependent parts of the organization may invite chaos. The ideal, rather, is a total effort at large-scale, systemwide change.

Zoffer (Chapter Ten) outlines a ten-point program for educating people for a competitive world. His ideal model includes improved scientific training, learning basic leadership skills, learning more than one language, learning more than one culture, learning the benefits of cooperative goal setting, and learning more about the government and other key stakeholders. Zoffer recognizes that not only must education be lifelong, but basic education must be designed as a ten-year package: four years of high school, four years of college, and two years of graduate study. Again a *total* approach is required for educational success, even if the current experience can only point to a little being done here and there. It is the dynamic *interconnection* among all human systems (due to political and technological change) that mandates holistic analysis and action.

Mackenzie (Chapter Eleven) offers the most explicit discussion of holistic—holonomic, as he calls it—approaches to competitiveness and outlines twelve processes that every organization should enact to bring about six desired ends. The key to his model is the explicit linkages among all twelve processes. It is clear that the chain is only as strong as the weakest link. Clarity of direction and structure, for example, would both be nonoperational if the measurement of key variables were unclear or simple unavailable. Similarly, results-oriented problem solving and successful goal achievement would not be possible without clear direction, structure, and measurement. It is the total package that needs to guide efforts at becoming more competitive, even if the ideal model was derived from bits and pieces of experience from different organizations.

Nathan and Cummings (Chapter Sixteen) present a normative — ideal — model for establishing productive linkages between companies and universities in order to foster technological innovation. Considering a number of current examples of such relationships, the authors outline four key phases of the process: identification (defining the R & D task and deciding whether a consortium of cooperative organizations can accomplish it), convention (establishing goal consensus among the interested parties), organization (establishing agreements, procedures, and plans for working together), and evaluation (assessing the results of the joint effort and informing the appropriate parties). The authors then consider the practical obstacles to forming an effective consortium among organizations. As a result, any set of companies and universities considering a joint venture for technological development can benefit from the normative guidelines outlined by this model.

Models and frameworks are presented by other authors, as well, to provide organizations with road maps for proceeding with new approaches to competitiveness. Bowen, Siehl, and Schneider (Chapter Eighteen) present a systems approach to linking manufacturing more closely in time and space to the ultimate customer. Their ideal model indicates how both the formal and informal aspects of the organization must be altered and what crucial interfaces must be established across functional units. Chandler and Khuen (Chapter Nineteen) present an ideal model for integrating the functions of sales and marketing. Through a centralized information system, they bring together such interrelated activities as corporate promotions, field-generated leads, sales activities, account management, and repeat business — with information on customers, prospects, products, sales forces, distributors, customer service, forecasts, and other pertinent marketing data. Their ideal model of a sales and marketing information network directly connects the central office with the sales representatives with the regional/branch sales office — all with a telemarketing center.

Kilmann, Shelleman, and Uzzi (Chapter Five) review the great variety of approaches to competitiveness in order to isolate their essential distinctions and then integrate these key features into one all-encompassing model. Specifically they synthesize the extensive literature on competitiveness that has developed during the past five years by reviewing academic journals from a variety of business disciplines, relevant publications for the professional manager, and popular business magazines and newspapers. Their integrating model distinguishes human from technological factors and *intra*-organizational (internal) from *inter*-organizational (external) stakeholder relationships. From these core distinctions, their model provides a systematic examination of nine separate approaches that have received the most attention in a diverse literature — which can now be combined into a comprehensive approach to competitiveness. Briefly the nine approaches are (1) computer technology in production, management information systems, and artificial intelligence; (2) cooperative linkages among research and development and manufacturing functions; (3) women in the work force; (4) management commitment and focus; (5) the manager's awareness of new technology; (6) the role of government in technological development and utilization; (7) government, business, and labor partnerships; (8) educating managers; and (9) synergistic management that fosters coordination and teamwork. While many of these topics are examined throughout the book in greater detail (with even more elaborate models), the literature review does highlight important avenues to competitiveness that are not explicitly addressed in subsequent chapters.

Developing New Linkages out of Old Categories

The long-standing boundaries around groups, organizations, industries, and nations are slowly eroding. The implicit sense that these boundaries are physical (because we have "always" agreed to such geographical and legal realities) is giving way to the recognition that most of our boundaries are in fact perceptual (since we have learned that psychological and cultural

processes define reality, especially for organizational and institutional phenomena). People in groups or departments in traditional organizations are finding that they are spending more
time dealing with people from *other* groups or departments than
with their own immediate colleagues. Organizations are finding
that *external* groups, organizations, and institutions are now
deciding their success or failure even more than their own
internal efforts. For many organizations, in fact, it is not even
clear any longer what industry a firm is in. The boundaries of
the "industry" are now blurred and constantly changing. The key
questions, then, for many organizations are: What kind of organization do we want to be, and what customers and markets do
we wish to serve?

Even countries, which have traditionally made safe assumptions about national loyalty, political sovereignty, and geographical boundaries, are no longer quite so certain what is
inside versus what is outside their domain. Even the Berlin Wall
is down, and the former distinctions between East and West
Germany and Eastern and Western Europe are fading. All Europe is now adjusting to the prospect of one economic reality
for the continent (circa 1992), which significantly affects the
Americas and Asia as well. The oceans that used to divide
continents are becoming more and more irrelevant by sweeping
political and technological change. Even the U.S.S.R. and China
have opened their doors in response to economic, political,
and technological forces that seemed unlikely just a few
decades ago.

Thus an overarching theme emerged at the conference:
The old categories for thinking about organizational functioning are being replaced by new linkages. In fact, what used to be
neatly contained *within* clearly defined boundaries is now flowing smoothly across these very same boundaries. Structures are
giving way to processes; conditions are being modified into
events. And ironically, in many instances, it seems that it is easier
to make contact with someone on the other side of the world
than to set up a meeting with a fellow employee down the hall.

Galbraith's discussion of matrix overlays (Chapter Three)
recognizes that functional boundaries can no longer contain

independent pieces of work in a dynamically interconnected world. Instead, multiple group memberships via matrix teams enable organizational members to coordinate the wor¹ that now flows across functional—and organizational—lines. Kelley (Chapter Nine) suggests that organizational structures should be reorganized around new categories such as identifying consumer needs and attracting resources—categories that were not even regarded as relevant functions decades before. Mackenzie (Chapter Eleven) also suggests that organizations should be redesigned to pursue core processes rather than traditional—functional—pursuits. The same concern about transcending traditional frames of reference is addressed by Helfgott's (Chapter Fifteen) redesign of labor–management relations and Nathan and Cummings' (Chapter Sixteen) redesign of university–industry relations. Similarly, redesigning functional relationships to encompass a whole business–customer orientation is best illustrated by Gunn's (Chapter Four) view of what it takes to become a world-class manufacturer, Pasmore and Gurley's (Chapter Seventeen) cross-departmental integration of R & D, Bowen, Siehl, and Schneider's (Chapter Eighteen) view of service-oriented manufacturing, and Chandler and Khuen's (Chapter Nineteen) integration of sales and marketing.

Any organization that continues to see its role in today's world according to yesterday's artificial categories (believing, wrongly, that organizational categories are a fixed reality) will be at a severe competitive disadvantage. Many of the contributors underscore the point that the present-day information technology and the political changes that have deregulated industries and nations are conjointly shattering our previous ways of categorizing—and, hence, seeing—what is and what is possible. The firms that choose to redefine their opportunities according to new frames of reference and then proceed to form new linkages that cut across all the old categories will create the new industries and organizing principles for tomorrow—to *their* competitive advantage.

Redefining the Role of Top Management

Many at the conference were concerned about the new role of top management in a competitive organization. Developing a high-involvement organization, becoming a world-class manufacturer, establishing cross-boundary associations and relationships around the world—all have significant implications for top management's new job. If the role of top management is not redefined, it will be most difficult for anyone to lead an organization down a new path with a new way of doing business.

Deal (Chapter Seven) addresses the role of leadership from the perspective of culture, quality, and competitiveness. Using well-known business leaders as examples, Deal suggests that leading by example does more to establish and maintain a quality culture than just about anything else an executive can say in a speech or write down in a memo to the masses. The CEO who "walks where he talks" conveys the values of the company and what is expected from every member of the organization. Critical incidents, if handled well, will have years if not decades of positive influence on everyone's behavior and commitment. But if a crucial event is handled poorly—if the president or CEO responds to a loyal customer in a rude or uncaring manner, for example—the damage to the culture can last twice as long.

Lawler (Chapter Eight) considers the new role of top management in a high-involvement organization. He suggests several types of executive behavior that must be consistent with all the principles of participative management. Special executive responsibilities would include, for example, being responsible for the strategic direction of the firm, managing the firm's culture, benchmarking results against the competition, monitoring and modifying the decision-making process (more so than a decision outcome itself), sharing information, and setting the example for organization-wide feedback and learning. Kelley (Chapter Nine) draws the distinction between leaders and followers and suggests that the development of a partnership between them is what is really required for a competitive organization. Such a partnership would also help to overcome the many dysfunctions of an autocratic management hierarchy and would, therefore, facilitate the development of high-involvement organizations. Mackenzie (Chapter Eleven), rather than referring to subordinates as workers or employees, suggests the term *associates* to describe the necessary partnership among *all* organizational members.

Helfgott (Chapter Fifteen) puts special responsibility on top executives to initiate cooperative efforts between labor and management. Similarly, a vital part of top management's new role will be to initiate all the other kinds of linkages, interfaces, and cross-boundary associations—rather than waiting for another executive in another firm to make the first move. In a fast-pace, interconnected world, top management must be exceptionally bold in its effort to establish new associations and cooperative efforts. Ansoff and Sullivan (Chapter Two) suggest, in fact, that environmental turbulence (ranging from repetitive to unpredictable) must be matched by a strategic response (ranging from stable to creative).

In sum, then, top management must ward off the temptation to continue a top-down mindset of superior/subordinate relationships. They should replace this tradition—behaviorally and symbolically—with collaborative partners all seeking to stay in constant touch with each other through information, feedback, and influence. Moreover, top management must take the initiative to establish the appropriate strategic, structural, and contractual groundwork for environmental challenges and opportunities.

Developing Global Mindsets and Competitive Skills

Sparked by all the discussions at the conference about creating new models, breaking down walls, and redefining leadership, considerable attention was given to the new "mental orientation" and mix of skills demanded by a competitive world. Significant concern was voiced about people's perceptual bias toward their own little part of the world versus a broad-based, cosmopolitan orientation toward the whole universe. Apparently many Americans see their own locale with a rigid set of blinders. Not surprisingly, their organizations have evolved with this same parochial mindset—nurtured by the arrogance of success and national policies of protectionism and isolationism. By way of comparison, it was suggested that people in Europe, especially in the urban areas, are more international in outlook and, in fact, are fluent in more than one language and experienced with many cultures. Perhaps one of the most frequently asked questions was: How can the United States compete globally if everything is seen from an American perspective and most Americans are not attuned to the unique needs, styles, and customs of people from other cultures?

At the conference Jay Galbraith cited the little-known fact that only 9 percent of the U.S. population has passports (and, of course, a much lower percentage actually uses its passports), compared to a much higher percentage for European countries. Perhaps this difference in cross-national exposure reflects the old geographical distances and oceans that once isolated the United States from the rest of the world. But the technology (people *and* information travel) is now readily available and affordable to cross these old physical boundaries. Galbraith suggested that corporations should hire recruits directly from high school and then provide them with the international experience to learn languages and cultures "before it is too late." H. Igor Ansoff reinforced this point during his presentation, as did Terrence Deal. Ajami (Chapter Fourteen) offers the most explicit scenario for what is in store for companies that plan to compete with international trade blocs and other multinational configurations. Such transnational networking demands a sophisticated appreciation of political and social history, national cultures, and foreign languages.

Zoffer (Chapter Ten) believes that business schools should require fluency in at least one foreign language (and experience in the culture as well), yet he notes that the trend in the past two decades has been to *remove* foreign language requirements from business school programs. The audience at the conference generally agreed that unless a global mindset is developed early in the educational process and is utilized by corporations in their recruiting, there may be limits to the kinds of networks and relationships that American firms can establish overseas. And the development of other skills would certainly be curtailed if a global mindset were not internalized in the first place. The audience seemed to appreciate that people will not bother to learn new skills if they do not see any use for them.

Apart from this concern about global mindsets, perhaps the one skill receiving the most attention at the conference was *trust building*—not as a value but as a behavioral skill, things that people do that either foster or undermine trust. Since so many of one's relationships in a competitive organization are with "strangers around the world," it seems essential that people learn how to create and sustain trust: the social glue that holds promises, expectations, and, hence, people together.

Zoffer (Chapter Ten) puts major emphasis on learning behavioral skills (personal and social sensitivity, communication and negotiation skills, and humor) and criticizes our formal educational system for focusing almost exclusively on content and cognitive skills. Galbraith (Chapter Three) puts special emphasis on developing the skills for making deals, since the outcome of cross-boundary arrangements will not be based on the formal authority of job positions *within* a clearly bounded unit. Instead, influence and control will be based on interpersonal skills, information, expertise, and trust. Galbraith, in fact, suggests that "everything" is negotiable in the future and little will be decided by formal authority.

A related skill that received considerable attention at the conference was *collaboration*—working together in partnership, from different but equally considered perspectives, in order to arrive at joint goals, strategies, tactics, and deals. It was again noted that universities do not seem to teach the *behavioral* skills that support collaboration, even if they do teach the concept. As highlighted by Kilmann, Shelleman, and Uzzi (Chapter Five), however, developing organization-wide participation and enhancing cross-boundary influence demand collaboration, interpersonal skills, trust building, and international skills—in practice. The requirements for collaboration are most evident in Helfgott's discussion (Chapter Fifteen) of labor–management relationships, which traditionally have been adversarial in nature. The same issue of developing more collaborative behavior and relationships emerges in Nathan and Cummings's (Chapter Sixteen) discussion of university–industry relationships, Pasmore and Gurley's (Chapter Seventeen) efforts to improve the use of R & D across organizational units, Bowen, Siehl, and Schneider's (Chapter Eighteen) approach to bringing together the functions of manufacturing and marketing, and Chandler and Khuen's (Chapter Nineteen) efforts at integrating the often separate (if not opposing) views of sales and marketing.

Redefining Organizational Goals and Performance

How does one assess goal accomplishment in a competitive world? Is the standard of profitability the answer? What about market share? If becoming more competitive calls for new models, boundaries, leaders, mindsets, and skills, perhaps the topic of goal accomplishment must be approached in a new way as well. Hess (Chapter Twelve) discusses how goal setting is often ignored in the process of aligning everyone's efforts in the same direction, and several of the other chapters highlight the importance of clear strategic direction—for example, Ansoff and Sullivan (Chapter Two), Galbraith (Chapter Three), Lawler (Chapter Eight), and Mackenzie (Chapter Eleven). But in addition to improving the processes of forming strategic plans and translating these plans into operational goals, the issue of goal *content* still deserves special attention.

A core theme throughout the conference was the importance of *value-added* goals and assessments. It was apparent that market share, for example, would become more and more difficult to define (let alone measure) with the continuing erosion of old industrial and national boundaries. And the old standard of profitability as a well-defined yardstick no longer suffices. Profitability does not capture the firm's ability to respond to *future* environmental challenges and opportunities. If conditions suddenly change (what old stakeholders want now and what new stakeholders will need), recent profitability may be a poor predictor of what kinds of products and services will lead to future profitability. Worse yet, profitability in the short term may give everyone a false sense of security. Such a self-assured posture does not generally inspire the radical organizational adjustments that might be essential for adapting to stakeholders' shifting needs and expectations. Alternatively, striving to gain (and assess) value-added contributions to products and services (involving everything inside and outside the organization) would focus attention on constantly improving the functioning of the organization in a dynamic, changing world.

Lawler (Chapter Eight) stresses value-added management as a way of considering whether executives do indeed contribute to organizational processes or if their functions should be distributed to autonomous teams throughout the organization. On a similar note, Kelley (Chapter Nine) suggests that followers should be concerned whether their leaders are indeed adding value to the organization and should, ultimately, distribute rewards to their leaders based on such value-added assessments. Galbraith (Chapter Three) considers the value-added perspective from the point of view of comparative advantage: Ideally an organization should focus on a single function or specialty it can do better than anyone else, while it develops cross-boundary associations with other organizations that can do all the remaining things better than the organization itself.

Ulrich (Chapter Six) concentrates on the people side of the organization when it comes to value-added considerations. He argues that it is rather easy in this information-intense world to copy how other firms acquire capital. It is also easy to copy technology and to clone products and services. But the one thing that is most difficult to copy (or acquire) from other firms is their particular approach to managing human resources. Since the culture of each organization is essentially unique, it is nearly impossible to transplant the culture of one company onto another — and make it work. Consequently, Ulrich suggests that the best way to add value to an organization is to nurture its human resources above everything else: What makes each organization a value-added system of cooperative effort is its special approach to managing people. It is the processes by which people interact, how they set goals, and how they make and implement decisions that primarily determine the ultimate quality of the firm's products and services. Therefore, setting value-added human resource goals and assessing the extent to which the organization has added value to the development and utilization of all its people might be one of the key ways, besides ROI, to determine an organization's prospects for long-term survival and prosperity.

Zoffer (Chapter Ten) uses the value-added approach to question what each level of formal education (from high school to graduate school) is really adding to the mix of skills needed for people to succeed at global competition. Most educational institutions set goals with regard to enrollments, average scores on entrance exams, the percentage of students who went on to the next educational level, the percentage of graduates who got jobs, and their average starting salary. But the fundamental question is: Has the educational institution added value to each student's repertoire of skills for meeting the challenges of the present job *and* his or her future career? (Or was it the reputation of the school or the prestige of the degree that made the difference?) Apparently, most educational institutions have been functioning in a rather protected environment and, therefore, have been free to pursue traditional goals that do not mesh with the changing needs of a broader set of (old and new) stakeholders. Educational institutions, however, just like the people and organizations they are attempting to serve, may soon face strong market pressures that threaten their long-term survival. Shifting to value-added, dynamic goals and performance assessments may ultimately save them from their own—and their clientele's—internally generated demise.

Conclusions

In this chapter we have summarized both the conference and chapter discussions on five key themes: creating new models of organizations and institutions; developing new linkages out of old categories; redefining the role of top management; developing global mindsets and competitive skills; and redefining organizational goals and performance. A major challenge emerging from all five themes is how to design the twenty-first-century organization: What will the organizations of the future look like? Can old-time companies that were successful in a noncompetitive environment be transformed into new structural forms that will enable them to compete in the future? What is the transformation process, and how can it be conducted while the organization is fighting to survive in the present? Is there indeed enough time to switch from a traditional to a new form of organization?

Explicitly and implicitly, questions of designing organizational *structure* lie at the heart of every discussion about making organizations more competitive. Perhaps structure suggests a tangible quality that people can get their hands on. With all the abstract discussions about crumbling boundaries and redefining organizations, industries, institutions, and nations, there seems to be an uneasiness about the unknown state toward which we are heading. If there is not some concrete end point, what does it mean to have arrived? Or can a transformation *ever* be complete if the environment keeps changing? Before these fundamental questions are answered (if ever they can be), it seems important to have a structural model to depict our vision of the new organization.

Network is the term heard repeatedly during the conference to describe the new form of organization for global competitiveness. It represents a highly elaborate but flexible system of relationships among organizational members and their associates around the world—held together by interpersonal *and* electronic connections. These associates represent any external person, group, organization, or nation that can contribute to the focal organization's value-added goals. Thus— in sharp contrast to the traditional organization that focuses most of its attention on itself—the network organization develops cross-boundary relationships with its shifting external environment. In a sense, the network organization integrates all the basic themes of this chapter by designing an interrelated system of cooperation, collaboration, and trust that will make any organization more competitive as we enter the next century of human endeavor.

But rather than present the ingredients of this "perfectly competitive organization" at this time, let us learn from the contributors themselves about the different challenges associated with becoming competitive. When we return to the topic of the network organization in the concluding chapter, the reader will be in a better position to appreciate how the ideal attributes of the network organization provide the basis for making use of everything we know about competitiveness.

PART ONE

UNDERSTANDING AND MANAGING COMPETITIVENESS

2

STRATEGIC RESPONSES TO ENVIRONMENTAL TURBULENCE

H. Igor Ansoff
Patrick A. Sullivan

It is strange, indeed frightening, to observe how much of the concern with American profitability is based on a socioeconomic doctrine that was enunciated in 1776 — in an age as different from today as horse-drawn vehicles are different from the automobile, supersonic airplanes, and levitating trains. This doctrine, propounded by Adam Smith and since then elaborated by many generations of brilliant economists, logically leads to the conclusion that a firm's competitiveness is optimized when it offers undifferentiated products at the lowest price. Hence the plethora of prescriptions for gaining competitiveness through minimizing costs by personnel reduction, automation, integrated manufacturing systems, robotics, and the like. And yet even a casual glance at today's reality reveals many successful firms that are not low-cost producers. One example is the Rolls Royce Company, which succeeds by maximizing rather than minimizing its prices. Other examples are IBM, Digital Equipment, and Apple, firms that can hardly be accused of being the lowest-priced competitors in the computer industry.

This chapter has three aims: to demonstrate that cost minimization, while important, is not the only determinant of competitiveness; to show that the factors that determine competitiveness vary from firm to firm, from industry to industry, and from one country to another; and to present a research-tested instrument that can be used to determine the winning combinations of factors for a firm. After defining competitiveness, we identify three clusters of factors that determine competitiveness and then focus attention on one of these clusters: the firm's response to the marketplace. Next, we propose a strategic success formula for a firm's business behavior that will optimize its competitiveness. We then present a diagnostic procedure a firm can use to develop a strategic response that will optimize its future competitiveness. Finally, we discuss empirical research showing that firms that demonstrate behavior consistent with the strategic success formula are likely to be the top competitors in their industries.

Here we will measure competitiveness not by the relative price of a firm's product, nor by its market share (remember the recent history of General Motors?), but by the return on the resources invested in the firm (ROI). A firm can be said to be *minimally competitive* in an industry when its ROI derived from this industry is marginally above zero. It is *maximally competitive* when the ROI is the highest in the industry. When a firm's ROI from an industry is consistently below zero, the firm is noncompetitive. As we will see, there are industries in certain countries that are inherently noncompetitive—that is, there is no competitive behavior in these industries that can ensure a positive ROI. We will refer to such inherently noncompetitive industries as industries in a *strategic trap*.

Environmental Impact on Competitiveness

Figure 2.1 shows the environmental forces that affect a firm's competitiveness. As the figure shows, these forces can be grouped into three categories: (1) the *rules of the game* under which the firm must operate, rules determined by the power structure, culture, stakeholders' expectations, and accounting conventions under which the firm must do business; (2) the *characteristics of the marketplace*, determined by the country's economy, its technological potential, and consumer needs, wants, and buying power; and (3) the *behavior of the firm's competitors*, which affects the firm in two ways: indirectly through the marketplace and directly through mergers, acquisitions, takeovers, joint ventures, strategic alliances, and similar activity. The three clusters of forces determine both the potential for competitiveness and the conditions the firm must follow in pursuing it. These forces can have a severe impact on a firm's or even an entire industry's competitiveness. For example:

- Pressures from shareholders, security analysts, mutual funds, and others for near-term profitability suppress the firm's long-term performance by inhibiting investment in innovation.
- Rules promulgated by the accounting profession inhibit investment in research and development by requiring that R & D be expensed rather than capitalized.
- Invasion of a market by new technology can destroy demand for products offered by an industry that has "owned" the market in the past—for example, the transistor industry destroyed the vacuum tube industry.
- Unfriendly takeovers can divert management's attention from pursuing competitiveness to fighting off takeovers and trying to preserve their jobs in the process.

As shown in Figure 2.1, firms respond to these environmental forces in three complementary ways:

- The *sociopolitical response* seeks to influence the rules of the game. If firms in an industry do not try to influence the rules of the game, they take a highly probable risk that society will impose rules that will put the industry into a strategic trap.
- The *interactional response* to competitors can be a confrontational response to predatory moves against the firm or a cooperative response such as a strategic alliance or joint venture. As noted above, the energy consumed by a confrontational response can have a severely depressing effect on the firm's competitiveness.
- The *business response* to the opportunities and threats offered by the marketplace, as discussed previously, is receiving the lion's share of attention given the present concern with competitiveness. The prescribed response, as noted, is cost reduction. In the following pages we will show that while cost

Figure 2.1. Determinants of Competitiveness.

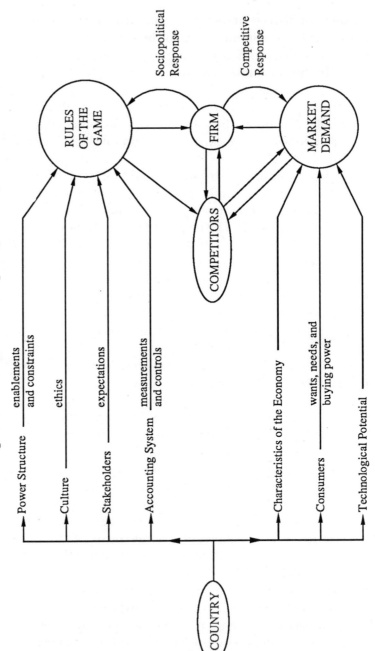

minimization is important, it is only one of several responses necessary to ensure a firm's competitiveness.

We can summarize our discussion of environmental impact and business responses by means of a verbal equation:

Competitiveness is a multiplicative function
of the firm's responses.

Or written somewhat formally:

Competitiveness = f(rules of the game × interactive response
× business response)

The significance of the multiplicative relationship among the three major determinants of competitiveness is that all three must be favorable in order to ensure a firm's competitiveness. Put somewhat differently, unless the rules of the game favor the firm's success, unless competitors are prevented from predatory actions, and unless the firm is responsive to the needs of the marketplace, it cannot hope to remain competitive, no matter how brilliant its management.

Therefore, all three types of responses are vital to a firm's competitiveness. Since our space is limited here, we will confine our discussion to the business response. (The problem of societal response is discussed in Ansoff, 1984; Lamm, 1988; Starr and Ullmann, 1988; Duffey, 1988; Tyson, 1988.)

Evolution of the Business Success Function

The contribution of the business response to competitiveness can be described by the following equation:

ROI = operating effectiveness × strategic responsiveness

Operating effectiveness is a measure of how well the firm is run. It can be divided into two submeasures:

- Efficiency of the firm's production function from purchasing to production of goods and services to distribution to sales outlets.
- Effectiveness of the marketing function, which includes promotion, advertising, sales, and after-sales follow-up. Marketing effectiveness also requires a sensitive response to the sociopolitical rules of the game that govern the marketplace.

Strategic responsiveness is a measure of how well the firm has related itself to the environment. It too can be divided into two submeasures:

- Attractiveness of the markets in which the firm does business, which includes the potential growth and profitability available to successful competitors and the potential turbulence that may produce major threats or opportunities
- Responsiveness of the firm's products and services to customer needs, wants, and buying power

Thus the preceding ROI equation can be rewritten as follows:

ROI = (production efficiency + marketing effectiveness)
     × (market attractiveness + product/service
     responsiveness)

At first glance it might seem that ROI can be optimized only if all four factors are continually optimized by management. Historical experience shows otherwise. The pattern of this experience is shown in Figure 2.2, which shows that production efficiency was the key success factor between the turn of the century and the 1930s. The reasons can be found in the firm's environment during that period: Demand grew at an attractive rate; successful growth led to high profitability; products were largely undifferentiated; and customers sought to satisfy their basic needs at the lowest price. As a result, the 1900s–1930s period in America's business history became known as the period of *production orientation*. It was during this period that the concept of management by exception was elaborated. Suc-

Figure 2.2. Evolution of Key Success Factors.

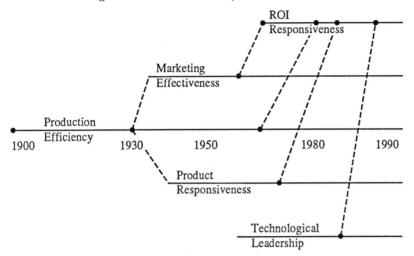

cessful firms were those that single-mindedly focused on competitive management.

During the 1930s the key success factor began to shift away from production efficiency. In consumer goods industries, *marketing effectiveness* emerged as the key factor because the customers' basic demands were becoming saturated, the buying power of the upper, middle, and lower classes was becoming differentiated, and the firm had to respond to this differentiation of demand and develop effective mass marketing technology. In some producer goods industries, demand remained undifferentiated (this was typically the case in process industries) and production efficiency remained the key success factor. But other producer goods industries shifted to *product responsiveness* as the key driving force in the firm. Typically these were machinery-producing industries whose customers demanded continual upgrading of products to incorporate the progressive evolution of the underlying technologies. The 1940s saw the blossoming of new industries based on novel technologies spawned by the second technological revolution. In such industries customers were prepared to pay the price for the most advanced technology. Here *technological leadership* was the key success factor.

By the 1950s four different success styles were observable in practice, each emphasizing a single success factor from the ROI equation presented above. Typically firms in all four categories were decentralized and managed by exception. With the exception of the production-oriented firms, all categories were now engaged in strategic activity. This activity, however, was typically decentralized. In marketing- and production-oriented firms, strategic development was incremental and followed the logic of historical development. In technology-oriented firms, creative insights and technological discoveries determined the evolution of the firm's products. Thus, in all categories general management was the recipient rather than the guide of the firm's strategic development. As a result, attention remained focused on competitive management and there was little evidence of purposive strategic management.

The 1950s ushered in the era of the New Ball Game. As shown in Figure 2.2, the increasing complexity, discontinuity, and turbulence of the new environment made it impossible to succeed by optimizing a single success factor. It was even more significant that strategic responsiveness acquired an importance at least equal to competitive effectiveness. This emphasis produced two results: Management by exception became inadequate and general management had to give direction and guidance to the firm's competitive work; general management had to assume a central guiding role in the firm's strategic activities. As noted earlier, a growing number of industries experienced saturation of demand during the 1950s. The consequent excess of capacity over demand caused declines in profitability in these industries. In some industries that were still growing, overcapacity was created by an influx of competitors from low-cost countries. In some industries the influx of new and alien technologies depressed or even destroyed the profitability of products and services based on the now obsolete technology.

As a result of all these changes, firms from different industries began to shift to the new and much more complex *ROI responsiveness* shown in Figure 2.2. Firms that are ROI responsive have the following characteristics:

- General management plays a proactive role in the firm's competitiveness.
- General management plays an entrepreneurial, creative, and directive role in guiding the firm's strategic development.
- No single function dominates the firm's behavior.
- Production efficiency, marketing responsiveness, market attractiveness, and product/service responsiveness are all important determinants of the firm's success.

As Figure 2.2 shows, the convergence toward ROI "bottom line" orientation did not initially affect the technology-driven firms. But in the 1970s these industries began to shift to strategic responsiveness—relatively recent examples are Apple, Hewlett-Packard, Texas Instruments, and Digital Equipment—as their customers became "technology saturated" and increasingly demanded "user friendliness" from products and services.

This brief survey of the evolution of competitiveness brings us to the 1980s and 1990s. As our discussion shows, general management managed by exception and focused its energies on competitive management until the 1960s. Since then, general management in an increasing number of successful firms has shifted from management by exception to a proactive management role. While strategic activity has long been a part of the firm's work, it too was managed by exception before the 1960s. Both the competitive and the strategic roles of general management are undergoing significant changes as a result of the increasing turbulence of the second half of the century. In the remainder of this chapter we will focus attention on the firm's strategic management. The right-hand side of Figure 2.2 shows that all the historical management behaviors are still being practiced and still bring success to firms. Therefore, the key questions we need to answer are: How can a firm choose the behavior that will ensure its future success, and under what conditions does strategic management become essential to success?

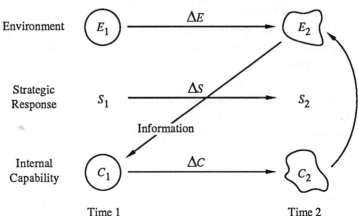

Figure 2.3. How Firms Adapt to the Environment.

Strategic Success Formula

Figure 2.3 shows a model of the way firms adapt to the environment. The model is based on three variables:

- The *environment* that presents the firm with opportunities and threats
- The *strategic response* the firm uses to capitalize on the opportunities and avoid the threats
- The *internal capability* the firm develops and uses to execute the strategic response

Figure 2.3 demonstrates how the three variables interact over time. As threats and opportunities change, both the strategy and the capability must change to ensure the firm's continued success. We now state a basic strategic success formula: For optimum ROI potential, both the aggressiveness of the firm's strategy and the responsiveness of its capability must match the turbulence of the environment. The formula is simple and sounds plausible. But before it can be applied in practice we need instruments for assessing the states of the environment, strategy, and capability, as well as a method for determining the degree to which the three variables match.

The *environment* can be assessed in terms of the level of environmental turbulence, ranging from a stable environment to a highly turbulent environment full of surprises. *Strategy* can be assessed in terms of the firm's strategic aggressiveness appropriate for each turbulence level, ranging from stable to creative. *Capability* can similarly be assessed in terms of the organizational responsiveness appropriate to each turbulence level, ranging from precedent-driven to creative. Thus the future success of a firm can be determined by using a simple diagnostic procedure:

1. Assess the level of future environmental turbulence.
2. Assess the level of the firm's present strategic aggressiveness.
3. Assess the level of the firm's present organizational responsiveness.
4. Determine the gaps in strategy and capability:

$$G_1 = \text{turbulence} - \text{agressiveness}$$
$$G_2 = \text{turbulence} - \text{organizational responsiveness}$$

These gaps must be zero if the firm is to be a successful competitor in the future environment.

In terms of these results, the strategic turbulence formula can be rewritten as follows: The firm's ROI potential will be optimum whenever the sum of the gaps is equal to zero; the ROI will depart from the optimum in proportion to the sum of the gaps.

Strategic Diagnosis

To execute this procedure requires diagnostic instruments. In this section we present instruments that have proved useful for practical application in business firms and have been tested by empirical research. *Environmental turbulence* is a measure of the changeability and predictability of the firm's environment. It is described by four characteristics: complexity of the firm's environment; relative novelty of the challenges the firm encounters in the environment; rapidity of change, measured by the speed with which challenges evolve in the environment compared to the speed of the firm's response; and visibility of the future, which measures the adequacy and the timeliness of information about the future that is available at decision time.

A scale of environmental turbulence is shown in Figure 2.4. Level 1 turbulence describes a placid environment in which a firm can confine its attention to its historical marketplace, successive challenges are a repetition of the past, change is slower than the firm's ability to respond, and the future is expected to replicate the past. Level 1 environments are rarely seen in free-market economies in which natural forces of competition are at work. The reason is that the key to success in today's competitive environment is continual substitution of new products and services that are superior to the historical products and services. Firms that do not innovate do not survive. While Level 1 turbulence is rarely seen in a free-market economy, the other levels shown in Figure 2.4 are all observable today. As turbulence rises, the environment becomes more complex, events in the environment become less familiar, change becomes faster relative to the firm's response, and it becomes more difficult to predict the events in time for an effective response.

Over the past ten years we have used Figure 2.4 with more than a thousand managers to diagnose the level of turbulence they expected in the environment of their firms during the 1980s and 1990s. A sample of recent results is shown in Figure 2.5. It is worthy of notice that roughly 80 percent of the managers expected their future to be at turbulence Level 4 or higher. At Level 4 and above, as we will see, strategic management becomes vital to a firm's success and, indeed, even its continued survival.

A firm's *strategic aggressiveness* is the second key element in strategic diagnosis. We describe it by two characteristics. The first is the degree of discontinuity in the future environment from the firm's historical products and services, competitive environments, and marketing strategies. The scale of discontinuity ranges from no change at all to change that has not been observed previously. The second characteristic of aggressiveness is the timeliness of the firm's new products and services relative

Figure 2.4. Turbulence Scale.

	National Economic	Regional Technological	Global Sociopolitical
COMPLEXITY			
FAMILIARITY OF EVENTS	Familiar	Inferable	Discontinuous familiar	Discontinuous novel
RAPIDITY OF CHANGE	Slower Than response	Comparable to response	Faster Than response
VISIBILITY OF FUTURE	Recurring	Forecastable	Predictable	Partially predictable	Unpredictable

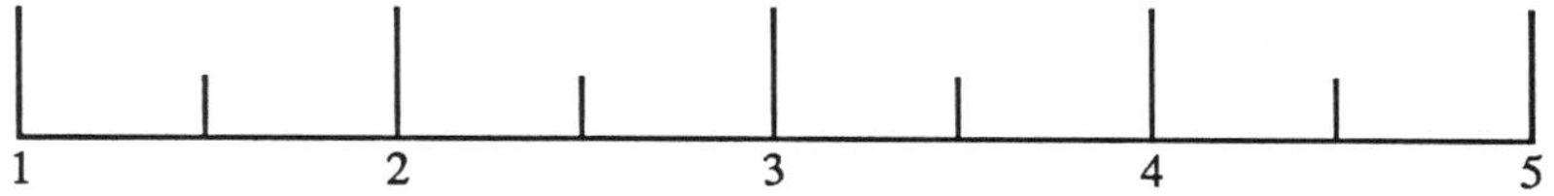

Turbulence Level

1   2   3   4   5

Figure 2.5. Managers' Expectations.

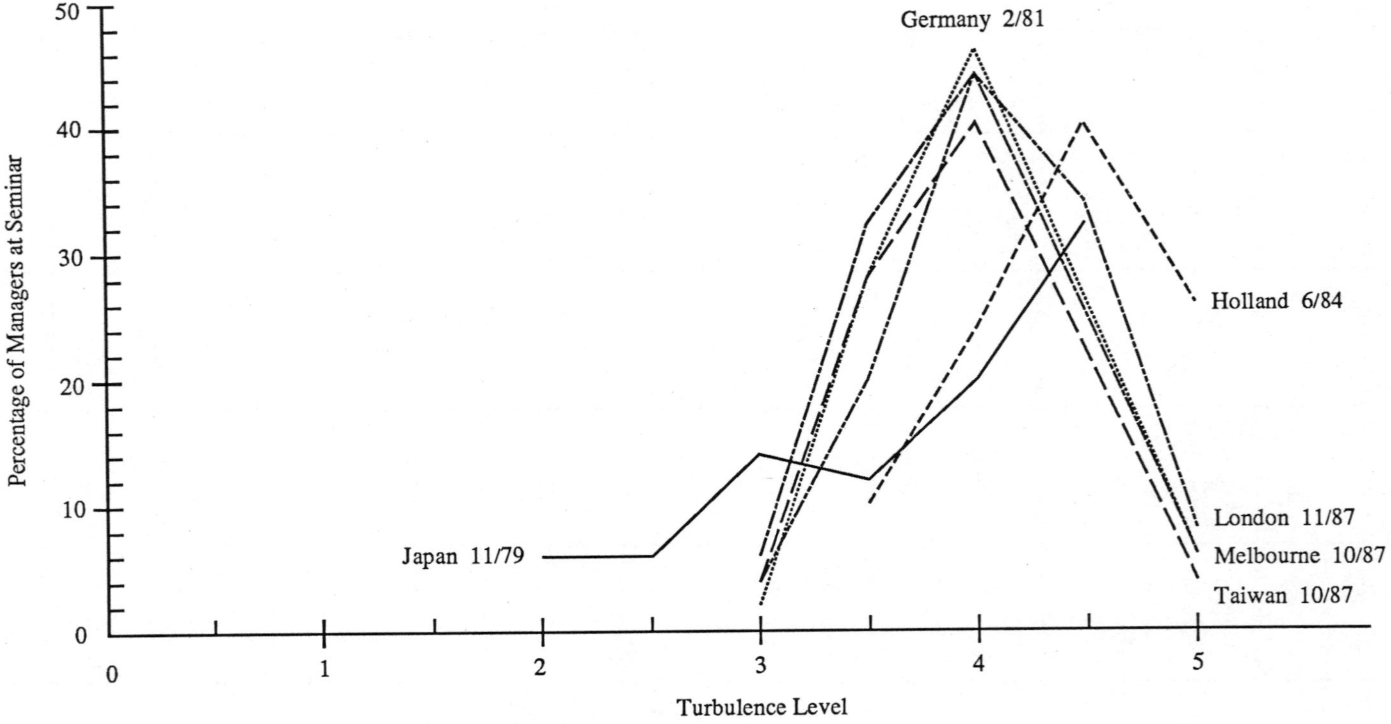

to other new products and services that have appeared on the market. Timeliness ranges from reactive to innovative.

Figure 2.6 describes the appropriate strategic aggressiveness necessary for success at each turbulence level.

Level 1 aggressiveness is rarely observed in the business environment, but it is common in the not-for-profit organizations that do not change their products and services unless forced to do so by a threat to their survival. At Level 2 the environment changes slowly and incrementally, and a firm succeeds if it changes its products only in response to competitors' moves. In the absence of threats from competition, such firms stick to their traditional products and services. Level 2 was typical of the business environment of the first quarter of this century. The great hero of the period was Henry Ford, who gave his customers the Model T in any color so long as it was black. At Level 3 the stars are firms that progressively improve their historical products and services in anticipation of their customers' evolving needs. The superstars are firms that discover the secret of shaping the customer's wants (for example, through artificial obsolescence). These heroes are celebrated in the Peters and Waterman (1982) book *In Search of Excellence*. The book's prescription for success is to "stick to the firm's [historical] strategic knitting" and to "sit in the lap of the customers."

Firms at Level 4 are in an environment that is subject to frequent discontinuities and poor predictability. This is the aggressiveness level for which a systematic response—which we call strategic management—has been developed by progressive business firms. Firms that apply strategic management demonstrate five key characteristics:

- The firm continuously scans its environment to discover future economic, competitive, technological, social, and political discontinuities.
- The principle of "sticking to one's strategic knitting" is replaced with "being where the action is." The firm stays in an industry only as long as it expects the prospects to be attractive and its own competitive position to remain viable.

Figure 2.6. Matching Aggressiveness to Turbulence.

ENVIRONMENTAL TURBULENCE	REPETITIVE	EXPANDING	CHANGING	DISCONTINUOUS	SURPRISING
	Repetitive	Slow Incremental	Fast Incremental	Discontinuous Predictable	Discontinuous Unpredictable
STRATEGIC AGGRESSIVENESS	STABLE	REACTIVE	ANTICIPATORY	ENTREPRENEURIAL	CREATIVE
	Stable based on precedent	Incremental based on experience	Incremental based on extrapolation	Discontinuous based on expected futures	Discontinuous based on creativity

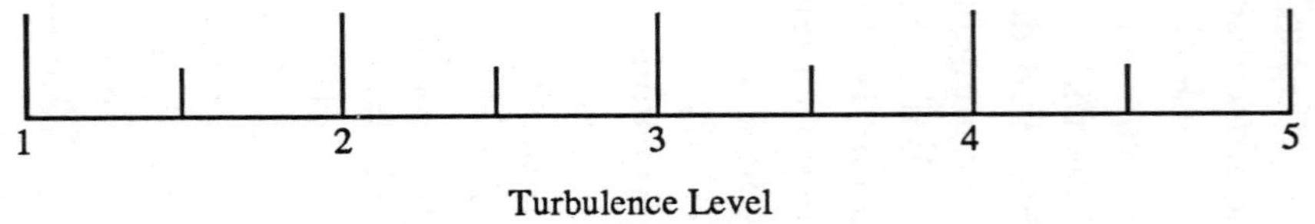

Turbulence Level

1   2   3   4   5

When the industry loses attractiveness or the firm can no
longer compete, it exits the industry in a timely manner.
- The firm continually seeks other industries in which the
promise is bright and the firm can succeed.
- Thus the firm continually repositions its resources from
markets and industries that will become unattractive into
growing and profitable industries of the future.
- In every industry in which it participates, the successful firm
continually reassesses the competitive factors that will bring
future success. Whenever the old success strategies do not
match the future success factors, the firm either develops
new strategies or leaves the industry.

The success formula at Level 5 is straightforward: to remain a
technological leader in developing products and services incorporating the cutting edge of innovation and technology.

The firm's *organizational responsiveness* is the final element
that must be measured for the strategic diagnosis. The responsiveness appropriate to different environmental levels is shown
in Figure 2.7. At Level 1, where the environment is repetitive, the
optimal organization suppresses strategic change. The precedent-driven organization is highly structured with hierarchical,
centralized authority. At Level 2, the efficiency-driven firm permits strategic change to occur, but only after management has
failed to meet the firm's goals. The organization is introverted; it
focuses on internal efficiency and productivity. Little attention
is paid to the environment, since it is assumed that minimization of costs will ensure success in the marketplace. The power
center is usually in the production function. Successful firms at
Level 3 are extroverted and future-oriented. Here the focus is on
serving the future needs of the firm's traditional customers by
using the historical strengths of the firm. The word *our* is frequently heard in such firms: "our products," "our technology,"
"our customers." The firm's strategic planning is based on extrapolation of historical success strategies. The marketing function typically drives the firm—hence the frequent use of the
term *market-driven* to describe such firms.

A distinctive characteristic of a strategically oriented firm

Figure 2.7. Matching Responsiveness to Turbulence.

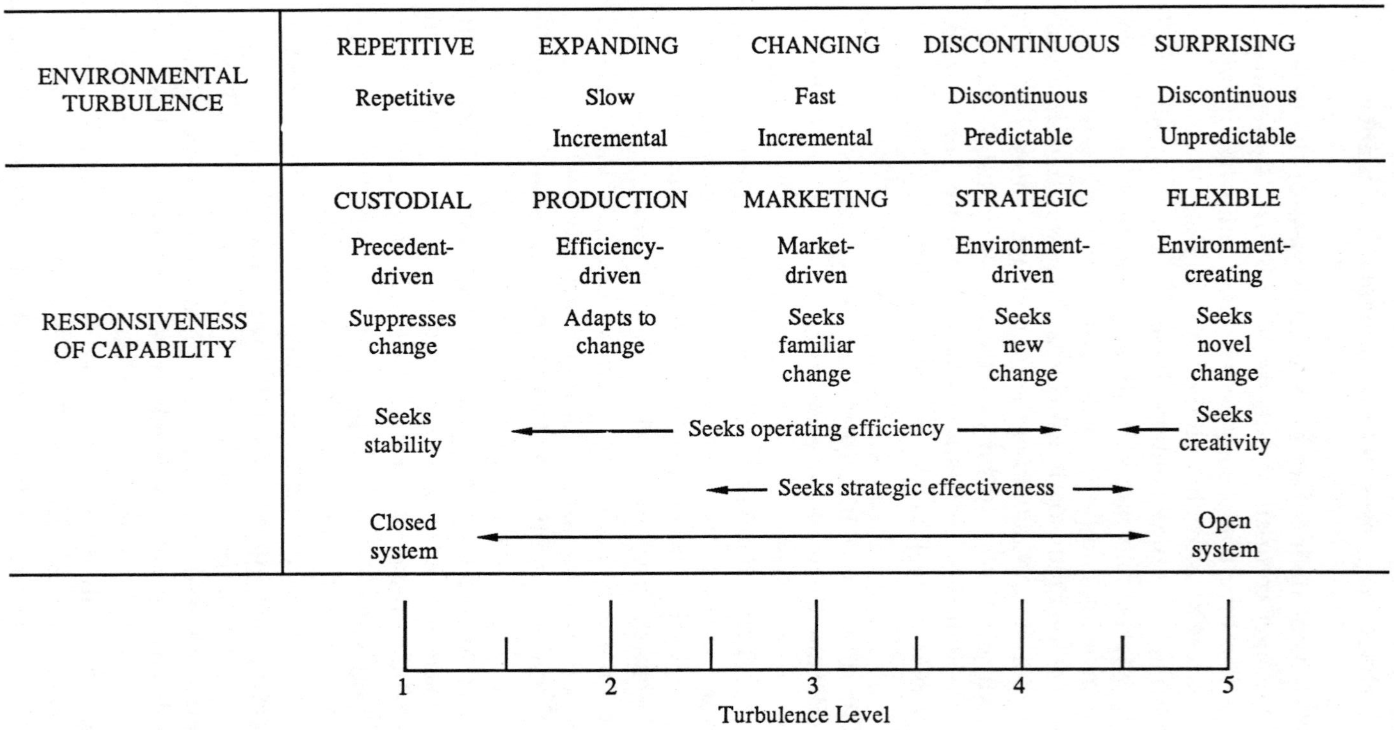

	REPETITIVE	EXPANDING	CHANGING	DISCONTINUOUS	SURPRISING
ENVIRONMENTAL TURBULENCE	Repetitive	Slow Incremental	Fast Incremental	Discontinuous Predictable	Discontinuous Unpredictable
RESPONSIVENESS OF CAPABILITY	CUSTODIAL	PRODUCTION	MARKETING	STRATEGIC	FLEXIBLE
	Precedent-driven	Efficiency-driven	Market-driven	Environment-driven	Environment-creating
	Suppresses change	Adapts to change	Seeks familiar change	Seeks new change	Seeks novel change
	Seeks stability				Seeks creativity
	Closed system				Open system
Turbulence Level	1	2	3	4	5

Seeks operating efficiency →

Seeks strategic effectiveness →

at Level 4 is that, unlike the market-driven firm, it has no attachment to prior history but is environment-driven. The future validity of historical success strategies is continually challenged and so is the future attractiveness of historically attractive markets. Unlike the other levels of responsiveness, no single function guides the behavior of an environment-driven firm. Power over strategic activity is exercised by general managers who balance the contribution of the functional areas. This balance is determined by the nature of the future environmental challenges and not by political influence of a single function.

The flexible firm at Level 5 seeks to create its own environment and has a feature in common with efficiency-driven and market-driven firms: All three are usually driven by a single function. This may be a creative market development function or a creative R & D department. A characteristic that distinguishes the flexible (environment-creating) firm from production-driven or market-driven firms is its total commitment to creativity. The past is merely something not to be repeated.

The strategic activity ("doing the right thing") and the operating activity ("doing the thing right") compete for both resources and management attention at Levels 3 and 4. The last line in Figure 2.7 shows that on Level 1 a successful organization is an introverted closed system that focuses on internal problems. As the turbulence level rises, the organization progressively becomes an extroverted open system that is focused on the demands of the environment.

Diagnostic Procedure

Figures 2.4, 2.6, and 2.7 translate the strategic success formula into specific instruments that can be used to identify combinations of turbulence level, strategic aggressiveness, and organizational responsiveness that will produce optimum ROI. At turbulence Level 3, for example, firms using anticipating aggressiveness and market-driven responsiveness are going to be top competitors. The three figures can be used to diagnose a firm's current preparedness for the environmental challenges of the

Figure 2.8. Strategy–Capability Gaps.

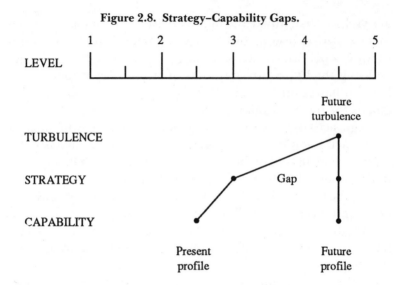

future. The procedure is demonstrated by using a hypothetical firm in Figure 2.8. Here are the steps of the diagnosis:

1. Figure 2.4 is used to diagnose the future turbulence level, which in Figure 2.8 is found to be 4.5.
2. The vertical line on Figure 2.8 connects the future turbulence to the strategic aggressiveness and organizational responsiveness that will be necessary for future success.
3. Figure 2.6 is used to diagnose the present aggressiveness, which in Figure 2.8 is found to be 3.
4. Figure 2.7 is used to diagnose the present responsiveness, which is shown to be 2.5.

The results of the diagnosis shown in Figure 2.8 indicate that the hypothetical firm is poorly prepared to meet the future. If it aspires to be a leading competitor, significant gaps will have to be closed.

Implementation of Strategic Change

If the strategic diagnosis reveals significant gaps between the firm's present profile and the future success factors, a change program will have to be designed and implemented. To identify the specific areas within the profile that need to be changed, a more detailed diagnosis will be required and a strategy for managing the change will have to be devised.

A detailed diagnostic procedure has been developed and used successfully (Ansoff, 1984, chap. 3.4). This is not the place for a complete description of the procedure, but we can offer an example showing the kind of information that would be available for changing management's capability to improve organizational responsiveness in our hypothetical firm. Figure 2.9 shows the four components of management capability that should be analyzed to improve organizational responsiveness: the behavior patterns of the firm's managers, the firm's organizational climate, the firm's organizational competence, and the firm's ability to get management work done.

The present capability profile shown in Figure 2.9 indicates that the four components are at different levels; as shown in Figure 2.8, the average level is 2.5. The priority assigned to reducing the gap for each element would depend on two factors: the size of the gap and the importance of the element to the overall success of the change. A more detailed diagnosis provides the information needed to identify the specific individuals and elements within the firm that will have the greatest involvement in a change program. If resources are not available for all the changes, they can be concentrated on the elements with the highest priority.

The first component of management capability addresses the general managers of the firm. The elements of this component are shown in Table 2.1. A management style appropriate for a low-turbulence environment will not be successful in coping with the demands of a more turbulent environment. The next component, climate, is an organizational component. Climate considers the factors that influence the firm's behavioral response to strategic change. Diagnosis of the firm's climate involves assessing the elements shown in Table 2.2. Climate is one of the key considerations in strategic change. It is also the most difficult feature of an organization to change. Changes in climate must be carefully planned and executed. Similar pro-

Figure 2.9. Management Capability Profiles.

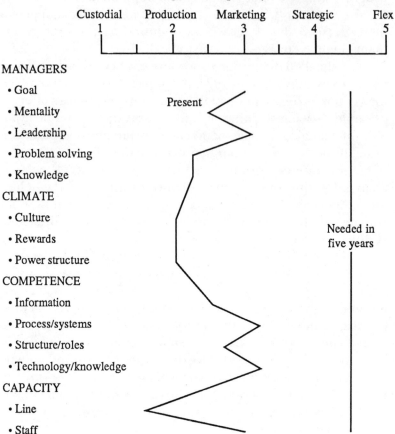

files can be developed for competence, which describes the firm's structure and dynamics, and capability, which is a measure of the firm's ability to complete management work. The detailed strategic analysis includes similar scales, aligned with environmental turbulence, for the two major components of strategic aggressiveness: marketing strategy and innovation strategy. These scales are used to develop detailed profiles to pinpoint the specific changes that must be made to close the gap between the present aggressiveness profile and the behavior required for future success.

Table 2.1. Manager Profiles.

Turbulence Level Manager Type	1 Custodian	2 Controller	3 Growth Leader	4 Entrepreneur	5 Creator
Goal	Status quo	Minimal cost	Optimal profit	Profit potential	Creation
Mentality	Custodial	Production	Marketing	Strategic	Creative
Risk	Suppress	Control	Familiar	New	Novel
Leadership	Political	Rational	Inspirational	Charismatic	Visionary
Problem Solving	Change control	Diagnostic	Optimizing	Opportunity finding	Creativity
Key Knowledge	Internal politics	Internal operations	Historical markets	Global environment	Emerging possibilities

Table 2.2. Climate Profiles.

Turbulence Level Climate Type	1 Custodial	2 Production	3 Marketing	4 Strategic	5 Creative
Culture					
• Norm:	"Don't rock the boat"	"Roll with the punches"	"Grow"	"Innovate"	"Create"
• Success model:	Stability	Low cost	Response to need	Strategic position	Technological leadership
Rewards	Longevity	Cost control	Profitability	Entrepreneurship	Creativity
Focus of power	Bureaucracy	Production	Marketing	General management	R & D

The final aspect of strategic change is management of the change process. In the 1960s, a number of firms found that extrapolative long-range planning did not accommodate the discontinuous changes caused by the increasing levels of turbulence. These firms replaced long-range planning with strategic planning that recognized the need to adjust to discontinuous changes by corresponding changes in strategic aggressiveness. These forward-looking firms were again disappointed when their strategic planning produced impressive plans but few results. We now recognize that two key factors were omitted from the strategic planning solution: the design of adequate management capability to support the increased strategic aggressiveness and management of the change process to ensure that the changes are really implemented. Let us look at this second factor in greater detail.

Resistance to change is a phenomenon that has long been recognized. Change creates uncertainty in people and in organizations that leads inevitably to resistance. Systemic resistance results from the inability of the organization to accomplish the required work—either because the managers do not know how to perform the new tasks or because the change workload is superimposed on the regular workload without adding capability. Resistance to change is increased when less time is provided to accomplish the change. If those involved do not fully understand the change, resistance is also increased. The traditional top-down, coercive approach to change produces maximum resistance; the gradual, adaptive approach used in low-turbulence environments produces minimum resistance. A realistic middle ground called the "accordion method" of change management (Ansoff, 1984, pt. 5) expands or contracts the change timetable according to the time available. It also provides for maximum participation of those involved in the change. Other major features of the accordion method include careful planning and preparation of change participants and concurrent planning and implementation of change projects.

The complete strategic success package, therefore, includes strategic diagnosis to identify gaps between a firm's present aggressiveness and capability profiles and the behavior required to succeed at the expected level of environmental turbulence. This step is followed by a detailed diagnosis to provide the information needed to close the gaps that were identified in the initial diagnosis. The final step is managed implementation of the change to minimize resistance and maximize acceptance.

Proof of the Strategic Success Formula

The strategic success formula is derived from the strategic success hypothesis (Ansoff, 1979). As its name implies, a hypothesis remains an assumption until it has been validated by applying it to business reality. One way to test a hypothesis is to apply it in practice. This is a costly and dangerous method. If the hypothesis is proved valid, all goes well. If it is not valid, serious costs may have been incurred and the firm's success may have been jeopardized by the time the lack of validity becomes apparent. Therefore, less costly approaches for testing the success hypothesis are preferable.

One such approach is the *plausibility* test in which experienced managers are shown the strategic success formula in a seminar or workshop and asked to judge its validity for planning a firm's future. Strategic diagnosis has been repeatedly exposed to the validity test by senior managers, and it has passed the test. Another validation method is the *empirical* test of the numerical validity of the success hypothesis. During the past two years the strategic success hypothesis and the strategic diagnosis instruments have been tested in doctoral dissertations by students at the United States International University in San Diego. The four tests highlighted here involved very different enterprises: U.S. manufacturing, wholesale, and retail firms (Hatziantoniou, 1986); banks in the United Arab Emirates (Salameh, 1987); state-owned enterprises in Algeria (Chabane, 1987); and U.S. federal agencies (Sullivan, 1987). The results of the tests are shown in Figures 2.10 and 2.11.

In these figures the columns class the enterprises into either two or three groups according to the gap between their strategic response and the environmental turbulence. The ver-

Figure 2.10. Validation of the Strategic Success Hypothesis:
U.A.E. Banks and Algerian State-Owned Enterprises.

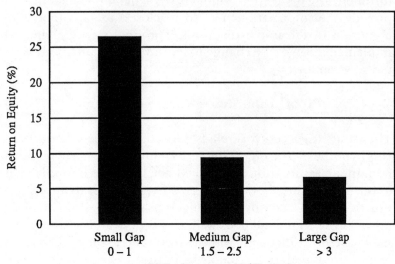

(a) Performance of 25 Banks in
United Arab Emirates vs. Strategic Gap

Source: Salameh (1987). Reprinted with permission.

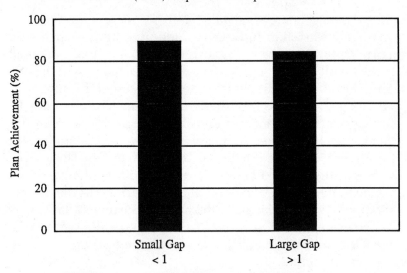

(b) Performance of 34 Algerian
State-Owned Enterprises vs. Strategic Gap

Source: Chabane (1987). Reprinted with permission.

**Figure 2.11. Validation of the Strategic Success Hypothesis:
U.S. Firms and Government Organizations.**

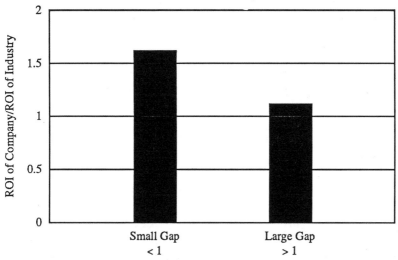

(a) Performance of 59 U.S. Firms vs. Strategic Gap
(43 Manufacturing, 16 Wholesale/retail)

Source: Hatziantoniou (1986). Reprinted with permission.

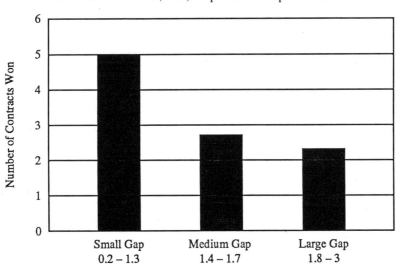

(b) Performance of 69 U.S. Federal
Public Works Organizations vs. Strategic Gap

Source: Sullivan (1987).

tical scales measure the success attained by the groups of enterprises: Banks and firms are measured by the return on investment (ROI); Algerian state-owned enterprises are measured by percentage of goals achieved; the U.S. federal agencies are measured by the percentage of contracts won in competition with for-profit firms. Note that enterprises whose aggressiveness and responsiveness are closest to the level of turbulence attain substantially better performance than enterprises with serious gaps. (All results were significant at the 0.05 level or better.)

U.S. firms with small gaps between environmental turbulence and strategic aggressiveness/organizational responsiveness had ROIs that were 50 percent higher than firms with large gaps. United Arab Emirates banks with small gaps had returns on equity that were three times as large as banks with medium gaps and four times as large as banks with large gaps. Algerian state-owned enterprises with small gaps had plan achievements that were 10 percent better than enterprises with large gaps. U.S. public works organizations with small gaps won twice as many competitive contracts as organizations with medium and large gaps. The consistency and strength of these results with such a diverse group of research samples provide strong support for the strategic success hypothesis and the resulting strategic success formula. In summary, then, the results of empirical research on the strategic success hypothesis strongly suggest that strategic diagnosis is indeed a valid instrument for diagnosing the type of strategic aggressiveness and organizational responsiveness a firm will need to optimize its future profitability.

Summary

This chapter began with a bird's-eye perspective of the problem of competitiveness. We have challenged the popular notion that competitiveness is attained through minimizing costs of the firm's products and services and shown that cost minimization applies only in a very special case in which the sociopolitical forces are favorable to the firm, competitors are well behaved, the firm's markets are growing, and the customers demand undifferentiated low-cost products. Thus we have proposed a more general concept in which the potential for competitiveness is determined by three clusters of environmental factors: the rules of the game under which the firm must operate, the behavior of competitors vis-à-vis the firm, and the characteristics of the firm's marketplace. A firm converts this potential (and to some extent can modify it) through three responses to the environment: its business response to the market, its interactional response to competitors, and its sociopolitical response to the environmental forces that shape the rules of the game. As we have demonstrated, a firm can optimize its competitiveness by modifying its business behavior.

References

Ansoff, H. I. *Strategic Management*. London and Basingstoke: Macmillan, 1979.

Ansoff, H. I. *Implanting Strategic Management*. Englewood Cliffs, N.J.: Prentice-Hall, 1984.

Chabane, H. "Restructuring and Performance in Algerian State-Owned Enterprises: A Strategic Management Study." Unpublished doctoral dissertation, School of Business and Management, United States International University, 1987.

Duffey, J. "U.S. Competitiveness: Looking Back and Looking Ahead." In M. K. Starr (ed.), *Global Competitiveness: Getting the U.S. Back on Track*. New York and London: Norton, 1988.

Hatziantoniou, P. "The Relationship of Environmental Turbulence, Corporate Strategic Profile, and Company Performance." Unpublished doctoral dissertation, School of Business and Management, United States International University, 1986.

Lamm, R. D. "Crisis: The Uncompetitive Society." In M. K. Starr (ed.), *Global Competitiveness: Getting the U.S. Back on Track*. New York and London: Norton, 1988.

Peters, T. J., and Waterman, R. H., Jr. *In Search of Excellence: Lessons from America's Best-Run Companies*. New York: Harper & Row, 1982.

Salameh, T. T. "Analysis and Financial Performance of the Bank-

ing Industry in United Arab Emirates: A Strategic Manage-
ment Study." Unpublished doctoral dissertation, School of
Business and Management, United States International Uni-
versity, 1987.
Starr, M. K., and Ullmann, J. E. "The Myth of U.S. Industrial
Supremacy." In M. K. Starr (ed.), *Global Competitiveness: Getting
the U.S. Back on Track*. New York and London: Norton, 1988.
Sullivan, P. A. "The Relationship Between Proportion of Income
Derived from Subsidy and Strategic Performance of a Federal
Agency Under the Commercial Activities Program." Un-
published doctoral dissertation, School of Business and Man-
agement, United States International University, 1987.
Tyson, L. D. "Competitiveness: An Analysis of the Problem and a
Perspective on Future Policy." In M. K. Starr (ed.), *Global
Competitiveness: Getting the U.S. Back on Track*. New York and
London: Norton, 1988.

3

STRUCTURAL RESPONSES TO COMPETITIVE STRATEGIES

Jay R. Galbraith

The 1980s continued the competitive trends that began in the 1970s. The 1990s appear to be more of the same. This chapter examines the environmental forces that are driving today's and tomorrow's strategies. Although there are many environmental forces, the primary force in today's business environment is global competition. Simply put, more and better contestants are all vying for their piece of the pie. The new competitive environment is driving three strategic changes. First, companies tend initially to adapt their core business in an effort to recover their cost and quality competitiveness. They then move internationally to extend those businesses from country-by-country strategies (multidomestic) to global business unit strategies. Eventually recovery gives way to development as the top strategic priority. Companies look for new revenue sources by concentrating on service, software, and high-technology businesses.

These new strategies naturally lead to new social structures through which to implement the new business directions. The first is *today's matrix* organization. Increasingly the choice is not whether to use matrix but how to make it work. Second is the emerging *network* organization. No longer are businesses vertically integrated, monolithic, hierarchical organizations. Instead they are becoming flexible networks of suppliers, com-

Note: The author would like to thank Gianfranco Gambigliani and FIAT-ISVOR for supporting the research reported in this chapter.

51

petitors, and customers who cooperate and coordinate among each other. The third social structure is the *neoconglomerate* organization. Before, there was a divisional structure that managed synergies between related businesses and holding companies that invested in unrelated companies. The new form mixes these styles so that the corporation manages synergies between unrelated or less related businesses. Moreover, the expansion of financial services and trading subsidiaries gives today's corporation a structure very similar to the Japanese Zaibatsus, which are built around a bank and trading company.

The other two changes are taking place inside the corporate umbrella. One is the *clean-sheet* organization through which a company introduces change by starting some activity from the very beginning. It is easier to introduce a radically different business practice by starting fresh than by transitioning from the old practice to the new. The other is the *new business development* organization. Organizations continue to build new businesses internally by separating the running of existing businesses from the starting of new ones.

The framework in Figure 3.1 shows how the environmental forces of slower economic growth, more and faster changing technology, new competitors, deregulation, government participation, and takeovers are creating a more intense level of global competition. Firms respond strategically by restoring the quality and cost competitiveness of their core businesses, creating global businesses, and formulating new developmental strategies. These new strategies get implemented by perfecting matrix-type organizations, developing network organizations, evolving toward the neoconglomerate, employing clean-sheet units, and promoting new business development activities. Each of the five organizational forms is being implemented via trial and error. The forms are emerging to relative degrees and still present significant implementation and adjustment problems. This chapter presents what we know about them and speculates on future developments.

The New Business Environment

There are many environmental forces, such as oil prices and demographics, affecting today's business strategies. But the

Figure 3.1. Framework for Analysis.

ENVIRONMENT ⟶	STRATEGIES ⟶	ORGANIZATIONS
Technology	Recovery of the core business	Overlays
Oversupply		Networks
New competitors	Extension of core to global reach	Neoconglomerate
New government role	Development of new business	Clean-sheet start-up
Deregulation		
Takeovers		

force having the greatest impact on the largest number of businesses is global competition. This new level of competition is the result of slower growth, larger investments in technology, new competitors, the new role of government, and takeovers.

Slower Growth

The developed world in the 1980s was characterized by slower economic growth than the decades following World War II. According to statistics, the West European countries have grown at 2 percent a year or less for the last ten years. This pattern is likely to continue. Neither Japan nor West Germany wants to replace the United States as the engine to lead world economic growth. As a result competitors will have to fight for existing markets. Growth will not provide more for everyone. Companies will have to look outside their slowly growing domestic economies to search for volume and new sources of revenue.

New Technology

Starting in 1975 the countries of the developed world stepped up their spending on research and development (Hage, 1988).

In that year spending increased (after inflation) by 6 percent. Since then the spending has been increasing by 5 to 6 percent a year. This compounded growth in research and development (R & D) spending has greatly increased the fixed costs of doing business. It cost Ford $3 billion and took five years to develop the Taurus and Sable car lines. The result is that companies, even in the United States, must increasingly go outside their domestic economies to pay off these fixed investments in new technology. So both slower growth and investments in R & D are driving companies to seek volume on a worldwide basis. But there is less worldwide volume available. With less volume and more seekers of that volume from traditional Western sources, the new competitors greatly heat up the global competitive arena.

New Competitors

The new competitors, Taiwan, Korea, India, Brazil, and others, are targeting industries, protecting home markets in those industries, providing cheap long-term financing, and using exports to provide economic growth. All of them are following the Japanese model. Initially they use lower labor costs and an educated work force to produce a cost advantage. They then invest in world-scale plants using the latest process technology to reduce their dependence on a temporary labor cost advantage, produce quality products, and still maintain a cost advantage. They borrow, license, copy, and even steal new technologies and avoid the costs of developing their own. As a result there is not only less volume to go around but there are more and more formidable competitors for that volume.

New Government Role

One of the reasons the new competitors are formidable is that they are teamed with their governments. There is still competition between companies, but increasingly competition is between countries or trade blocs. Since World War II, countries have been evolving their role in the economic process from one of regulation of markets to negotiation and participation. Most international trade was initially carried out by merchants and traders. The trade was largely in raw material commodities. Governments intervened with market mechanisms like tariffs, quotas, and subsidies. Now the trade is in industrial and increasingly consumer products. The trade is carried out by the manufacturers themselves, who are multinational oligopolies. It is easier for countries to achieve their economic objectives by negotiating directly with IBM, Daimler-Benz, or Sony.

The biggest change, however, is that governments are becoming partners in the economic process with their own multinationals. Using subsidies, reduced taxes, reduced anti-trust regulation, cheap capital, protected home markets, research consortia, forced joint ventures, and so on, governments promote the cause of their domestic companies. They use their international diplomatic networks as sales offices and for negotiating leverage. The role of government makes the new competitors more competitive. Deregulation is another force increasing the intensity of competition. Ironically governments are becoming both more and less active. The financial markets, the media, telecommunications, and the Common Market are clear examples. It is quite possible for governments to regulate markets less but help their firms compete more effectively.

Takeovers

The time for sleepy managements is over. The competitive pressures have increased substantially. If the competition does not cause change, investors who see undervalued opportunities will bring about change. Takeovers will continue in the United States, the United Kingdom, and increasingly in Europe. Combined, these competitive forces increase the power of the shareholders and customers among the stakeholders. In most industries it is a buyers' market. If companies do not respond to the discriminating customer, their owners will act or sell.

In summary, five environmental changes are acting in concert to make the world markets much more competitive places to do business. Slower growth combined with occasional recessions in the developed world plus a debt crisis in the developing world mean less demand volume for those seeking it. Slower growth and higher investments in technology are driving companies outside their domestic markets to seek the more limited volume. In seeking international volume, these companies are encountering new competitors from the newly industrialized countries seeking economic development through exports. In partnership with their governments the new competitors are competing with more than just low labor costs. They are global competitors. This competition is increasingly global and increasingly more difficult.

Whether this scenario will continue is subject to future changes in the world's economic and diplomatic environment. If the United States turns more protectionist in the post-Reagan environment, the world could repeat the 1930s scenario and competition would return to country-by-country contests. But a likely scenario is that increased global competition based on cost, quality, and new technology will drive business strategies for some time to come.

The New Strategies

The new global competition and the recession of 1981–1982 acted together to severely depress corporate performance in the United States and Europe. Manufacturing firms were particularly hard hit. The American firms were also subject to an overvalued dollar. The hard times caused them to make major changes in their core businesses. Initially the focus was on recovering their competitive position, particularly with respect to cost and quality. They then extend their core businesses from country-by-country strategies to more global strategies. Eventually, development of new revenue sources becomes the high priority.

Recovery

The policies to reduce costs were initially the obvious cuts, closings, and concessions. The cuts involved layoffs of the work force, early retirement, layoffs of managers, reduced corporate staffs, reduced levels of organization, and so on. Inefficient facilities were closed or sold. Concessions on wages were negotiated with unions. These changes immediately dropped the break-even points of the business.

Over the longer term, companies are continuing their efforts to become and stay cost competitive. They are attacking all types of cost. Quality has been a consistent focus not only to raise quality as perceived by the customer but also to reduce costs of rejects, rework, customer service, and warranties. Quality directors were appointed at corporate level, and quality programs of all sorts were launched and maintained. With high interest rates in the United States, chief financial officers shopped the world of lower-cost money in the form of Eurodollars or yen.

Since the new competitors used lower labor costs as a competitive advantage, labor was an early and obvious target. Concessions on wages, automation to reduce labor content, and employee involvement policies were all introduced. The employee involvement approach has been the least utilized of these policies. The reason is that it is extremely difficult to change traditional factories to the new high-involvement work systems. Instead, the new work practices are introduced when new plants are constructed. Companies are therefore migrating slowly to the new, more productive work systems. At some companies, these new plants are 40 percent more productive. Although progress has been slow in introducing employee involvement at existing plants, it is now starting. Companies are recognizing that recovery is permanent. The dramatic reductions are giving way to continuous improvement based on employee involvement. Employee involvement represents a significant source of future improvement. In the developed countries with educated work forces, people are underutilized and overpaid. The approach can also be used for professional, clerical, and even managerial work improvement. All these approaches have been successful to the point where labor cost is becoming less of an issue. In some assembly operations labor cost has dropped from 25 to 7 percent of total costs. As a result, cost reduction efforts are focusing more on management productivity than labor productivity.

The initial cost recovery efforts attacked the obvious sources of cost improvement. While useful, these efforts have been only the beginning of real recovery of competitiveness. Profit recovery has also been a function of recovery of economic conditions in the United States, a reevaluation of the dollar, and various protectionist efforts against the Japanese. Experts question whether Ford, for example, can weather a recession, the dropping of quotas or starting of U.S. production by Japanese carmakers, and the entry of Korea, Yugoslavia, and others into the small-car market. As a result, companies are now searching for the less obvious and harder to achieve cost reductions. These reductions involve interface management, consolidation and pooling of resources, debureaucratization, outsourcing and alliances, and continued automation.

Many companies are discovering that there are hidden costs in the interfaces between business functions like engineering and manufacturing. Under cost pressures companies are adopting programs for "design for manufacturability." Previously engineers were unconcerned or unaware that trivial design changes could often produce major savings in manufacturing costs. Attempts to achieve faster time to market are also forcing tighter integration across functions. If General Motors (GM) is able to reduce product launch time from five years to three, it will achieve enormous cost reductions. Use of cross-functional teams has generated the tighter integration and "simultaneous engineering" efforts. In another company the sales force, measured on revenue and sales expense, was unconcerned and unaware that many of their practices raised manufacturing costs. The introduction of product teams measured on "total delivered cost" produced significant cost reductions. Thus managing the interfaces has made functions more aware of how their actions can reduce costs incurred in other functions.

Businesses that have highly specialized labor and use expensive equipment have found that consolidating and pooling those resources into a single unit can reduce the numbers of people and investment levels to do the work. At General Electric (GE) the business units are centralizing and returning to functional organizations in order to reduce the number of managers as demanded by Jack Welch. Unless managed properly, however, consolidated functions can also become unresponsive monolithic empires that pursue their own parochial goals. In this case, costs are not reduced.

Another source of cost improvement, so far underutilized, is the reduction of bureaucracy. Many companies have paperwork systems requiring eight to ten signatures for a new hire or capital expenditure. In another company a project office hired an engineer, not to do any engineering, but to check on the engineering department and act as an independent information source to the project office. This company estimates that bureaucracy and redundancy groups increase management by 20 percent. Removing this cost is as difficult as implementing employee involvement, however. The checks result from lack of trust, status seeking, hierarchical thinking, an inability to delegate, or a need to know everything. Like employee involvement, less bureaucratic organizations are best created by using a new start-up facility. These clean-sheet organizations start with little bureaucracy and stay small. Often these new plants implement automated processes like computer-aided design (CAD), employee involvement, paperless factories, and minimal bureaucracy all at the same time.

The final recovery technique is the increased use of sourcing arrangements and alliances with outside firms. These practices are becoming known as vertical disaggregation. Previously, high-performing companies did everything themselves. ("If you want something done well, do it yourself.") This policy led to extensive vertical integration managed by monolithic hierarchies like IBM or GM. Today the policy is changing. The belief now is that companies cannot do everything well. Companies should therefore perform only those activities at which they excel and outsource the rest. This policy applies to the purchase of parts, components, and subsystems as well as to support activities like maintenance, food service, printing, and design of test equipment. Costs get reduced and quality is increased by giving the activity to a specialist in that activity.

Costs also get reduced by establishing close working relationships with the firms to which activities have been sourced. Here the logic is the same as working on internal interfaces. External interfaces carry the same costs as the internal ones. Using new information technology, a company can link with suppliers and customers to fine-tune product flows, thereby reducing delivery time, inventories, shortages, and oversupplies. Even where parts were previously purchased outside, companies are reducing the number of suppliers, increasing volumes from a single supplier, working closely with them eliminating activities like incoming inspection, and reducing costs and sharing the gains.

The newest form of alliance is the increasing numbers of arrangements between competitors. Here large capital outlays for something like a semiconductor plant force competitors to share the investment. Companies cannot afford to remain at the cutting edge in all relevant technologies. In the aerospace industry, teaming arrangements allow the sharing of technologies and the reduction of development costs. The European auto business will be characterized by extensive cooperative design and manufacture of components and subsystems. These arrangements take place through agreements, contracts, minority investments, and joint ventures.

In summary, then, the manufacturing firms reacted to the profit problems of the early 1980s by focusing on a competitive recovery of their core businesses. Initially they pursued the obvious course of reducing employment and dropping their break-even points. They then focused on long-term efforts aimed at quality, automation, interface management (both internal and external), consolidation and pooling of functions, outsourcing of components and support activities, and alliances with competitors. To a lesser degree they have adopted employee involvement and debureaucratizing policies. These efforts are continuing as the companies see more and more formidable competitors. Most believe they have recovered their core business to the point where development of new business is becoming a higher priority. One strategy has been to extend the core business internationally.

The Global Business

Manufacturing firms extend their businesses internationally in order to get the necessary volumes, generate new sources of revenue, establish a presence in all key markets, and acquire a retaliatory capability for potential use against new competitors. They also convert their international strategies from country-by-country approaches (called multidomestic) to more global or worldwide strategies.

The primary force for international strategic change was initially the quest for volume to support higher break-even points on new product programs. The increased R & D investment requires that companies achieve sales volumes greater than the volume available in their country alone. Shorter product life cycles mean there are fewer years over which to amortize an investment. With fewer years of sales volume, companies seek more countries for sales volume now. With slower domestic growth in the West, companies are forced into international markets.

International sales volume is not achieved, however, if different products are desired in different countries. Different preferences in different countries for consumer products and to a lesser degree industrial products had always been the rule. Today markets are homogenizing across countries and products are becoming more universal. Consumer behavior for many products is determined more by disposable income and education than by nationality. The equalization of economic standards across the developed world has homogenized the demand volume. The lower cost of universal products also generates more value for the customer.

Ford is typical of the trend. It first homogenized demand within Europe. Then after the failure to make the Escort a world car, they have been moving to more universality with Sierra/Merkur and most recently Taurus and Sable. They cannot afford another $3 billion for European equivalents of Taurus and

Sable. Therefore new models are designed from the beginning to serve multiple markets.

World or multicountry volume is also needed in capital-intensive industries—for example, it now costs $200 million for a new semiconductor plant. As more activities become computer-aided and telecom-driven, the capital costs increase and along with them the need for world volume. This discussion suggests that companies should supply the world from one or two factories, have a single design center, and utilize a local multicountry sales force. Indeed, this model has served the Japanese very well. However, there appears to be a Newton's Law of International Business: For every economic and technological force, there is an equal and opposite political force. The countries of the world are happy to have a company supply the world from a single plant so long as that plant is in their country. If it is not, they insist on some offset to imports or value added within their country. The solution to the local value added but world-scale dilemma appears to be the use of multiple plants in multiple countries. Each plant produces and usually designs a limited product line and produces that line for the world. Each country gets a worldwide mission, local value added, and yet sufficient scale to support the fixed costs.

The other force causing a shift to more global strategies is the tactics of the new competitors. They compete on price. The price competition may cause a need for global integration even if the company has varied markets, local products, few economies of scale, and minimal investment in R & D. The new competitors start at the low end of the market where price is important and their low labor costs are an advantage. They go to private labels or distributors next and get more manufacturing share than market share. Next they build low-cost, world-scale plants and attack the middle and main markets using price and universal products to buy market share. If the Western company is domestic only or manages international business with a multidomestic strategy, the market share battle can only be waged in the attacked market. If the Western company has a large share and the new competitor a small share, the Western company cannot afford to have a large percentage of its revenue under margin pressure. A better strategy would be to retaliate in another country where the new competitor has a large share and the Western company a small share. But to retaliate or to have the threat to retaliate, the Western company must be in all the main markets and be able to manage the business cash flow across countries. That is, the company must manage the business on a global basis.

In summary, the environmental forces are causing companies to establish a presence in all key countries and to manage across these countries with a global strategy. Presence in key countries is required to get world volume and local value added. Presence is needed for retaliation capability. It is also needed for market intelligence. In order to introduce universal products to homogeneous markets and coordinate pricing across countries, the business needs a global strategy. Countries cannot be forgotten, either, as companies need a substantial presence in order to have negotiating leverage with host governments.

Development

The initial response of manufacturing companies to the increased competition was to recover or exit from their core businesses and extend those businesses globally. This process is continuing today. But at some point each company began to search for new sources of revenue. They believed that they could not survive by closing plants. The new developmental strategies are not yet fully configured, but some generalizations about them can be made.

The first strategy is simple: Some companies are choosing not to develop. The oil companies are returning excess cash flow to their stockholders and buying back their own stock. These companies went through their own difficult times in the 1970s when OPEC emerged, oil crises occurred, and corporate raiders tried to take them over. They diversified, performed poorly, and divested their ventures to stave off the raiders. Other companies promote revenue growth by managing on a portfolio basis. They fund faster-growing, cash-using businesses with money taken from mature, slower-growing cash generators. So far portfolio management has altered product mix and improved profits more than it has stimulated growth.

The new developmental efforts are targeted on service and technology-based industries. Services are attractive for manufacturers for several reasons. First, manufacturing companies already provide these services as product supports to their manufactured products. Second, services are the fastest-growing sector of the postindustrial economies. Third, they tend to be local businesses and less susceptible to foreign competition and the new competitors. And finally, many services are local or regionally fragmented businesses. A large company can bring capital for computer-aided delivery, provide a brand name for national advertising, and install sophisticated management. The example of mortgage banking shows how a fragmented industry can be concentrated by a large company like Ford.

Many companies kept their services units when they sold or closed the manufacturing portion of the business. General Electric's Credit Corporation, Nuclear Services, and Information Services are all examples. These units have then been expanded internally and through acquisition. Nuclear Services not only repairs and supports GE equipment but will now maintain any equipment, thereby giving a customer a single point of responsibility. From here they have taken over a customer's maintenance function and in some cases run the facility for them. GE Credit would finance the purchase of GE equipment. With deregulation of financial services, they can now finance or lend for any purpose. They can buy equipment and lease it back to the user. They have acquired other financial capabilities like investment banking and insurance to service the entire needs of the chief financial officer.

These businesses have been major sources of revenue growth. Currently the companies are encountering problems with further growth of the services they already provide. The problems arise because the units producing the products being serviced are still viable businesses. The manufacturers of the products still see service as a product support activity, not a moneymaking activity in its own right. The service activity may need to service competitors' products or take on activities that reduce the priority given to support activities for the manufacturing unit. The strategic question becomes one of whether the service activity is a vertically integrated portion of the manufacturing unit or another stand-alone business unit. The conflict is slowing the use of service units as a source of growth of new revenue. Usually the company's leadership has come from the older manufacturing portions of the firm and they are reluctant to promote the new service directions.

The second growth initiative is to pursue business opportunities in R & D or technology-intensive industries. There are several reasons for this focus. First it is believed that the United States and the developed countries have the infrastructure and education levels to use technology as a competitive weapon versus the new competitors. The new competitors have advantages in mature, cost-based industries. Second, technology leads give competitive advantages that reduce cost-based competition. Third, government partnerships to exclude foreign firms are most likely in new technologies. Even in the United States, the government is ignoring the antitrust implications of collaboration, encouraging joint research like Sematech for semiconductors, and sponsoring cooperative programs in superconductors. Fourth, the defense establishment in the developed world buys performance and technology over cost in its weapons acquisition programs. The companies in both commercial and defense businesses want to pursue spinoffs from their defense work.

And, finally, new products and new technology are the source of new industries and new growth. Semiconductors created Texas Instruments, Xerox came from copiers, Polaroid from instant photography, Digital from minicomputers, Intel from integrated circuits, and so on. So companies see technology as a means to enter the next sunrise industry like the factory, office, or home of the future. The initial markets for these sunrise industries will be the home markets of the developed countries, which would favor local manufacturers and could also be protected in the infant stages. Thus technology-based strategies can yield significant advantages to companies in developed countries.

The question then becomes how to pursue the new strategies. Companies could use acquisition or internal growth. They could use combinations of small acquisitions, minority investments, joint ventures, venture capital, and internal growth. A variety of patterns has emerged. The large acquisition made on a conglomerate, portfolio basis is rare. The institutional investor immediately trades the acquirer at a lower price/earnings multiple. The acquirer's stock price drops, making it a target of takeover and breakup. The acquisition must "fit" in some way with the current portfolio of businesses. Moreover an acquisition must be friendly, fair to the stockholders, and not subject to antitrust objections from the Justice Department. The number of acquisitions that are large enough to be meaningful to the big companies of the world and yet satisfy the criteria of fit, friendly, fair, and legal is quite small. The large acquisitions that have taken place have been caused by problems at the acquired firm or its previous owners. The firms had to be sold. The acquisitions of Kidder Peabody and Employers Reinsurance purchased by General Electric, Hughes purchased by General Motors, and MAN (the German engine manufacturing company), Dornier, and AEG (the German electric manufacturing company) purchased by Daimler-Benz were all motivated by problems at the selling organization. RCA, bought by General Electric, is still the subject of speculation as to why it was sold and whether it had to be sold. Only General Motors' acquisition of Electronic Data Systems (EDS) was initiated by the acquirer.

The acquisition of service firms is always undertaken to extend the acquirer's internal service unit into new products or new geography. The acquired firm builds on what the acquirer already does. TRW with its credit information systems is a good example. TRW had the internal seed plus the database technology and capital. It acquired several small regional firms and then grew the business internally. It concentrated a previously fragmented industry to become the dominant provider.

Firms have employed a wider variety of growth methods for the pursuit of technology businesses. The auto companies have used large acquisitions. Each acquisition, however, has been a potential supplier to the acquirer. The acquisitions have been analyzed from a supplier and an acquirer view. They all have some relation to the core business. The acquiring firm can benefit from the additional market share it gives to the acquisitions and from any state-of-the-art advances given to the acquisition from a state-of-the-art customer. Both GM and Ford are using the same logic for small acquisitions, joint ventures, minority investments, and venture capital activity. They seek to acquire the best of their vendors in the new high-tech components area. The acquisition of high-technology firms to enter new markets has not been successful for General Electric or Westinghouse. In fact, their attempts to enter the factory of the future market through the acquisition of small high-tech firms have been a failure. GE's acquisitions in computer-aided design and ceramics have not performed well either. The unfamiliar technology and small-sized units have presented difficulties to the large acquiring firm.

Companies have also pursued the growing of new business units internally and the extension of current ones from technologies transferred to them. The technologies are most successful when transferred to an existing business unit. The transfer of magnet technology to Medical Systems at GE is an example. The start-up of new business units from internal ventures or small acquisitions has been less successful. Only TRW, with a history of early identification of sunrise industries, has had some success. The potential of using technology is strong but the inability of large companies to manage small entrepreneurial units has been a major barrier. A similar pattern repeats itself in ventures to transfer technologies from defense to commercial applications. Products do not transfer. They are never cost-effective. Existing business units can adopt basic technologies and improve their product line or process experience. New ventures using basic technologies suffer the same problem of entrepreneurial units in a large company. Very little experience is available from the use of research consortia.

In summary, companies are targeting technology-based businesses as a source of future growth. These industries could provide an advantage to companies in the developed world. Our experience to date shows that existing businesses can exploit new technologies for line extensions and next-generation products. Using new technology to break into new markets and establish new industries has not yet been successful. Perhaps acquisition is a better vehicle for new market entry if the acquired management remains. Management is still searching for the formula for new business development in technology-based industries. Part of the problem with the implementation of new strategies is that the organizations for them have not been discovered. It is to these new organizations that the discussion now turns.

Today's Organizations

The environmental changes described earlier have brought new strategies that, in turn, require organizational changes for their implementation. Table 3.1 shows which strategies are causing the new organizations. The following discussion summarizes these organizational types: matrix, network, clean sheet, mixed corporate forms, and business development.

Today's Matrix

The forces promoting a return to matrix are twofold. First, the simultaneous need for consolidation and faster time to market is creating a need for better integration across functions in the business units. Second, the simultaneous pressure from global business strategies and active host governments creates a need for integration across countries. In both cases a reorganization to product profit centers or worldwide business units is counterproductive. What is needed is the simultaneous organization of matrix management in its various forms. Matrix permits the dimensions of product, functions, country, and business to be addressed simultaneously.

Matrix is not a new organization form (Galbraith, 1973). Although earlier versions existed, matrix became the means by which aerospace and defense contractors implemented fixed-

Table 3.1. How Strategy Dictates Organization.

Strategy	Organization
Recovery Cuts, closures, and concessions Quality Automation Cheaper money	} Today's Matrix
Management Productivity Interfaces Consolidation Outsourcing, alliances Debureaucratizing Employee involvement	} Network } Clean-Sheet
Global Expansion Presence in key countries Global business Active host governments	} Mixed Corporate Forms
Development Services Technology	} Business Development

price contracts in the 1960s. During the 1970s, it became a management fad. By the time the 1980s arrived, some 80 percent of the companies that tried matrix had become disillusioned with it. Part of the problem was that companies saw matrix as a structural issue. They would have emotional battles over solid-line or dotted-line reporting relations. These battles sabotaged the collaborative relationships on which matrix depends.

In the other 20 percent of the companies and in aerospace, matrix worked well. These companies developed sophisticated information systems and accounting systems for tracking both sides of the matrix. They used the planning system to resolve many of the inherent conflicts in the simultaneous organizations. Subordinates were thereby buffered from unnecessary conflicts. Goals from the planning process became the "managers" of two boss managers. Performance appraisal became a key joint process. Reward systems became more flexible and recognized the priority given to team players. People who were team players were selected and promoted. Understanding of both sides of the matrix was promoted by career paths that gave managers experience on both sides. Matrix—the simultaneous organization—became manageable when managers became capable of managing on either side and decision processes were put in place for simultaneous management. The key to managing "today's matrix" is not structure. It is simultaneous processes and the development of managers with experience on both sides. Sophistication in management processes—performance appraisal, planning, information systems, reward systems—is the foundation to making functions and countries responsive to business needs without reporting to a business unit or product manager. The key to simultaneous implementation of global business integration and strong country presence is sophistication in matrix skills. The same skills are required for implementation of the network organization.

Network Organization

The second organizational form required for today's strategies is the network organization (Miles and Snow, 1986). Instead of the monolithic management of vertically integrated empires through hierarchical structures, more economic activity is being managed though flexible, often temporary, arrangements between suppliers, customers, and even competitors. These arrangements may be contracts, subcontracts, alliances, teaming arrangements, joint ventures, or minority investments.

The network organization results from two strategic sources. First the search for cheaper sources of supply or support and better quality has caused companies to look outside their organizations. With the fixed costs of technology and capital intensity rising, it is increasingly difficult to stay on the cutting edge of everything. Instead companies are focusing on fewer activities at which they excel and subcontracting the rest. The second pressure comes from global strategies to have a presence in all key countries. Usually the best (and sometimes the only) approach to entry is a joint venture or strategic alliance with a local firm. Some alliances are combinations of both strategic pressures. Success at managing the network organization demands the same sophisticated management systems and managerial skills as those required in the matrix. Managers must work across interfaces with peers that they do not and cannot control. Authority, control, and majority ownership are like structure. They are old-fashioned thinking in the new organizations.

The network organization involves two stages of development. The first is the negotiation stage. Alliances and joint ventures require considerable up-front work in searching for compatible partners. Like acquisitions, partnerships may be struck opportunistically, but their success will depend on foundations laid before the opportunity appears. Then virtually everything is negotiable. Who pays for what? How much profit can be repatriated? What technologies are involved? How are revenues split? And so on and so on. A great deal of negotiating skill is involved. In international environments a great deal of linguistic and cross-cultural skills is also involved. Management selection and development processes must reflect the new need for these international skills.

The second stage is the management of the relationship after it is established. As in any relationship, the problem arises when those who negotiate leave. New people arrive to manage with someone else's contract. The managers of the relationship need to be involved early in the negotiations. Then they need the same skills at managing interfaces as managers managing in a matrix. The benefits of a joint venture are extracted daily. The day-to-day managers need the skills of negotiating just as the up-front negotiators do. Our biggest problem is finding managers for this day-to-day negotiation. We need good matrix managers. Most companies lack the skills for an internal matrix. An external interface is more difficult. An external international interface is the most difficult. If the managerial skills for the matrix are not developed, the network organization will become the next management fad to replace the matrix.

Clean-Sheet Organization

The clean-sheet organization is a way around the lack of managerial skill and entrenched power centers. The implementation of employee involvement also requires managers who can operate without relying on authority, power of the office, and status differentials. The nonbureaucratic organization requires trust of others, nonhierarchical processes, and less acknowledgment of position. All of these social hierarchical features are difficult to take away from those who have worked to attain them. So rather than convert existing organizations, companies are creating new self-contained units to implement employee involvement, nonbureaucratic management practices, and automated management activities. When starting with a clean sheet of paper for the organization and carefully selecting new managers, these new strategies are more likely to be successful.

Top management needs to orchestrate the use of these experimental centers. They are usually successful on performance criteria but unsuccessful on conformance criteria. The clean sheets therefore need protection from the established order. They function best with little publicity. The graduates of the unit should not be made "elite troops." In time the establishment of many clean sheets and the promotion of the graduates may convert the company to the new strategies. The process is slow and painful.

Mixed Corporate Forms

The new development strategies are generating a new corporate form: the neoconglomerate. In the 1970s there were two distinct types of diversified companies. The first was the divisionalized company that diversified through internal growth into related businesses. Hewlett-Packard and Procter & Gamble are classics of this type. The other type of company grew through acquisition by buying companies in many unrelated industries. These companies, such as ITT and Textron, were managed through holding companies.

Today diverse enterprises like GE and TRW are diverse but are being managed to achieve synergies between businesses. In addition they buy and sell companies just like the old conglomerates. Many related businesses or single businesses like Ford and GM are acquiring and growing into less related areas.

This intermediate form is referred to as the "mixed corpora-tion." It is organized into clusters of related businesses. The cluster manages itself through a group structure with group or sector staffs and a holding company structure at corporate level. Policies and careers are oriented around related clusters. Inter-nal joint ventures across the clusters are the new phenomena that corporate units are trying to promote.

One way to promote the internal joint ventures is to use the financial services subsidiary as an internal bank. This inter-nal bank, the international divisions, and the trading subsidi-aries along with the mixed corporation become the neo-conglomerate. General Electric, Daimler-Benz and Deutsche Bank, and the Mitsubishi Group all look alike on paper. Is this neoconglomerate the corporate structure of the future? The prevailing opinion would say it is not. The conglomerates have not performed well in the United States. The investment com-munity trades conglomerate stocks at a discount. Academic research says corporate headquarters must provide value added. Otherwise the collection of businesses in freely com-petitive capital markets is better off being separate.

Recent evidence from academic studies, however, shows that diversity pays off. The Japanese Zaibatsu model has also performed well. In technology-based competition a long view is needed. Having friendly long-term shareholders like the Jap-anese Zaibatsu or German banks may be an advantage. As competition shifts to country versus country, the neoconglomer-ate may be a superior form. It permits the acquisition of cheaper money on a worldwide basis. But the U.S. conglomerate has not been as successful at accomplishing internal joint ventures as the Japanese Zaibatsu. Additional implementation work needs to be done.

Business Development Organization

The final organizational form needed for the new strategies is the new business development unit. Like matrix, the new busi-ness or new venture groups are not new. They were popular in the late 1960s and again in the early 1980s. Companies became fascinated with internal entrepreneurship. The oil companies were the most obvious promoters of these units and the biggest failures.

The development dilemma still exists. Managers responsible for running today's businesses are not successful at creating tomorrow's businesses. Yet new business development units have not been successful. Part of the problem is this: At what stage in the development of a new business or industry should the large firms enter? The prevailing view now is that start-up should be left to the free market and venture capitalists. Big companies can participate but as part of venture capital funds, minority investors, and customers. Then during the shakeout period, when access to resources and management skills become competitive advantages, the large firm should enter via acquisitions. Thus the new business units should be searchers for sunrise industries, new technologies, and likely acquisition candidates for the neoconglomerate.

In the meantime the growth that is occurring comes from offshoots of the current businesses. These were mentioned earlier as service units and software units. The firm already performs these activities. In areas where the firm has an advantage, these units can be spun off and acquisitions added to build a business unit. This approach is currently being followed by GE and TRW.

Summary

In sum, then, the new strategies demand new organizations for their implementation. Some of the new organizations are not really new. They are resurrections of previous forms that need to be perfected. The new organizations—matrix, network, clean-sheet units—all require managers who can influence without authority or 100 percent control. Many of the barriers to implementing these new strategies involve our limitations in implementing these new organizations. The corporate form that is partially implemented and still evolving is that of the neoconglomerate. Its ultimate form is a matter of debate. The new business development unit is still being perfected. Where in the development cycle should the big firm enter? This is the key question being addressed. These issues appear to be the primary ones facing manufacturing organizations in the United States and Europe today.

References

Galbraith, J. R. *Designing Complex Organizations.* Reading, Mass.: Addison-Wesley, 1973.

Hage, J. *Futures of Organization.* Lexington, Mass.: Lexington Books, 1988.

Kotler, P., Fahey, L., and Jatusripitiak, S. *The New Competition.* Englewood Cliffs, N.J.: Prentice-Hall, 1985.

Miles, R., and Snow, C. "The Network Organization." *California Management Review,* Spring 1986.

Prahalad, C. K., and Doz, Y. *The Multi-National Mission.* New York: Free Press, 1987.

4

INCREASING COMPETITIVENESS THROUGH WORLD–CLASS MANUFACTURING

THOMAS G. GUNN

Countless books and articles written over the past decade
have delineated the declining competitiveness of U.S. manufacturers. Study after study has documented our weakening
competitive position in global markets, the decline of our manufacturing base, and the continued closing of manufacturing
plants across the United States. This chapter reviews some of the
causes of the declining competitiveness of U.S. manufacturing
and examines why executives have been slow to turn it around.
After discussing the impact of technological advances in manufacturing and changes in markets and globalization, the focus
shifts to what can be done to reverse the decline in manufacturing so that U.S. manufacturers can begin to compete more
effectively in global markets and to satisfy the increasingly strin-
gent demands of their global customers.

The Declining Competitiveness of U.S. Manufacturers

Of major concern, from a manufacturing viewpoint, is the
American motor vehicle industry. In 1960, the United States
produced 48 percent of the world's total supply of new motor
vehicles. In 1980, U.S. manufacturers supplied only 20 percent.
For Japan these numbers were 3 percent and 28 percent, respec-

Note: This chapter is adapted from Thomas Gunn's *Manufacturing for Competitive Advantage*, copyright © 1987 Ballinger Publishing Company, by permission of Ballinger Division, Harper & Row, Publishers, Inc.

tively. Foreign car imports to the United States in 1960 represented only 6 percent of the total U.S. automobile marketplace. In 1980 this number had grown to 27 percent. In 1985, foreign imports, despite substantial restrictions, only declined to 25 percent of the U.S. marketplace. Today Japanese carmakers produce over one-third of the world's motor vehicles. The Korean motor vehicle industry is emerging right behind them. Further behind the Koreans, of course, will come the production of motor vehicles in other Far Eastern countries such as India and China.

Many U.S. manufacturing companies are barely surviving. Many cannot hope to compete successfully with the increasing sophistication of world-class manufacturing plants (Schonberger, 1986). The return on sales of U.S. manufacturing companies, according to a 1985 *Fortune* 500 study, was only 3.9 percent. Return on total assets in 1985 for the same group of manufacturers was only 4.6 percent, and it has been less than 7 percent since 1970. Many manufacturing companies find themselves burdened with obsolete plants and equipment, with distribution facilities that are totally outmoded, with work environments for human workers that need substantial improvement, and with manufacturing plants that are no longer close to America's desirable locations for work and education. There is little question that in years to come even more manufacturers will be hard pressed to stay in business as major players in their (former) markets.

On a global basis, Americans have unwittingly encouraged the growth of manufacturing in foreign countries, particularly in the Far East. This has come about from two practices. First, in the 1950s and 1960s U.S. manufacturers licensed a great deal of technology to foreign competitors in a quest for quick and easy dollars and with the belief that the people to whom we were licensing this technology would be hard pressed to make effective use of it and would never offer a substantive threat to U.S. manufacturers. Thus it was with total arrogance about our manufacturing supremacy in those days that we mortgaged our future for the present. Compounding the error, in a misguided attempt to reduce production costs, U.S. manufacturers chased cheap labor all over the world. This was a result of management's preoccupation with reducing direct labor costs. Even in the 1950s and 1960s, direct labor as a percentage of total manufactured cost was at most 20 to 25 percent, less than half the typical cost of materials. Rather than focusing on reducing the cost of materials, American management took the easy way out and moved manufacturing abroad, where wage rates for direct labor were often only one-eighth to one-fourth of U.S. rates. In the long term, this strategy gave further impetus to the growth of manufacturing expertise in foreign countries.

The past few years have seen overhead increase markedly in manufacturing companies. With recent changes in manufacturing technology and the further automation of many industries, we find that direct labor currently represents only 3 to 20 percent of total manufactured cost. Yet U.S. manufacturers continue to chase cheap labor and temporary tax relief deals around the world. This temporary approach to lowering overall manufacturing costs is not a viable long-term solution. Even if direct labor costs were *zero* in many companies or industries that are not competitive today, that would not solve the problem. The problem of reducing costs is far more fundamental and structural. Often the reduction of labor costs achieved by setting up manufacturing plants overseas was merely traded for increased costs of communication, distribution, and management.

The Shortcomings of Current U.S. Business Management

One of the real problems with the management of U.S. manufacturing companies is their complacent attitude toward the need for change in the way they operate. In part, this attitude stems from focusing inward instead of using the external world as a frame of reference. Far too many executives are content to measure their company's progress against last year's baseline of performance over the past five to ten years. This will not suffice. In any competitive endeavor, the benchmark for performance and progress has to be the competition's performance. This is all that matters. How well a company did last year is irrelevant to its success in contest with its global competitors. By failing to understand the capabilities of *all* their firms' competitors, American executives have been lulled into a false security. They fail to grasp the urgency of the need to improve the effectiveness of their operations. They wonder what all the fuss is about. They just do not understand the changing world around them.

Hiring Practices

Certainly a major impediment to the increase of competitive effectiveness in global markets has been the background of many of today's manufacturing top executives. Until very recently, the great majority of corporate senior executives in the United States have come from marketing, financial, and legal departments. People from these backgrounds tend to have little interest in manufacturing operations. Hardly understanding manufacturing as it was five to ten years ago, they are even less likely to understand manufacturing as it will have to be five to ten years from now. Only in the mid-1980s has the pendulum begun to swing the other way and have people of manufacturing and engineering backgrounds begun to emerge at the top in many U.S. corporations. In Europe, senior managers are more likely to have a technical background and to have come from the manufacturing or engineering side of the company. This is also the case in Japan, although most chief executives who reach the top there have managed to rotate through the major functions of their company in fulfilling long-term careers within the firm. Belatedly, the boards of U.S. manufacturing companies are discovering that if the company is in business as a manufacturer, then it might be worthwhile to have as CEO someone who understands the business of manufacturing.

Short-Term Goals

Perhaps the most publicized shortcoming of American management is its excessive focus on producing short-term results. While apparently fueled by Wall Street's pressures for short-term performance, so many U.S. manufacturing executives have grown up in this environment that they can conceive of no other way to look at manufacturing performance. Most spending, improvements, projects, and plans for the future are subordinated to results that can be produced this week, this month, or this quarter. In marked contrast to Japanese manufacturers especially, we subvert long-term strategy in quest of competitive advantage to initiatives that produce short-term results (Abegglen, 1984). Often these quick results are in direct conflict with the strategic long-term goals of the business.

Far more pernicious, however, is the short-term orientation shown by management with regard to their job tenure. Many studies have pointed out the short-term tenure of the average job assignment in U.S. businesses, whether it be the CEO or other senior manufacturing executives. Many job assignments last for only two to three years—and often for an even shorter period in so-called high-growth companies. It is often not unusual for people to change jobs in such businesses every nine to twelve months. Thus the manager has barely begun to learn the current job before being promoted to a new one. Short tenure does not bode well for technologies and practices that require years to implement. Under such managements, some people's sole preoccupation is "what short-term results do I need to get my bonus?" rather than "what tasks should I be performing for the long-term good of the company?" Preoccupied with obtaining short-term results, many managers also assume that their successors will be able to handle whatever problems they are creating today.

By the time many executives reach the CEO level in a company, they have but two or three years to work before retirement. Many of them are reluctant to interrupt a stream of earnings or dividends demonstrated by their predecessors— especially since their retirement pay may be based on their highest-paid five years, for example. Many of them want to *enjoy* their relatively short tenure at the top. Their motto might well be "Don't rock the boat." Another reason they avoid disturbing the status quo is that they grew up in the current environment. Indeed, more often than not, they were *responsible* for the current environment. To change it would imply they were wrong. Too often the attitude, perhaps unconscious, is "Let me get my two or three years in until retirement, and I'll let my successor deal with the problem." The concern voiced at lower levels of the company, particularly by younger people, is "Will there be any company left by the time we're in the driver's seat or approaching retirement? Will there be any pension fund left for us when today's managers are through playing with our company's future?"

Closely associated with senior management's nearsighted outlook is a rather simplistic way of looking at things that prevails in American business today: the two-bullet mentality. Senior managers say: "Don't present anything to me that has any more than two bullets on a slide. I can't deal with any issue that cannot be reduced to two bullets." Unfortunately, many of the real world's problems cannot be reduced to two bullets. Particularly in manufacturing, executives must deal with complex issues about complex products and processes—and with demands of customers that are not only complex but often totally insensitive to whatever the manufacturer must do to satisfy the customer. Seldom can life be reduced to two bullets. And when it is, the two bullets are so general in nature that to select one will not provide much direction, vision, or focus for the company. Senior management must be willing to tackle complex issues, to exert leadership, and to advance the company toward effective solutions that gain it a competitive advantage.

Career Perception

Compounding the woes of American management is the fact that manufacturing still is not considered by many to be a desirable career. Colleges and business schools are graduating people who select the fields of consulting, investment banking, or marketing. Manufacturing is still considered a career backwater—a place full of dirt, noise, confusion, long hours, and the punishing pressure of meeting daily schedules and sometimes unreasonable customer expectations. Manufacturing is regarded as a "low-pay" career in contrast to a career in sales and marketing, consulting, or investment banking. For all these reasons, the career of manufacturing has not appealed to the top talent of U.S. colleges and business schools over the last two or three decades.

Educational System

Closely aligned to the notion of manufacturing as an undesirable career has been the almost total lack of attention paid to manufacturing by teachers in our colleges and graduate business schools. To be kind, most such schools have been offering totally inadequate programs. Until very recently it was not at all unusual to be able to obtain an M.B.A. degree where no more than two or three courses in operations management, manufacturing, or even operations research were offered, much less required. Moreover, because these courses were such a minor part of the overall M.B.A. program, they were often taught by instructors who had lost touch with what was going on in the real world of manufacturing around the world.

Leading business and technical schools are now establishing innovative programs to educate students in modern manufacturing. In attempting to do so, however, they run into the problem of finding qualified staff to teach these programs. For as a prominent Dutch college professor once said to me: "Who will teach the teachers?" Most research programs in colleges and universities focus on "leading-edge" applications of technology, whereas the answers that lead to competitive advantage in manufacturing in the real world often entail the application of *proven* ideas and technology. Moreover, academicians tend to be advocates of particular schools of thought concerning the solution to manufacturing problems, and the courses they teach often suffer as a result of that narrow view. Thus the growing number of students who desire an up-to-date education in manufacturing will not receive it, for many schools just do not have the programs to address this need.

Industry has been slow to realize that investment in support of college and graduate school research both with real-world projects and with technology-based equipment might add to the pool of talented people available for hire. Only recently have major U.S. corporations begun to contribute computer-based equipment in substantial quantity to universities and to sponsor research projects relevant to today's manufacturing problems.

Manufacturing Process

American management has been remiss in its neglect of the manufacturing *process*. The major preoccupation of managers in the United States has been with the design of the product, not the process (Harrington, 1984). In many cases, the process has been taken for granted. In the frenzied product development atmosphere that exists in many companies today, there is rarely time to plan the process adequately because product design is always so far behind schedule. Either design resources are insufficient or last-minute marketing and engineering changes to the product specification are too numerous—or both.

One symbol of the lack of attention given to process design in this country is the weakness of the manufacturing engineering function found in many companies, compared to the product design function. The ratio of product design engineers to manufacturing or process design engineers in American companies is often 5 or 10 to 1. But to implement the kinds of factories required for competition in world markets of the future, the experience of many leading manufacturers shows that this engineering ratio must be brought much closer to 1 or 2 to 1. The Japanese have been successful in getting the most out of manufacturing—not only by maximizing operational efficiency and human talent but especially by designing quality into the product and knowing which aspects of the manufacturing process to control in order to guarantee product quality (Schonberger, 1982). Attempts at improving manufacturing in the United States, especially in Detroit, have usually focused on redesigning the product—to lighten its weight, improve its performance, and the like—instead of improving the design of the manufacturing process itself.

Manufacturing Culture

Still another reason for the recent lack of progress in American manufacturing is that the culture in manufacturing precludes paying careful attention to planning. Manufacturing in the United States and often in other parts of the world is a very macho environment. There is a great preoccupation with getting the product out the door in this hectic, male-dominated environment. Manufacturing has a kick-ass mentality that says: "Make it happen on time and on budget." Planning is generally viewed as something that M.B.A.'s and consultants and sissies do or as a function performed by staff. There is little appreciation of the value of planning among manufacturing managers and little tolerance for those who do it. The culture reinforces the feeling: "We're manufacturing people. We've got to get the product out the door. We don't have time to plan." Thus a "work harder, not smarter" culture often prevails in manufacturing companies.

Management reinforces this culture when it hires full-time staff or consultants to put together a plan into which the line managers have little input. Without serious involvement by the users (the line managers) in their creation, such plans have little chance of successful implementation. Thus the vicious circle of the notion that "planning is no good—it doesn't work here" becomes reinforced. Only recently have CEOs of some major U.S. corporations begun to disband their corporate planning staffs and push the planning process down to their operating groups where line managers are forced to become directly involved in the company's strategic planning.

Keeping Up to Date

Regrettably, most line managers in the United States today (or staff for that matter) seldom devote sufficient time to maintaining their own education and training programs to ensure they are at the state of the art in their own job function or industry, much less in broad business terms. Far too few corporations have adequate education and training programs for their personnel. Many managers fail to stay current with changes in technology, new practices, and new philosophies and ways of doing things. Many are lucky to read two or three journals a week or a month. Many no longer attend seminars and trade shows. Few have observed advanced factories in this country or abroad or have been exposed to people from other parts of the world who have different ideas on how to manufacture effectively. Few have enrolled in continuing education programs in colleges and graduate schools or taken advantage of those available from vendors in certain technological fields. It seems that many, when they graduated from school, made a conscious decision never to open another book again.

Many managers today are insufficiently aware of the increasing rate of technological change in science and business and the increasing rate of globalization of business. They lack a sense of the competitive pressure of today's global business environment. They are used to a slower pace of doing things. That simply will not suffice in the global markets in which they currently compete. The subject of continual education and training at all levels of the company for all the company's personnel is critical, for experience shows that such education and training is the key element in enabling companies to gain competitive advantage in manufacturing.

The Increasing Rate of Change of Technology

At no time in history has the rate of change been greater in technology than since the 1960s. In manufacturing, technological change has occurred primarily in three areas: information technology, materials technology, and manufacturing process technology.

Information Technology

Information technology has existed only since the early 1950s. In less than forty years, the science of computing and information systems has emerged as the major driver of change in business and indeed in society. In spite of this rapid progress, much remains to be accomplished. We are just beginning to understand information processing as a science, not as an art. We are just beginning to realize that the common thread throughout business and manufacturing is data—data not only in the alphanumeric form of numbers and letters, but data in geometric form. The tangible objects that we manufacture are manifestations of these geometric data. We are just beginning to understand the application of structured analysis to business and the concepts of data flow modeling and to develop more sophisticated software more productively. Only recently has major progress been made in the development of relational database management systems that inject more mathematical and logical rigor into the way we define, store, access, and manipulate data.

Many companies are beginning to realize that they are really in the software business, not the hardware business. In the manufacture of material handling products, for example, companies for years have thought that they were in the business of building steel racks, or storage units, or transportation devices. Today these hardware-based devices are commonplace and are almost commodity items. What differentiates the value of these products to customers is the sophistication of the software that lies behind the operation of the *total* material handling system.

Yet to come is the application of artificial intelligence (AI). Manufacturing companies of the future will be able to use decision support systems and expert systems that capture permanently in software the knowledge base, as well as the reasoning base, of people. Thus as experienced people—process planners or design engineers in manufacturing—leave companies today, their knowledge can be captured and embedded permanently in the software-based expert systems that will be used to make intelligent decisions in manufacturing and business applications in the future. An entire AI-based industry is in its infancy today.

Materials Technology

Many new materials developed since the 1960s are available to manufacturers, as are new forms of older materials. A prime example of changing materials technology is the use of plastics in automobiles or in other forms of industrial output, where plastics in many different varieties are replacing steel, aluminum, die-cast zinc, and other expensive metal parts. In 1950 there were very few plastic parts in an automobile. In 1975 plastics were responsible for about 4 percent of a car's total weight. In 1986 the average automobile produced in the United States contained about 300 pounds of plastic (about 9 percent of its weight), and the ratio of plastic material to total car weight continues to increase.

In the production of airplanes and aerospace vehicles, major new materials made from organic or metal matrix composites, ceramics, and high-strength and high-temperature metal alloys continue to rise in importance. Composite materials make up some 10 to 30 percent of the weight of new military aircraft and some 3 to 10 percent of the weight of commercial aircraft. These numbers are projected to rise significantly in the next decade or two. In the telecommunication industry, fiber optics is replacing copper for conducting bits of data throughout the world. A typical fiber optics cable has some 250 to 500 times the data-carrying capacity of a copper wire. In the world of semiconductors, gallium arsenide is replacing silicon in certain very specialized semiconductors.

The adoption of new materials has been hastened by the underlying cost structure of particular industries and the cost of one material compared to another. A major limitation to the adoption rate for many new materials has been the manufacturing process to which they are tied. In the substitution of plastics for other kinds of material in manufacturing industries, for instance, the adoption rate may be paced more by the *process* than by the cost of the material itself. One of the limitations in the adoption of plastic to make many complex products is the complexity of the molds and dies required in manufacturing the plastics. It used to be cheaper for the part to be produced by fastening together many different mechanical products to form a large product. With the advent of computer-aided design in engineering and computer numerically controlled (CNC) based machining, we now have the ability to design and machine sophisticated dies quickly and accurately to produce one plastic part that substitutes for an assembly of many metal parts used previously (Gunn, 1981). Thus the advent of more sophisticated design and mold production equipment will enable an accelerating rate of adoption of new *material* technology in the future.

Then, too, entirely new materials are available to fasten products together. Traditional technology used mechanical fasteners such as nuts, bolts, screws, nails and rivets to hold components together. The advent of new adhesives has enabled the assembly of many different parts without the traditional fasteners. Not only are costs saved in production, but the product is often stronger, lighter, and more esthetically pleasing. The use of these new design and assembly methods may have major implications for the after-sale service of new products, however. In fact, the rate of change of materials technology has tremendous implications for the entire business world. Consumers demand products that are made out of cheaper materials that perform better, last longer, and are of better quality. Manufacturers in turn demand materials that are cheaper, easier to work with, and made by processes more amenable to obtaining higher quality (as defined by the consumer) at lower overall cost. Thus the adoption of new materials in manufacturing is a driving force for the adoption of new manufacturing processes in industry.

Process Technology

The material changes described here are having a dramatic effect on the rate of change of manufacturing technology in industry. Whereas the aircraft factory used to be peopled by metal cutters and sheet metal benders, now machine tools and presses are being replaced by CNC tape-laying and epoxy-coating equipment and huge autoclaves to cure large parts made of composite materials. The autoclaves are large ovens that not only help bond the materials but relieve the stresses in the product as well. Entirely new processes now achieve results in more traditional parts of industry, such as metalworking. The industrial laser can be used to cut metal—either a piece of sheet metal from which a special design is to be cut or a metal part in which a hole is to be drilled. Lasers can also be used for heat treatment.

New processes can be used for the production of other kinds of metal parts, as well. Near net shaping is gaining momentum in the casting and forging of many metal parts. In this process, the amount of excessive metal and flashing is minimized so that the part produced is as close to the final shape and size as possible. This minimizes the amount of metal removal that will have to be performed by some sort of machining process. Among other new methods of producing and treating materials is hot isostatic processing (HIP). This process is used to create metals of strengths that we could only dream about a few years ago. Photolithography is used to produce conventional silicon-based semiconductors with circuit line widths of approximately 1 micron (one-millionth of a meter). An emerging manufacturing process uses X-ray lithography to embed circuit lines of about 0.25 micron width in the silicon material with a moving X-ray beam. Moreover, manufacturing processes carried out in the absolute vacuum of space are just emerging. A new science of zero-gravity manufacturing will be developed to manufacture pure chemical elements, perfectly round bearings, and new medicines, for example. Thus many chemical processes that simply cannot be used in an atmosphere where gravity exerts even the minutest effect will become available for use in manufacturing.

The rate of technological change in manufacturing and business seems to be advancing at an increasing pace. In part this is due to the greater amount of communication occurring today. An event regarding technology in a foreign country—for instance, Japan or China—is immediately newsworthy to the concerned followers of that field in other parts of the world whether they be manufacturing people or scientists. High-speed communication and the increased publishing of scientific and business information around the world increase the availability of such information to people who would otherwise not have had access to it in the past.

Despite the increasing rate of discovery, the time it takes to implement new technology or develop it into a viable business, ironically, remains much the same as in the past. Many studies have shown that the average technological innovation requires some thirteen years between its origin and its first commercial success. It is little wonder, then, that the new tool of computer-integrated manufacturing (CIM) is taking so long to be implemented throughout the industrial world (Gunn, 1986a).

Changing Markets and Globalization

Without a doubt, the most significant occurrence in the world of business over the last decade has been its increasing globalization. The world continues to shrink as communication and travel become easier and faster and as we open up major new areas of the world as markets and production bases. In the first seventy years of this century, U.S. manufacturers faced competition that was primarily regional or at best national. Today U.S. manufacturers compete with rivals around the world. In the Far East, the competition used to be just Japanese. Now the competition has spread to Taiwan, India, the Philippines, Korea, Singapore, and mainland China. South America, Brazil, and to a lesser extent Mexico have become major manufacturing competitors. In Europe there is an increasingly competitive manufacturing base in the Scandinavian countries, Italy, West Germany, Switzerland, and France.

The new concept of designing global products for global markets has emerged in the last five to ten years. Increasingly the United States, Western Europe, and Japan are looked upon as a relatively homogeneous body of some 600 million consumers, all with relatively similar tastes and education and spending levels. People in these three geographical areas produce and consume some 80 percent of the world's goods. Increasingly, product designs are targeted on this market. All we need to do is to look at the range of nondurable consumer-related products that span these three market areas: Levi's, McDonald's, Coke and Pepsi, hi-fi and stereo equipment, camera equipment, video recorder equipment, and a wide variety of other consumer products. Not only has market globalization happened to consumer products, but it is happening to industrial products such as forklift trucks and durable consumer goods such as power tools. The design of global products for global markets entails a major shift in both marketing and design philosophies for most U.S. manufacturing companies. Currently many companies are struggling to accomplish this change and achieve successful global design and distribution of their products.

Decreasing Product Cycle

With the increased pace of life today and the increased competition in global markets, another major trend is the decreasing product life cycle of today's products, whether consumer or industrial. In automobiles and trucks, for instance, major redesigns of engines, cars, axles, and brakes used to occur every six or seven years or longer and would last at least that long in their product life cycle. Today, product life cycles have decreased to just three or four years. Nowhere is the abbreviation of product life cycle more evident that in computer-based equipment. One example is the engineering work station, which used to have a product life cycle of some three years. By 1988 this was reduced to eighteen months, and now it is down to four to six months. This may be a harbinger of things to come for all kinds of products.

I have developed a hypothesis, recently, that the ratio of new product design lead time to product life cycle is constant. If this hypothesis is true, the ability to design and change products ever more quickly (thanks to computer-aided design and engineering and to group technology) means ever-shortening product life cycles in the future for almost every product. Recent studies have shown a correlation between business success (in terms of profit and market share) and a company's ability to innovate and bring new products to market more quickly and at a faster rate. So it seems there are a number of major forces that are moving us toward a continual decrease in the life cycle of products.

Sophisticated Consumers

Coupled with increasing global competition and a decrease in product life cycles is the increasing sophistication of the customer. The advanced educational level of consumers, particularly in Japan, Western Europe, and the United States, means that they are (or can be) more knowledgeable about the products they seek and able to discriminate more easily among differing product specifications, performance features, and quality levels. Moreover, such sophisticated customers are becoming increasingly demanding about what they want in a product—not only from the technological or functional point of view but with respect to esthetics and styling as well. Learning to cope with the increased demands of customers presents a major change for many U.S. manufacturers and their marketing managers.

Perhaps the greatest change in the global marketplace has been the consumer's increased emphasis on product quality as a criterion for purchase. Today's educated and sophisticated customers are more willing to pay more money and invest in a higher-quality product that will deliver better performance over a longer life. Moreover, increased global competition has led many manufacturers, particularly those in Japan, to differentiate their companies and products by emphasizing product quality. They have defined product quality in its broadest sense, not just by conformance to a specification (Ishikawa, 1979).

Channels of Distribution

No discussion of changing markets would be complete without looking at the changing expectations of the channels of distribution that exist in many markets. Just as the individual consumer is becoming more discriminating, the managers of successive stages of the distribution channel are becoming more sophisticated. Distributors too are more aware of the need for accurate business records, the need to increase return on assets, the need to avoid tying up working capital in their businesses, and the need to turn their inventory faster, among other things. Distributors are also acutely sensitive to the issue of quality and the demands of their customers. The last thing they want to do is spend all their time handling customer complaints about quality and hassling over quality problems with the manufacturer.

Thus distributors are placing additional burdens on the manu-facturer to hold their inventory for them, to give quicker deliv-ery, to design new or specialized products for their markets more quickly, and to produce higher-quality products that will result in fewer customer complaints. These demands all place a heavier burden on the original manufacturer to be a more effective competitor and to be much more responsive to cus-tomer demand.

A New Vision of Manufacturing and Business

Beset by calls for a change in manufacturing, business manage-ment also finds its own environment changing. The needs and skills required to manage today's businesses in a global environ-ment are far different than they were just a decade ago. Today's businesses need people who have a state-of-the-art education and understand such things as information systems and global trading. With markets changing rapidly, the old ways of market-ing—more often, in past years, selling—in global markets sim-ply will not suffice. Not only is sophisticated marketing needed to identify the demands of global consumers, but increasingly sophisticated design and manufacturing and distribution pro-cedures are needed to service today's and tomorrow's markets. In short, the business of manufacturing has become far more demanding.

To simplify the task of improving manufacturing ac-tivities, large-scale problems in a factory were divided into many smaller boxes, from a functional as well as a process aspect, as illustrated in Figure 4.1a. This was done in order to understand the process in each box, to gain control of it, and then, it was hoped, to optimize the performance of each box—whether that box was a work center, a department, or an entire functional organization such as design engineering or production. The result over the past two or three decades has been some improve-ment in manufacturing effectiveness, but we have also been left with certain negative side-effects of this approach. One is that we end up with a wide variety of uncoordinated boxes. Moreover, optimizing the performance of each box does not necessarily optimize the performance of the total system—and, even more damaging, we have built enormously counterproductive walls around each box. If this approach is insufficient to sustain our competitive advantage, what approach might now be effective?

We now must look at the total manufacturing system—and at manufacturing as a total system—as illustrated in Figure 4.1b. This approach offers several benefits:

- We consider the performance of the system as a whole.
- The entire manufacturing process, all five major activities, is involved.
- Solutions are coordinated across the total manufacturing function.
- We consider our suppliers, who, in most cases, play a major role in most manufacturing companies' activities.
- Most important, we dissolve those counterproductive walls between functions and departments and promote a sense of teamwork throughout the manufacturing organization.

This new way of looking at manufacturing is merely a start toward gaining our competitive advantage. Additionally, today's manufacturers must understand the nature of the change all around them, create a strategic plan to thrive in this new environment, and come up with a program of action to move their companies from wherever they are today to where they must be in the future to compete in global markets. What is needed is a *vision* of manufacturing as it will exist in the world, in their industry, and in their company in the next five to twenty years—and then, even more important, a *process* by which they can plan and implement the many changes in their organizations necessary to survive and prosper as successful competitors in the future. (See Gunn, 1987, for the details of this process.)

The Manufacturer of the Future

Eventually firms will establish global networks of new, flexible, fixed-cost, variable-output manufacturing plants. A firm wishing to compete globally will build such world-class manufactur-

Figure 4.1. The Old and New Ways of Looking at Manufacturing.

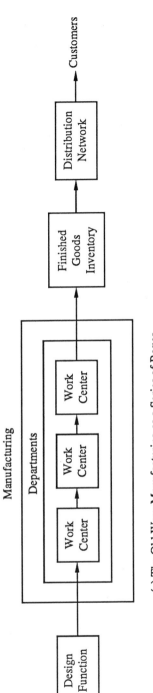

(a) The Old Way: Manufacturing as a Series of Boxes

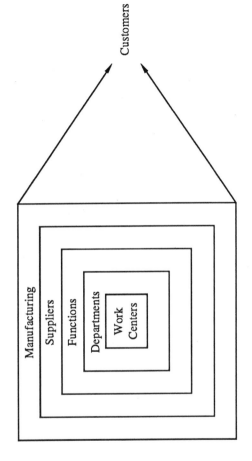

(b) The New Way: Manufacturing as a Total System

ing plants around the globe in many different countries that are located next to key suppliers or key markets. For political reasons, the firm may select certain countries regardless of the closeness of the market supplier. Like McDonald's hamburger franchises, every plant will be identical in every way — its production equipment, its computing equipment and software, and its (small) staff of interchangeable engineers and technicians. The company will espouse a fairly simple design and manufacturing philosophy: There will be one global product design that will be produced by one production process and that will be identically utilized throughout the world.

A global control room will be needed for the global network. This control room may be at corporate headquarters somewhere in the world, or in a satellite orbiting the earth, or in a cave a mile underground. There may be two or three people in this global manufacturing plant control center who are charged with the operation of the company's manufacturing plants. Of course, all of these plants and the control headquarters are tied together in a global satellite-based network of total communications capability, and all of them are nodes in a highly integrated information system. The entire company is operated with one integrated logical database design and with databases distributed geographically as well as hierarchically.

Any plant in this global network can execute the production of today's global products. Any of the plants can try out the production of any one of next year's products if the product fits within the current group technology classification for either the product design or the process design. It would probably be most beneficial to locate the product tryout plant nearest the company's R & D or design center for more immediate feedback during the design and production trial stage.

The firm will be able to respond to a wide variety of global competitive challenges. It can quickly respond to political upheaval or to changes in currency values in various areas of the globe. It can quickly fulfill product demand in increasingly volatile world markets. It can respond to increasingly volatile supply sources and adapt quickly to the availability of raw materials and products that make up the product it sells. It can respond quickly to changes in tariffs or trade laws.

One or two people can sit in the global corporate control room and allocate the production of products among this global network of factories. They can respond quickly to changing business conditions. At the touch of a button, the assignments to build products can be transferred to any one of the plants around the world. The prototyping of new products — and particularly the production process that will produce them — can be going on in any one of these factories. Once the software and system are configured to produce that product on one line, senior management can, at the touch of a button, send that product design and production process to any or all of the plants. When the global bill of materials for a given product design changes — because of an engineering change to the product design or for that matter in the manufacturing process — it can be communicated instantly around the network of plants.

Now the reader might think we have wandered off to the realm of hyperthink and speculation here. Yet the predecessors of such global networks are with us today. IBM has about fifty-five plants and design centers tied together in a global network. Each one of their products has a single bill of materials used for the manufacture of that product on a global basis. Any engineering change necessary may be transmitted to all of those fifty-five plants and design centers electronically within seconds. Even more prophetic is an emerging series of factories that Fanuc Ltd. is establishing in the remote regions of Japan. The items produced in the first of these factories will be products for electric spark machines (EDM machines) and electric motors. Fanuc has chosen to call these "village blacksmith" factories. Each one of these factories is on a site of only about 54,000 square feet. Each one of these factories has a floor space of approximately 1,800 square feet. Each one of these factories has four CNC machine tools and three robots. Each facility has only two employees, both engineers. The total facility cost of each one of these factories, using a conversion rate of 176 yen per dollar, is approximately $370,000. The goal of Fanuc's president, Seiuemon

Inaba, is a "future network of small-scale automated factories." Note that he has left out a significant word: *global*. For once you achieve this kind of manufacturing plant network in Japan, there is no reason why these factories could not be duplicated at will around the world.

Thus the world of tomorrow is here today, at least conceptually. The sooner other companies begin the same experience curve with such manufacturing facilities, the closer they will be to becoming world-class competitors five or ten years from now. But the ultimate question of long-term strategic importance for all corporations is this: What will happen when every company is a world-class manufacturer? How then will your company differentiate its products and services as a manufacturing competitor in global markets? The new bases of competition will be price, delivery, service, distribution, flexibility, and how quickly companies can respond to the increasingly fickle and sophisticated customer. As a result, the entire emphasis in business will be shifted back to products' features, functions, and value and the other aspects of quality that David Garvin (1984) mentions in his classic article, "What Does Product Quality Really Mean?"

Companies are going to have to start concentrating on product or market *areas*, not product lines. A classic example of this shift toward market areas can be observed by looking at Black & Decker over the last forty years. Originally, Black & Decker started making quarter-inch drills for consumers to use in their home workshops. Later they expanded their product offerings to other power tools for the home workshop, and still later to industrial areas where such products could be used. Then they discovered that they could offer electrical products for other places in the home besides the basement or garage workshop. Along came products like the Dustbuster, the scrub brusher and the spot lighter, and other products that were not only for the home but geared to the women customers more likely to be their purchasers and users. Most recently Black & Decker has bought General Electric's housewares division to expand its presence in the home to other small electrical appliances that can be used by several different members of the family. The products they acquired range from men's hairdryers to electric coffeemakers and from small ovens to irons. Apparently Black & Decker has decided to concentrate on the home market for small electrically powered products, whether they be powered by 110 volt AC or by battery. This represents a major change from producing quarter-inch drills.

Thus we see that the very bases of competition in manufacturing and indeed for manufacturing companies are going to change substantially over the next half century. As usual, the race will be to the swift and strong. But equally important, the race will go to those manufacturing leaders who are cognizant of these emerging changes in the bases of competition in manufacturing and who can incorporate this kind of knowledge into their plans to obtain more competitive advantage for their companies in global markets during the next fifty years.

The Business of the Future

Parallel to the radical changes in manufacturing are developments taking place in all the other functions in the business environment. We hear much today about the factory of the future. We also hear much about the office of the future. But generally we hear about the factory of the future *or* the office of the future as if there were a vast wall between them as shown in Figure 4.2. Yet the computer is a tool that can be used to integrate the functions of sales and marketing, accounting and finance, human resources, and the office. Aren't we really talking about the *business* of the future? Doesn't that wall disappear when we look at this subject in a broader context, as shown in Figure 4.3? Isn't that wall only conceptual, and will it not vanish as we improve our ability to look at a total business system in a logical sense and then mirror that view in a physical sense?

Consider marketing. If we look at the four classic marketing functions shown in Figure 4.4, we see that these too are being integrated by information technology. Particularly if we expand this picture in detail as in Figure 4.5, we see that it is the electronic links to other parts of the business world that are crucial. Obviously distribution forms the front end for manufacturing. Sales needs electronic interfaces with customers, with

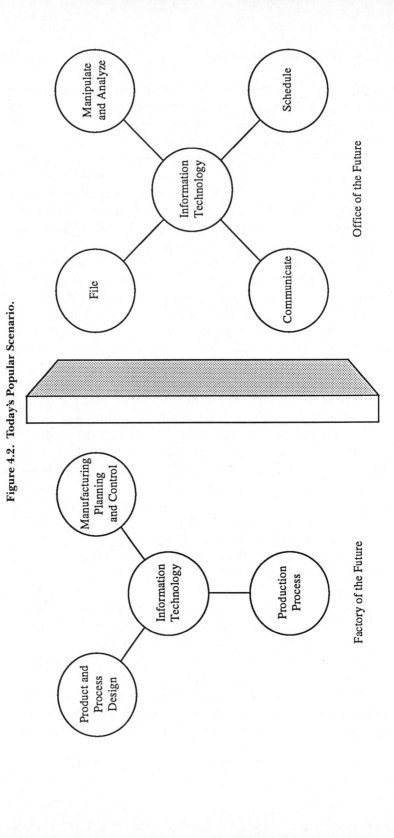

Figure 4.2. Today's Popular Scenario.

Office of the Future

Factory of the Future

Figure 4.3. The Business of the Future.

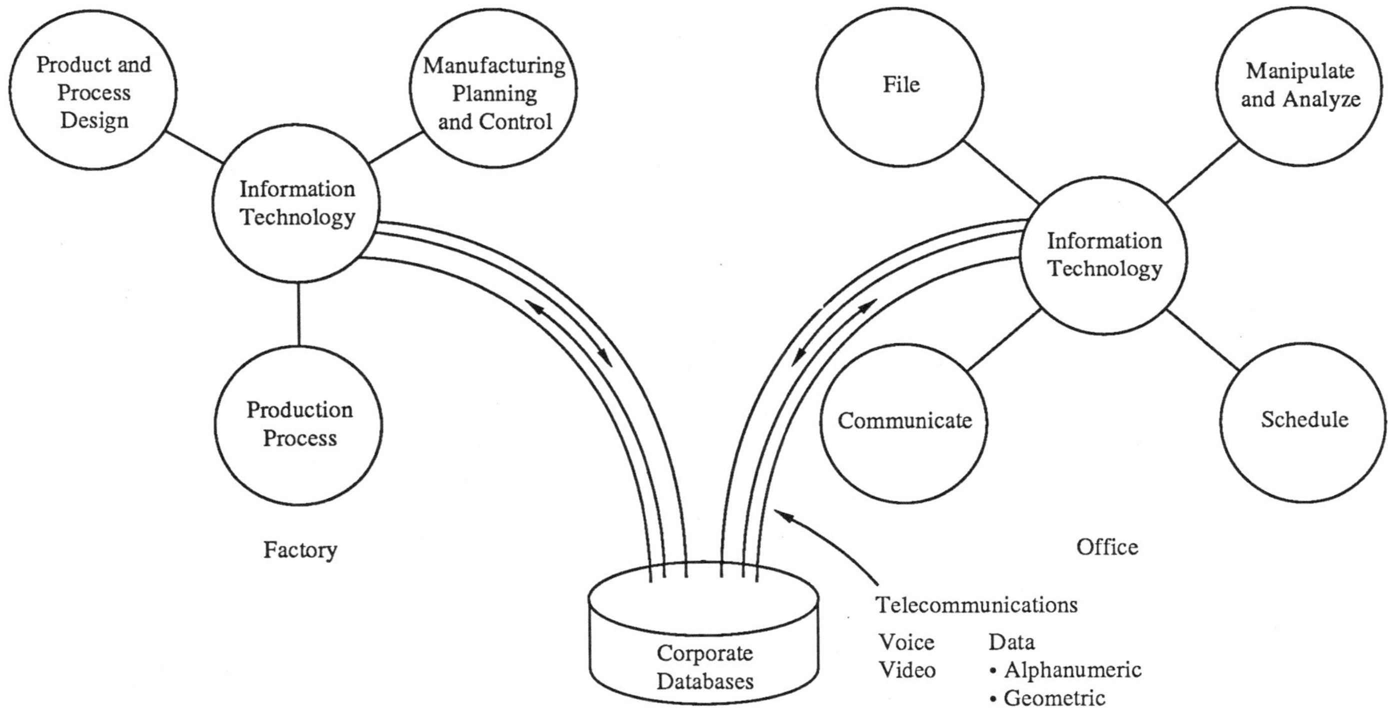

Figure 4.4. Computer-Integrated Marketing.

officers, and with salespeople in the field. Accountants need links to virtually all parts of the business. Consider the marketing function. New-product planning needs electronic access to information in engineering and R & D. Market research needs links to R & D and engineering as well. Equally important, it needs software links to other parts of the external business world. Market researchers need to be able to access Compustat and Standard & Poor's financial databases, for instance. They may need to access Nielsen test market data. They may need to access technical data in a database such as Lockheed's Dialog. They may need to access legal and patent data that might be contained in a database such as Lexis. The list goes on.

Figure 4.6 illustrates a two-step or three-step distribution process and its problems. The plant is at the back of the line, two steps removed from the final customer. In many cases, manufacturing is subject to the order and inventory control practices and policies of the distributors and retailers in between. Thus managers at the plant are generally ignorant of real-time sales to their final customers.

Current distribution presents a number of problems in

Figure 4.5. Computer-Integrated Marketing in Detail.

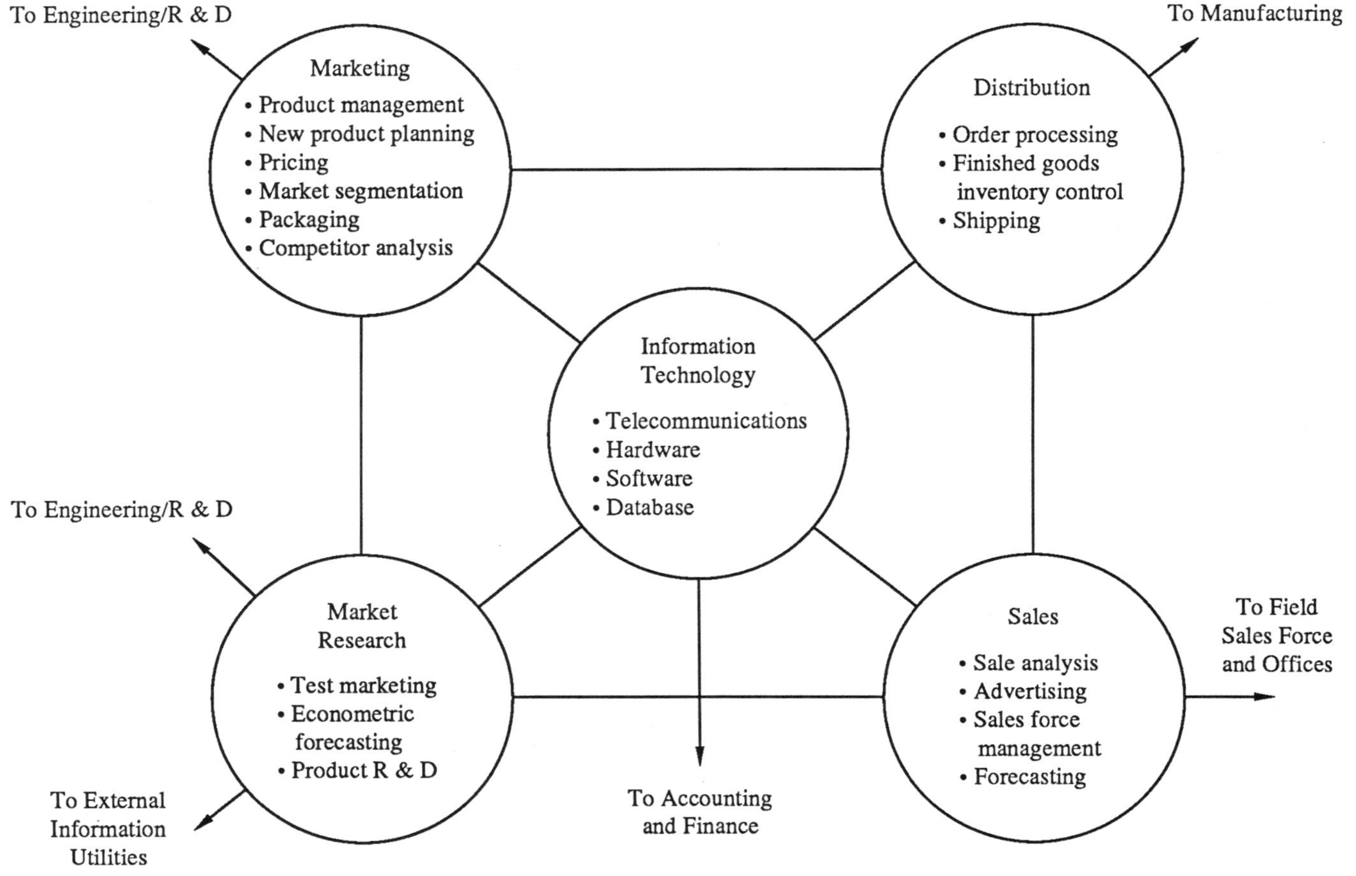

To Manufacturing

Distribution
- Order processing
- Finished goods inventory control
- Shipping

Sales
- Sale analysis
- Advertising
- Sales force management
- Forecasting

To Field Sales Force and Offices

Information Technology
- Telecommunications
- Hardware
- Software
- Database

To Accounting and Finance

Marketing
- Product management
- New product planning
- Pricing
- Market segmentation
- Packaging
- Competitor analysis

Market Research
- Test marketing
- Econometric forecasting
- Product R & D

To Engineering/R & D

To Engineering/R & D

To External Information Utilities

manufacturing and in marketing. First, plants become whip-sawed by the uneven demand of distributors and retailers between plant and final customer. Traditionally, at the end of the calendar year, distributors wish to reduce their inventories to avoid inventory tax or to facilitate taking a physical inventory. They either tell their suppliers to minimize order size or they place no further orders until after the first of the year. The plant responds by cutting its output, perhaps even laying off workers. Yet, at the same time, product sales in the marketplace might be quite strong. Come the first of the year, distributors want to fill their pipelines and shelves by ordering a great deal from their suppliers. Suddenly the plant is deluged with orders from all its distributors. Meanwhile, sales to the final customer have been relatively constant, so the plant has been whipsawed needlessly by intermediate agents, the distributors. With this kind of distribution, the sales forecast time horizon is generally long, which automatically results in greater uncertainty as we try to forecast further and further into the future. Finally, and perhaps most damaging, product sales patterns cannot be discerned in detail. What we really would like to know is what *individual* products sold, from what store, in what town, in what region, and when—what hour, day, week, month—and to whom.

The solution to this scenario lies in computer-integrated marketing that reaches out electronically over the heads of

Figure 4.6. Current Distribution Practice.

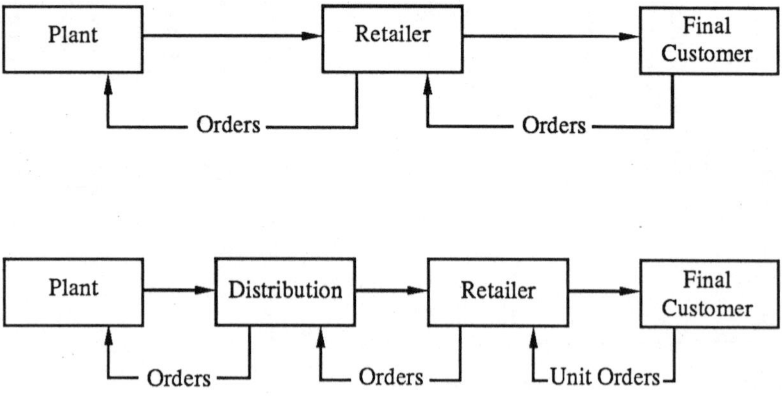

Figure 4.7. The Solution: Computer-Integrated Marketing.

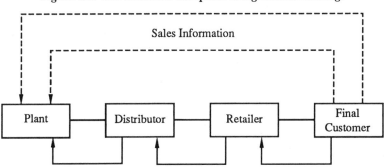

distributors and retailers to the final customer, as shown in Figure 4.7, to obtain information about the sale as it occurs. Today we talk about reaching out over the head of the distributor or retailer. Tomorrow, in many cases, we will eliminate the distributor or retailer in a distribution channel and go directly to the final customers in their homes.

In any event, there are distinct advantages to be gained from this computer-integrated marketing approach. We capture more detailed sales information *as the sales occur* to the final customer. Gaining detailed knowledge about sales aids the forecasting process. Reducing the forecasting time horizon automatically improves the accuracy of the forecast. But computer-integrated marketing also brings a host of other benefits. Customer service improves. Customer service can be maintained with lower inventories. Eventually, perhaps, when combined with the capabilities of a flexible, highly automated factory, a make-to-order environment will be possible and we can eliminate the concept of finished goods inventory altogether. Management of plant resources and capacity is better. The batch-to-flow move in manufacturing improves to the point where the ideal manufacturing environment in discrete part manufacturing is a flowlike process with the capability of handling a lot size of one. Last, and perhaps most important, market research improves remarkably. This is truly getting closer to the customer — one of our key goals as a world-class manufacturer. The

Figure 4.8. The Enterprise of the Future: Computer-Integrated Business.

task that lies before us in manufacturing is only a small part of the far larger evolution (or revolution!) of the computer-integrated enterprise, the business of the future, as portrayed in Figure 4.8.

Conclusion

When we try to imagine a truly integrated business environment in which each integrated business is electronically linked forward to its customers and backward to its suppliers, the implications are truly staggering. It is difficult to envision how this globalized network of businesses will interact and operate fifty or a hundred years from now. We can hardly cope with the implications of world-class manufacturing, much less those in the scenario suggested by computer-integrated business. With the advent of artificial intelligence and expert systems, one wonders about the degree to which human beings will be required (or even be able) to interface with this complex, global business environment.

Yet we cannot let our lack of knowledge and our uncertainty about the future hold us back in our progress toward such an environment. Only one thing is certain: The business environment will continue to change. We have barely begun to harness the power of the computer. Although we still have those Luddites who wish to deny the kind of progress painted in this chapter's scenario, progress is inevitable. And it is to be hoped that this new way of doing business will persevere to the benefit of all people everywhere.

References

Abegglen, J. C. *The Strategy of Japanese Business*. Cambridge, Mass.: Ballinger, 1984.

Garvin, D. A. "What Does Product Quality Really Mean?" *Sloan Management Review*, Fall 1984, pp. 25–43.

Gunn, T. G. *Computer Applications in Manufacturing*. New York: Industrial Press, 1981.

Gunn, T. G. "The CIM Connection." *Datamation*, Feb. 1, 1986a, pp. 50–58.

Gunn, T. G. "Integrated Manufacturing's Growing Pains." *Electronic Engineering Times*, Feb. 1, 1986b, pp. 1–8.

Gunn, T. G. *Manufacturing for Competitive Advantage*. Cambridge, Mass.: Ballinger, 1987.

Harrington, J. J. *Computer Integrated Manufacturing*. Huntington, N.Y.: Krieger, 1978.

Harrington, J. J. *Understanding the Manufacturing Process*. New York: Marcel Dekker, 1984.

Ishikawa, K. *What Is Total Quality Control?* (D. Lu, trans.) Nagaya: Central Japan Quality Control Association, 1979.

Schonberger, R. J. *Japanese Manufacturing Techniques*. New York: Free Press, 1982.

Schonberger, R. J. *World Class Manufacturing*. New York: Free Press, 1986.

5

INTEGRATING DIFFERENT APPROACHES FOR ACHIEVING COMPETITIVENESS

RALPH H. KILMANN
JOYCE SHELLEMAN
BRIAN UZZI

The topic of competitiveness has been addressed by several academic fields and most business specialties. As one might expect, however, each expert is much more familiar with his or her own area of study than with the work being done by others— even if it is on the same topic. This state of affairs is not only a common experience with regard to virtually every complex phenomenon, but it is also understandable given limitations of time, energy, and the human mind. What is so unfortunate, nevertheless, is that opportunities are missed to learn from and, thereby, build upon what others are discovering (or inventing). And besides these additive possibilities, perhaps the most overlooked benefit from cross-disciplinary efforts is the opportunity for *synergy*: Several experts working on the same complex topic can jointly develop a synthesis of insight that is much more than the sum of their individual contributions.

Because the topic of competitiveness is so vitally important to the quality of life everywhere (and not just a theoretical topic that is left to fill the spaces of academic journals), it seems of paramount importance not to risk overlooking synergistic contributions that derive from working across disciplines and specialties. Indeed, there is a special irony in pursuing a synergistic approach to studying competitiveness: The lessons learned from a look across the different approaches to this topic, as we will see, underscore the importance of synergy, integration, and cross-boundary relationships. Thus the ingredient that is essential for making organizations more competitive is the very same approach needed to tackle such a complex problem in the first place.

While we, the authors, are naturally limited by our own biases and experiences, we made a concerted effort to cross our educational boundaries. We sought to review a much more diverse literature on the topic than would ever have been our inclination otherwise. Although such an effort is by no means the same, for example, as establishing a true interdisciplinary team of different industry experts, business-functional experts, government officials, representatives from foreign nations, and a diverse set of academic faculty specializing in all the areas that are germane to competitiveness (broadly defined), we do believe that even a purposeful examination across different literatures is a step in the right direction. The reader will have to judge from the ideas presented here whether this effort at synergy has gone far enough. At a minimum, the references at the end of the chapter provide a broad (but certainly not complete) sampling of the diverse literature on the topic. At a maximum, the key distinctions, insights, and approaches to the topic — captured in our synthesis and models of the literature — will provide a helpful integration for further efforts at understanding and managing this important cross-disciplinary problem.

Here we present a model to integrate key distinctions in the literature for both understanding and managing competitiveness. The model was derived by noting the recurring themes that cut across the great variety of discussions on the topic. Specifically we examined not only our own literature in the behavioral sciences but also the following areas: labor relations; education; business–government relations; market, legal, and economic structures; technology; management skills and styles; accounting, management information, and expert systems; marketing; and strategic planning and business policy. We examined these specialties as reported in academic journals and books, publications for the professional manager, and popular business magazines and newspapers — all published in the last five years.

A Model for Understanding Competitiveness

Figure 5.1 highlights nine major themes related to organizational competitiveness as defined by two key distinctions. The

Figure 5.1. A Model for Understanding Competitiveness.

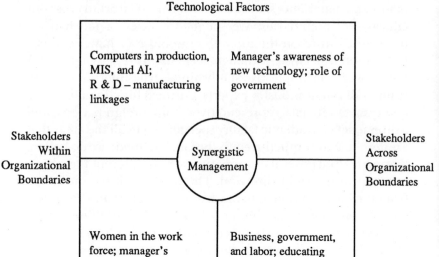

Technological Factors

	Computers in production, MIS, and AI; R & D – manufacturing linkages	Manager's awareness of new technology; role of government	
Stakeholders Within Organizational Boundaries	Synergistic Management		Stakeholders Across Organizational Boundaries
	Women in the work force; manager's commitment and focus	Business, government, and labor; educating managers	

Human Concerns

nine themes are (1) computer technology in production, management information systems (MIS), and artificial intelligence (AI); (2) cooperative linkages between R & D and manufacturing; (3) women in the work force; (4) management's commitment and focus; (5) the manager's awareness of new technology; (6) the role of government in developing and utilizing technology; (7) government, business, and labor partnerships; (8) educating managers; and (9) synergistic management. While a great variety of issues are reflected in the literature we reviewed, these themes seem to capture the critical success factors for global competitiveness. Teamwork and coordination touch upon every aspect of the model, and management's commitment and focus emerged as the unifying concepts needed to pursue improvements in organizational competitiveness.

Regarding the underlying distinctions that define each of the nine themes, the model consists of two axes: technological

and human factors and intraorganizational (internal) and interorganizational (across) stakeholder relationships—with an integrating core referred to as synergistic management. Although
no conceptual framework can accommodate all behavioral and
technological phenomena exactly into categories, this model
seems to capture the essential meaning of the literature on
competitiveness we reviewed.

The first distinction, along the vertical axis, shows the
technological and human factors currently influencing organizational competitiveness. Technological themes relate to those
advances in technology that affect the efficiency and effectiveness of the organization in producing an output. Thus technology encompasses production processes, computer and information systems, research and development, and product
innovations. On the other side, human themes concern individual behavior and the ways in which people work with one
another. Are managers participative or nonparticipative in
their management style? Do union leaders and management
have an adversarial or a cooperative relationship? What are the
implications of more women in the workplace?

The horizontal axis focuses on *where* the major changes
affecting competitiveness are primarily taking place—that is,
among stakeholders within the boundaries of the traditional
organization (intraorganizational) or among stakeholders both
inside and outside the organization's traditional boundaries
(interorganizational). This distinction is important for two reasons. First, much of the literature on organization development
has directed managers' attention to managing only intraorganizational issues (Motamedi, 1985). Yet major technological
advances and social and economic developments outside the
firm may have an equally important impact on its performance.
If an organization is to manage all the forces affecting success
within the global marketplace, these relationships with external
stakeholders must also be managed. The second distinctive
feature of the horizontal dimension concerns the linkages
across the quadrants: ways of managing the stakeholder relationships within the firm as well as across its boundaries.

Synergistic management is the integrating theme at the

heart of the model. It represents the appropriate orientation to action suggested by the two primary distinctions of the model and the themes within each quadrant. The literature dealing with competitiveness clearly suggests that an integrated and team-oriented approach to management is required in the dynamically complex environment facing today's organizations.

In the following discussion, we summarize each of the four quadrants of the model that are defined by the two distinctions of technological versus human and stakeholder relationships within versus across organizational boundaries. We simplify these quadrants as (1) technology within organizational boundaries, (2) technology across organizational boundaries, (3) human concerns within organizational boundaries, (4) human concerns across organizational boundaries, and (5) synergistic management.

Technology Within Organizational Boundaries

The literature on competitiveness repeatedly stresses the importance of up-to-date and specialized technology as a major competitive tool. Yet it has become apparent that many American organizations lag behind worldwide competition in the development and adoption of new technology (Hayes and Wheelwright, 1984; Porter, 1986; Wheelwright, 1985) — especially production process technology (Ross, 1985). A number of issues emerge relative to technology and relationships within the bounds of the traditional organization. These fall into two major categories: (1) a need for increased coordination between R & D and manufacturing managers in order to improve manufacturing process technologies and (2) the growing use of computer technology and its related impact on individual workers, relationships among workers, and relationships between workers and managers.

Although the American industrial system has paid a great deal of attention to product innovation, critics say that little attention has been given to innovation in manufacturing processes (see, for example, Steele, 1984). Close cooperation between R & D and manufacturing divisions or assemblers and their suppliers (an external stakeholder relationship) is advocated as a means of implementing advanced manufacturing techniques (Flynn, 1984–85). A number of technological means for improving the manufacturing process have been proposed. These include computer-assisted design (CAD), flexible manufacturing, and similar innovations (Ross, 1985; Cohen and Zysman, 1987). Within the organization, each of these technologies is founded on increased communication, understanding, and cooperation between R & D and manufacturing managers. Such a partnership will become increasingly essential if firms are to be competitive (Hoerr, 1987).

Computer or automated technologies are perceived as important to boost productivity in the United States. For example, a study conducted by Booz, Allen & Hamilton, Inc., suggests that moves to automated systems typically trim production time, scrap and rework, inventories, and direct labor costs by 50 to 85 percent (Jonas, 1987). Similarly, management information systems, both for internal control and decision-making purposes and for external strategic information gathering, are becoming essential as well as sophisticated (Reimann, 1985; Stone and Shaw, 1987). Moreover, artificial intelligence technology in the form of expert systems continues to expand the frontiers of decision support tools (Bulkeley, 1986; Rhines, 1985). All of these new computer technologies in production, management information, and decision support are creating pressure for new accounting and human control systems within the organization (Abramson, 1986; Jayson, 1986).

With the increasing dependence of business on such advanced technology and its growing use in nearly all functions, managers will increasingly be called upon to ease the anxiety many workers will feel during the transition to an automated workplace (Port and Wilson, 1987). Consequently, managers must develop human relations skills that will enable them to understand and alleviate the problems associated with major change, a sense of loss, retraining, and, in some cases, relocation or termination of workers. Moreover, managers will need to work more closely with employees who actually use the technology, since these workers' daily exposure and level of expertise provide an important source of information about the technology and its characteristics. This is especially true in today's environment where integrating the work of robots and other computer-controlled machines requires a team effort in managing the technology as well as the employees who operate it (Hoerr, 1987).

The widespread use of computer technologies creates new relationships among workers and between managers and workers. Workers who interface directly with computers will, in most cases, gain increased autonomy. This will lessen the role of middle management, flatten the organizational hierarchy, and mandate greater team effort and worker participation in decision making ("ISM Interviews Peter F. Drucker," 1987; Salerno, 1985).

Technology Across Organizational Boundaries

The management of technology across boundaries is central to competitiveness. Specifically, managers must become aware of the technological advances in their environments and learn to interface with stakeholders regarding technology (Porter and Millar, 1985). For example, companies will need managers who can match computer technologies with job requirements on a project-by-project basis. This step will help to bridge the long-standing gap between computer professionals who operate a centralized mainframe and the unique needs of project managers, thus transforming computer technology into a strategic tool.

This movement seems to require two things of managers. First, managers will need to know the technological needs of the firm so that the proper selection of technologies can be made and they can be brought into the firm. Second, managers must keep well informed of the technological changes in the environment that can have a direct effect on the organization's production processes. Hence managers should develop expertise in managing the latest technology and its application within the organization by technical workers. This expertise may be predicated on relationships developed with sources for new technology, such as government-funded R & D efforts, or governmental policymaking bodies that encourage technological development.

Although these requirements may significantly broaden the manager's role, managers (particularly division or department managers) are in a key position for accomplishing this critical part of a company's technological objectives. Since managers usually are close to the technological needs of their departments, they are best able to decide on critical technologies. Moreover, this role complements the top-down approach to technology development and adoption by offering a bottom-up process founded on the expertise of departmental managers and skilled professionals. Critical interfaces between production managers and R & D managers, as noted earlier, may be essential to the manager's role in facilitating these technological interfaces with external stakeholders.

A related issue for managers will be the degree to which technological innovations are shared with other firms, both American and foreign. Increased global competition will foster an environment of difficult technological decisions among international stakeholders (Rivers, 1987). Along with the question of sharing technology, managers may face difficult ethical decisions in regard to the use of information acquisition strategies to gain knowledge of competitors' technologies (Beltramini, 1986).

Human Concerns Within Organizational Boundaries

Human concerns in this quadrant fall into two primary categories: (1) teamwork and coordination achieved through the manager's commitment and focus and (2) the increasing numbers of women in the permanent work force. Regarding teamwork and coordination achieved through the manager's commitment and focus, the human resource management literature cites participative management as one example. It is reflected in such concepts as employee participation in the form of new compensation schemes, employee ownership, and innovative uses of internal labor markets (Stiener, 1981; Rosen, Klien, and Young,

1986). In the general management literature, participative management is reflected in such practices as consultative management, quality circles, career planning, and the broadening of job contributions.

Another example of teamwork and coordination is the new "design for assembly" (DFA). This process is based on teamwork among designers, manufacturing managers, and marketing managers (Nussbaum, 1988). In DFA, the number of parts is minimized in order to cut assembly costs, which typically account for two-thirds of the total manufacturing cost of products. Design teams that involve all of the relevant managers in the production and marketing process are increasingly seen as the way to improve competitiveness in manufacturing. Manufacturers view this teamwork as important not only to cutting production costs but also to producing higher-quality products.

For quality control to achieve its objectives, teamwork and coordination are critical. Although product quality and productivity have historically been considered as separate, if not adversarial, at least one recent study has demonstrated that quality improvements can actually reduce production costs (Shetty, 1986). Lowering production costs has the effect of making manufacturing processes more efficient, thus enabling the firm to increase its output given the same inputs to production (that is, its productivity). The decline in production costs implies that efforts to improve both productivity and quality may be complementary. Although design is essential in effecting quality improvements, equally essential is a need for consistency and comprehensiveness in monitoring quality. Consistency and comprehensiveness come largely through cooperative efforts by workers and managers and through teamwork around a common goal.

Similarly, the strategic planning literature, with its emphasis on costs and products, calls for flexibility, risk sharing, communication, and appropriate incentives—both inside the firm and with external parties and stakeholders. (See, for example, Schwartz and Saville, 1986; Doz, 1980.) Cooperative effort is necessary both with internal stakeholders and with business divisions in other countries, other firms, and governments (interorganizational stakeholder relationships) (Rivers, 1987). Within the firm, strategic information gathering can be accomplished through the use of task forces that involve key decision makers throughout the organization (Kilmann and Covin, 1988). Strategic economic, legal, financial, social, political, marketing, and technical intelligence will be increasingly essential to organizational survival. Incorporating a wide array of individuals in the intelligence-gathering process may help to ensure the comprehensiveness and validity of information that will be used to guide strategic decisions.

Fundamentally, teamwork represents a movement away from the traditional autocratic management model. Some of its underlying propositions are that increased worker participation in decision making, career planning, or ownership of the firm will promote higher levels of commitment, job variety, autonomy, career choice, career stability and security, bottom-up information flow, and group accountability. These outcomes contribute to increased organizational productivity (Lawler, 1986).

Regarding the increasing numbers of women in the permanent work force, the literature on organizational change has often ignored the particular needs of women in organizations and their potential influence on organizational behavior (Alderfer, 1982). But with the major demographic and social changes that have led to the increased representation of women in key organizational roles (Taylor, 1986) and as key participants in overall economic growth (Appelbaum, 1985), the literature on organizational competitiveness has begun to place great importance on the role of women in the work force.

Presently a significant percentage of new jobs are being filled by female workers. In five key occupational classifications—managerial and administrative, sales, professional and technical, food and health, and clerical—women have been found to constitute from 30 to 79 percent of the work force, with an average participation of 53.7 percent across all of the classifications (Pennar and Mervosh, 1986). Trends suggest that women will continue to attain higher levels of education and have fewer children. Given the increasing number of two-income families and an economy dominated by service- and information-based industries, one is led to conclude that women workers must be accepted as permanent additions to the traditionally male work force in American companies. Yet despite women's increased participation and importance in the work force, only two women were chief executives in the top thousand companies in 1987 (Ehrlich, 1987) and only four women were among the top thousand chief executives in 1988 ("A Portrait of the Boss," 1988). Women's representation in top positions implies that much remains to be accomplished in integrating women into the work force.

If organizations are to meet changing societal needs, some observers have suggested the provision of more flexible work options and institution of equitable pay systems for men and women. Parental leave and child care, for example, are major concerns. Provision of child care has been defined as a competitive issue. Research suggests its role in reducing worker stress, absenteeism, and turnover and in increasing productivity (Friedman, 1986). Organizations will also have to decide how to confront potential future labor shortages in clerical and secretarial positions as women attain equity in their access to other organizational roles.

A secondary issue concerns the influence these increased numbers of women may have on the character of traditionally male-oriented corporate life. Some have predicted that increased numbers of women in organizations may lead to the feminization of corporate values (Colwill and Erhart, 1985). These new values could translate into more cooperation, freer emotional expression, and greater trust evident in organizations. Managers must begin devoting time and resources to maximizing the benefits to be gained by the entrance of greater numbers of women into the work force and managing the potential effects of this change on the character of their organizations.

Human Concerns Across Organizational Boundaries

Increasingly, human concerns across the boundaries of the organization must be managed more deliberately. Our review of the literature revealed two major categories of critical relationships outside the primary organization: those between business, government, and labor and those between business and the management educational system. Other critical relationships will involve foreign divisions, firms, and governments.

The most basic linkages lie between business and labor and between business and government (Lodge and Crum, 1985), both domestically and internationally. Repeatedly authors have stressed that the problem of U.S. competitiveness cannot be solved unless there is a concerted effort by all three groups. At the core of this linkage is the need for these relationships to become less adversarial and more cooperative. A fundamental dilemma for business involves pricing products for a competitive marketplace yet providing the wage structure to which American workers have grown accustomed. The solution will require the effort of both organized labor and business if U.S. firms are to be successful. A second arena for closer relationships is that between business and government (Halal, 1987). Government policies and incentives can be crucial to the ability of American organizations to compete with foreign firms; again, close coordination in developing and implementing national investment and trade policies is essential.

The literature on management education seems to stress two major factors relative to competitiveness: what is being taught and how it is being taught (Damzsa, 1982). With regard to the first issue, it is becoming clear that students of management need broader leadership skills. These broader competencies would include course work in areas only indirectly related to the functioning of business, such as psychology, political science, and anthropology. In addition, course work would emphasize qualitative skills (interpersonal skills, conflict management skills, family/business relations skills, career counseling skills, and so on) as well as the more traditional skills directed toward analytical decision making. A competitive environment demands managers "who can sense and define critical problems before turning to analytical methods for their solution" (Kilmann and Covin, 1988, p. 533).

The second issue—how students of management are

being taught—carries with it a set of more complex and interrelated concerns. On the side of the educator, clearly more needs
to be done in blending management experience with management theory (Gibson, 1986). This includes the publication of
research with both practical and theoretical utility. To attain this
goal, the present system of "publish or perish" will require modi-
fication (Stoever, 1987), and greater emphasis, with corresponding rewards, may need to be placed on teaching quality. Lastly,
there must be a greater recognition that management education
is a lifelong process that transcends the boundaries of knowledge provided by the M.B.A. curriculum (Damzsa, 1982).

These changes in management education can best be
realized through the support and involvement of business in
university programs in a joint-venture relationship (Bloch,
1987). If the educational system does not provide the necessary
training for professional managers in a competitive environment, then corporations may seek to fill that void, though it
would be costly for organizations to attempt to provide the
equivalent of a university-based management training program
(Kilmann and Covin, 1988). Universities and businesses working
together in a complementary fashion—each contributing
unique expertise and resources to develop the necessary management skills—is the most productive course to follow.

Synergistic Management

The integrating theme of our model is synergistic management.
Our review of the literature on competitiveness offered a striking mandate for approaching organizational reality as a complex hologram. (See, for example, Bartlett and Ghoshal, 1987.)
The variety and number of stakeholders and the nature and
complexity of the technological and human challenges demand
a new type of manager. This new manager is not a renaissance
person but a coordinator and team player who realizes that
participative management coupled with a holistic approach to
problems is the only way to become more competitive.

Besides the management skills cited earlier, the literature
on technology suggests that managers must learn how to man-

age internal stakeholders in a participative manner in order to integrate new technological systems that cut across functional areas. Furthermore, the management literature suggests that managers must be growers and supporters—as opposed to the Tayloristic manager who directs, controls, watchdogs, and delegates (Byrne, 1986). Thus the notion of teamwork and coordination presents a new guiding principle for managers. The manager must be responsible for orchestrating the change in the workplace culture from one of nonparticipation to one of participation. Another important new skill the manager will need is that of dialectical reasoning (see Kilmann, 1985). Dialectical reasoning gives managers the skills they need to expose, test, and reformulate, if necessary, outdated and dysfunctional assumptions. In short, dialectical reasoning allows the manager to analyze the full variety of opinions on a problem (whether it be the choice of a new technology, the desirability of entering an interorganizational relationship, the issues involved in hiring more women, or the implications of new regulation) and thus, through debate among the viewpoints, to expose the underlying assumptions. Once unstated assumptions have been made explicit, they can be tested and acted on with confidence.

Furthermore, dialectical reasoning offers the manager a technique for resolving the competing demands posed by a diversity of stakeholders and a myriad of technological factors and human concerns. Because dialectical reasoning creates a debate among contending parties, the manager is better able to choose among alternatives by guiding the parties themselves toward agreement as faulty assumptions become apparent to all.

Conclusions

We have sought to go beyond our own boundaries of specialization, just as competitive organizations must do, in order to develop a comprehensive understanding of this highly complex topic. It seems clear to us that many different experts, in both academia and the business world, have offered important and unique perspectives. Our hope is that the model we propose will stimulate even more systematic efforts at cross-disciplinary integration, since such an approach has not generally been pursued in the past. We have identified nine key issues that organizations must consider in order to be competitive: computer technology in production, management information systems, and artificial intelligence; cooperative linkages between R & D and manufacturing; women in the work force; management's commitment and focus; the manager's awareness of new technology; the role of government in developing and utilizing technology; government, business, and labor partnerships; educating managers; and synergistic management.

If one central theme can be said to capture the essence of our model, we would have to choose the theme of teamwork and coordination. None of the critical issues on competitiveness can be solved in isolation; none of the relationships can be forced. Further, management's commitment to new cooperative relationships is critical. The tension between technology and humans, and among diverse internal and external stakeholders, is not amenable to a quick fix or to top-down intervention in one segment of the organization. In the face of unprecedented global competition, a holistic, integrated, and collective approach is not only desirable but also imperative.

References

Abramson, D. H. "The Future of Accounting: Scenarios for 1996." *Journal of Accountancy*, Oct. 1986, pp. 120–124.

Alderfer, C. P. "Problems of Changing White Males' Behavior and Beliefs Concerning Race Relations." In P. S. Goodman and Associates, *Change in Organizations: New Perspectives on Theory, Research, and Practice.* San Francisco: Jossey-Bass, 1982.

Appelbaum, E. "Alternative Work Schedules for Women." Working paper, Temple University, Department of Economics, 1985.

Bartlett, C. A., and Ghoshal, S. "Managing Across Borders: New Organizational Responses." *Sloan Management Review*, Fall 1987, pp. 43–53.

Beltramini, R. F. "Ethics and the Use of Competitive Information

Acquisition Strategies." *Journal of Business Ethics*, 1986, *5*, 307–311.

Bloch, E. "Economic Competition: A Research and Education Challenge." *Research Management*, Mar.–Apr. 1987, pp. 6–8.

Bulkeley, W. M. "Expert Systems Are Entering into Mainstream of Computers." *Wall Street Journal*, Dec. 5, 1986, p. 33.

Byrne, J. A. "Business Fads: What's In and What's Out." *Business Week*, Jan. 20, 1986, pp. 52–61.

Cohen, S., and Zysman, J. *Manufacturing Matters: The Myth of the Post-Industrial Economy*. New York: Basic Books, 1987.

Colwill, N. L., and Erhart, M. "Have Women Changed the Workplace?" *Business Quarterly*, 1985, *50* (1), 27–31.

Damzsa, W. A. "The Education and Development of Managers for Future Decades." *Journal of International Business Studies*, Winter 1982, pp. 9–18.

Doz, Y. L. "Strategic Management in Multinational Companies." *Sloan Management Review*, Winter 1980, pp. 27–46.

Ehrlich, E. "What the Boss Is Really Like." *Business Week*, Oct. 23, 1987, pp. 37–44.

Flynn, M. S. "U.S. and Japanese Automotive Productivity Comparisons: Strategic Implications." *National Productivity Review*, Winter 1984–85, pp. 60–71.

Freeman, R. E. *Strategic Management: A Stakeholder Approach*. Boston: Pitman, 1984.

Friedman, D. E. "Child Care for Employees' Kids." *Harvard Business Review*, 1986 (2), 28–34.

Gibson, M. D. "Managerial Experience and Management Teaching: Some Theoretical and Practical Considerations." *Journal of Further and Higher Education*, Spring 1986, pp. 9–19.

Halal, W. E. "Business and Government—A New Partnership?" *Long Range Planning*, 1987, *20* (1), 120–130.

Hayes, R. H., and Wheelwright, S. C. *Restoring Our Competitive Edge: Competing Through Manufacturing*. New York: Wiley, 1984.

Hoerr, S. "Getting Man and Machine to Live Happily Ever After." *Business Week*, Apr. 20, 1987, pp. 61–62.

"ISM Interviews Peter F. Drucker." *Journal of Information Systems Management*, Spring 1987, pp. 92–96.

Jayson, S. "Cost Accounting for the '90s." *Management Accounting,* July 1986, pp. 58–59.

Jonas, N. "Can America Compete?" *Business Week,* Apr. 20, 1987, pp. 45–47.

Kilmann, R. H. *Social Systems Design: Normative Theory and the MAPS Design Technology.* New York: Elsevier North-Holland, 1977.

Kilmann, R. H. "A Typology of Organization Typologies: Toward Parsimony and Integration in the Organizational Sciences." *Human Relations,* 1983, *36* (6), 523–548.

Kilmann, R. H. *Beyond the Quick Fix: Managing Five Tracks to Organizational Success.* San Francisco: Jossey-Bass, 1984.

Kilmann, R. H. "Understanding the Matrix Organization: Keeping the Dialectic Alive and Well." In D. D. Warrick (ed.), *Contemporary Organization Development: Current Thinking and Applications.* Glenview, Ill.: Scott, Foresman, 1985.

Kilmann, R. H. *Managing Beyond the Quick Fix: A Completely Integrated Program for Creating and Maintaining Organizational Success.* San Francisco: Jossey-Bass, 1989.

Kilmann, R. H., and Covin, T. J. "Conclusions: New Directions in Corporate Transformation." In R. H. Kilmann, T. J. Covin, and Associates (eds.), *Corporate Transformation: Revitalizing Organizations for a Competitive World.* San Francisco: Jossey-Bass, 1988.

Lawler, E. E., III. *High-Involvement Management: Participative Strategies for Improving Organizational Performance.* San Francisco: Jossey-Bass, 1986.

Lodge, G. C., and Crum, W. C. "U.S. Competitiveness: The Policy Tangle." *Harvard Business Review,* Jan.–Feb. 1985, pp. 34–51.

Mitroff, I. I. *Stakeholders of the Organizational Mind: Toward a New View of Organizational Policy Making.* San Francisco: Jossey-Bass, 1983.

Mitroff, I. I., and Mohrman, S. A. "The Slack Is Gone: How the United States Lost Its Competitive Edge in the World Economy." *Academy of Management Executive,* Feb. 1987, pp. 65–70.

Motamedi, K. "Transorganizational Development: Developing Relations Among Organizations." In D. D. Warrick (ed.), *Con-*

temporary Organization Development: Current Thinking and Applications. Glenview, Ill.: Scott, Foresman, 1985.

Nussbaum, B. "Smart Design: Quality Is the New Style." *Business Week*, Apr. 11, 1988, pp. 102–108.

Pennar, K., and Mervosh, E. "Women at Work: They've Reshaped the Economy and Now Their Wages Will Rise." In D. R. Hampton (ed.), *Inside Management: A Selection of Readings from Business Week.* New York: McGraw-Hill, 1986.

Port, O., and Wilson, J. W. "Making Brawn Work with Brains." *Business Week*, Apr. 20, 1987, pp. 56–60.

Porter, M. "Why U.S. Business Is Falling Behind." *Fortune*, Apr. 28, 1986, pp. 255–262.

Porter, M. E., and Millar, V. E. "How Information Gives You a Competitive Advantage." *Harvard Business Review, 63* (4), 1985, 149–160.

"A Portrait of the Boss." *Business Week*, Oct. 21, 1988, pp. 27–32.

Reimann, B. C. "Decision Support Systems: Strategic Management Tools for the Eighties." *Business Horizons*, Sept.–Oct. 1985, pp. 71–77.

Rhines, W. "Artificial Intelligence: Out of the Lab and into Business." *Journal of Business Strategy*, 1985, *6* (1), 50–57.

Rivers, L. W. "Time Is Past for Studying Industrial Competitiveness." *Research Management*, Jan.–Feb. 1987, pp. 7–8.

Rosen, C., Klien, K. J., and Young, M. "When Employees Share the Profits." *Psychology Today*, Jan. 1986, pp. 30–38.

Ross, I. M. "R&D for a Competitive Edge." *Research Management*, Jan.–Feb. 1985, pp. 6–8.

Salerno, L. M. "What Happened to the Computer Revolution?" *Harvard Business Review*, Nov.–Dec. 1985, pp. 129–138.

Schwartz, P., and Saville, J. "Multinational Business in the 1990s: A Scenario." *Long Range Planning*, Dec. 1986, pp. 31–37.

Shetty, Y. K. "Quality, Productivity, and Profit Performance: Learning from Research and Practice." *National Productivity Review*, Spring 1986, pp. 166–173.

Steele, L. W. "Meeting International Competition." *Research Management*, Mar.–Apr. 1984, pp. 36–41.

Stiener, R. E. "Labor Relations." *Personnel Journal*, May 1981, pp. 344–346.

Stoever, W. A. "Management Teaching Isn't *Fun* Any More." *Business Horizons*, Jan.–Feb. 1987, *30* (1), 85–86.

Stone, M., and Shaw, R. "Database Marketing for Competitive Advantage." *Long Range Planning*, Apr. 1987, pp. 12–20.

Taylor, A. "Why Women Managers Are Bailing Out." *Fortune*, Aug. 18, 1986, pp. 16–23.

Wheelwright, S. "Restoring the Competitive Edge in U.S. Manufacturing." *California Management Review*, 1985, *27* (3), 26–42.

PART TWO

MANAGING PEOPLE AND PROCESSES
WITHIN ORGANIZATIONS

6

USING HUMAN RESOURCES FOR COMPETITIVE ADVANTAGE

DAVE ULRICH

Almost every organization today professes some form of the creed "People are our most important asset." Since disagreeing with the doctrine is tantamount to apostasy, the difficulty becomes one of translating the dogma into action. As has been suggested by others, if strategic planning is to move from concepts to actions then people and people management programs must become more than credos. In the last few years, it has become popular to talk about "strategic human resource management" as a way to think about managing people programs (Dyer, 1984; Schuler, 1987; Tichy, Fombrun, and Devanna, 1982, 1984). Using human resources to gain and sustain a competitive advantage goes beyond strategic human resource management—it requires new approaches to managing people. Companies that have gained a competitive advantage have done so, in part, through judicious allocation and management of human resources. This chapter suggests that assessment of human resources as a competitive advantage not only improves our understanding of competitive advantage but extends the role of strategic human resource management to competitiveness.

The Nature of Competitive Advantage

Competitiveness has been a national agenda (witness President Reagan's 1987 State of the Union Address), a hot topic for research, and a primary challenge for many executives. Porter (1981, 1985) has clarified many elements of gaining and sustain-

129

ing competitive advantage. He suggests that a firm must focus not only on strategies but on how strategies build competitive advantage, which he defines as customer-perceived value, not merely technological progress. He also suggests that industry forces (threat of entrants, concentration of suppliers, substitutability of products, buyer concentration, and rivalry within the industry) create a more or less favorable industry structure that influences competitive advantage.

Within industry structure, a firm's strategies and executive choices influence competitive advantage. A firm's strategies may be classified as some mix of cost or differentiation; executive choices exist in inbound logistics, operations, outbound logistics, marketing and sales, and service. Through managing strategy and executive choices, firms may build a competitive advantage. Figure 6.1 simplifies Porter's analysis: Competitive advantage is the expected outcome of the firm's strategies; executive choices in each of the five areas allow for the establishment of these strategies.

Porter's work installs competitive advantage as a major challenge for scholars and executives, yet his model may not encompass all the components of creating and sustaining competitive advantage. First, in addition to choices about strategies, executives also make a myriad of choices about culture, management style, and structure. The set of executive choices dealing with the organization's practices may create its capability—a component of competitive advantage not thoroughly discussed in Porter's model. Although Porter (1985) does recognize the importance of an organization's structure and human resource management—"HRM affects CA in any firm. . . in some industries it holds the key to CA" (p. 43)—his work does not elaborate on the specific practices that create organizational capability and influence competitive advantage. In fact, in a 536-page book, only 8 pages discuss human resources and part of one chapter reviews organizational structure. While Porter acknowledges what needs to be done with organizational practices, his analysis focuses on economic, technological, strategic, and product capabilities of firms and does not elaborate *how* to create organizational capability. In this chapter I not only sug-

Figure 6.1. A Model for Creating and Sustaining Competitive Advantage.

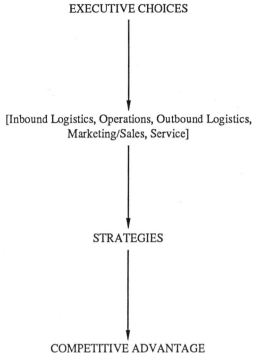

EXECUTIVE CHOICES

[Inbound Logistics, Operations, Outbound Logistics, Marketing/Sales, Service]

STRATEGIES

COMPETITIVE ADVANTAGE

Source: Adapted from Porter (1985).

gest what needs to be done (for example, pay attention to organizational capability) but review *why* and *how.*

Second, Porter's model emphasizes a static view of competitive advantage. Often the factors that enable a firm to compete successfully today will not be the same tomorrow. Although Porter acknowledges that his five industry forces, general strategies, and five executive choices must adapt to continual change, he does not specify how. Without the organizational capability to respond to change, competitive advantage may be found only in historical documents, not in current and future needs. Companies that rely exclusively on general strategies or the five executive choices miss the essence of sustained competitive advantage — the organization's ability to respond to con-

tinuous environmental changes such as customer product demands, technological breakthroughs, competitor strategies,
and federal legislation.

Third, Porter's model says little about the role of people in
creating and sustaining competitive advantage. Organizational
capability—represented by the firm's capacity to respond to
change and to implement executive choices and general strategies—derives from people and organizational practices that
affect people. Organizations do not think, make decisions, or
gain competitive advantage; people do. Many organizations
proclaim with almost religious fervor the importance of people
but fail to link the management of people to sustained competitive advantage. Porter's model would benefit from an assessment of how people and organizational practices affect competitive advantage, and those who advocate the importance of
people in organizations would benefit from linking people not
merely to strategies but to competitive advantage.

Human Resources as a Competitive Advantage

Two criteria must be satisfied in creating and sustaining a competitive advantage. First, a firm must produce a good or service
that is valued by customers. Technologically elegant products
that do not satisfy customer needs will not translate into competitive advantage because customers will not use them. Second,
competitive advantage comes from activities that are unique to
the firm and cannot easily be replicated by competitors. These
activities create a firm's distinctive competence. If an activity can
be copied easily, there is no competitive advantage because
customers have equal access to competitors' goods or services.

The second criterion highlights the importance of organizational capability. It is not merely a new technology but the
organizational ability to use it that creates a competitive advantage. In the automobile industry, each firm examines competitors' products to improve design. The organization's ability
to learn from competitors and implement new technologies
becomes a major source of competitive advantage. The Japanese
have the organizational capability to interpret new information,

design a new automobile, and deliver it in less than two years, while General Motors estimates a minimum of four years to deliver new products. The organizational capability to deliver the new automobile becomes a major source of competitive advantage.

The management of people plays a major role in creating organizational capability that satisfies these two criteria and creates and sustains competitive advantage. People and organization practices affecting people translate to customer value and are unique to each firm, thus leading to competitive advantage for three reasons: cost, competence, and change.

People Costs

First, people costs often represent one of the firm's major controllable costs. These people costs translate directly into price, and price may determine how customers value a product. Thus if a major category of controllable costs is people costs, the management of these costs may lead to competitive advantage. The large number of companies that have gone private (Beatrice, Fred Meyer, FMC, Metromedia, Uniroyal, and others) and dramatically reduced their costs by cutting layers of management and people illustrates the importance of people as a major cost factor. In addition, people costs are unique to each firm and depend on the firm's hiring practices, number of people, number of layers in the organization, and compensation systems. Thus the cost of managing people in one firm may be difficult to replicate in another firm—thereby meeting the second criterion of competitive advantage.

Some firms have recognized that people represent a major controllable cost that is reflected in price and competitive advantage. The annual report of United Parcel Service reveals that people costs (salary, benefits, and other direct costs, such as travel time, development, moving) represent approximately 60 percent of the overall operating budget. For government agencies, the percentage of operating budget allocated to people may go as high as 80 percent. The Federal Aviation Administration (FAA), for example, even in the midst of an enormous buildup of technology and computer systems, found that 75 percent of its operating budget went to people costs. As a result, managers in the FAA realized that how they worked with and developed their people became a critical factor in accomplishing their safety goals (Ulrich, 1986). In the airline industry the major cost elements determining price include equipment (about 25 percent of budget), fuel (about 25 percent), maintenance (25 percent), and people (25 percent). After deregulation in 1978 when competitiveness increased throughout the industry, airline executives examined these four categories of costs and realized that the only place they could gain a competitive advantage over their competitors was people. Competitors could purchase essentially the same aircraft, fuel, and maintenance, but the ability to manage people costs became a primary variant in creating distinctive competence and building competitive advantage. Almost all major air carriers, Continental, TWA, United, American, and Delta, began to reexamine their organizational practices and adjust direct salary costs with two-tier pay systems or lower pay and to reexamine organization designs with fewer layers of management and overhead. The reasons for these changes were straightforward—in order to create a distinctive competence that translated into competitive advantage, people and people management systems became the central lever.

Distinctive Competence from People

People and organizational practices affecting people create a distinctive competence that leads to competitive advantage because skills deriving from organizational practices become nearly impossible to copy. For example, one of the Japanese practices that have influenced their competitiveness has been career management systems. Consider the U.S. and Japanese automotive industries. Executives in U.S. firms have experience in only a few functional areas whereas executives in Japanese firms have broad experience in many functional areas (Pucik, 1984). The traditional U.S. career track encourages specialization and allows employees to move from one firm to another as functional specialists. Japanese employees become specialists in the firm, not the function. They learn how to make things happen within the firm because they have a range of experience and a diversity of knowledge that allow them to help the firm respond to changing conditions. The organizational practice of managing career tracks creates competitive advantage through employees who have broader experiences and more dedication to the firm—which in turn translates to products that better meet customer expectations.

Managing Change Through People

People and organizational practices create competitive advantage because they become the foundation upon which organizational changes are made. Whenever an organization adopts a new strategy or program, it must be implemented through people. The FAA spent three years preparing its strategy for the next two decades (called the National Airspace System Plan). Yet in the 300-page document not one page communicated the changes that would have to occur in people and organizational practices to implement this strategy. Currently this technologically elegant plan is years behind schedule, causing increasing turmoil throughout the airline industry. Without the careful assessment of how people changes need to be adapted to organizational changes, strategies remain blueprints.

Organizations that manage their people and practices carefully create a competitive advantage by establishing a capability that enables them to manage costs, generate distinctive competencies, and manage change. Organizational capability translates into customer value through products or services and becomes difficult for competitors to replicate because the organization's capability is embedded in its culture (Barney, 1986). Copying one element of an organization's practices without an overall framework will not create the same competitive advantage. Some firms attempting to implement management by objectives, behavioral rating scales, or other appraisal programs have been disappointed that their results did not match what other successful companies achieved with the same programs.

The reason lies in the fact that no isolated organizational practice may be used to achieve success. Successful companies using
management by objectives support the system with selection,
rewards, development, and organizational planning practices.
Since the overall infrastructure of a company cannot easily be
replicated, it thus becomes a potential source of competitive
advantage.

Human Resource "Primary Levers"

As we have seen, organizational practices may be used to create
and sustain competitive advantage. Many organizational practices may give rise to organizational capability. The practices
that directly affect people become a valuable focus for identifying key practices since people are critical in implementing
organizational change. Human resource practices offer managers *primary levers* for change that translate into customer satisfaction. These practices become uniquely identified with a firm
and are not easily copied by other firms. But before we can
suggest the specific ways in which human resources create and
sustain competitive advantage, we need a framework that encompasses human resource practices.

Six areas encompass human resource practices, and
within each area there are specific choices. These six systems are:

1. *Organizational Planning*: the practices of shaping and structuring an organization, including its structure, reporting
   relationships, and how it allocates responsibility. Specific
   choices include:
   • Centralization versus decentralization: How centralized
     or decentralized should different functions be?
   • Degree of specialization: How specialized should differ-
     ent departments and individuals be?
   • Locus of accountability: Which departments or indi-
     viduals should have primary accountability for accom-
     plishing projects?
   • Degree of routinization: How routinized should systems

be? Technology, budgeting, and other systems may be routinized or may vary from division to division.

- Degree of coordination between units: How much and what types of coordination should occur between and among departments in the organization? Coordination may be slight (granting great autonomy for each business unit) or extensive. Coordination may occur through liaison teams, matrix organizations, rules, or values (Galbraith and Kazanjian, 1985).
- Degree of horizontal and vertical integration: How diversified should the firm be (horizontal integration), and how much forward and backward integration should occur?

2. *Selection*: the practices of hiring, promoting, and outplacing employees at all levels of the organization. Specific choices include (Gerstein and Reisman, 1983; Olian and Rynes, 1984):

- Types of staffing criteria: How much weight in the hiring process is given to technical, job-focused skills versus interpersonal and company-focused skills?
- Skill level of new hires: How many new employees will come directly from college versus those experienced in the industry?
- Sources of promotion candidates: How many promotions will come from within the organization versus recruiting outside?
- Types of career paths: What career paths will be encouraged (working in one functional area and becoming a specialist, for example, versus becoming a generalist by working in many functional areas)?
- Extent of succession planning: What content (forms, criteria) and processes (meetings, responsibility) will be used in developing succession planning systems?

3. *Rewards*: the practices of compensation, both base salary and incentive salary, and nonfinancial rewards that motivate employees to behave consistently with organizational goals. Specific practices may be used to shape reward systems:

- Types of rewards used: How much consideration will be given to financial recompense, recognition, and the work itself as possible reward systems?
- Criteria for rewards: What criteria will the organization establish for allocating rewards—for example, equality (everyone in the organization receives a similar reward) versus equity (reward according to performance)?
- Term for determining rewards: What length of time will be used—short term (annual results) or longer term (more than a year)?
- Collaboration: How much will rewards be based on individual versus team contributions?

4. *Development*: the practices associated with building employee competencies through training, job rotation, counseling, cross-functional moves, or task force assignments.
   - Types of training: What types of training (technical versus managerial, for example) will be highlighted?
   - Purposes of training: What results are expected—conceptual, skill building, attitude change, team building, problem solving, or intervention?
   - Delivery of training: Who will deliver the training—human resource staff, line managers, or outside experts?
   - Location of training: Where will the training be held—on-site or off-site?
   - Alternative development programs: How much formal attention will be given to cross-functional moves, task force assignments, job rotation, and counseling?

5. *Appraisal*: the practices that set standards, give feedback, and assess performance according to a set of expectations:
   - Criteria for standards: How much of the standards will emphasize outputs (results such as a management by objectives system) or behavior (behavioral rating scales)?
   - Frequency of feedback: How often should feedback be given to the employees from the appraisal process?
   - Participation in standard setting: Should standards be

set jointly by manager and employees or should they be set by the manager and then shared with the employee?

- Focus of standards: How much do the individual's standards reflect the strategic thrusts of the organization?
- Form of feedback: What kind of feedback will the employee receive (written, verbal, group)?

6. *Communication*: the practices of telling employees not only what needs to be done but why and how.

- Content of communications: What information should be given to employees?
- Recipient of communications: Who should receive what communication—for example, how far down the organization should information about the strategy be spread?
- Deliverer of communications: Who should deliver the messages—corporate or local managers?
- Delivery systems for communications: How can communications be delivered—talks, memos, meetings, videos, newsletters?

Human resource practices in each of these six systems complement Porter's model and create competitive advantage in three ways: They affect a firm's strategy, they affect all executive choices within the firm, and they allow for a sustained competitive advantage.

Effect of Human Resources on Strategy

To pursue a new business strategy, human resource practices may have to be modified. Table 6.1 describes the human resource implications for the cost and differentiation strategies suggested by Porter. These two strategies are not representative; they simply indicate how human resource systems may be modified to affect strategies. Far more than these two strategies may exist, of course, but the same logic can by applied to any strategic position.

Cost strategies create competitive advantage by offering

Table 6.1. Effect of Human Resources on Strategy.

Human Resource Issue	Impact on Cost	Impact on Differentiation
Cost and quality of people	• Percentage of budget dedicated to people	• Quality of people hired who can guarantee quality outputs
Organizational planning	• Flat organization • Multiskilled employees • Many generalists • Small staffs • Broad and deep delegation and accountability • Routinize the work	• Specialists in product design and development • High budget for R & D • Work on integration across business units to deliver product
Selection/ staffing	• Hire the less experienced • Find technological substitutes • Use a narrow net to find new employees • Have little socialization effort • Generate incentives to stay • Create loyalty to organization • Source from lower-paying other jobs	• Hire the technically superb in all areas • Hire for quality in each functional area (marketing, manufacturing, R & D) • Allocate resources for hiring • Plan the process of succession carefully for symbolic reasons and quality reasons
Rewards	• Lag industry norms • Focus on incentive or performance-based pay • Build in long-term (stock) options with lower base • Offer bonuses rather than additions to base • Offer nonfinancial incentives (pride, work opportunities) • Create peer pressure to perform • Share cost savings	• Set industry norms • Tie reward to quality in all parts of the business • Offer creative rewards for quality (start your own business) • Reward innovations (conferences, money, trips) • Measure quality as well as quantity • Encourage innovation with time off to pursue ideas
Development	• Emphasize efficiency theme in all training	• Emphasize quality theme in all training

Table 6.1. Effect of Human Resources on Strategy, Cont'd.

Human Resource Issue	Impact on Cost	Impact on Differentiation
	• Focus on technical training • Lean training staff—use line managers or subcontract • Require dual technical competence • Highlight on-the-job training	• Use training to generate new ideas and procedures (bring new people and customers to training) • Train beyond technical area to include management development, customer relations, and so on • Use line managers to communicate key quality themes
Appraisal	• Set cost standards • Report feedback on cost • Identify and watch for cases of efficiency and talk about it • Share cost attainment information and benefits • Keep feedback immediate and specific • Assign individual goals and accountability	• Set quality standards in important areas • Report attainment of quality standards publicly • Include user data as an indicator of quality (customer can become part of appraisal team) • Encourage team appraisals to build team quality • Use upward appraisal
Communication	• Share cost data of organization and competitors • Focus every message on efficiency and cost savings • Use slogans, videos, speeches, and other tools to highlight costs • Show cost focus in work setting, bids for equipment, lunchroom, executive offices (communicate nonverbally)	• Compare quality data with self and with competitors • Focus every message on primary quality theme • Invite users to talk about quality standards • Show quality in all areas of the organization (nonverbal communication of quality)

buyers lower prices. These strategies might be characterized by flat organizational structures with fewer levels of management, technologically driven and automated systems with routinized work and fewer employees, and delegation and accountability further down the organization to reduce the need for large staffs. Moreover, cost strategies imply certain human resource practices: hiring less experienced (and thus less expensive) employees, basing rewards on incentives that increase commitment (and may lower base salary costs), ensuring that performance monitoring systems focus on control of costs, and making sure that development programs cross-train employees to allow for substitutability and contain modules on cost control as a critical strategy (see Table 6.1). One organization that uses these primary levers to pursue cost strategies is Continental Airlines, where the human resource practices are designed to reduce the cost of operations; these cost savings may then be passed on to passengers in the form of lower fares.

Differentiation strategies create competitive advantage by attempting to distinguish in the buyers' minds one organization from another based on quality, service, or some other factor. Human resource practices may be designed to further this strategy—through organizational plans that encourage specialists in product design and development, through staffing practices that ensure the highest-quality employees entering the organization, through reward systems tied to quality and service, through development programs that focus on quality and service, and through appraisal systems that set high standards and abide by them. John Akers, chairman of International Business Machines, attributes IBM's high regard for quality and service to the company's people and people management program.

Human resource practices serve as primary levers for executives who want to pursue strategies directly. In managing strategic change, human resource practices often become the key to success. When Exxon Corporation failed in its attempt to enter the office automation market through acquisitions in the late 1970s, much of the failure could be attributed to Exxon's inability to build human resource competencies that would create and sustain competitive advantage in office automation. The merger of Baxter Travenol and American Hospital Supply (Ulrich and others, 1989) and General Electric's acquisition of RCA were accomplished, to a great extent, through the integration of two different cultures by using human resource levers: restructuring the organization, making careful staffing assignments, forming work teams, redesigning reward systems, and communicating a new ideology through development programs.

Making sure that human resource practices are systematically reviewed according to how they further the strategy helps to translate strategy from formulation into implementation. In lieu of focusing on strengths, weaknesses, opportunities, and threats and positioning strategic alternatives, strategic analysis should examine how the firm can create an organizational capability for accomplishing strategies.

Effect of Human Resources on Executive Choices

While human resource practices affect business strategy, they also affect executive decisions. The five executive choices noted by Porter (see Figure 6.1) depend on human resource practices. To accomplish inbound logistics, operations, outbound logistics, marketing/sales, and service, human resource practices must be not only considered but managed. Table 6.2 shows these five areas of executive choice and the human resource decisions in each area. I use the five areas of executive choice to illustrate that *any* area of executive decision making must be accomplished through people. The idea is to identify specific choices in managing people to demonstrate not only the importance but also the application of human resources to competitive advantage. To accomplish operations, for example, human resource decisions may be made about *organization planning* (for instance: what type of assembly line or work flow — centralized versus decentralized assembly or manufacturing?), *selection/staffing* (for instance: what types of career paths, what sources may be used to identify employees?), *rewards* (for instance: what pay systems to use — base, incentive, or skill-focused), *development* (for instance: what skills are needed and how do we train those skills?), *appraisal* (for instance: what standards do we set in the organization and how do we provide employees feedback on their performance?), and *communications* (for instance: what messages to share with what employees?). As these practices are considered for each executive choice, they become the means of translating executive decisions into practice.

If a department or function in an organization is to operate effectively and efficiently, human resource practices must be managed. If procurement, manufacturing, distribution, marketing, sales, or service departments are to accomplish their goals, they must do so through people. People management systems become the primary levers for executives attempting to direct and focus people's attention and behavior.

Effect of Human Resources on Sustained Competitive Advantage

As discussed earlier, one of the main challenges is translating strategies into sustained competitive advantage. Long-term competitive advantage comes from organizational members recognizing, accepting, and personally committing themselves to strategic continuity. Strategic continuity occurs when strategic thinking emphasizes not only technology, market niche, and industry but focuses as well on organizational capability. Strategic continuity requires that strategies focus on positive rather than negative activities. Negative strategies emphasize what organizations should *stop* doing—stop selling certain products, stop organizing in traditional hierarchies, stop rising labor costs, and so forth. Although these negative strategies may affect competitive advantage in the short run, they cannot lead to sustained competitive advantage.

Positive strategies emphasize what organizations should *start* doing to sustain a competitive advantage. Rather than stop selling old products, positive strategies emphasize the new products that should be started. Rather than stop old organizational forms, positive strategies highlight the positive value of forming strategic alliances. Rather than stop rising labor costs, positive strategies focus on meeting customer needs. Positive

Table 6.2. Effect of Human Resources on Executive Choices.

Areas of Executive Choice

Inbound Logistics	Operations	Outbound Logistics	Marketing/Sales	Service
		Organizational Planning		
• Vertical Integration • Location of purchasing department • Routinization of purchasing department	• Type of assembly line • Relationship of production and engineering and how they report through the hierarchy • Centralized versus decentralized manufacturing • Means of sharing information from marketing to manufacturing	• Location of distribution facility • Reporting relationship of distribution manager • Coordination of distribution with other areas • Organization by territory, district, region, or nation for distribution • Subcontract or own shippers	• Marketing in region or national accounts • Marketing to customers or within product lines • Advertising inside or outside and length of relationship with vendor • Sharing market information with all groups in company	• Local or national service reps • Joint service contracts • Location of service centers • Sharing information with rest of functions in company
		Selection/Staffing		
• Ensure right personnel in job • Determine career sources of personnel • Work for future career moves	• Hire new or experienced employees for the job • Define job evaluations and standards for jobs • Prepare for career mobility of operations personnel	• Hire new or experienced employees for the job • Ensure that job evaluations describe critical job elements • Consider career opportunities	• Assign employees who have sales profile • Build future sales competencies • Promote those with managerial skills, not just the best sales record	• Hire service reps with correct skills • Prepare fair and equitable job evaluation • Prepare career counseling and paths

Table 6.2. Effect of Human Resources on Executive Choices, Cont'd.

Areas of Executive Choice

Inbound Logistics	Operations	Outbound Logistics	Marketing/Sales	Service
	• Promote managers who have correct skill mix		• Plot career track of sales force	
		Rewards		
• Balance base and incentive pay • Link salary to job performance • Create work conditions that motivate • Structure individual and team rewards	• Design pay system to elicit desired behavior • Make pay system consistent with technology • Manage individual and team rewards	• Make sure that pay creates an incentive to perform • Use a variety of reward systems • Reward teams as appropriate	• Design incentive system for sales to meet goals • Use financial and nonfinancial rewards to drive behavior • Make sure employees know basis of reward system • Create rewards to motivate advertisers	• Design rewards for service personnel • Use mix of incentives to maintain output
		Development		
• Train to ensure needed skill mix • Ensure that technical skills match the job • Allow for cross-training to develop a strong team	• Offer training in technical areas so that employees can do the job • Upgrade skill training for job changes • Cross-train to build a team of qualified	• Train in areas where more skills are needed • Look for cross-training opportunities to develop labor force • Train to make sure	• Train in technical areas as needed by sales force • Train in becoming a better sales force • Train for awareness of overall organization	• Ensure quality technical training • Allow for new skills to be taught as career changes • Cross-train for stronger team

• Ensure enough development time to work on team morale	• individuals • Train managers as they are promoted	that all work areas are included		

Appraisal

• Set standards to link procurement with company strategies • Provide employees immediate feedback on performance • Measure employee behavior against standard	• Set standards that integrate operations with overall company strategies • Observe employee behavior by manager, peer, and subordinate to meet standard • Provide timely and honest feedback to employee for positive and negative behavior	• Set standards to ensure excellent distribution and match overall company goals • Ensure that managers watch employees and offer timely and constructive feedback	• Set sales goals that are accepted by all members of sales team • Provide feedback to sales team to ensure progress toward sales goals	• Set standards of service consistent with company strategy • Ensure that all service employees know and accept standards • Offer feedback on attainment of standard

Communication

• Explain what needs to be done and why inbound work builds competitive advantage • Have senior executives deliver message	• Ensure that operations employees know importance of their role in overall company success • Use many ways to communicate message	• Ensure that outbound employees see what they need to do and why it builds competitiveness • Use many communication techniques	• Make sure that sales force sees overall company perspective and their unique role • Use a variety of communication techniques	• Help service see the overall issues of business success • Use many communication tools

strategies are critical to sustaining strategic continuity. Positive executive choices must be built into the fabric of the organization so that its members recognize, accept, and personally commit to strategic continuity.

Strategic Unity

Strategic unity exists when everyone inside and outside the organization understands, accepts, and acts on the organization's strategy to create and sustain a competitive advantage. Strategic continuity — sustained competitive advantage — comes when there is strategic unity. There must be unity regarding the nature of the environment. Members of an organization need to understand the transitions occurring within an industry and how the industry affects what the organization is currently doing. Understanding externalities allows members to accept the rationale behind organizational transitions. Too often organizational members see what transitions are expected of them without understanding *why*. Unity regarding externalities allows members to commit to strategic continuity. There must be unity regarding customer values as well. The value chain suggested by Porter (1985) implies a framework for thinking about strategic unity. The organization's output must provide value added for the buyer. Understanding this value chain leads to unity.

Examining the value chain in greater detail, we find unity regarding both absolute and instrumental values (Brockbank and Ulrich, 1987). Absolute values represent the organization's goals. All parties to an organization must recognize its valued outputs. Buyers receive a value product (their goal) while the organization receives a profit (its goal). Absolute values create unity around the outputs of the organization. Instrumental values represent the processes an organization uses to accomplish its output. Organization members and buyers must have unity on not only the output (the absolute values) but the process (the instrumental values). When buyers accept the norms, processes, and activities of an organization that lead to a valued output, then unity exists. This unity allows strategic continuity, which leads to sustained competitive advantage.

There must be strategic unity between external stakeholders and internal organization members and among different internal stakeholders. Externally, buyers, suppliers, financiers, and others must share absolute and instrumental values. They need to see how the firm's output and processes provide value added to each stakeholder. Internally, unity means different departments working cooperatively to accomplish organizational goals. Manufacturing, marketing, engineering, R & D, and other departments accept their differences but realize that there must be unity regarding organizational strategies. Unity comes when departmental roles and specialties become subservient to overall organizational goals. External and internal unity allows members to understand, accept, and act on an organization's strategy to sustain a competitive advantage.

Developing Strategic Unity

Executives play a key role in developing strategic unity. First they need to identify the absolute and instrumental values of an organization around which strategic unity can be built. These core values may be characterized as an organization's culture: the mindset and expectations established for those inside and outside the organization. The mindset focuses on how people think about the organization; it evolves from executives continually emphasizing key success factors. At McDonald's, for example, an employee is continually tutored in the mindset of "quality, service, cleanliness, and value." This mindset suggests that employees and customers think about the key success factors at McDonald's coming from these four basic values. From this mindset, expectations are created about how employees behave. Thus a strategic unity exists among employees at all levels and between the firm and its customers. This strategic unity communicates to customers what they may expect to receive from this visit to McDonald's. The strategic unity communicates to employees absolute and instrumental values that must be followed if the employee is to succeed.

To develop strategic unity, executives must identify the distinctive competencies in the organization's culture. Then they must articulate and communicate them inside and outside the organization through formal and informal talks, customer and employee meetings, training programs, or newsletters. Strategic unity comes as external and internal stakeholders work to define, establish, and build distinctive competencies. In one study (Brockbank and Ulrich, 1987), these distinctive competencies became the focus of discussion between sales representatives and key customers. By having customers help define the firm's competencies, they became increasingly committed to the firm, strategic unity between customers and the firm increased, and the firm's market share increased from 19 percent to 31 percent over a two-year period.

To create these distinctive competencies, executives may use human resource practices as primary levers. Innovation growth, cost consciousness, and entrepreneurship may be created and sustained through human resource practices. Organization plans, staffing (new employees and succession planning), rewards, appraisal, development, and communication may serve as primary levers in establishing and maintaining competencies. Innovation, for example, may come if employees see the opportunity to create and operate a division based on their product (organization planning done at 3-M, for example); if employees with entrepreneurial skills are hired and promoted; if employees are rewarded for new ideas and product introduction; if employees are offered the training programs for acquiring new skills; and if formal and informal communication programs encourage innovation.

Thus executives can use human resource practices to translate strategies into long-term competitive advantage by creating and sustaining an organizational culture that leads to distinctive competencies that lead to strategic unity of external and internal stakeholders around absolute and instrumental values. Following this logic, human resource practices lead to strategic continuity and long-term competitive advantage.

Implications and Conclusions

Everyone accepts that people are important to organizational performance; that organizations do not think, make decisions, change, or act; that people do. The challenge, then, becomes one of discovering which human resource programs should be institutionalized to create and sustain competitive advantage. How do human resource practices create and sustain competitive advantage? To answer this question we must go beyond strategic human resource management and focus on the relationship between human resources, strategies, and competitive advantage. Human resource practices help to create and sustain competitive advantage by affecting strategy, executive choices, and strategic unity. These three additions to Porter's framework, presented in Figure 6.2, complement the econometric models of strategy and reveal the important role of human resource practices in competitive advantage. This perspective also requires new roles for line managers, planners, and human resource professionals.

Implications for Line Managers

Line managers who seek competitive advantage, recognize the importance of organizational capability as a source of competitive advantage, and understand the role of human resource practices in establishing organizational capability may be well served by learning more about specific human resource practices. They may gain competitive advantage by understanding how the human resource levers of change can be used, by asking challenging human resource questions when considering new ventures, and by measuring competitiveness in terms of market share gain, financial gain, and organizational capability. Jack Welch, chairman at General Electric, believes that "people are GE's most important asset." But rather than leaving this statement as a creed, he spends time managing General Electric's human resource practices. He personally reviews slates for staffing positions; he personally visits executive training programs and meets with managers; and he continually asks how to improve the organization's ability to be competitive through management of people. As line executives become more involved in human resource practices, they learn the infrastructure of the firm and how to manage changes for competitive advantage.

Figure 6.2. A Model for Creating and Sustaining Competitive Advantage Through Human Resources.

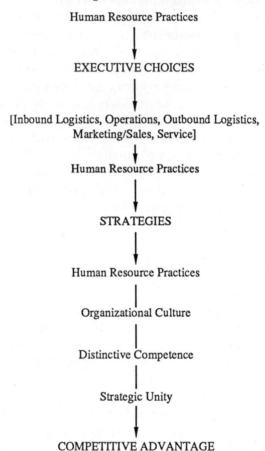

Human Resource Practices

↓

EXECUTIVE CHOICES

↓

[Inbound Logistics, Operations, Outbound Logistics, Marketing/Sales, Service]

↓

Human Resource Practices

↓

STRATEGIES

↓

Human Resource Practices

|

Organizational Culture

|

Distinctive Competence

|

Strategic Unity

↓

COMPETITIVE ADVANTAGE

Implications for Planners

Planners often build barriers between themselves and other staff functions. Rather than perpetuate barriers, competitive advantage requires that they be replaced by cooperation. Planners may find insights from incorporating human resource practices into the plans. At Sumitomo Metals in Japan, the planning group reports to the human resource group. The logic is that the most difficult aspect of planning is not what needs to be done but how to do it. *How* requires a careful assessment and sensitive understanding of people and organizational practices. At Sumitomo even acquisitions are managed through human resources, since a major challenge to an acquisition is the integration of diverse cultures and people management systems.

Implications for Human Resource Professionals

Human resource professionals may need to learn new skills. Rather than being passive participants observing strategy, they need to become strategic partners. As such they need to know strategies, be able to communicate business needs, and see the broad role of human resources in building competitive advantage, not in a policing role. Rather than being the last to know about strategies, they should be continually involved in strategic thinking. In this way creeds become actions that enhance performance in both the short and the long term.

References

Andrews, K. R. *The Concept of Corporate Strategy.* Homewood, Ill.: Dow-Jones-Irwin, 1971.

Barney, J. B. "Organizational Culture: Can It Be a Source of Sustained Competitive Advantage?" *Academy of Management Review*, 1986, *11* (3), 656–665.

Bower, J. L. *Managing the Resource Allocation Process.* Boston: Division of Research, Harvard Business School, 1970.

Brockbank, J. W., and Ulrich, D. "Strategic Unity: A Theory of Strategy Implementation." Ann Arbor: Division of Research, School of Business Administration, University of Michigan, 1987.

De Bejar, G., and Milkovich, G. T. "Human Resource Strategy and the Business Level Study 1: Theoretical Model and Empirical Verification." Paper presented at the Academy of Management, Aug. 1986.

Dyer, L. "Studying Human Resource Strategy: An Approach and

an Agenda." *Industrial and Labor Relations Review*, 1984, *23*, 156–169.

Galbraith, J., and Kazanjian, R. *Strategy Implementation*. St. Paul, Minn.: West, 1985.

Gerstein, M., and Reisman, H. "Strategic Selection: Matching Executives to Business Conditions." *Sloan Management Review*, Winter 1983, pp. 33–49.

Lorange, P. *Corporate Planning*. Englewood Cliffs, N.J.: Prentice-Hall, 1980.

Olian, J. D., and Rynes, S. L. "Organizational Staffing: Integrating Practice with Strategy." *Industrial Relations*, 1984, *23*, 170–183.

Porter, M. E. *Competitive Strategy*. New York: Free Press, 1981.

Porter, M. E. *Competitive Advantage: Creating and Sustaining Superior Performance*. New York: Free Press, 1985.

Pucik, V. "White-Collar Human Resource Management in Large Japanese Manufacturing Firms." *Human Resource Management*, 1984, *23*, 257–276.

Schuler, R. S. "Personnel and Human Resource Management Choices and Corporate Strategy." In R. S. Schuler and S. A. Youngblood (eds.), *Readings in Personnel and Human Resource Management*. (3rd ed.) St. Paul, Minn.: West, 1987.

Schuler, R., and MacMillan, I. "Gaining Competitive Advantage Through Human Resource Management Practices." *Human Resource Management*, 1984, *23*, 241–255.

Tichy, N. M. *Managing Strategic Change: Technical, Political, and Cultural Dynamics*. New York: Wiley, 1983.

Tichy, N. M., and Devanna, M. A. *The Transformational Leader*. New York: Wiley, 1986.

Tichy, N. M., Fombrun, C. J., and Devanna, M. A. "Strategic Human Resource Management." *Sloan Management Review*, 1982, *23* (2), 47–60.

Tichy, N. M., Fombrun, C. J., and Devanna, M. A. (eds.). *Strategic Human Resource Management*. New York: Wiley, 1984.

Tsui, A., and Milkovich, G. "Dimensions of Personnel Department Activities." Paper presented at Academy of Management, Aug. 1985.

Ulrich, D. "Specifying External Relations: Definition of and

Actors in an Organization's Environment." *Human Relations*, 1984, *37*, 245-262.

Ulrich, D. "Human Resource Planning as a Competitive Advantage." *Human Resource Planning*, 1986, *9* (1), 1-15.

Ulrich, D. "Strategic Human Resource Planning: Why and How?" In R. S. Schuler and S. A. Youngblood (eds.), *Readings in Personnel and Human Resource Management*. (3rd ed.) St. Paul, Minn.: West, 1987.

Ulrich, D. "Organizational Capability: Competitive Advantage Through Human Resources." In H. Glass (ed.), *Handbook of Business Strategy*. New York: Warren, Gorham, and Lamont, 1989-90.

Ulrich, D., and Brockbank, J. W. "Institutional Antecedents of Shared Cognitions." Ann Arbor: Division of Research, School of Business Administration, University of Michigan, 1988.

Ulrich, D., and others. "Human Resources at Baxter Healthcare Corporation Merger: A Strategic Partner Role." *Human Resource Planning*, 1989, *2* (12), 87-103.

7

DEVELOPING A QUALITY CULTURE

TERRENCE E. DEAL

One very large U.S. electronics company found itself with the need to order a number of small electronic [components]. . . . So a bunch of clever managers said to themselves: "O.K. these Japanese companies are supposed to be such hotshot makers of quality products. Let's give them a chance to prove that they are really as good as everybody says they are."

So they placed an order for the 10,000 [components] with one of the Japanese hotshots, but as a condition of the order stipulated what was by typical American standards of the day an unheard-of quality criterion. In the order, they said, "We will accept three bad components in the entire lot of 10,000." Really tough stuff. You can almost see them sending off the order with a sort of stick-that-in-your-pipe-and-smoke-it swagger.

Several weeks later, on the exact date shipment was promised, . . . the order of [components] arrived. When the box was opened, a note was found with the

Note: Many of the stories and other material about organizations included in this chapter relate to company lore and were obtained during my years as a consultant. My interest in symbolism and corporate culture motivated me to speak with many people concerning issues relevant to business and the professions. Through these informal interviews, and through the help of some able assistants who also conducted informal interviews, I compiled this material concerning quality in organizations.

[components]. It began: "Thank you very much for your order. We are honored to have been given the opportunity to serve you. We were confused about one aspect of your order, though. We couldn't understand why you *want* three defective [components]. But we made them, and we packed them separately on the assumption that you would not want them to get mixed with the rest, thereby polluting your manufacturing operation" [Guaspari, 1988, pp. 47–48].

To most Americans, this story strains the boundaries of believability. Perhaps it is an apocryphal story. But stories, like myths, stand above truth; they are truer than true. Stories such as this help to reinforce the myth of Japanese superiority in the world of business and commerce. While we may not believe each individual story, we come to accept the overarching mythology.

The other possibility is that the story's credibility is undermined because American standards of quality have actually eroded over the years. Such a commitment to quality is unbelievable because we know that even our highest standards cannot equal those of the Japanese. Our concerns are supported by contemporary business journals. According to many cover stories and headlines, American companies have lost their competitive edge. There are many reasons given for our inability to compete with the Japanese and other foreign rivals. Some reasons are largely economic; others relate to differences in the respective work forces.

This chapter argues that competitive advantage ultimately rests on quality—a characteristic that an organization can control (Barney, 1986a). Too often competition is seen mainly as rivalry among companies in the same marketplace. To compete means to keep your eye glued on competitors, rather than on the quality of your own product or service. In the short term, such rivalry may increase market share. But in the long term it is impossible to compete successfully without delivering high quality—or at least value (where cost is an important variable) to clients, customers, or consumers. Becoming more competitive is ultimately linked to questions of quality: What is it? How can we ensure it? How can organizations produce quality products or services on a continuous basis?

Competition as an Absolute Value

Americans, in particular, assume that competition is an ultimate good. Our sporting events stress the importance of vying successfully with opponents. Irrespective of their moral character or methods, winners are deified and losers are scorned. Childhood memories of such principled phrases as "It's not whether you win or lose, it's how you play the game" are forgotten in favor of an obsession for short-term victories. How opponents were treated or what principles were violated in winning are irrelevant—"nice guys don't win." Beating one's opponent becomes the only object of playing the game.

These same cultural attitudes spill over into the way Americans conduct business. We come to see competition as absolute. With the help of economists we accept, without question, such propositions as the following: Competition improves efficiency; competition improves individual productivity; competition improves quality. Competition thereby becomes the pathway to quality, rather than the other way around.

Does Competition Improve Quality?

Chester I. Barnard ([1938] 1968) argued many years ago that the essence of an organization—business or otherwise—is cooperation. In many respects, Japanese management practices reflect an emphasis on consensus, cooperation, and the group. Americans, unlike the Japanese, seem to overemphasize decision making, competition, and the individual. Competition is a cultural value that becomes reflected in our business practices and policies. Assumptions about the link between competition and quality, for example, contributed to recent changes in American commerce: the deregulation of the communications and airlines industries. Two previously regulated domains were opened to the vying forces of the marketplace.

How have these assumptions held up? Are air travel and telephone service better? At the macro level, the question is open to debate. Proponents on both sides of the competition issue take predictable stances. But to passengers and telephone users, the impact of increased competition seems reasonably clear. Most frequent commuters who compare air travel before and after deregulation argue that the quality of service has declined. Anyone who has flown abroad one way on an American carrier and another on SAS, Singapore Airlines, or Swiss Air would testify that the high-quality carriers are seldom the airlines of this country. Unless one tries to make a telephone call in Europe or Mexico as a basis of comparison, most telephone users would argue that the quality of phone service has declined since the breakup of AT&T. The assumption that competition improves quality seems relatively weak if these two examples are any indication. Perhaps competition has had an impact on cost. But if quality has declined, whether competition has produced greater value in communications or airline travel is little more than an interesting question.

The Downside of Competition: The Cola Wars

No sector of the economy displays more rivalry than the soft drink business. Competition between the two giants — Coke and Pepsi — is particularly keen. Each company has nourished a competitive, hard-driving approach to business. Pepsi, for example, was singled out by *Business Week* as one of the classic examples of a macho culture where competition and winning are at a premium. The prize is market share; the arch rival is Coca-Cola.

In the early 1970s, Pepsi launched several new market initiatives and was gaining market share from Coke. The Pepsi Taste Difference Campaign was making inroads into Coca-Cola's business — a situation that Coke's new chairman could not tolerate. The preoccupation with winning back a large share of the soft drink market caused Coke's executives to consider a radical move. Diet Coke's earlier success persuaded them that to best Pepsi's challenge they needed to do something very differ-

ent. The company decided to alter its flagship product. Changing the secret hundred-year-old recipe produced New Coke as a
challenge to Pepsi.

In hindsight, it appears foolhardy to have changed the
basic character of Coke to compete with Pepsi. But, for a moment, Coca-Cola's executives were riveted on their competitor,
not on the quality of their own product. In their urge to beat
Pepsi, they overlooked industry standards of quality assurance
and underestimated the symbolic importance of Coke—either
in the eyes of the consumers or those of their own employees.
Taking their eyes off the ball and focusing on their opponent
caused Coke to make a serious and costly mistake (Enrico, 1987).

Competitiveness does not always lead to success. Another
potential downside of competition has been felt recently within
Pepsi. To maintain the company's competitive edge, Pepsi has
encouraged competition internally. Working long hours, best-
ing one's colleagues, and anticipating a short career within the
company have been among the dominant cultural attributes of
the firm. But these same attributes take their toll in the quality of
life that employees can expect. As a consequence, turnover at
Pepsi has always been high. To counter the costs of internal
competition Pepsi has launched a new program designed to
emphasize cooperation, personal satisfaction, and expectations
for a lifelong career with the company. Internal competition will
remain a way of life at Pepsi, but counterbalanced by other
values that encourage a high quality of life at the workplace or in
one's personal life. Pepsi's cultural transition is reflected in the
following list (Deal, 1986):

From	*To*
• Competition	• Teamwork
• Individualism	• Cooperation
• Discrimination	• Equity
• Work	• Play
• Career	• Family
• Expedient	• Ethical
• Profit	• Distinctive character

Increasing a company's ability to compete may improve the quality of its products or services. But excessive competition can also threaten quality—either in the business sense or in the personal lives of employees. Pepsi's move is based as much on sound business interests as on its concern for employees. Pepsi believes that the right values will result in better quality and a more competitive organization.

What Is Quality?

The issue of quality has been the subject of discussion and debate since the advent of civilization. Philosophers have tried to penetrate its inner core and raised questions about whether quality can exist independent of perceptions—"does a tree falling in a desolate forest make a sound?" Concerns about quality are certainly evident in the modern business world. Ford's "Quality Is Job One" campaign is a prime example. But contemporary discussions of quality continue to wrestle with age-old questions: What is it? How do we know it? Can we measure it?

Robert Pirsig's (1974) essays on the application of quality to motorcycle maintenance underline its importance in human experience: "Quality is the Buddha. Quality is scientific reality. Quality is the goal of art. I remain to work these concepts into a practical down-to-earth context; and there is nothing more practical or down-to-earth than what I have been talking about—the repair of an old motorcycle" (p. 248). As modern organizations begin to apply the concept of quality to products—computers, automobile parts, cookies, or toys—or to services in restaurants, schools, banks, or airliners, two different sides of quality begin to take form.

In some areas, there is a tangible, technical side to quality on which people can agree. Consensus makes possible standards that can be specified, quantified, and measured. It is this side of quality that typically captures our attention and is embedded in quality control or assurance programs. But measuring the antecedents of quality does not have to involve sophisticated formulas or techniques. As Philip Crosby (1986, p. 108) notes:

One company ran into problems with its management people, who said that there was no way that
their jobs could be measured. So the quality improvement team issued each manager a measurement chart of standard size and color, and a crayon
for marking, and asked each manager to think of
one thing that could be measured and hang it on
the office door. There was a long period of silence
for several hours, and then one manager put,
"Getting to meetings on time" out there. Soon another one put, "Articles of mail left over at end of
day." Another put, "Time secretary needs to find
me and cannot find me." Soon everybody had a
measurement.

Measuring performance can leave a positive effect on quality.
Consider, for example, the impact of blood pressure readings,
cholesterol counts, and other laboratory measurements on the
quality of health care a hospital can provide.

But quality also has a more elusive side. Rooted in preferences, expectations, and perceptions, this aspect of quality is
difficult to articulate and measure. The softer side of quality is
strongly influenced by the total context in which products and
services are produced, delivered, used, and evaluated. As an
example, groups of hospital administrators were recently given
an assignment to eat lunch at a restaurant and then return to a
seminar and reflect on the experience. In their reflections, the
administrators mentioned the attitudes of the people who
parked their cars, the ambience of the building's exterior and
interior, the greeting by the maître d' or hostess who welcomed
them and took them to their table, the demeanor of the people
who poured their water, the poise, knowledgeability, and timing
of the waiter or waitress, the pace of the service, the continual
attention without obtrusiveness. Only late in their presentations
was the quality of the food mentioned—and then only if it was
exceptionally good or abysmally poor. The administrators reported on the quality of their *experience*, of which the food was
only a part. Quality, in their eyes, was intimately related to

people. And any individual in the dining service could affect the perceived quality of the restaurant — even the chefs, dishwashers, and others backstage.

Arguments over whether quality is measurable, specifiable, and controllable through routine procedures or elusive, governed by perceptions, and influenced by the situation are really irrelevant. Quality is both real and imagined:

> Actually this whole dilemma of subjectivity-objectivity, of mind-matter, with relationship to Quality was unfair. That mind-matter relationship has been an intellectual hang-up for centuries. They were just putting that hang-up on top of Quality to drag Quality down. How could *he* say whether Quality was mind or matter when there was no logical clarity as to what was mind and what was matter in the first place?
>
> And so: he rejected the left horn. Quality is not objective, he said. It doesn't reside in the material world.
>
> Then: he rejected the right horn. Quality is not subjective, he said. It doesn't reside merely in the mind.
>
> And finally: Phaedrus, following a path that to his knowledge had never been taken before in the history of Western thought, went straight between the horns of the subjectivity-objectivity dilemma and said Quality is neither a part of mind, nor is it a part of matter. It is a *third* entity which is independent of the two [Pirsig, 1974, p. 213].

Approaches to Quality Assurance

If we can accept quality as an independent entity, neither purely subjective nor completely objective, we can begin to examine where in an organization quality can be compromised. Companies with quality troubles often have the following symptoms (Crosby, 1986):

- The outgoing product or service normally contains deviations from the published, announced, or agreed upon requirements.
- The company has an extensive field service or dealer network skilled in rewards and resourceful corrective action to keep customers satisfied.
- Management does not provide a clear performance standard or definition of quality, so the employees develop their own.
- Management does not know the price of nonconformance.
- Management denies that it is the cause of the problem.

In a sense, the symptoms of poor quality are systemic, not the fault of any one part of a business. Because of this, many approaches to quality control do not work. Statistical quality control attacks only part of the problem. Quality circles focus on several but not all. Both are plausibly helpful approaches to improve quality, but they are tools, not a program. For the most part, companies try to implement a solution before knowing the problem and prescribe a remedy for the symptom rather than finding and eradicating the root cause. Often this makes things worse because the only pathway to high quality, over time, is a strong commitment to quality from the top in both words and deeds, a company-wide understanding that each function and role can add to or detract from quality, and a commitment from everyone that quality is the ultimate end.

Producing Quality on a Regular Basis

Quality of products, service, or anything else cannot be realized overnight. A commitment to quality must be articulated and embodied at the top—"This is the way we do it around here." The commitment must be woven day in and day out into everyday activity at all levels: reinforced, celebrated, and embellished in shared examples. The commitment to quality must become part of the collective mindset and ways.

Recently I selected several companies known for their commitment to quality as well as their ability to deliver high quality on a regular basis (Deal, 1986). The companies are Hallmark Cards, American Airlines, Anheuser-Busch, L. L. Bean, Procter & Gamble, Marriott Hotels, Federal Express, and Chrysler Corporation. Brief profiles of each company show how a commitment to quality pervades past, present, and future operations.

Hallmark Cards

"When you care enough to send the very best" is a statement about quality reflected in both external marketing and internal workings at Hallmark. Hallmark's commitment is expressed in a shared sense of our "artistic sense of pride, dignity, and beauty" and "conviction that there must be more to business than making a profit." Mr. Hall, the company's founder, summed it up by saying "if a man goes into business with only the idea of making a lot of money, chances are he won't" (Hallmark n.d.a, n.d.b). Hallmark's commitment to quality is reinforced in celebrations at the company headquarters and signaled through sponsorship of the Hallmark Hall of Fame. Creativity as the wellspring of quality in the greeting card business is encouraged by Thursday afternoon cartoon matinees for employees. Quality control is also encouraged at lower levels—lithographic operators can send a greeting card back to design if they feel it does not measure up to Hallmark's standards (Levering, Moskowitz, and Katz, 1984).

American Airlines

C. R. Smith, the founder of American Airlines, once remarked: "It's my airport, my airline, my industry." This competitiveness has been carried on in recent times by Robert Crandall, the current CEO responsible for much of American's domestic and foreign expansion. The airline's competitive position is anchored on its "commitment to quality which is at the cultural core of what this airline is...something special in the air." Regular passengers themselves are unpaid quality control inspectors. Gold Advantage members are given "You Are Someone

Special" coupons each month. These can be awarded to any employee of that airline who displays the standard of quality for which the airline is widely recognized. One regular passenger remarked: "These coupons are a way of recognizing what I have come to expect from American. I know what quality is— . . . pilots, ticket agents, cabin attendants, and anyone that I have contact with in the company. I know what a textbook American flight looks like—from making reservations to claiming baggage at the end of my trip. I often make a big deal out of awarding an employee one of my coupons."

Poor quality is not tolerated at American. One regular passenger tells of writing a letter to Robert Crandall complaining about the service and the attitude of one cabin attendant aboard an American flight. The receipt of the letter was formally recognized. The chief flight attendant from American called the passenger before sitting down with the flight attendant to discuss the complaint. A final call from one of Crandall's personal aides informed the passenger of the disposition of the case and rechecked some details. "Holy smokes!" the passenger remarked, "they practice what they preach!"

Anheuser-Busch

The Anheuser-Busch eagle has been a symbol of the company for over a hundred years. In response to every competitive challenge Anheuser-Busch has staunchly refused to alter the quality of its flagship beer—Budweiser. Challenges above or below the quality level have occasionally been matched with new products—Michelob or Busch Bavarian. But at any cost level, Anheuser-Busch delivers the highest quality possible. Their phrase "someone still cares about quality" reflects a long-standing pledge to deliver top value to the consumer.

In response to a competitive challenge by Miller, August Busch III, the company's chief executive officer, remarked: "Tell Miller to come right along, but tell them to bring a lot of money" (Levering, Moskowitz, and Katz, 1984, p. 8). Around the current CEO, who took over control of Anheuser-Busch by replacing his father, whirls story upon story about his obsession with quality. Two examples convey the essence of his concerns.

While touring a brewery, Busch found a flaw in the label of Budweiser bottles coming off the bottling line. He pointed out the flaw to the plant manager, who reportedly shrugged his shoulders: "Only a millimeter, sir." August Busch immediately ran to the emergency switch and stopped the bottling operation. He pulled off his coat and motioned to the maintenance workers to follow him into the intricacies of the machinery. When the operation resumed, Busch in shirt-sleeves held up a bottle to the employees on the floor. "Now there," he exclaimed, "that is a bottle of Budweiser — no flaws." Reportedly, a week later a woman inspecting bottles coming off the line spotted another small flaw and herself stopped the machine.

On another occasion Busch was having a draft Michelob at a local St. Louis pub with some executives and important customers. Upon being served he exclaimed, "The head's not right!" He pulled off his coat and to the astonishment of the bartender raced behind the bar, grabbed a screwdriver, and fiddled with the tap. He finished, drew a beer, held it up to everyone to see, and said, "Now there's a Michelob."

In addition to slogans and lore, Anheuser-Busch relies on Clydesdale horses and other symbols to convey its commitment to quality to employees and customers. Yearly "dialectics" bring executives and managers together to ensure that quality standards are being upheld ("When You Say Busch...," 1984).

L. L. Bean

Like the other three companies, quality has been a way of life at L. L. Bean since the beginning. The Maine Hunting Boot, the company's most visible product, is itself a symbol of quality. One hundred pairs of the hunting boots were the company's first product. Faulty materials caused ninety pairs to fall apart after a few wearings. L. L. Bean returned each customer's money along with a personal letter. The legend of quality at the company had begun (Gorman, 1981).

Much of the emphasis on quality centers on L. L. Bean

himself, who although deceased is still an important part of the contemporary operations. Employees remember that "to hear that one of his products failed was a genuine shock to his system" (Gorman, 1981, p. 9). Always contrite about any lapse in quality, Bean was renowned for taking disappointed customers fishing if they were ever in the neighborhood. He always did everything he could to make it up to the customer when the expected level of quality was not reflected in one of the company's products. His motto was simple: "Sell good merchandise at a reasonable profit. Treat your customers like human beings and they will always come back for more" (Gorman, 1981, p. 11). L. L. Bean emphasizes the human element in its business, arguing that "people don't break down" (Prokesch, 1985). Yearly "roundtable discussions" give employees an opportunity to renew their shared commitment to L. L. Bean's expectations for higher quality.

Procter & Gamble

In many respects Procter & Gamble (P&G) has set a standard for quality. Beginning with their "moon and stars" symbol, fashioned by an illiterate deckhand to keep Procter & Gamble's merchandise separate on the dock, the company has emphasized the high quality of its products. Ivory Soap's "99.44/100% pure" was more than a guarantee of purity; it became a symbol of quality maintained over time. This is Procter & Gamble's "legacy of research. . . world class products to meet a wide variety of consumer needs" (Deal and Kennedy, 1982).

The company relies heavily on research to develop and produce quality products. This commitment to the scientific side of quality is reflected in their "Armpit Research" story. Reportedly, scientists working in research and development were developing a new deodorant. They were so intent on a vigorous field test of two possible products that they sought help from P&G employees. A sample of workers reported to the lab each day before work to receive Brand A under one arm and Brand B under the other. By creating various experimental and control groups and sniffing armpits at the end of each shift as a posttest, the scientists were ultimately satisfied that Brand A was the better of the two deodorants.

Customer expectations, the more elusive side of quality, are reinforced in the "Bad Batch That Floated" story. When an early batch of Ivory was mistakenly aerated by an employee, the shipment received rave reviews throughout the country. "Please send us more of the soap that floats" became a popular order. (In the days of heavy industry, shifts would bathe in murky river water and bars of soap that stayed on the surface were easier to find.) The story reminds P&G employees of the importance of perceived as well as actual quality ("Celebrating 100 Years . . . ," p. 3).

Harley and Procter, the founders of the company, agreed: "If you cannot make pure goods, and full weight, go to something else that is honest, even if it is breaking stone" (Terrence E. Deal, personal communications, 1986). Their words are indelibly carved in the day-to-day experience of P&G today.

Marriott Hotels

For many frequent travelers the Hyatt and Marriott companies provide hotels of choice. The Marriott chain, founded by William Marriott, Sr., began with cold A&W root beer and hot western food served in Washington, D.C., Hot Shoppes. "We do it right" became an early pledge to high quality—a promise that was transferred from root beer and hot tamales to restaurants and hotels around the world (Lee and Lambert, 1985).

One of William Marriott, Sr.'s, promises was: "Take good care of your employees, then they will take good care of your customers." Care begins early, as new employees are indoctrinated with Marriott's high standards. When asked recently how Marriott consistently delivered such high-quality service, a company vice-president responded, "We get our new employees together, tell some good stories about Marriott Sr. and Jr., and send them into the properties. The culture there supports them and shapes them up."

Good stories about the Marriotts are not difficult to find. One in particular demonstrates the importance of quality

within the company. According to legend, William Marriott, Sr.,
visited a property each time a new general manager took over.
He would always ask the new GM to walk with him on a tour of
the property. As they walked, Marriott would take note of problem areas, pebbles on the walk, a broken rhododendron branch,
guests waiting at the cashier's desk, a piece of paper on the lobby
floor. At the end of the tour the new GM would have a long list of
things requiring his or her attention. On one occasion, a new
GM refused a call from a guest in order to ask questions about
her list. Marriott then quickly added another item: "Make sure
that you never neglect a guest for less important matters." He got
his point across.

Marriott's periodic Escort to Excellence ceremonies reward employees who have received high in-room guest evaluations. In countless ways, Marriott instills in its employees the
idea that quality is everyone's business (Einhorn, 1985).

Federal Express

Federal Express is the brainchild of Fred Smith. Years ago he saw
an opportunity for a reliable overnight delivery system. While
his brainchild received a *C* from his business school professors,
it quickly became a multi-million-dollar business, and within a
shorter time span than the preceding companies, Smith has
captured a major share of the overnight mail market (Meltzer,
1984).

The Federal Express Overnight Package symbolizes the
high quality that customers can expect from the company:
"When it absolutely, positively has to be there overnight." The
quality guarantee is anchored in the company's three primary
values: "people, service, profits . . . in that order." Putting people
and service ahead of profits ensures the latter. As employees of
Federal Express echo: "That's what Fred wants" (Meltzer, 1984,
p. 34).

Bravo Zulu are semaphore flags that can be affixed to any
FedEx memo or document to reward service and commitment
to people. The Golden Falcon award provides the celebrating

occasion for rewarding employees who contribute to Federal Express's high-quality performance.

As in other companies, stories reinforce the commitment to quality. One involves a vice-president who reportedly came to Fred Smith to report a suspicious claim by a customer. The company had lost his Overnight Envelope. When asked about its contents, the customer replied, "It contained $5,000 in cash." After hearing the circumstances, legend has it, Smith responded immediately: "Give him his money, we lost a package."

Chrysler Corporation

This last company is different from the others. Instead of a history or legacy of quality, Chrysler's products had sunk to a lower level of mediocrity. The company was in danger of bankruptcy because its products were neither valued nor purchased by the consumer. The new chairman, Lee Iacocca, quickly sensed the core problem and launched an effort to improve the actual and perceived quality of automobiles produced by the company.

Iacocca himself quickly became the public embodiment of quality: "If you can find a better car, buy it" (Glassman and Hompe, 1984). In Chrysler ads he touted, "We have one and only one ambition. To be the best. What else is there?" A joint agreement between the UAW and Chrysler established the Quality Improvement Program, a joint commitment on behalf of both labor and management (UAW–Chrysler, 1981). Iacocca's bravado was welcomed by the public. He encouraged production of the LeBaron convertible, capitalizing on his personal experience of driving around in one with a cut-off top instead of relying on surveys to measure the potential market.

Iacocca's commitment to quality was reportedly exemplified in a story about the ceremony surrounding the introduction of the first LeBaron convertible. Knowing that he was to receive the keys to the first automobile publicly, vice-presidents reportedly showed up on the assembly line to ensure that the first car would be perfect. During the ceremony, as planned, Iacocca was awarded the keys to the first car by the plant manager. The manager proudly announced: "Here you are, sir, the keys to the first LeBaron. You'll find the car perfect for you." Iacocca, in front of a big crowd of celebrities and employees, quickly replied, "I'll take the fourth one"—a signal that if the fourth one is not of the same quality as the first, they cannot compete.

Building A Culture of Quality

None of these companies developed a shared commitment to quality overnight. Nor did any rely mainly on statistical controls or quality circles to ensure high quality. Each has cultivated, in its own way, a culture of quality inside the company. Quality is instilled in employees, reinforced from top to bottom, rewarded and attended to by everyone on a regular basis. Quality has become a way of life and employees take pride in delivering high-quality goods and services to customers. Their advertising lets customers know what to expect, and each company delivers on its promises.

The management literature constantly swings from one approach to another. Underlying each new set of ideas is a set of assumptions and terminology that focuses management's attention and provides a direction for improvement. For a while, "culture" was in vogue. Departing from rational management techniques, cultural approaches encouraged managers to pay attention to the symbolic, existential, human side of business organizations. Now, like so many other management trends, culture has become an overworked concept giving way to a different set of fashionable ideas in good currency. Once a term that *had* to be used by top managers, *culture* is now a word that is often avoided in management articles and seminars. "It's not cool anymore," one executive recently remarked.

But many companies, working on the cultural side of the business before the idea was "cool," have continued to cultivate, reinforce, and transform the uniquely human creation that gives meaning to the workplace. In each of the companies profiled here, building a culture of quality has a high priority. As one considers these companies, it is the elements of culture shaped around quality that stand out. Quality is mentioned or implied in pithy statements of core values. Quality is embodied in the words and deeds of visible heroes who are well known to managers and employees. Quality is reinforced in meaningful rituals and celebrated in significant ceremonial occasions. The commitment to quality is communicated in stories that are told to new employees and retold on a regular basis. As one looks closely at the recent transformation in Ford Motor Company, the same elements appear. "Quality Is Job One" has become a cultural commitment, a new way of life, at Ford.

Competition, Quality, and Culture

It is always important to entertain new ideas. But entertaining new ideas does not necessarily mean discarding old ones that work. Competition is a key issue in today's business world. The competitiveness of American businesses will become even more important as commerce in the global marketplace begins to flow more freely.

The key argument of this chapter is that the core of competition is quality. Cost, of course, is important. But quality at a reasonable cost represents value. Marriott Hotels, for example, compete in the luxury hotel market, and the quality of their service is second to none. At the same time, Marriott Courtyard Hotels compete in the less pricey guest hotel market. The cost is lower and many of the amenities that one comes to expect at the New York Marriott Marquis are not available at the Denver Marriott Courtyard. But the core of quality service, the Marriott way, is evident at both places. In a similar way Marriott is in the airline catering business. Most people who fly are not impressed with the quality of airline food. When asked how Marriott's commitment to quality is reflected in the airline meal business, one vice-president remarked: "Within that market we deliver the highest quality we can." Cost may be an issue in competitive advantage, but quality is the mainstay on which competitive advantage needs to be built.

If you want to build a factory or fix a motorcycle, or
set a nation right without getting stuck, then classical, structured, dualistic, subject–object knowledge, although necessary, is not enough. You have
to have some feeling for the quality of the work. You
have to have a sense of what's good. *That* is what
carries you forward. This sense isn't just something
that you are born with, although you are born with
it. It's also something that you can develop. It is not
just intuition, not just unexplainable "skill" or "talent." It is the direct result of contact with basic
reality. Quality, which dualistic reason in the past
tended to conceal [Pirsig, 1974, p. 255].

To be competitive, a company must come to terms with
the tangible and elusive sides of quality. To ensure a continuous
flow of quality goods and services, a culture of quality must be
woven into the basic fabric of everyday life.

References

Barnard, C. I. *Functions of the Executive.* Cambridge, Mass.: Harvard University Press, 1968. (Originally published 1938.)

Barney, J. B. "Organizational Culture: Can It Be a Source of
Sustained Competitive Advantage?" *Academy of Management
Review,* 1986a, *11* (3), 656–665.

Barney, J. B. "Types of Competition and the Theory of Strategy."
Academy of Management Review, 1986b, *11* (3), 791–800.

"Celebrating 100 Years of Ivory Soap as America's Favorite."
Procter & Gamble brochure (n.d.).

Crosby, P. B. *Quality Without Tears: The Art of Hassle-Free Management.* New York: New American Library, 1986.

Deal, T. E. "Quality Is the Key." Presentation to AT&T Administrative Conference, N. J., 1986.

Deal, T. E. "Managing Cultural Change." Presentation to Pepsico
Leadership Conference, New York, 1988.

Deal, T. E., and Kennedy, A. A. "Corporate Culture: The Rites and Rituals of American Business." Reading, Mass.: Addison-Wesley, 1982.

Einhorn, D. "Hotel Motivation." *Incentive Marketing*, Apr. 1985, pp. 72–73.

Enrico, R. *The Other Guy Blinked: And Other Dispatches from the Cola Wars.* New York: Bantam Books, 1987.

Glassman, J. K., and Hompe, J. T. "The Iacocca Mystique: Would You Buy a New Car from This Man?" *New Republic*, July 16, 1984, p. 20.

Gorman, L. *L. L. Bean, Inc.: Outdoor Specialties by Mail from Maine.* New York: Newcomen Society of America, 1981.

Guaspari, J. *The Customer Connection: Quality for the Rest of Us.* New York: American Management Association, 1988.

Hallmark. "Hallmark History Is Story of Birth of an Industry." Press release, n.d.a.

Hallmark. "Joyce C. Hall: 1891–1982." Press release, n.d.b.

Hayes, R. H., and Wheelwright, S. C. *Restoring Our Competitive Edge: Competing Through Manufacturing.* New York: Wiley, 1984.

Lee, D. R., and Lambert, D. B. "How They Got Started: The Growth of Four Hotel Giants." *Cornell HRA Quarterly*, May 1985, pp. 22–32.

Levering, R., Moskowitz, M., and Katz, M. *The 100 Best Companies to Work for in America.* Reading, Mass.: Addison-Wesley, 1984.

Meltzer, M. "Fedex Reflects Fred Smith." *Air Cargo World*, Dec. 1984, pp. 34–37.

Pirsig, R. *Zen and the Art of Motorcycle Maintenance.* New York: Bantam Books, 1974.

Prokesch, S. E. "Bean Meshes Man and Machine." *New York Times Business Day*, Dec. 27, 1985.

UAW–Chrysler. *Preserving Markets and Saving Jobs: Product Quality Improvement Program.* Detroit, Mich.: Joint International Union/Management Steering Committee, 1981.

"When You Say Busch, You've Said It All." *Business Week*, Feb. 17, 1984, pp. 58–59.

8

EXECUTIVE BEHAVIOR IN HIGH-INVOLVEMENT ORGANIZATIONS

Edward E. Lawler III

T he increasing popularity of participative management has led to an extensive literature on the topic. This literature typically makes the case that increased use of participative management can improve international competitiveness and offer a competitive advantage to many firms. This seems to be particularly true for high-technology companies that face stiff international competition. Companies like Motorola, Microsystems, Compaq Computer, and Digital Equipment are often cited as premier examples of organizations that use participative management throughout their operations. Along with the increasing adoption of participative management has come an extensive literature on how to make it work. Books on high-involvement management, high-performance work systems, and participative leadership tend to focus extensively on the lower levels of the organization and specify in some detail how work should be structured, how people should be paid, and how supervisors should behave.

Missing in most discussions of participative management is a clear view of what must happen at the upper levels of management in order for it to provide a competitive advantage. Many have pointed out that traditional supervisors often have trouble adapting to a participative management style. Typically they go on to describe how lower-level managers should behave in order to be effective in a participative or high-involvement work setting. (See, for example, Walton and Schlesinger, 1979.) Much less has been written about the role of senior management. There is, however, a growing literature on the role of leaders in organizations. (See, for example, Bennis and Nanus, 1985; Tichy and Devanna, 1986.) This literature is, of course, relevant to high-involvement organizations since they, more than most organizations, need leadership that provides a sense of purpose and vision.

This chapter is not about leadership per se. It is about how senior managers in organizations should structure and carry out their jobs in order to be consistent with a high-involvement approach to management. Demonstrating certain leadership behaviors certainly is a part of this task, but only one part. There are also structural issues, reward issues, and other parts of the job that need to be done in a certain way if a participatively managed organization is to be effective. As more and more organizations are managed along high-involvement lines the roles of executives and senior managers will undoubtedly come into even sharper focus. If our knowledge is limited at present, it is because so few senior managers have managed a high-involvement organization. Little effort has been directed to working out the kind of behavior and support structures that are necessary at the executive level in order to make a high-involvement organization so effective that it gains a competitive advantage. Nevertheless some points can be made here based on our knowledge of organizations and the experience of a limited number of cases.

Setting the Overall Direction

There is one function that must be led from the top of the organization: It is the unique responsibility of senior management to set the firm's overall direction. This issue has less to do with how an organization is going to operate than what an organization is trying to accomplish and in what direction it is heading. It involves decisions about which mountain the organization is trying to climb—or, even more broadly, whether the organization is in the business of mountain climbing rather than underwater exploration.

In a high-involvement or participative organization it is

up to the senior levels of management to lead the decision process in this regard and to ensure there is a consensus in the organization about the direction in which the business is heading. This does not mean, however, that the decision has to be made in a unilateral top-down manner. It does not have to be made, for example, by a few senior executives going off to a retreat and coming back with a statement of objectives. Nor does it have to be made by a single executive who has an inspiration about the business and its direction. Input should be sought from a number of levels of the organization, and ideas should be tested throughout the organization once they have been proposed. This is an ideal place for an organization to use task forces and form study groups. It is easier to get acceptance of an idea when the development process has been participative. Moreover, a participative development process can reinforce the overall commitment of the organization to participative management.

Often the strategic direction of an organization is best captured in a written document. There are a number of successful examples of this approach, particularly in large organizations such as Johnson & Johnson, Ford Motor Company, and the 3M Corporation and smaller ones such as Herman Miller. The role of the senior executive should be to have everyone in the company understand its objectives and embrace them as a guiding focus. The best statements tell people the right things to do in their jobs, how to behave toward one another, and how to behave toward customers, suppliers, and others. Since establishing such statements is clearly a difficult process, this is where leadership skills as well as managerial skills are crucial.

Once the strategic direction of an organization has been set, senior management must keep it in the forefront of the organization's consciousness. They are the only ones who can bring it to life and keep it as an important theme of the organization's culture. There are no prescribed formulas for doing this, but in some organizations certain kinds of activities have clearly helped. For example, meetings of the right kind can help. Similarly, certain kinds of publications and other symbolic activities can highlight the direction that the organization is taking. Symbolic events can range all the way from senior executives meeting new employees to tell them about the firm's goals to employees meeting with customers and suppliers to discuss quality. Indeed, TV advertising and other forms of media attention can help capture and communicate the strategic direction. Ford has done this very effectively with their advertising efforts on the subject of quality; SAS airlines has done it with their service-oriented advertising.

As part of the focus on strategic direction, senior management needs to develop certain feedback mechanisms that make everyone aware of the progress the organization is making. One particularly useful process is competitive benchmarking. Xerox, for example, has used this process very skillfully to specify what the organization is striving to achieve and then to keep the organization up to date about how well it is doing. Thus senior management must put into place some mechanism to ensure that everyone in the organization gets a sense of how they are doing competitively and whether in fact they are meeting the firm's strategic agenda.

Structure at the Top

Most models of organizational design stress congruence and fit. In essence, the argument is that although there is no perfect set of practices for an organization, there are practices that tend to fit and reinforce each other. The key to organizational effectiveness, therefore, is having an organization in which the different pieces fit together and support each other and, of course, also fit the strategy. This thinking has interesting applications for the kind of organizational structure that should exist at the senior management level in a participative organization.

Perhaps the best place to start discussing structure at the top is with the highest level of the organization: the board of directors. Typically boards of U.S. companies are made up of senior managers and some outside board members. Boards need to be structured quite differently, however, in the case of the high-involvement organization. As in traditional organizations, one issue is the degree to which the board is dominated by internal versus external members. The argument for having outside board members—who are more than tokens, that is—is particularly compelling in the case of high-involvement management. They should be powerful enough, in both numbers and stature, to check any tendencies on the part of executives to act arbitrarily or unilaterally on issues that directly affect employees and, of course, issues that are clearly in the self-interest of senior managers (issues such as pay). More than in traditional organizations, they should be experts in management and be able to help the organization measure itself against the outside world in terms of its managerial effectiveness.

Perhaps the most important issue in high-involvement organizations is the presence of lower-level employees on the board. They have a significant stake in the success of the organization and thus would seem to warrant a position on the board. Since it is a major axiom of high-involvement organizations that information, power, knowledge, and rewards should spread to the lower levels in the organization, clearly one way to do this is to have lower-level employees represented on the board. In large organizations this may be more symbolic than practical in the sense of giving nonmanagement employees, as a whole, a chance to participate directly in the decision making, but they can at least be assured that someone is there speaking for them. In short, it can be a kind of representative democracy.

The idea of lower-level members being on boards is far from new. It has been practiced in Europe for a considerable period of time and by a few U.S. corporations. In the United States it has been adopted by companies such as Chrysler that have been in financial trouble and needed union support for restructuring and by some Employee Stock Ownership Plan (ESOP) companies that have employee representation on the board. If it has not become an accepted practice in the United States, the reason, undoubtedly, is that it is inconsistent with the way most American companies have been run. Since they have been managed in a top-down manner it is hardly surprising that they regard the idea of employee representation on boards as not being particularly appropriate.

There has, however, been some experimentation in the

United States with the idea of a junior board. Typically junior boards have been made up of promising managers who have not yet reached the executive level. They look at many of the same issues as the board of directors and, in many cases, make recommendations to the board for use in their final decision making. In most cases this idea has been used in association with a management development program rather than as a means of participative management. It may be appropriate at this point to use it as a way of getting employees throughout the organization more involved in the company's major decisions. It represents a powerful way to spread new kinds of information, power, and knowledge downward in the organization. Like employee membership on the board, it is limited in the number of people that are directly affected but, nevertheless, it can be a symbolic and practical way of involving a broader range of people in the decision-making processes of the organization.

A second important structural issue concerns the reporting relationship of the senior human resource executive. Although precise figures are not available, a good estimate is that in as many as 50 percent of U.S. corporations the senior human resource executive reports to an executive one or two levels below the chief executive office. This reporting relationship is quite inconsistent with an organization model that stresses high-involvement management. Indeed, it suggests that other features of an organization are more important to its success than are its human resources. This implication is directly contrary to the typical statements made by high-involvement organizations: "People are our most important asset," for example, and "We are committed to the growth of our human resources." Although this issue is partly symbolic, there is also a practical side to it. If a human resources executive is not in the senior management decision-making process, human resource issues are less likely to be considered and the organization's actions are less likely to align themselves with a focus on high-involvement management.

The whole issue of the reporting relationship of the human resources function leads to the question of how the rest of the senior management team should be structured. One intriguing possibility is to structure it as a work team (Nadler,

1989). The literature on employee involvement is full of cases on the success of self-managing work teams in production and service areas (Lawler, 1986). A great deal is known about how to structure them and manage them at the lower levels. Virtually absent, however, is any discussion of work teams at the senior management level. There may be a good reason for this: They simply do not fit the kind of work that needs to be done at the top. But before we conclude that they are entirely inappropriate at this level, some experimentation would seem to be in order.

Some organizations have adopted structures including an office of the president that has two or three members and operates on a limited work-team model. It may not be too difficult to extend this idea to a somewhat larger group that in fact covers the major functions of the corporation. Given the level of technical specialization that is required in some aspects of senior management responsibility, clearly some people must take primary responsibility for specific areas, but a more flexible deployment of people may be possible here. Those who have come up to senior management through cross-functional rotation programs, for example, should be able to operate in more than one functional area. This notion could lead to a senior management group in which individuals take responsibility for projects as well as functional areas. The projects could cover multiple functional areas; indeed, the idea could lead to executives taking supervisory responsibility for more than one function and sharing responsibility for functions. One of the major advantages of this approach could be to create a senior management group that is familiar with the total functioning of the organization and is a much better decision-making body when dealing with issues involving functional competition and differences. It also could help the group make better decisions when issues involve several lines of business.

One more structural issue must be considered here: the use of task forces. Task forces that include people from multiple levels in the organization, particularly the lower levels, are a powerful way to spread new information downward in the organization. They can be used to address many of the decisions that must be made in an organization. Depending on the issue, task forces can be given the power to make a final decision or just to make a recommendation to senior management. They can be effective in a number of areas, but one place where they seem to be particularly appropriate is in developing such human resource management programs as career development structures, pay systems, and training programs. They can also be quite useful in doing organizational design work and deciding on certain types of new capital investments. These are all situations where people have knowledge by virtue of their work in lower-level jobs. Participating on task forces is not only a way for the organization to utilize this knowledge but also a way to get improved decision making and broader input into decisions.

Structure at Lower Levels

Senior management is uniquely responsible for the overall structure of an organization. They, for example, are in a position to create an organization that is structured around products, services, customers, or functions. The use of high-involvement management has clear implications for the kind of structure that is appropriate for an organization. Specifically, high-involvement management demands an organizational structure that allows people at the lower levels to have a customer/supplier relationship so that they can get feedback and be held accountable for the delivery of a product or service. The implication for senior management is clear. They must be sure that the organization is structured in a way that allows all employees to have a customer/supplier relationship. In most cases this means the overall structure of the organization should be based on a customer, product, or service (Galbraith, 1977).

The success of high-involvement management also depends on having a relatively flat organizational structure. If there are many levels of management, it is virtually impossible to move power, information, and knowledge to the lower levels in the organization. In essence, power gets picked off by each level of management so that by the time it gets to the lower levels there are very few decisions left to be made. Related to the issue of flatness is the role of the staff organization. Moving decision-making power to lower levels requires more than a lean staff; the staff must see its role as facilitating and supporting decision making by the line organization. Staff organizations are likely to adopt this role only if senior management keeps the staff small and gives it direction.

Participative Behavior

Much of the writing on participative management emphasizes that senior managers must exemplify the kind of behavior they expect from lower levels of the organization. The argument generally says that role modeling the behavior will give people at the lower levels an example and establish a culture in which this behavior is acceptable and even demanded (DePree, 1987). It is hard to argue with this point of view, but we need to go one step further and talk about the kinds of behavior that are appropriate at the senior levels of management.

One of senior management's most obvious tasks is to hold meetings and convene groups. How these are run can be an important symbol of the type of information exchange and decision-making processes that prevail at the senior management level (Peters, 1978). In a traditional organization, for example, staff meetings frequently are sessions in which executives make long, formal reports on what is going on in their area. Little discussion takes place, except for a few questions, and the meetings are run by a senior executive in a top-down "efficient" manner. Organizations, such as Xerox, that have adopted more participative management styles have made a significant effort to alter the activities that take place in these meetings. They have tried, for example, to incorporate many of the principles of good group decision making into their meetings. Instead of focusing on information exchange, they have used the meetings for decision making and have, in fact, trained the executives in group process and decision-making techniques. Moreover, they have tried to change the highly formal presentation by using flip charts and discussions and encouraging debate.

One final point should be made here. Often the decision process at the top is the critical event in determining whether or not people throughout the organization see participative management as sincere. Particularly important is the manner in which the key organizational decisions are made. Often these decisions concern capital expenditures and budgeting. If they are made in a traditional top-down manner, the organization is likely to get the impression that employee involvement is all right for trivial decisions but not for the crucial ones. Senior management, therefore, must take a careful look at how these decisions are made and be sure to give lower levels an opportunity to influence the capital expenditure and budgetary decisions for their work unit.

Even in a high-involvement organization it is unlikely that all decisions should be made in a highly participative manner. Indeed, one of the most important decisions a senior manager must make concerns which decision style to use (Vroom and Yetton, 1973). Admittedly, the high-involvement model argues that, in many cases, the decision style should be participative. But when time is of the essence or information rests uniquely at the top, a participative decision process may not be the best way to go. In such cases, the senior executive should explain why a nonparticipative decision-making approach will be used. Even the most ardent advocates of participative decision making recognize that the decision-making style depends on the problem being addressed and the firm's situation. What differentiates top-down management from participative management is that top-down management is not obliged to explain why it is using a traditional autocratic decision style. High-involvement management, by contrast, does have such an obligation, and the best place to start modeling this behavior is with senior managers.

Another aspect of managerial behavior that should be modeled at the top concerns feedback about managerial effectiveness. Critical to the high-involvement approach is the willingness of managers to find out how effective they are in their decision making and leadership (Argyris and Schön, 1978). At the lower levels in many organizations, information can be obtained through attitude surveys and other means and then be given to the manager. It is always hard for supervisors to ask for feedback because of the risk involved. Further, it is often difficult for subordinates to give valid feedback because they, too, perceive a risk. If feedback is going to occur in an organization, it is best to begin by having senior managers ask their subordinates about the leadership of senior management. This is an area where senior management can take a dramatic step forward by modeling the behavior that is needed throughout the organization.

Senior management is in a particularly good position to share results throughout the organization. They are in the best position to talk about overall operating profits, goals, and performance. Because an important part of high-involvement management is the sharing of information about financial results, it is critical that senior managers do this type of communicating. There are a number of ways this can be done — informal discussions with employees, interactive video sessions that cover an entire organization, and, of course, large meetings with groups of employees invited to hear reports about the organization and its performance. In most organizations, a diversity of methods is probably appropriate and should be carried out on a regular basis. Indeed, it is hard to imagine too much downward communication taking place with respect to operating performance and results.

Precisely because an important part of every participatively managed organization is the employees' knowledge base, executives need to be particularly concerned about the kind of training that is offered. This concern should extend beyond simply being assured that the organization offers good training opportunities. Executives must look at their own behavior and ask whether they are modeling the kind of learning they expect from people at lower levels.

A good way for managers to be assured that they are in fact supporting the right kind of training is to develop an organization policy that supports everyone, themselves included, having at least a week of training per year. IBM has done this for decades. In addition, managers should be the first to experience any training programs that focus on leadership style, decision processes, and the development of participative management behavior. They in turn should participate in these programs when they are given to their direct subordinates. This cascading process can be extremely valuable in reinforcing the importance of managerial behaviors throughout the organization. Xerox, to mention just one organization, has done an excellent job of developing training approaches that in fact give superiors a key part in developing and supporting participative behavior from the top to the bottom of the organization. In other organizations — for example, General Electric — senior executives attend management training programs at all levels in order to reinforce the right culture and find out how the organization is performing.

Finally, Nadler (1989) has pointed out that executives' everyday behavior as well as "grand gestures" can shape organizational behavior. The following behavior, he says, can have a great impact:

- Allocation of time and calendar management
- Shaping of physical settings
- Control over agendas of events or meetings
- Use of events such as lunches and meetings
- Summarization of what has occurred
- Use of humor, stories, and legends
- Small symbolic actions, including rewards and punishments

To this list I would add:

- The type of questions asked in meetings and tours of company facilities
- Rejection of status symbols and signs of hierarchical difference

These are all things an executive can do to signify what is important and what type of behavior is expected in the organization. Used skillfully, they can strongly support the effective practice of high-involvement management.

Monitoring Decision Processes

In participative organizations a number of decisions are made at lower levels. Because of this, people at all levels often have to take responsibility for decisions that they do not directly influence. Indeed, one of the stressful aspects of participative decision making is that people are often held accountable for decisions they have not directly made. The emphasis here is on *directly* because senior managers do have an opportunity to influence how decisions are made in a participative organization, just as they do in a traditional structure. They have the chance to influence them because they are responsible for the kind of decision-making processes that exist in the organization. Indeed, one of their main tasks should be to monitor the kinds of decision processes that go on. They need to gather systematic data about how effectively the organization is operating at levels considerably below them.

There are a number of techniques that senior managers can use to find out how their organization is operating. In addition to the customary financial and quality data available to senior managers, they can use formal opinion surveys and sensing sessions throughout the organization. Beyond this, in certain organizations they can actually do lower-level jobs in the organization. Some organizations have used this approach quite effectively for decades. At Federal Express, for example, senior executives are expected to do a nonmanagement service job in the organization on a regular basis. This gives executives a unique opportunity to see how the organization is working at a different level and gives them experience with customer contact. In many ways this approach is vastly superior to the idea of wandering around the organization and sensing how people feel by watching them and having casual conversations with them (Peters and Waterman, 1982). Wandering runs the risk of being superficial and, in some ways, a condescending interruption of important work. Actually getting out and *doing* the work demonstrates to employees that everyone in the organization is willing to participate in production and gives senior managers a much more intensive experience in how the organization actually operates.

Sometimes senior managers need to do more than just listen to recommendations from lower levels. They need to check personally on how the decision was made and to ask decision makers how they feel about the process. Executives must be sure that affected employees are given the opportunity to participate in decisions when their expertise is relevant. Again, senior management is in the best position to test the decision processes and ensure they are operating effectively. Only then can they fully commit themselves to the decisions made at lower levels of the organization.

Especially relevant here is the issue of access. Senior managers must be regarded as accessible to those at the lower levels of the organization. One means of access is a formal appeal process that allows employees who feel they have been overlooked in the decision process or have been unfairly treated to raise this issue with senior management. In a number of organizations, such as IBM, this practice has been used for years and allows the organization to resolve a number of complaints short of a lawsuit or union grievance.

Access must go beyond the formal appeal process, however. Senior managers working in lower-level jobs can help, as can eating in a dining room with other employees. Even arranging office space so there is informal contact among people throughout the organization can help. The specific ways of creating access will differ from organization to organization. The overall point, however, remains: Senior managers need to be sure they are accessible through both formal and informal communication channels.

Reward Systems

Senior executives are in a particularly good position to design and influence their firm's reward system. Pay increases, promotion, and recognition are an important element in the motivation and control systems of organizations. Because they are so important, the rewards must align with and support participative management if a high-involvement organization is to be successful.

Senior management is especially well positioned to give recognition for outstanding performance. Indeed, from several perspectives, one of the most important things that senior management can do is to reward the kind of performance that contributes to the organization's strategic direction. The rewards need not be of material or financial value; they can simply be symbolic. Particularly when senior management is involved, attention is in and of itself often rewarding. Because senior managers have the unique ability to give certain kinds of recognition, it is particularly vital that they recognize performance and, in the process, become the role model for the kind of behavior they expect from managers lower down in the organization.

As suggested earlier, senior executives should be accessible and need to convey a sense that their behavior and their decision processes are consistent with a participative approach. This notion has strong implications for perquisites. In high-involvement organizations, extensive perquisites are simply inappropriate. There is little room for reserved parking spaces, executive dining rooms, and the other benefits that set senior executives apart from the rest of the employees. It is not that perquisites, per se, are bad. Rather, they simply do not fit a style of management that stresses minimal social distance and behavior patterns involving upward communication.

There is one other feature of high-involvement organizations that argues for minimal perquisites. High-involvement management implies that decisions should be made by those who have the most expertise on the issue. Sometimes this is indeed senior management; but sometimes it is not. When senior managers are set apart by symbols indicating that they are the most powerful and prestigious members of the organization, there is a tendency to look to them for all the answers. The difference between high-involvement management and traditional management centers on this very point. In traditional management, decisions belong to positions and the key element of a position is its place in the hierarchy. Thus the big decisions clearly belong to high-level executives. High-involvement management, however, argues that decisions ought to go where the expertise is and this may or may not relate to the hierarchy. Thus status symbols and hierarchical reward structures ought to be minimized so they do not channel decisions to the top of the organization.

Perhaps the greatest impact of senior managers on the spread of high-involvement management throughout the organization comes through the promotion and pay systems. Organizations that preach the importance of participative management and then disregard it in promotion and pay decisions do not elicit much participative behavior from managers. If senior management wants to encourage participative management, it needs to ask questions and demand that data be gathered about how managers behave throughout the organization. These data, in turn, should be an important part of decisions concerning promotion and pay changes. Data on managerial performance can be obtained from subordinates and by observing the behavior of managers. The important point is that managers throughout the organization must realize that their behavior has an important influence on their career direction and their pay increases. Senior management, in particular, should reinforce this theme and send a clear message that this is the way the organization operates.

Executive Effectiveness

So far I have emphasized a number of areas where senior managers must be particularly effective if they are to succeed in managing a high-involvement organization. We are now ready to look at the question of how senior executives can tell whether they have been effective. Clearly there are a variety of indicators. Here the intention is simply to focus on a few key signs that an organization is in fact a high-involvement operation.

Perhaps the key communication change concerns the upward flow of information. Simply stated, executives should find much more upward communication taking place — from direct feedback about their own behavior from subordinates to informal communication from people throughout the organization about how things are going. In the effective high-involvement organization, senior levels should feel they are in touch with what is going on throughout the company—particularly with respect to how decisions are made and the overall operation of the organization.

The second sign concerns understanding of the business. Executives should be able to ask people throughout the organization how the business is performing and get informed answers. Further, they should notice a high level of ownership of business results—that is, employees should feel responsible for how their business unit is operating and, indeed, how the total organization is operating. One of the most striking aspects of the successful high-involvement organization is the degree to which people at all levels can talk about the condition of the business, its cost, its performance, and its customers.

Responsibility for the business leads to the third element. In a high-involvement organization, people recognize and reward each other for effective performance. Management alone should not have to be responsible for acknowledging good performance. Peers should recognize peers and subordinates should recognize bosses for good performance. Effective high-involvement organizations rely on this mutual recognition as an important method of control. Indeed, to a substantial degree this means of control is critical in replacing the traditional controls one finds in top-down organizations. It comes about only when people are committed to the effectiveness of the organization and feel a common responsibility for its operation.

Finally, senior managers should be able to observe that employees have a strong and accurate sense of the right thing to do in a particular situation—and, of course, the willingness to do it. They should not, for example, talk about what their job description calls for or "what they are responsible for." In effective high-involvement organizations, people worry about what needs to be done to make the organization effective. Not only do they need to think about what to do, of course, they need to make good decisions about the right course of action. Again, senior management needs to monitor this aspect of the organization's culture to be sure it is performing its role as a senior management group.

Overall, the idea is that if senior management performs its role effectively the effects should be observable throughout the organization. Employees at all levels should take responsibility for the company's effectiveness and make a strong commitment to its long-term performance. In the absence of effective senior management, this commitment is hard, if not impossible, to inspire. Thus, in a very direct sense, the effectiveness of senior management is ultimately visible in the effectiveness of the organization and can prove to be a decided competitive advantage.

References

Argyris, C., and Schön, D. *Organizational Learning: A Theory of Action Perspective*. Reading, Mass.: Addison-Wesley, 1978.

Bennis, W., and Nanus, B. *Leaders: The Strategies for Taking Charge*. New York: Harper & Row, 1985.

Burns, J. M. *Leadership*. New York: Harper & Row, 1978.

Carlzon, J. *Moments of Truth: New Strategies for Today's Customer Driven Economy*. Cambridge, Mass.: Ballinger, 1987.

DePree, M. *Leadership Is an Art*. East Lansing: Michigan State University Press, 1987.

Galbraith, J. R. *Organization Design*. Reading, Mass.: Addison-Wesley, 1977.

Johnston, R., and Lawrence, P. R. "Beyond Vertical Integration — The Rise of the Value-Adding Partnership." *Harvard Business Review*, 1988, (4), 94–101.

Lawler, E. E., III. *Pay and Organization Development*. Reading, Mass.: Addison-Wesley, 1981.

Lawler, E. E., III. *High-Involvement Management: Participative Strategies for Improving Organizational Performance*. San Francisco: Jossey-Bass, 1986.

Nadler, D. "Leadership and Organizational Change." In A. M.

Mohrman, Jr., and others, *Large-Scale Organizational Change*. San Francisco: Jossey-Bass, 1989.

Peters, T. J. "Symbols, Patterns and Settings: An Optimistic Case for Getting Things Done." *Organizational Dynamics*, Autumn 1978, pp. 2-23.

Peters, T. J. *Thriving on Chaos*. New York: Knopf, 1987.

Peters, T. J., and Waterman, R. H., Jr. *In Search of Excellence: Lessons from America's Best-Run Companies*. New York: Harper & Row, 1982.

Rosen, C., Klien, K., and Young, K. *Employee Ownership in America*. Lexington, Mass.: Heath, 1986.

Tichy, N. M., and Devanna, M. A. *The Transformational Leader*. New York: Wiley, 1986.

Vroom, V. H., and Yetton, P. W. *Leadership and Decision-Making*. Pittsburgh, Pa.: University of Pittsburgh Press, 1973.

Walton, R. E., and Schlesinger, L. A. "Do Supervisors Thrive in Participative Work Systems?" *Organizational Dynamics*, 1979, *8* (3), 25-38.

9

COMBINING FOLLOWERSHIP AND LEADERSHIP INTO PARTNERSHIP

ROBERT E. KELLEY

ompetitiveness and *leadership* were two of the busiest business buzzwords of the 1980s. Each still frequently headlines the covers of major U.S. business publications and is invoked in speech after speech. Ironically, they seldom appear together. These two topics are treated as distinct subjects with little relation to each other. Leadership has its own voluminous body of literature (Bennis and Nanus, 1985; Burns, 1978), as does competitiveness (Cohen, Teece, Tyson, and Zysman, 1985; Scott and Lodge, 1985; Porter, 1985). The link between these two topics is the concept of followership. This chapter articulates the concept of followership, examines how followers and leaders can form effective partnerships, and delineates how these partnerships can lead to greater competitiveness.

Followership

Followership and leadership are roles, not people. People assume the followership or leadership role as one of the many roles they play in our society. Most of us play simultaneous leader and follower roles. Since few of us are always in one role

Note: This chapter is adapted from the author's book-in-progress *From Followership and Leadership to Partnership.* Some of the ideas have appeared in his article "In Praise of Followers" (*Harvard Business Review*, 1988) and his previous book *The Gold-Collar Worker: Harnessing the Brainpower of the New Workforce* (Addison-Wesley, 1985).

or the other, we need to learn to play both. In this chapter, *leader* and *follower* refer to roles, not people.

Organizational success is as much the result of effective followership—those forgotten supporting players who seldom get notice for their contributions—as it is effective leadership. In fact, effective followers can achieve an organization's goals despite an ineffective leader. Yet all the attention is given to leadership and to the romantic notion that leaders are the cause of all organizational success. Thousands of studies have analyzed leadership from every possible perspective. All this research has found, however, only one characteristic that effective leaders share in common: the ability to attract followers. Meanwhile, few research studies have examined followers (Kelley, 1988c; Lippitt, 1982).

The reality is that most of us will more often be followers than leaders. Even when we have subordinates, we will still have bosses above us. For every committee chair we hold, we will sit as a "follower" member on several other committees. In our society, however, we do not teach the skills and attitudes that most of us will need most of the time. Have you ever heard of a course that teaches, active, intelligent, and ethical followership? Before I began teaching such a course three years ago, a survey of business schools and corporate training programs uncovered none. All had leadership courses.

Since followership dominates our lives and since followers with different motivations can perform equally well, my research examined the behavior that leads to effective and less effective following (Kelley, 1988c). How, for example, do executives distinguish between the performance of the best, average, and worst followers? How do people describe when they performed well as a follower and when they did not? Two underlying behavioral dimensions emerged from my analysis. As illustrated in Figure 9.1, one dimension separates followers according to whether they exercise independent and critical thinking vis-à-vis the leader versus dependent and uncritical thinking. The other dimension characterizes followers according to how passive or active they are in carrying out the followership role.

Figure 9.1. Organizational View of Followers
Committed to the Organization.

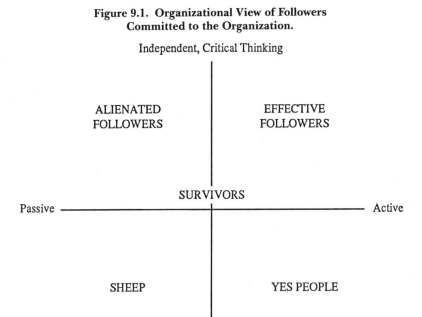

Independent, Critical Thinking

ALIENATED   EFFECTIVE
FOLLOWERS   FOLLOWERS

SURVIVORS

Passive ———————————————————————— Active

SHEEP   YES PEOPLE

Dependent, Uncritical Thinking

From these two dimensions, five different followership patterns emerge.

The *effective followers* in the top right-hand quadrant are independent, critical thinkers who actively carry out their follower role. Because they are self-starters, independent problem solvers, and risk takers, they are consistently rated the best by others. Their specific behavior is described more fully later.

Yes people depend on the leader and do not exercise critical thinking. They conform and passively go along with whatever the leader wants. The *survivors* hover near the center of the figure trying to figure out which direction the wind is blowing. Their motto, "better safe than sorry," underscores the political game playing they use to survive any leader and changes in leadership. These two types are perceived as typical in most organizations but are rated considerably less effective than the best followers.

The small minority of *alienated followers* and *sheep* represent the worst. The former think for themselves but are passive when carrying out the follower role. Viewed as capable but antagonistic, they frequently hold back their effort even though they are committed to the organization. They are a constant thorn in the leader's side. The sheep are dependent, passive followers who require direction and motivation from the leader.

Effective following does not happen automatically. It involves a set of skills that enable people to serve what they follow and the organization in which they follow. From my research, distinctions between effective and less effective followers become apparent. When I contrasted the effective followers in Figure 9.1 with the other types, a consistent pattern of effective followership emerged. Rather than stating these findings as principles of effective following, they are better viewed as propositions:

- Effective followers self-manage.
- Effective followers are committed.
- Effective followers build competence.
- Effective followers focus their contributions.
- Effective followers establish credibility.
- Effective followers exercise a courageous conscience.

Self-Management

Effective following is grounded in the central notion of self-management—the ability to think for oneself and to take appropriate action. Effective followers manage themselves, their job activities, and their relationship with the leader. They also exert great control and independence over their actions, whereas ineffective followers require close supervision. They pinpoint critical issues and suggest the steps to resolve them, especially if other departments are involved. This self-management frees the leader to attend to important activities best handled at the leader's administrative level.

Effective followers proactively manage their relationships with the leader. They find out what the leader is trying to accomplish and what the leader's needs are. They understand that their leader is generally a follower to someone else and that the someone else may also have a boss. Less effective followers have a more limited worldview that considers their own immediate needs but not the pressures facing their leader.

Effective followers pay attention to the chemistry between them and the leader. Since effective followers see themselves as social equals to the leader, they carry on mature adult-to-adult interactions. Thus they can encourage and reward the leader for good work, just as the leader encourages them. Ineffective followers, by contrast, accept the vertical hierarchy. Because they perceive themselves as subservient, they vacillate between feeling powerless and manipulating the leader to gain a sense of power. They are prone to say "I knew it was a bad idea, but I'd get fired if I stuck my neck out" or "things will never change around here, so why bother making waves?" Their assumptions become a self-fulfilling prophecy that reinforces their sense of powerlessness.

Not all leaders like having self-managing followers. It makes some of them nervous. Effective followers protect themselves from such bosses by self-managing their careers. They obtain the skills and experience necessary to stay attractive to other leaders and organizations. Being desirable in the marketplace allows effective followers to choose freely to stay in their current situation. As an additional safeguard, some followers develop multiple sources of income to reduce their economic dependence on the leader. These self-managing strategies eliminate the traditional weapons that threatened bosses use to keep followers in line.

Self-managed followers give their organizations a significant cost advantage. Self-managing eliminates the capital spent on managers and supervisory control systems designed to motivate and keep tabs on followers. These controls cost money and alienate the followers, lowering their morale and productivity.

For these reasons, one large midwestern bank has redesigned its personnel selection system to attract self-managed workers. The bank expects to trim its management ranks and administrative costs while improving productivity and performance. Given fierce banking competition, they know that self-managing can give them a considerable advantage.

Commitment

Effective followers have a purposeful sense of commitment regarding their lives and work. They care about something—the leader, the cause, the product, their co-workers. They know what they care about, and they actively support it. Caring is infrequently fostered in business. In attempting to rationalize the workplace, companies root out followers' emotional energy. If caring is allowed, it is directed solely at the bottom line.

Some leaders are surprised to learn that followers care about something other than the leader. Although effective followers still acknowledge the leader's role and their horizontal relationship to each other, this recognition should not be confused with loyalty. Many top-rate followers simply view the leader as a co-adventurer on a worthwhile cause. Leaders are facilitators to achieve mutually desired goals. If the facilitation works, the leader is followed; if not, the follower continues the pursuit without that leader or seeks another leader. On the other hand, when less effective followers do not care about the leader, they become adversarial. These followers act as if their cause is the most important agenda for both them and the leader. A leader invites disappointment by assuming that followers have a single-minded and exclusive commitment to the leader. By perceiving followers in the context of what they care about, it is easier to determine their loyalties.

A noteworthy by-product of caring is that it is contagious. Effective followers have their heart in their work. People, for the most part, like being around others who are energized and committed. Caring followers help keep morale up and negativism down. They get others involved and keep projects on track. These followers have a significant effect on the leader and co-workers.

Competence

Effective followers build and demonstrate competence. They actively become great at something, mastering skills that are useful and advance what they care about. This distinctive competence sets them apart from other co-workers and makes them more valuable.

Since dedicated incompetence is still incompetence, effective followers work hard at having something positive to offer. They generally hold higher performance standards than those required by the work environment. Also, they are good at judging their strengths and weaknesses. Since they know their competence better than anyone else, they participate in decisions about how it is used. When asked to perform at something they are unqualified to do, they inform the boss that they are not right for the job. This saves the boss and the organization time, lost energy, and poor performance. This does not mean that they adhere rigidly to a narrow job description, are unwilling to take on extra work, or are afraid of failure. Like athletes stretching their abilities, they do not mind failing if they know they can succeed. They simply shy away from activities that set them up for failure.

Effective followers keep up in their areas of competence. They approach life with a sense of learning, continually discovering how to improve their talents and use their gifts. Continuing education is a staple in their professional development. Investing in themselves makes them more valuable. Less effective followers expect others to develop them. If the leader does not send them to a seminar, they do not go. They let their competencies depreciate and then act surprised when they are no longer valued.

Contributions

If they are caring and competent, effective followers are well equipped to contribute actively. By consciously choosing environments whose requirements of success match their talents, they work to make success happen. At their best, they become active players in the destiny of the enterprise.

Effective followers do many extras on their jobs, but first they do a superb job on their core responsibilities. Activities outside their job description are pursued only after they have done what they are paid for. They continuously focus their contributions on activities critical to the leader or what they care about. Since conservation of energy is an important characteristic of effective followers, they pick additional activities carefully. Often they search for overlooked problems—whatever may have fallen between the cracks of assigned responsibilities.

Effective followers contribute as team players. They do not usurp the leader's role, for they know that little gets done when several people vie for the leadership position. They get along well with co-workers and try to help the group win. Less effective followers contribute for their own advancement; co-workers are seen as competitors rather than colleagues.

In our rapidly changing world, effective followers are flexible and expansive. Although they understand the constraints of organizations and leaders, they are less bound by the traditional way of doing things. Since they often can anticipate change, it does not throw them off balance. Instead, by assessing what the impacts of the change will be, they figure out ways to use the change to the organization's advantage. Ineffective followers are bound by tradition and procedures. Change is threatening and therefore resisted.

Credibility

An essential element of contribution is building credibility. We all know competent people whose contributions are not fully valued because they are not viewed as credible. This is primarily because they are not regarded as independent, critical thinkers whose knowledge and judgment can be trusted. Effective followers know how to establish credibility with their peers and leaders.

Effective followers determine early and accurately the

criteria for success in the environment, distinguishing between the apparent criteria and those that really count. They demonstrate their competence through focused contributions that build a quick record of success in tasks that are important to the leader and the group. Rather than the big bang achievement that takes a long time to pull off, they seize smaller victories that accumulate into a "can do" aura.

Honesty is a critical element of credibility. Effective followers are honest about communicating their accomplishments. When informing another, they tell the whole story, not just the part that makes them look good. They give credit where it is due and own up to their part in any mistakes. Whereas less effective followers claim more than they are entitled to, effective followers take credit only for their actual accomplishments. By framing their successes and failures in positive ways, they further their credibility. Those who stretch the truth undermine theirs. Edward R. Murrow summed it up in the following way: "To be persuasive, we must be believable; to be believable, we must be credible; to be credible, we must be truthful" (Peter, 1977, p. 474). Credibility grows day by day through consistent demonstration of trustworthiness.

Conscience

Effective followers are courageous. They independently form their own views and ethical standards, stand up for what they believe in, and exercise an active conscience. Unlike less effective followers, who might carry out the leader's orders regardless of legality or morality, effective followers maintain their own standards. One follower reported that he asks two questions when considering the ethics of his actions. First, can he face himself in the mirror? Second, can he face his spouse, family, and friends if his actions are held up to the hard light of public scrutiny?

Effective followers can conduct themselves in this manner because they have self-managed their careers. They know they can create other options if necessary. Elliot Richardson could say no to Richard Nixon during the Watergate coverup because he was not dependent on Nixon for his income or job. Ineffective followers feel trapped. They have too much at stake to stand up for what they believe in.

Effective followers keep the leader and their colleagues honest. Rather than collude in a leader's self-delusion, they take a stand and hold firm on their version of reality. Rather than allow authoritarianism or groupthink to permeate the group, they push for individual participation and respect. An effective follower's credibility allows him or her to question a bad or unethical decision.

When effective followers find themselves ethically disagreeing with their co-workers or the leader, they search their consciences to pinpoint the source of the disagreement. They ask themselves if the issue would cause them to resign. They seek advice on the situation from people they respect. Before taking formal action, they try to resolve the situation informally. If possible, they work from within, following the accepted norms and protocol for dissenters. If the circumstances require going outside the system, they assess the risks and benefits of their actions. They do not go off half-cocked, use their ethics as a self-righteous sledgehammer, or turn personal disagreements into ethical sensationalism. This requires courage not to be found in ineffective followers.

Leadership

Just as the followership role has skill requirements, so does the leadership role. Contrary to popular belief, leadership is not one skill; it can be divided into three sets of skills: meta-leadership, macroleadership, and microleadership (Kelley, 1985). These three skill sets correspond to the three major contexts facing an organization. (See Table 9.1.) The external environment—social, economic, political, and technological forces—is the domain of the meta-leader. The industrial environment, which includes competitors, customers, and suppliers, is the domain of the macroleader. The organizational environment of employees, systems, and productivity tools is the domain of the microleader. These three sets of skills are seldom embodied in

Table 9.1. Relationship Between Leadership Skills
and Areas of Organizational Concern.

	Leadership Skills		
Areas of Concern	Meta	Macro	Micro
External			
Global/political	Foresight		
Sociocultural	and		
Technological	insight		
Economic			
Industrial			
Competitors		Vision	
Customers		and	
Technology		strategy	
Resources/distribution			
Organizational			
Management practices			Trust
Staff			and
Technology			tools/
Structure			systems

one person. Most people who play leadership roles are gifted in only one area. My research has yet to find someone capable in all three. Leaders get in trouble when they surround themselves with likeminded people — associates who duplicate their skills — rather than rounding out the team with the other two skill areas.

Meta-Leadership

At the global level, there are meta-leaders who are sensitive to the outside world. They have foresight regarding societal trends and insight into the dominant social mood of the times. These are big movements — the G. I. Bill, the flight to the suburbs, television, jet travel.

Because the public prefers to believe that true leaders can change the course of history by their pure force of character and will, meta-leadership is sometimes confused with the myth of charisma. Yet historical evidence demonstrates that well-known twentieth-century leaders such as Mao, Lenin, Gandhi, and Martin Luther King did not truly change the course of history—what they did was to understand how society was changing and then put themselves in the forefront of that change. Thus great leaders are able to interpret for others diverse and fragmentary inputs regarding current events. They compare these snapshots with projections made in the past and use them as the basis for projections into the future. Comprehending the larger context, they know how to redefine it when circumstances begin to shift. In this way, they have an instinct for the unknowable and are able to foresee the unforeseeable. They possess skills that qualify them to show their followers the way.

After World War II, for example, the leaders of Sears, Roebuck and Montgomery Ward demonstrated considerably different meta-leadership skills. Ward at that time was the industry leader, but its top managers made several incorrect assumptions about the future. They believed that a deep recession would follow the war, that urban centers would continue to be the principal shopping areas, and that consumers would be cautious buyers as a result of their experience during the Great Depression. Thus they decided to build only a few new stores and to locate them only in downtown areas. Sears, on the other hand, realized that cars and the sprawling development of housing would lead to the growth of suburbia and shopping centers. They also believed that consumer demand, pent up by World War II, would explode.

Sears used the meta-leadership findings to develop their macro-level vision and strategy. They adopted an ambitious expansion plan by placing stores throughout suburban shopping centers. They complemented this move with aggressive hiring and compensation systems to ensure the right staff, which could capitalize on the quick growth facing the company. Their meta-leadership skills paid off handsomely as they became the dominant retailer. Montgomery Ward, on the other hand, became an expendable, stepchild division of Mobil Oil Company.

Meta-level leadership dissolves if its proponents lose the advantage of foresight and insight. The beginning of the end is signaled by their failure to foresee what reasonably could have been foreseen and their failure to act on that knowledge while freedom to act exists. Once they merely react to immediate events, leaders fail.

The oil industry provides a startling example of what happens when meta-leadership skills are lacking. During the oil crises, the industry failed to appreciate the social character of the United States. Instead of responding in helpful ways during the shortages, they appeared as ruthless robber barons capitalizing on society's misfortune. The backlash resulted in the creation of the windfall-profits tax, a tarnished public image that has yet to recover, and a wave of energy conservation that Americans hope will end the energy monopoly of OPEC and the oil companies. In addition, the oil industry (and almost everyone else) failed to forecast oil supplies accurately. They predicted a shortage, but in fact a glut occurred in the 1980s. These meta-leadership mistakes cost the United States an estimated $500 billion. Because bad management decisions were made on the basis of incorrect forecasts, Americans paid excessive energy prices; high costs for new plants that were built to be more energy-efficient but proved to be unnecessary; and increased costs for cars, food, and other energy-sensitive consumer products.

Macroleadership

The major macro-level leadership skills—vision and strategy— are employed to transform meta-level forecasts into clear, cohesive images of the opportunities and dangers that lie ahead. By establishing a common purpose, a shared sense of identity, and a sense of excitement about the future, effective macroleaders can mobilize their followers to march together into that future.

A good vision incorporates several components. It offers idealistic followers a view of what the world is or can be. It is compatible with dominant social and environmental trends, the prevailing social character, and the spirit of the changing times. It delineates exactly how followers can fit into, contribute to, and benefit from the world of the future. It is both concrete and holistic, appealing to both the linear left side of the brain and the insightful right side. It identifies clearly the rules, structure, and values necessary for survival and success in the new world. Finally, it replaces naive cause-and-effect theories with an original interpretation of events and their consequences that followers accept as both viable and valid. When Alfred Sloan led General Motors, for example, he dreamed that one day every American adult would own a car tailored to his or her tastes and needs; different social groups could select different models in different colors and with different features. The founders of Apple Computer envisioned every child in the United States having access to an Apple computer at home or at school. As the research efforts of pharmaceutical companies demonstrate, an enlightened corporate vision can encompass both doing good and making money.

Visions do not necessarily concern the creation of something new; instead, they can reveal what already exists or offer a more positive view of what is already in place. It is demoralizing to followers if the organization or the world itself is perpetually seen as deficient when compared to the strategic ideal. Eventually they come to consider themselves on a treadmill of endless striving for an impossible goal of perfection. For this reason, a leader's foresight is crucial not only for articulating the goal but also for identifying all the steps required to reach that goal.

Sometimes insight is as important as foresight. Michelangelo maintained that he never created new works of sculpture; he merely discovered the statue already contained within a block of marble. Lenin often observed that he did not create the Russian Revolution; he saw that the revolution was in progress, simplified this concept so the common people could grasp it, articulated it in a way that lent them a feeling of power, and then installed himself as the leader of the new revolutionary wave.

Whether a vision is a matter of creation or discovery, it inspires an entire organization and infuses it with a welcome sense of direction. Many experts believe that followers within an organization that clings tenaciously to its vision are more contented and more productive and that the organization itself meets with greater success. The Apollo Moon Project is an excellent example. Despite overwhelming obstacles to their objective of a manned lunar landing by 1969, group members held their vision firmly in mind. This unifying force engendered enormous creativity and resulted in an astounding array of technical and logistical breakthroughs that otherwise might never have occurred.

The success of a particular strategy should not be gauged by whether or not each step is completed or whether budgets are met. A strategy is successful only if the organization has made progress relative to its guiding vision. Far too often, managers become obsessed with budgets and performance plans. If they overemphasize maximization of the parts instead of optimization of the whole, the result will be disappointing: All the parts may perform, but the whole will not progress. Organizations are like engines: Each part can be tuned to run at maximum efficiency; yet a maximized carburetor puts such a strain on the other components that overall performance is reduced. To attain optimum performance from an engine, the parts must run at a submaximized level but be carefully attuned to one another.

Microleadership

Microleadership skills assist in the realization of an organization's vision as well as its strategy by providing the requisite trust and tools. A microleader's primary task is to foster group cooperation in identifying and solving problems. For this to occur, trust is crucial. A leader's attitudes greatly affect how well he or she and others in the organization work together. Both the leader and the follower compress their attitudes and impressions into one powerful belief: How much can each trust the other person? The leader's access to existing or newly created knowledge in the organization, for example, largely depends on how much others trust him or her. Ultimately, how much leaders and followers trust or mistrust each other significantly shapes decisions. When they trust each other, the quality of decisions improves, their implementation is facilitated, and commitment is effortless. When they mistrust, quality and implementation suffer. Leaders and followers sense they must trust some people more than others, but they underestimate the corrosive effects of that mistrust. To improve their decision process, both leaders and followers must understand the meaning and pervasive effects of trust.

The divisive effects of mistrust are frequently underestimated. Mistrust provokes rejection and defensiveness. People tend to act on their suspicions and apprehensions rather than discussing them, thereby rendering them more difficult to track and control. Trust, in contrast, stimulates originality and intellectual development and facilitates emotional stability and freedom of expression. Both trust and mistrust are expressed through inference, control, and the exchange of information. Leaders, as well as followers, who do not trust others will conceal or distort relevant information, causing colleagues to act on the basis of a false portrayal of reality. Because they suspect the motivations of others, they reject opposing views, deflect suggestions, and limit the influence of other people. Those who mistrust also minimize their dependence on others and consequently undermine the cooperation necessary to achieve mutual goals. Even worse, their defensive responses make their mistrustfulness contagious.

Because participants are not always perfect, an important element of microleadership is teaching group members to handle failures and mistakes. Traditional management has a low tolerance for error—either a worker who cannot achieve a goal is replaced by someone who can or it is assumed that the task is impossible. Microleadership, in contrast, avoids negative self-fulfilling prophecies. It helps individuals and groups to keep the vision on track during times of despair. We would have neither genetic engineering nor fifth-generation computers today if researchers had not persevered in the face of numerous naysayers.

At the same time that microleadership sustains a group's vision, it teaches group members to question the rules, assumptions, and norms that contributed to its creation. A vision can become static and lose its force unless it is continually updated in accordance with changes in the external environment, changes in underlying group norms, and changes in the relationship between the leader and his or her followers. It is as essential to reject an outmoded vision as it is to adhere to one that remains valid. Passengers—or group members—on the *Titanic* have a responsibility to jump ship rather than convincing themselves that they are only stopping to stock up on ice. They also are responsible for bringing lurking icebergs to the attention of their leader. If microleadership tools had been widespread throughout General Motors, group members might have abandoned the vision of large-car production earlier in order to meet changing consumer markets. Without microleadership, leaders lose a major source of wisdom and support: feedback from their followers.

Microleaders must also provide the tools and design the systems that increase the productively of followers. This includes organizational structures, technology, communications, corporate cultures, incentives, and the other necessities that lead to success. These require day-to-day linking of societal trends with the company's vision and the company's vision with the needs and preferences of the followers. Microleadership, then, teaches everyone how to participate as equals in decision-making settings, provides them with the information they need to act, lets them share in formulating the vision, and gives them skills with which to measure progress against the vision rather than against budgets or plans. These skills do not simply come from humanistic ideals. Instead, they are essential for the success of the joint undertaking, since success depends on the active participation of the followers.

Follower–Leader Partnerships for Competitive Advantage

Given the skills required for effective followership and leadership, we need to focus on the interactions between them and how they influence competitive advantage (Figure 9.2). The bottom right quadrant of Figure 9.2 captures our societal bias of viewing the leader as effective and the followers as ineffective. This bias is reflected in writings about the "transformational" leader who turns followers from nothing into something, from

Figure 9.2. Follower–Leader Interactions.

	Ineffective Leaders	Effective Leaders
Effective Followers	Transform Leader or Subvert Leader	Winning Situations
Ineffective Followers	Losing Situations	Transform Follower or Reject Follower

something worse into something better (Burns, 1978; Tichy and
Devanna, 1986). Whether the myth conjures up Gandhi mobilizing the masses or General Patton disciplining out-of-shape recruits into fighting soldiers, leaders are perceived as struggling
to bring mightiness out of mediocrity. They motivate, develop,
cajole, discipline, and overcome resistance from bloblike followers to achieve superordinate goals. In this view, leaders are
the molders and followers are the clay.

After researching followers and leaders, I have discovered
that the upper left quadrant occurs where the followers play a
powerful role in making or breaking the leader. We may ignore
the way followers can contribute to the leader's development, but
they often are instrumental in "transforming" ordinary people
into leaders. Ronald Reagan's followers, including his wife,
played critical roles in transforming him from an actor into

president of the United States. Some political analysts believe that the 1988 presidential election was won and lost, not on the basis of leadership, but on the basis of followership (Perry and Langley, 1988). Bush's followers served him well; Dukakis's followers served him badly. Leaders supported by their followers often become more than they were. If they cannot be transformed, then the followers subvert them, either by withdrawing support or by active sabotage.

In reality, most followers are reasonable and responsible adults who succeed in their lives without a strong leader. They are capable of using their talents to promote a healthy and stable environment for everyone. Many followers believe they offer as much value to the organization as the leader, especially in project or task force situations. In their roles, they simply do equally important but different activities. Leaders are no longer viewed as superior people; they only happen to be higher on the administrative ladder. In the top right quadrant, the leader is more an overseer of change and progress than a hero. The followers are adult participants, not children needing guidance.

To create the competitive advantage resulting from effective follower/effective leader interactions, we must replace the traditional "topdog/underdog" model with a new concept: partnership. With strong, successful followers and leaders complementing each other, this arrangement is not only possible but desirable. Partnership implies mutual sharing and responsibility for risks, success, rewards, and power. In true partnerships, competent people join together to achieve what they could not achieve alone. Drawing from its legal roots, partnership requires the partners to be individually and collectively accountable for the actions and liabilities of the firm. Unless explicitly negotiated otherwise, partners are viewed as equals. As equals, they decide how to work together, to share power, and to reward individual and joint contributions so that the partnership succeeds.

Since leadership and followership are roles, not people, these roles transfer from partner to partner based on expertise, interest, availability, and the nature of the task. A key skill of all partners is moving back and forth between followership and leadership with ease and high performance. Although individual partners may do different activities at different times, they value all contributions as important to getting the job done right. Partners respect each other as equal adult participants, synergize success, and protect each other from failure.

Effective follower–leader partnerships resonate with the needs of the United States at this turning point in our economic and social development. The traditional models have become a competitive liability in the fast-changing international marketplace. America's economic vulnerability can no longer afford narcissistic leaders who alienate their followers nor floundering followers who drag down productivity and quality. The new partnership is required if we are to regain our advantage. This partnership needs to extend beyond followers and leaders to include labor–management, supplier–customer, and government–industry partnerships.

The key to follower–leader partnerships is making the previously designated leadership skills a joint responsibility and utilizing followers in the process. We make a strategic mistake in neglecting followers as potential contributors. At best it is inefficient use of a huge asset. For example, one Midwest firm looking for ideas got only six from the executive team. When they finally asked the workers, fifty-three were submitted. If this company had never reached out to its followers, it would have unnecessarily limited its capacity to innovate. By taking this first step toward follower–leader partnerships, it increased its competitive capability. Japanese companies such as NEC and Korean companies like Samsung have demonstrated that the combined contributions resulting from follower–leader partnerships can lead to significant competitive advantage.

Follower–leader partnerships can occur at the meta level, macro level, and micro level. At the meta level, followers along with leaders can be on the lookout for future trends. At SRI International, for example, every employee is encouraged to submit to a committee any observation, hunch, article, or signal of a future shift. The committee sifts through these monthly and synthesizes them into themes. Each month's themes are compared to the cumulative themes from previous months to spot any recurring ones. Recurring themes are validated against a cross section of the organization. In this way, the entire organization participates in the meta-level activities of foresight and insight.

At the macro level, a vision forged by followers and leaders increases its probability of success. A CEO of a furniture company conducted twenty-six successive vision-building workshops for all employees on weekends. The major purpose of each workshop was to build a cumulative vision for the company using the output of the previous session. At the end of the twenty-six weeks, a collective vision was established. Over the next six years, revenues soared from $6 million to over $70 million. Likewise, when leaders develop a strategy without the help of followers, they are asking for trouble. A major money-center bank asked outside consultants to devise a new strategic plan. When top management unveiled it to the bank's loan officers, they gave it a thumbs down. These loan officers spend their entire careers analyzing strategic plans of companies seeking financing. They unanimously agreed that if their own bank asked for a loan on the basis of the new strategy, they would turn down the request. Rather than use this reaction to modify the strategy, top management shrugged off the criticism as due to the "Not Invented Here" syndrome and implemented the strategy. Consequently, many of the bank's top performers left rather than go down with what they called a sinking ship. The bank's high-risk strategy of energy and Third World loans almost drove it to insolvency.

At the micro level, follower–leader partnerships dovetail with corporate America's restructuring. In the past five years, firms from Wall Street to Silicon Valley have eliminated over 1.2 million "leadership" positions. After cutting layer upon layer of management, flatter and leaner organizations emerged as the norm. With fewer leaders, companies now depend on followers to operate successfully on their own. High numbers of effective followers reduce the need for microleadership. Self-directed work teams and leaderless work groups have filled in the leadership vacuum, yielding successes unheard of under the old model.

Figure 9.3. Customer–Follower–Leader Partnership.

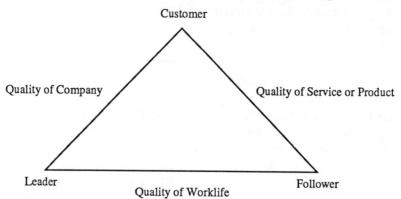

The competitive power of partnership can also be extended to include the customer (Figure 9.3). Follower–leader partnerships often involve serving a customer. For elected leaders, citizens are the customer; in business, consumers are the customer. The resultant customer–follower–leader triangle helps tie together three major competitive threads: quality of service or product, quality of worklife, and quality of company. Since followers generally have the greatest amount of direct and indirect contact with the customer, their work usually determines the quality of the service or product received by the customer. If the customer–follower link of this partnership is strong, then the resultant quality of service or product provides both a source of competitive advantage and the profits of repeat purchases. Likewise, leaders symbolize the kind of organization the customer is encountering. Through their values and public projections, they influence the company's image and reputation as being customer-driven and customer-responsive. If the customer–leader link is strong, then the quality of the company is improved in the public's eye, yielding a competitive advantage.

The follower–leader link shapes the quality of worklife, as well. When this link is strong, the other two links are strengthened. Schneider (1980) has demonstrated that high employee satisfaction leads to high customer satisfaction. When followers are served poorly by their leaders, they serve the customer poorly (Kelley, 1987). Quality of worklife can lead to significant competitive advantage when it is connected to the other two links.

When organizations manage from a customer–follower–leader perspective, an added competitive advantage occurs: The customer becomes an active partner in the destiny of the enterprise. Rather than passively accepting, they begin making contributions to product design, delivery systems, and pricing strategies. At a minimum, they become loyal customers. At their best, they become volunteer marketing representatives, increasing the organization's market share via word-of-mouth advertising. The distinctions between customer and follower and leader may even begin to blur since all partners are concerned with ensuring that the partnership succeeds.

Cultivating Competitive Partnerships

Organizations can foster follower–leader partnerships in several ways. First, they must redefine followership and leadership as a partnership. If motivating followers is the leader's defined responsibility, he or she is likely to treat followers as if they need motivation. If transformation is the leader's job, then the follower's job is to be the clay. If followers by chance do not need transformation, the leader looks ineffective. Our definition of the roles clearly dictates the relationship's outcome.

Second, during employee orientation each individual can be instructed in the importance of follower–leader partnerships. Tell them what it takes to succeed in each role and explain that they will be expected to move back and forth between them. Expected competencies and contribution levels should be communicated so that employees can self-manage their performance levels in both roles. Illustrations of effective versus ineffective following and leading provide benchmark comparisons. Then make it clear that everyone, regardless of the role played, is responsible for the organization's overall success. It is not enough to do one's job and stop. After all, this is a partnership. Individual success in a failing firm does not increase competitiveness.

Third, organizations can train their people in the skills necessary to make the partnership work. Most organizations focus on leadership training but assume that everyone knows how to follow. If followers and leaders learn the skills to work *with* each other as partners, rather than followers being worked *on* by the leader, organizations can alleviate the need for much current leadership training. A program of partnership training can correct this state of affairs by focusing on certain key topics:

- Improving independent, critical thinking
- Enhancing self-management and motivation
- Disagreeing with others agreeably
- Making ethical choices and avoiding groupthink
- Acting responsibly toward the organization, the leader, co-workers, and oneself
- Aligning personal and organizational goals and commitments
- Understanding similarities and differences between followership and leadership roles
- Moving between the two roles with ease

Fourth, performance evaluations must focus not only on leadership skills but also followership and partnership skills, including the ability to shift easily from one role to the other. Evaluations can come from peers, subordinates, and oneself, as well as from supervisors. Anyone who comes into regular contact with the person being evaluated is asked to complete brief, periodic questionnaires.

Finally, companies can use rewards to underscore the importance of follower–leader partnerships. If partnership activities do not receive recognition and compensation, they do not surface nor do they remain. Organizations that encourage "yes people" and "survivors" through the reward system will not benefit from the powerful performance of effective followers. Organizations that spend all their time searching for and rewarding leaders, while simultaneously disparaging followers, will seldom find people willing to play both roles. To gain the benefits of partnership, the entire reward structure must send

the message that effective followership, leadership, and partnership skills are important to the organization.

Conclusion

The time has come to redefine the follower–leader relationship
in the context of our increasingly competitive world. The power
plays of the topdog/underdog system are dysfunctional. Rather
than viewing the relationship as a zero-sum game, we need to
view it as a partnership. To compete effectively, all parties must
join together and play either role when necessary. Partnerships
work best when all parties are strong in their own right, respect
each other's contributions, and share equal responsibility for
success and failure. The United States was founded and had
prospered as a society under these principles. It is time that our
corporations began to use them for competitive advantage.

References

Bennis, W., and Nanus, B. *Leaders: The Strategies for Taking Charge.*
    New York: Harper & Row, 1985.
Burns, J. M. *Leadership.* New York: Harper & Row, 1978.
Cohen, S. S., Teece, D., Tyson, L. D., and Zysman, J. *Global
    Competition: The New Reality.* The Report of the President's
    Commission on Industrial Competitiveness. Washington,
    D.C.: U.S. Government Printing Office, 1985.
Kelley, R. E. *The Gold-Collar Worker: Harnessing the Brainpower of the
    New Workforce.* Reading, Mass.: Addison-Wesley, 1985.
Kelley, R. E. "Poorly Served Employees Serve Customers Just as
    Poorly." *Wall Street Journal,* Oct. 12, 1987, p. 18.
Kelley, R. E. "A Society Can Succeed If It Has Effective Followers."
    Chicago Tribune, Oct. 26, 1988a, p. 23.
Kelley, R. E. "From Followership and Leadership to Partnership."
    Unpublished manuscript, 1988b.
Kelley, R. E. "In Praise of Followers." *Harvard Business Review,*
    1988c, *66* (6), 142–148.
Lippitt, R. "The Changing Leader-Follower Relationships of the

1980s." *Journal of Applied Behavioral Science*, 1982, *18* (3), 395–403.

Meindl, J. R., Ehrlich, S. B., and Dukerich, J. M. "The Romance of Leadership." *Administrative Science Quarterly*, 1985, *30* (1), 78–102.

Perry, J. M., and Langley, M. "Bush Thrives on One-a-Day TV Message Capsules Prescribed by His Skilled Poli-Tech Image Makers." *Wall Street Journal*, Oct. 27, 1988, p. A16.

Peter, L. J. *Peter's Quotations: Ideas for Our Time.* New York: Morrow, 1977.

Porter, M. E. *Competitive Advantage: Creating and Sustaining Superior Performance.* New York: Free Press, 1985.

Schneider, B. "The Service Organization: Climate Is Crucial." *Organizational Dynamics*, Autumn 1980, pp. 52–65.

Scott, B. R., and Lodge, G. *U.S. Competitiveness in the World Economy.* Boston: Harvard Business School Press, 1985.

Tichy, N. M., and Devanna, M. A. *The Transformational Leader.* New York: Wiley, 1986.

Zand, D. E. *Information, Organization, and Power.* New York: McGraw-Hill, 1981.

10

EDUCATING PEOPLE FOR A COMPETITIVE WORLD

H. J. ZOFFER

Determining who is at fault is a favorite American game. The culprit-versus-hero mentality seems to pervade our very essence as a nation. Thus it is no surprise that when the United States—that behemoth of countries—began to falter some years ago as the acknowledged leader of the world in competitive endeavors, the fickle finger of blame began to point.

It is a sobering thought, given the world scene today, to recognize that discussing how to improve organizational competitiveness in the United States would hardly have raised an eyebrow of interest only a few years ago. If some other country's organizations were being discussed, the topic would have had greater credibility. But it was hardly a fit subject for intellectual discussion in the heartland of the world's greatest producer of competitive products. What a difference a few years can make!

It hardly matters whose fault the current malaise is. We need to get on with the restructuring task to create competitive organizations. Certainly educational institutions have a crucial role to play. Certainly they have failed to realize their potential in the past. Certainly they must create agents of change who are compatible with today's organizations. Certainly it is unproductive to debate whether organizations are noncompetitive because the output of the educational establishment is incapable of making them competitive or because the entrenched organizations are incapable of utilizing their wisdom.

Note: The author wishes to thank Dr. Won Woo Park for his help in providing research assistance.

What *is* productive is to agree that organizations need to be made more competitive; that organizations do not become competitive by some natural process; that organizations are composed of people, educated and uneducated, experienced and inexperienced, younger and older, sensitive and insensitive; and that education has a crucial role in producing the kind of people who can make organizations more competitive than they currently are in the United States. Once these basic assumptions are digested, it may be helpful to suggest several more that are not universally applauded but are nevertheless necessary if we are to create an educational system that will address the competitiveness question.

First, education is a zero-sum game. As the game is now structured, there is only so much time available and an ever escalating flow of materials to be transmitted. Either the structure needs to be made more efficient or the time parameters must be relaxed.

Second, certain aspects of knowledge need comprehensive, integrated attention over extended periods of time. There is no sense in graduate schools being viewed as remedial institutions having to worry about ensuring the basic ability of students to read at proper speeds, to articulate effectively, and to comprehend basic mathematical skills.

Third, at the very least the high school, college, and graduate school system needs to be viewed as a smoothly running continuum rather than a highly segmented and fragmented series of experiences provided without regard to prior exposure, integration of effort, or results achieved.

Fourth, no educational system can ensure its graduates will have skills and knowledge that can be immediately translated into organizational competitiveness. But there are any number of incremental improvements, compared with current efforts, that will head the train in the proper direction. Any road will do—so long as it is going in the right direction.

Fifth, attitude and commitment are at the core of educational progress. As U.S. history amply documents, crisis is often required before educational progress takes hold. Major modifications proposed in the absence of crisis frequently produce patient smiles and studied acquiescence yet modest movement. Thus crisis may be a prerequisite to all but the most comfortably evolutionary modifications in today's educational systems. But even if one accepts all the foregoing assumptions, a program to enhance competitiveness may run aground on the shoals of the rigid structural conditions pertaining in the United States.

Structural Factors Blocking Improvement

There are a number of factors supporting improved organizational competitiveness in the United States that should encourage the development of new programs to enhance competitiveness. There are many excellent subsystems, such as transportation, that create a supportive infrastructure. In many areas there are sufficient natural resources. Graduate programs in many areas are state-of-the-art, and the level of technology is generally high. But the list is not as long as it should be.

On the other side of the ledger are some serious environmental conditions that hamper the development of educational programs that could enhance competitiveness by improving the operation of society's organizations. Philip Condit of Boeing said recently:

> I am convinced that any true fix for the problems U.S. industry is experiencing in facing foreign competition must begin by taking a comprehensive look at our primary and secondary education systems, and discovering why our children are inherently fascinated with the way things work, but become, as adults, content to know only the size and shape of the things around them [Condit, 1988, p. 8].

B. J. White in an article in the *Academy of Management Executive* noted:

> On the matter of education, I firmly believe that the underpinning of a company's or nation's ability to

compete is the capability, the knowledge and skills of its people. Twenty-three million U.S. adults are functionally illiterate. The U.S. literacy rate is 49th of the 158 countries in the United Nations. Our high school drop out rate is a tragedy and a disgrace. The number of required school days is about 180 on average as compared with 240 in Japan. This is powerful evidence that our commitment to excellence in education, and therefore to long-term economic development and competitiveness, is inadequate [White, 1988, p. 32].

We thus have an educational system supposedly preparing our children for productive careers and certainly for the supposed rigors of undergraduate and graduate programs. Yet in a sixteen-nation survey of educational attainment conducted by the International Association for the Evaluation of Educational Achievement, American secondary school students ranked third from the bottom in reading and in science and ranked the lowest in math among industrialized countries (Sawhill, 1983). There is a serious deterioration in the ranking of American schools during the secondary school period.

What causes such results? Commentators suggest television, inadequate parental supervision, insufficiently demanding curricula at the secondary level, declining college entrance requirements, competing demands on students' time, and the qualifications of teachers. Clearly the solution has little to do with money spent on education. In 1986, a University of Rochester economist, Eric Hanushek, synthesized a number of empirical studies and concluded that there is no strong or systematic relationship between school expenditures and student performance or between student achievement and teacher-student ratios, the level of the teachers' educational background, or the amount of their prior classroom experience. First-rate schools do exist and they are often expensive, but putting money into a school does not necessarily provide excellence.

There are many other factors that make it hard to establish programs to promote organizational competitiveness.

Many of these factors are amenable to the charms of education, but most require significant periods of maturity. As a wise man once said, there are no quick fixes.

First, there is the inherent rigidity of society's structures and institutions. There are many older and largely matured mass production companies where institutional bureaucracies prevail and it is especially difficult to transform ideas into products that can be sold on world markets.

Second, management–labor relations in some manufacturing situations inhibit shop-floor flexibility. That is a somewhat intractable problem unless flexibility can be introduced with the trade-off of greater participation in broad-scale decisions within the plant.

Third, securing leadership consensus and willingness to take dramatic steps for change is difficult in a society where there is a noticeable lack of national leadership and where even presidential campaigns tend to obscure fundamental issues with image and trivia.

Fourth, there is little government support of dramatic changes.

Fifth, there appears to be a shortage of workers with adequate basic skills — owing to a serious high-school dropout rate, less emphasis on the need for learning than the enjoyment of life, and minimal use of time available for educational pursuits.

Sixth, the international vision of education has not taken hold in the United States. There is only modest interest in learning foreign languages and cultures. The emphasis is on internal rather than external problems.

Seventh, there is an unacceptable lack of emphasis on basic science and engineering, as evidenced by the decreased rate of American students majoring in these subjects in graduate school. It is even estimated that only about one-third of the high school students in the country are taking a science course in any given year. The continuing boom in student enrollments in business and law schools may have distorted a more appropriate balance of majors in terms of maximizing society's interests.

Eighth, there has been, in recent years, an inordinate interest in the United States in short-term financial results, in stock prices as opposed to innovative products, and in risk avoidance rather than risk acceptance. All of these results augur poorly for quick improvements in organizational competitiveness. The obvious manifestation of this shift in interest has been the merger mania.

Ninth, there seems to be a lack of incentive to improve, a lack of commitment to achieve, and a comprehensive complacency that is perhaps to be expected of a matured economy with a supportive welfare system.

None of these conditions separately or even together rules out educational improvements, but the path to competitiveness is certainly more arduous with these boulders in place.

How Education Can Help

What can the educational establishment do to change this state of affairs? Much of the criticism in contemporary society of those holding the M.B.A. degree — the elitist credential claimed by 70,000 new entrants per year and the supposed passport to management responsibility — reflects society's frustration with the entire educational process.

The M.B.A. is the coup de grace of the educational system. It comes at the very end of a process that takes more than a decade and includes four years of high school, four years of undergraduate work, and perhaps fifty-five to sixty credits in a graduate school as the terminus of the formal education experience. But it is the graduate school that bears the blame if the student lacks values and ethics, cannot speak or write with effectiveness, lacks risk-taking courage, fails to understand diverse cultures, and is devoid of the capacity for innovation.

And graduate schools all over the country are struggling to arrange that burden of criticism on their broad shoulders. They are busy pouring salve on the wounds. As a way of making silver-tongued orators out of formula-driven engineers, English professors are hired to help graduate students improve the quality of their papers and to evaluate videotapes of their class presentations. Harried linguists are scurrying around the halls of academe to offer language facility in various tongues to monolingual students who have enough trouble making themselves understood in their native tongue. Cases are being stuffed into the nooks and crannies which point out that ethics is not to be forgotten and values are good business. The list goes on. Fill the cracks, smooth over the inconsistencies, paint up the dingy exterior, and pour intellectual Alka Seltzer into the students so the system works better, emits no unseemly noises, and justifies the exorbitant salaries the product demands.

It is thus a jerry-built product that is offered as the panacea for the nation's troubles. But these graduates are struggling to work magic in a package marked intellectually sophisticated, smoothly cultured, broadly visioned, globally oriented, behaviorally responsible, flexibly positioned, technologically proficient, and ethically wrapped. Is it any wonder the product fails to deliver, the expectation outruns the reality, the fix often comes loose, and the effort leaves scars of defensiveness? It is too much to load on the structure, too late to load it, too disjointed in focus, and too sporadic in application.

If we are to produce an improved product at the end of the educational line, we need to plan the process better and organize it over a longer period of time. Segments need to be distributed over a ten-year period, at least, and the comparative advantage of each level in the educational hierarchy must be considered. Of course, exits need to be provided on this freeway so that alternative choices can be made. Not everyone will decide to opt for legal or business careers. Some will stop the educational process and pull off the road. Others will branch off to unexpected byways. But so much of the basic materials are broadly useful and relevant that little waste will occur in the system — if the structure is organized wisely.

I propose an educational program with ten major objectives. It could be nine or eleven. In fact, there could be any number and the points on the map could be varied. So long as the road goes in the right direction, it does not matter. What does matter is agreement on the expected outcomes, an organized and integrated approach to achieving those outcomes, some understanding of the timelines required to do the job in an effective fashion, concern for the comparative advantage of each level in the system, agreement as to who does what and when, and some accountability for the outcomes.

Indeed, a basic prerequisite for such an approach is to set expectations and to measure the value added by the process through designing instruments to assess the results achieved. Whether this assessment is made by written instruments, by assessment centers, by capacity testing, or by whatever means, each expectation for competence or understanding or sensitivity should be not only clearly articulated but evaluated. Where progress is less than optimal, modifications can be made in the approach or the content.

These possibilities are listed here without regard to priority. For convenience I postulate a management student, but the approach is general in application. Let us start with the goal of improving the student's level of scientific thinking and scientific training. Whether or not one becomes a scientist or manages scientists or is concerned with technological innovation or transfer of technology, the need for improved scientific training in the American educational system seems clear. It is not just the province of scientist types. And it is not just a response to the high proportion of foreign graduate students in these fields. The manager needs to understand the scientific process. Whether it is to manage R & D laboratory personnel or to discover how technology gets transferred from one environment to another, the educational process must include regular scientific course work that develops each student's capacities in mathematics and a variety of related cognitive areas as well as skills particularly important for the scientist-to-be.

Second, our educational programs should encourage the enhancement of that amorphous set of skills called leadership. Leadership has as many definitions as there are writers about it. My concept of the word in terms of its educational implications is a process of influence aimed toward positive outcomes and a set of attributes that are appropriately attached to it. There is the question of willingness to lead and the sequential task of being able to. In order to influence and convince and win over and encourage all aspects of leadership, one needs to understand how the human mind works, how people relate to one another, the roles of leaders and followers, and myriad related understandings. It is one thing to understand all of that and yet another to be able to do it. The attributes of leadership are well known, and many of the associated skills can be taught. Whether it is negotiation, delegation, listening, communicating, behavioral flexibility, perception of threshold social cues, levels of energy, sense of humor, social sensitivity, or whatever, there are educational components that must be identified, organized, and put into the process.

This leads us to the third educational goal: enhancing basic tools and skills. We will have arrived at an important point when we can admit that education is not only the teaching of information but the creation of an acceptable package in which to deliver that information. Viewing the educational milieu as a proper place where such skills are taught, honed, and enhanced is the first step. There is a whole cadre of faculty, however, prepared to suggest otherwise. They wish to preserve the educational milieu for techniques, formulas, data, materials, and whatever else has traditionally emanated from the hallowed halls. But competitive organizations must have people who have well-developed communication skills, quantitative skills, behavioral skills, reasoning and analytical skills, and decision-making skills. There are others, but the delineation is a detail. The issue is to have the identification, enhancement, measurement, and application of skills within the educational system.

Another major educational component involves what is needed to provide a one-world vision — a true understanding of the international environment. This includes facility with one's own language and fluency in at least one foreign language. The level expected would be that required to converse easily and negotiate in that language. Fluency in English may prove to be the most troublesome goal! Some companies today are beginning to think of bilingualism as a prerequisite for hiring. This goal also implies an understanding of foreign cultures, the global marketplace, the economic workings of a global society, and multicultural behavioral differences. One cannot operate in a world environment without experiencing and understanding at least certain aspects of the subenvironments.

A much more challenging issue—particularly so because the road to understanding is so poorly marked—is the need to create educational experiences that encourage creative responses in the student and lead to innovation. A major need in our economic environment is to reduce the gap between the development of innovations and the application of the technology. To solve this problem we must develop people who are willing to take risks and are prepared to seek the high rewards associated with high danger—and to do this we must counter the risk-aversive philosophies that permeate the educational establishments, particularly some of the graduate schools.

Moreover, we must provide incentives for a proper work ethic. The educational environment is an important location for that task. Complaints about the loss of pride in workmanship or the unwillingness of today's young people to "pick up the papers" and assume responsibility, to take charge, to volunteer for service, to carry through, to walk the last mile, are but surface indications of the problem. Standard setting in education is only a precursor to standards in other areas, and no one encounters the young person earlier and oftener than the teachers of the country. One could quote a string of statistics to prove that American students work less, try less, and achieve less (perhaps a predictable result) than students in other developed countries. Part of the solution is an educational set of demands that require commitment to the kind of work ethic that would set the standards for other areas of a student's life. Here again we have a goal of the educational process that is related to but distinct from the transmission of knowledge. It is the form in which that knowledge is transmitted, the difficulty of the transmission, and the discipline developed that are crucial.

Related to the discipline of the delivery system is the need to create an understanding of the role that improved productivity plays in the competitive equation. The question suggested here is not an easy one. How can educational programs be structured so that they stress the relationship of input to output, the importance of a commitment to excellence, and the outcomes that yield the best results without straining human or fiscal resources to the limit?

What about the conflicting roles of labor and management in a competitive society? So much is heard of stakeholder analysis, of participative management, of the tensions between labor and management, of employee stock ownership, all of which are part of the study of how organized and unorganized groups in our society relate to one another. What courses or experiences can be offered to provide an understanding of the constituent groups in our society, how they relate to one another, how they share mutual goals or pursue diverse approaches, what the benefits of cooperative goal setting or profit sharing are, or how incentives run counter to egalitarian concepts? There needs to be an ongoing educational dialogue about these relationships during the student's formative years. What forums should be used? What subject matter should be included? How should all of this be integrated? What conclusions should be anticipated?

Furthermore, we need to structure our educational process so that it relates to the importance of culture in competitiveness. This concept refers not only to what constitutes organizational culture, how it develops, how it is recognized, what it accomplishes, and how it is modified, but to an understanding of cross-cultural differences among diverse societies. Culture as an aspect of human endeavor is too seldom addressed and needs greater attention.

Finally, what is the role of government in a competitive society? How is the relationship between the society and its government structured? What are the components of an acceptable industrial policy? Should the government function as a protector or court of last resort, or is the safety net concept outmoded? How do we develop an educational program that educates students to take part in the dialogue? Government is a major player in society. An informed voter is our best customer, to paraphrase a current commercial. Competitive organizations need managers who can participate in the national dialogue. What should U.S. trade policy be? Should the United States government punish countries who run up chronic surpluses? How do we as a country help developing nations out of their debt mess? What is the role of tariffs and tariff barriers in competitive playing? How does the research sponsored by government get transferred to nondefense industries? What is the government's role in improving our 70 percent high school completion rate so that it competes with Japan's 98 percent (Jonas, 1987b)? What is the role of the government in ensuring job security and encouraging portable pension plans? What is the role of the government's tax policy in spurring competitive behavior? All these questions need answers and an informed citizenry to give them. Surely we can devise educational programs to produce graduates who can at least talk intelligently about the quandaries.

Conclusion

Education indeed has a role in making organizations more competitive. That role is to produce graduates who understand the problems and can contribute to the solutions. Designing an integrated program to achieve the appropriate levels of understanding and knowledge is no easy task, but it can be achieved if a national priority is declared. A commitment to excellence will enhance educational competitiveness and lead to greater organization competitiveness.

There is a direct relationship between the educational process and the development of a competitive society. But the current flowing through the present educational system is discrete, segmented, and short-circuited. What we need is a continuous, direct current that energizes the process through a long-term, outcome-oriented set of procedures that assign a different, but crucial, part of the task to each stage in the student's educational pattern. While this approach may suggest a more normative educational pattern than the current freedom of choice system, it rests on a basic, admittedly paternalistic assumption: If complex, comprehensive outcomes are expected, then well-designed patterns of experience and courses will have to be based on the judgment of those who have traveled the road.

Education clearly has a role in producing competitive

organizations, since those organizations are run by the products of education. But if education is not to be found wanting, it must get its house in order, mobilize its resources, and recognize that the task is formidable and the race to the finish line needs to be started now.

References

"American Investment in Education Faulted." *Education Week*, June 22, 1988, p. 5.

Berger, J. "Productivity: Why It's the No. 1 Underachiever." *Business Week*, Apr. 20, 1987, pp. 54–55.

Bloch, E. "Economic Competition: A Research and Education Challenge." *Research Management*, Mar.–Apr. 1987, pp. 6–8.

"Can America Compete?" *Business Week*, Apr. 20, 1987, pp. 45–52.

Condit, P. M. "Why U.S. Firms Cannot Compete with the Japanese." *Research Technology Management*, May–June 1988, *31* (3), 7–8.

Finn, C. E. "Education That Works: Make the Schools Compete." *Harvard Business Review*, Sept.–Oct. 1987, pp. 63–68.

Galagan, P. A. "Joining Forces: Business and Education Take on Competitiveness." *Training and Development Journal*, July 1988, pp. 26–29.

"Governors Report Says Key to Prosperity Is in a Global View." *New York Times*, July 26, 1987, pp. 1 and 14.

Harris, P. R., and Morron, R. T. *Managing Cultural Differences.* (2nd ed.) Houston: Gulf Publishing, 1987.

Hays, R. H., and Abernathy, W. J. "Managing Our Way to Economic Decline." *Harvard Business Review*, July–Aug. 1980, pp. 75–76.

Jonas, N. "Can America Compete?" *Business Week*, Apr. 20, 1987a, pp. 45–47.

Jonas, N. "No Pain, No Gain: How America Can Grow Again." *Business Week*, Apr. 20, 1987b, pp. 68–69.

Kempner, T. "Education for Management in Five Countries: Myth and Reality." *Journal of General Management*, Winter 1983–84, *9* (2), 6–23.

Lawler, E. E., III, and Mohrman, S. A. "Unions and the New Management." *Academy of Management Executive*, Nov. 1987, pp. 293–300.

Lewis, A. C. "Confucius Say, Learn from International Neighbors." *Phi Delta Kappan*, Mar. 1987, pp. 492–493.

Mitroff, I. I., and Mohrman, S. A. "The Slack Is Gone: How the United States Lost Its Competitive Edge in the World Economy." *Academy of Management Executive*, Feb. 1987, pp. 65–70.

Rosenfeld, S. A. "Education for the Factories of the Future." *Education Week*, June 22, 1988, p. 48.

Sawhill, I. V. "Human Resources." In G. W. Miller (ed.), *Regrowing the American Economy*. Englewood Cliffs, N.J.: Prentice-Hall, 1983.

Smith, M. R. "Improving Product Quality in American Industry." *Academy of Management Executive*, Aug. 1987, pp. 243–245.

Thurow, L. C. "America in a Competitive Economic World." In G. W. Miller (ed.), *Regrowing the American Economy*. Englewood Cliffs, N.J.: Prentice-Hall, 1983.

Weidenbaum, M. L. "Learning to Compete." *Business Horizons*, Sept.–Oct. 1986, pp. 1–12.

White, B. J. "The Internationalization of Business: One Company's Response." *Academy of Management Executive*, Feb. 1988, pp. 29–32.

11

HOLONOMIC PROCESSES FOR ENSURING COMPETITIVENESS

KENNETH D. MACKENZIE

Because competition forces change, firms must adapt in order to survive. Some are better than others in adapting to change. One of the tasks of organization theorists is to analyze why. What is it about the organization that distinguishes the efficient competitor from the failure? Is it possible to develop a theory of organizations that explains how and why some organizations are more adaptive?

This chapter summarizes a new theory for the efficiently adaptable organization that I developed jointly with Gerald W. Holder since we began working together in 1985. Both of us had noticed that out of the chaos of change in U.S. companies in the past decade, a new organizational form and new management practices were emerging. By a complex sequence of trial and error, imitation, and sheer necessity, organizations were beginning to learn how to manage change better. Our own experiences as theorists, consultants, and managers had led us to try to understand what was happening and why. The best of our organizations were doing things that seemed to be working but lay outside normal academic musings and theory. Thus our theory was induced from practice rather than deduced from principles. Once we were able to induce a general understanding of the outlines of the new emerging organizational form, we began a three-year effort to construct a theory about it. This

Note: The author wishes to thank the editor and Dr. Don Utter for comments on an earlier draft. They are not, of course, responsible for the final result.

theory seeks to explain the emerging organizational form in which the challenge is to become simultaneously more productive, adaptable, and efficiently adaptable. It represents an ideal toward which organizations can adapt to achieve. It is a way of thinking about organizational problems that we find very useful.

Perhaps a comparison with other words might help us express the nature of this theory. Consider the following words:

Monarchy— ruled by one
Oligarchy— ruled by a few
Anarchy— ruled by no one
Isocracy— ruled by everyone
Democracy— ruled by the people
Bureaucracy— ruled by bureaus

This theory is a new type. It is a rule by processes of adaptation and change. The new executive trying to manage rapid change operates more as a concertmaster who manages the processes of change and adaptation according to a shifting musical score determined by his specific condition. The object is to create good music continuously by managing the processes that produce the desired functional behavior of his managers. He does not play the violin, piccolo, trumpet, or french horn or operate the instruments of percussion. His job is to ensure that when each plays his or her part of the score they all, together, produce the desired results. Furthermore, each manager operates the same processes for his or her subordinates. Thus, as the whole set of players play their parts, the result is harmony and resonance according to the score. But because of change, the score is also changing. The challenge is to recognize and institutionalize the processes of adaptation and change so that changes can be made quickly and efficiently in order to produce desired outcomes.

This theory is very specific. It provides both the means for diagnosing organizational problems and the remedial actions that need to be undertaken. It identifies twelve basic processes that must be managed in order to become simultaneously more productive, adaptable, and efficiently adaptable. Moreover, it shows how each is based on underlying principles, propositions, definitions, and assumptions so that in every situation the user has specific issues upon which to base problem solving. The manager applying this theory has specific remedies that allow immediate problem solving in the context of an overall strategy for organizational transformation. He or she can take direct and specific actions and have a coherent program for the future. There is no single intervention that is right for all situations. Following an initial diagnosis, each manager can start where he or she thinks there is most need and then proceed later to the rest of the organization. One CEO might decide that the most pressing problem is establishing and maintaining a clear strategic direction. A second might be concerned with improving the organization's reward system. A third might be worried about making the process of problem solving more healthy. A fourth might think that the organization's design is the most pressing issue. Since these issues are not independent of one another, one should first "scratch where there is the biggest itch" and then proceed systematically to the rest of the organization. Thus effective change can begin anywhere and the results can be used to build consensus and support for later changes. Since more changes will occur and new opportunities and problems will surface, this work never ends. The theory provides the reasoning and the processes that need to be set into motion and managed. It shows that when these processes are working continually throughout the organization, it will be congruent, maximally productive, and efficiently adaptable.

The theory of the organizational hologram begins with the description of environments. The organization's environments consist of all the events and processes outside its boundaries that can affect its operation. The impact of these environments has implications ranging from the organization's strategic direction to how it organizes itself and how it adapts. The interdependencies of a firm with its environments are an integral part of organizational theory and strategic management. Organizations have always had to cope with environmental changes. Today, however, there seems to be an acceleration in the number of changes, a broadening of the variety of changes, and an upsurge in major, sudden changes to which an organization must adapt in order to survive. Furthermore, the impacts of these environmental changes and their ripple effects are felt in every industry and unit of government. From banking to robotics, from cities to the federal government, from the large *Fortune* 500 to the little start-up firms, one can sense and measure the successive impacts of environmental changes. These forces have sharpened management's awareness and concern for more effective management of change.

These environmental changes must be recognized and managed. They pose challenges to managers and to theorists attempting to explain and predict organizational behavior. A consensus is growing in both the business world and the scholarly community that we must rethink our theory and practice of management. One recognition of this is the growing concern for transformational management. Another is the growing interest in corporate culture.

It is interesting to track the conferences organized by Ralph Kilmann and his associates and sponsored by the Katz Graduate School of Business of the University of Pittsburgh. The 1982 conference, entitled "Producing Useful Knowledge for Organizations" (Kilmann and others, 1983), dealt with how to make academic research more relevant. This conference recognized the growing gaps between organizational reality and organizational research. The next conference, held in 1984 and entitled "Gaining Control of the Corporate Culture" (Kilmann, Saxton, Serpa, and Associates, 1985), was an effort to understand the significance of corporate culture and cultural change. This topic underscored the need for comprehending change and culture. The third conference, held in 1986, resulted in the book *Corporate Transformation: Revitalizing Organizations for a Competitive World* (Kilmann, Covin, and Associates, 1988). This conference examined the problems of transforming organizations suited to the conditions of the past to ones capable of competing in today's more dynamic environments. The 1988 conference continued the theme and focused on making organizations more competitive. It would seem that we are progressing from the task of encouraging relevant research to that of discovering how to make organizations more adaptable and competitive. One trend in these books is the need for *complete* organizational theories. Kilmann (1984) uses the phrase *dynamic complexity* to refer to the new reality. A system is said to be dynamically complex if it has a number of interdependent parts that are always changing. The very notion of dynamic complexity means that it is becoming less and less relevant to propose partial theories and rely on simple linear interdependencies. Rather, one must begin to think of organizations as open systems that are dynamically complex. Hence the need to propose more comprehensive models for describing and explaining organizations. Furthermore, the concept of dynamic complexity should be extended. What we face today is better described as a dynamically complex milieu.

A *dynamically complex milieu* has five characteristics: There are many different stakeholders who have vital interests and the power to enforce them; there is great uncertainty regarding the development, production, and marketing of new products and services; the organization has only partial control over the uncertainty involved in new products and services; the major decisions of the organization have multiple aspects, each of which must be factored into the decisions; and the major decisions of the organization involve a concatenation of subordinate decisions, each of which affects the uncertainty. The extension from dynamic complexity to a dynamically complex milieu recognizes the necessity to consider the interdependencies between the organization's environments and its decision making.

Another trend is the shift in emphasis from the simple idea of productivity and efficiency as the organizational desiderata to more dynamic concepts of its being adaptive and even efficiently adaptive. Because of the pace of change, efficiency alone is no longer enough to ensure competitiveness. Being adaptive helps cope with change. Moreover, as the rate and types of change accelerate, it is important to become efficient at being adaptive in a dynamically complex milieu. That is, firms need to become efficient at being adaptive.

Efficient adaptability, however, poses new challenges both to the practice of management and to organizational theory. This chapter summarizes the theory of efficient adaptability presented in *The Organizational Hologram: The Effective Management of Organizational Change* (Mackenzie and Holder, 1990). After outlining the main features of the theory, I will try to show that the real challenge in making organizations more competitive is to learn how to become simultaneously more productive, adaptable, and efficiently adaptable by becoming an organizational hologram.

The Holonomic Organization

A hologram is the exposed photographic plate onto which are superimposed the interference patterns of two beams of light from a coherent light source. The coherent beam is split by a beam splitter. One part bounces off mirrors onto the plate and the other off an object. The hologram appears as interference patterns that resemble swirls of lines rather than a direct image of the object. The image produced by incident light on the exposed photographic plate (the hologram) is the holographic image. The holographic image appears as a shadowy three-dimensional figure. One of the truly fascinating properties of a hologram is that it can be cut in half and both halves will produce the full holographic image. Whereas a photograph produces only half of the image, each part of a hologram contains the whole image.

Some scholars have used the notion of a hologram as a metaphor for organizations. Kilmann (1984), for example, uses the three-dimensional aspect of a holographic image to describe the complexity of organizational reality and to emphasize the unseen depths of its culture and each member's psyche. Morgan and Ramirez (1984) use the main property of the hologram to propose a way of thinking about action learning. Elsewhere Morgan (1986) develops the notion of a hologram in a chapter entitled "Towards Self Organization: Organizations as Brains." His idea is that, to the extent an organization can become like a hologram, the more it will take on the useful properties of the human brain. Morgan argues that if each part of the organization can contain the whole set of functions, then each part will, in this sense, contain the whole and thus be more holographic. This is called redundancy of function.

The main problems with such a use of the holographic metaphor are that holograms are static, people and social processes are not waves of light, and an organization is not a hologram. Furthermore, it is unlikely that redundancy of function is achievable because there are so many technologies and functions, most of which change. Human limitations in cognitive capacity preclude redundancy of function in most organizations. It would be most unusual, for example, to have a dean of a school of business who could understand the research papers produced by the faculty. Given a dynamically complex milieu, redundancy of function needs to be replaced by *redundancy of change processes*. It is easier to have all units adapting to change with the same processes than it is to have each capable of performing all the functions.

The word *holonomic* refers to the property of being like a hologram. Organizations can become holonomic, but they are not holograms. This theory derives twelve holonomic processes of change and adaptation that, if working throughout the organization, will result in efficient adaptability. An organizational hologram is a metaphor based on these holonomic processes. It is holonomic to the extent that all of the organization's units have all twelve holonomic processes working at all times throughout the whole organization. That is, the parts contain the whole in the sense that they change and adapt with the same holonomic processes.

Key Aspects of the Theory

The full theory of the organizational hologram contains an extensive set of assumptions, definitions, and an analytical pyramid of conclusions. The base rests on a set of definitions and assumptions. These are used to derive a set of thirty-five conclusions called propositions. The thirty-five propositions yield twenty principles that are like the propositions but more general. The twenty principles are then used to derive twelve holonomic processes. These allow the statement of six desired organizational characteristics. The top level of the analytical system includes something called a holonomic cube and four macroorganizational principles, one of which is the principle of the organizational hologram. While it is impossible to present the full theory here, it is possible to present the main ideas.

Combined Congruency

One bulwark of the theory of the organizational hologram is the concept of combined congruency. *Combined congruency* consists of fourteen organizational-level congruency conditions and eighteen bonding congruency conditions and exists when all thirty-two congruency conditions have been met. Each congruency condition examines the compatibility between a pair of elements. Combined congruency obtains when all of the elements are compatible and the organization as a whole has a good fit with itself, its environments, and its people.

Figure 11.1 depicts the ABCE model illustrating the organizational-level congruency conditions. The idea is that the organization lies embedded in its environments and has three main parts. Part A is called the *strategic direction*—the organization's mission statement and the organization's goals and strategies. Part B is called the *organizational technology*, which consists of three types of organizational assumptions (strategic, organizing, and environmental), the organization's logic (which describes the work of the organization, including the processes to establish long-range strategic, tactical, and annual operating plans), the organization's architecture, the organization's reward system, and the organization itself. Part C is called *results* and consists of current and expected future results. The means-ends flow is assumed to be clockwise and continual in a dynamically complex milieu. In Figure 11.1, each of the fourteen organizational-level congruency conditions is illustrated by an arrow. There are three types: strategic congruency conditions (labeled SC), organizational technology congruency conditions (labeled OT), and organizational results congruency (labeled

Figure 11.1. A Model of Organizational-Level Congruency Conditions.

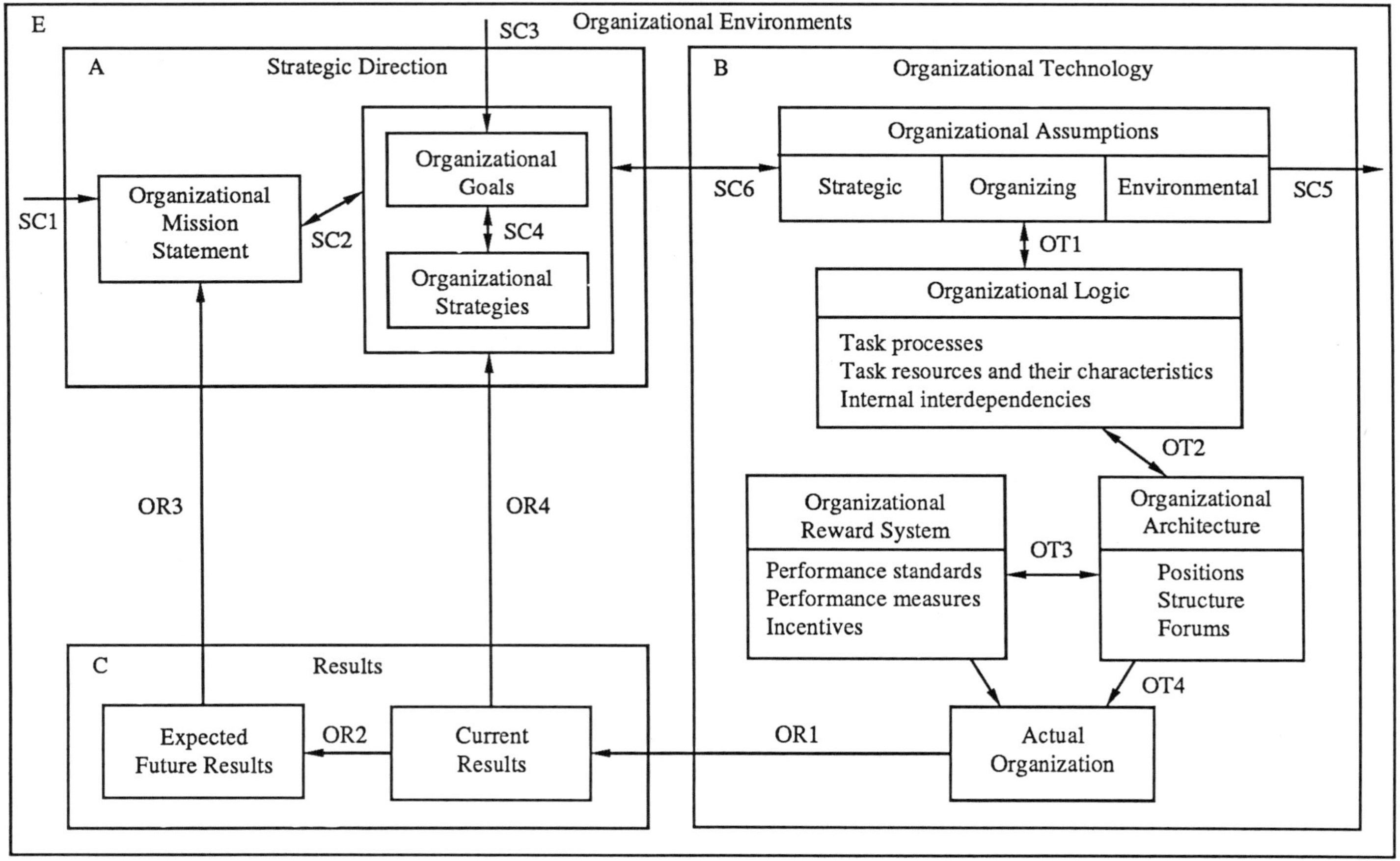

OR). For example, SC1 is the strategic congruency condition of the fit between the environments and the organization's mission statement.

The fourteen organizational-level congruency conditions do not involve the members of the organization directly. The members of an organization in a dynamically complex milieu are considered its main assets, however, so some provision must be made to ensure that each member (called an associate) is bonded to the organization as a whole and to the position held. Moreover, the position should be bonded to the organization. Thus there are three types of bonding congruency conditions: associate/organization (AO), associate/position (AP), and position/organization (PO). Think of bonding as the social glue that binds the associate to the organization. The theory assumes that the stronger the bonding, the better the organization will perform in a dynamically complex milieu.

Figure 11.2 illustrates the associate/position/organization bonding linkages. The upper level represents the organizational-level ABCE model (Figure 11.1); the lower level is called the abce model. The two are combined in Figure 11.2 to illustrate the full range of combined congruency built into the theory of the organizational hologram.

The theory contains a number of propositions concerning congruency conditions. The more important ones are:

Proposition 1:   Bonding congruency is a necessary but not sufficient condition for attaining and maintaining organizational-level congruency.

Proposition 2:   Organizational-level congruency is a necessary but not sufficient condition for attaining and maintaining bonding congruency.

Proposition 11:   An organization is maximally productive if and only if it has combined congruency.

Proposition 12:   The attainment of efficient adaptability is the result of managing to achieve and maintain combined congruency.

Note that Propositions 1 and 2 show that both bonding and organizational-level congruency are necessary for each other but that each, by itself, cannot guarantee the other. This means that it is necessary to manage *both* types of congruency. Propositions 11 and 12 state that the organization's productivity and adaptability are directly related to organizational-level congruency. Proposition 11 is very strong. It states that (1) if the organization is organizationally congruent then it will be maximally productive and (2) if it is maximally productive then it will be organizationally congruent.

Holonomic Process

The concept of combined congruency and the resulting propositions and principles that flow from it produce useful diagnostic tools for organizations. They have also proved useful as the basis for designing organizations to be more productive and adaptable. For example, the organizational audit and analysis technology (OA&A) for organizational design (Mackenzie, 1986) is based primarily on the notion of organizational-level congruency.

The design of an organization is more concerned with organizational-level congruency than it is with bonding congruency because it looks at the organization as a whole whereas bonding looks at each associate and his or her relationship with the organization. While it is true that organizational design must be concerned with the organization's reward system and with the bonding of each position to the organization, it is only indirectly concerned with the bonding of each associate to his or her position and to the organization. It focuses on creating the conditions for this bonding, but it does not directly specify mechanisms for achieving such bonding.

Another limitation of OA&A is that it views the design of an organization as a process guided by the chief executive officer only when there is a clear need for it. This means that the design of an organization is episodic rather than continuous. The OA&A approach is not holonomic because its impetus and direction are concentrated at the top of an organization rather

Figure 11.2. Associate/Position/Organization Bonding Linkages.

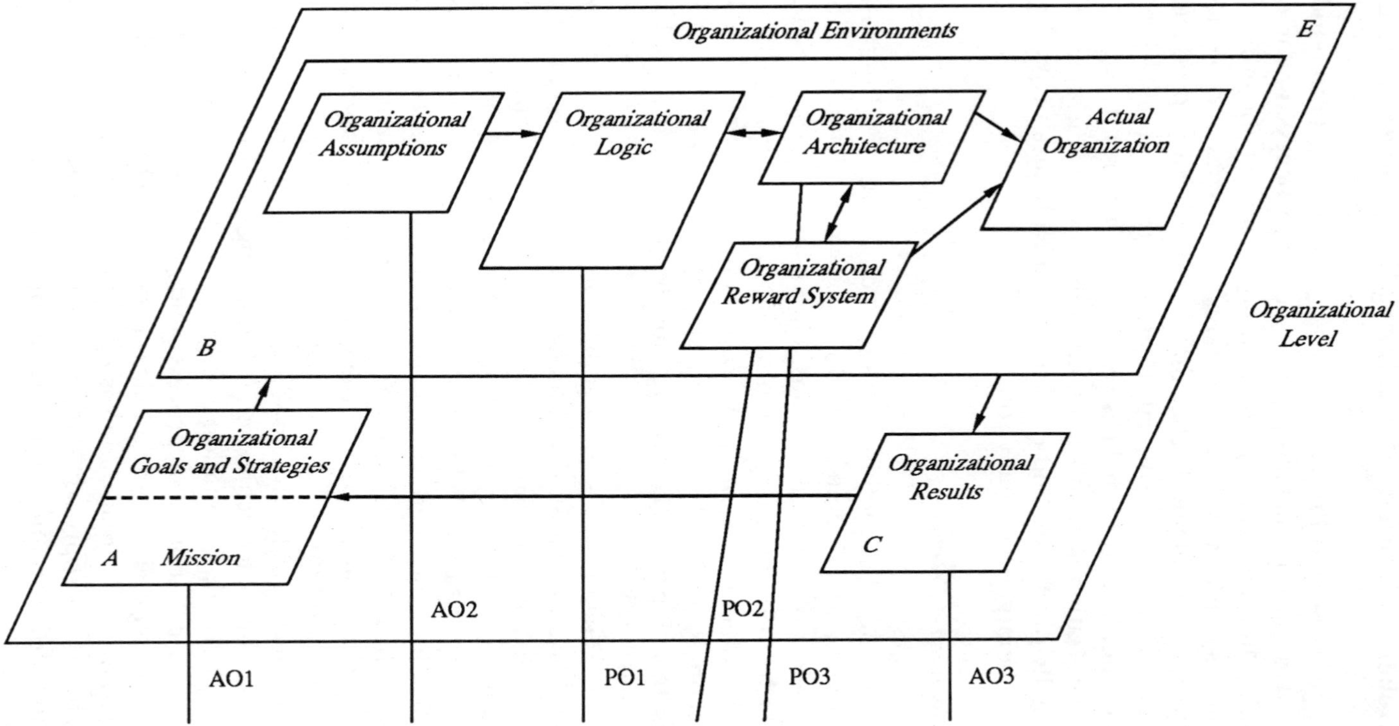

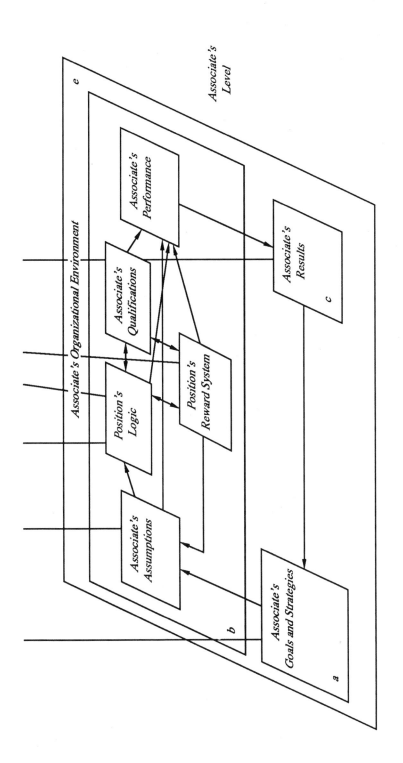

Associate's
Level

Associate's Organizational Environment

Associate's
Performance

Associate's
Qualifications

Associate's
Results

Position's
Logic

Position's
Reward System

Associate's
Assumptions

Associate's
Goals and Strategies

e

b

a

c

than distributed throughout. Consequently, a theory of the organizational hologram must provide mechanisms for continuous adaptations that are capable of working in every part of an organization. The OA&A approach provides a proven method for attaining organizational-level congruency, but it must be supplemented with other ongoing processes of change and adaptation.

The main result of the theory is its twelve holonomic processes and their implications. These twelve processes, if working throughout the organization, create combined congruency, productivity, and efficient adaptability as a by-product. These holonomic processes are dynamic and ongoing. The set of twelve includes:

HP1: Establishing and maintaining clear strategic direction
HP2: Defining and updating the organization's logic
HP3: Ensuring the best decision making
HP4: Adapting to ensure position clarity
HP5: Ensuring systematic planning that is workable, involved, and understood
HP6: Integrating associate selection, development, and flow with the strategic direction
HP7: Nurturing and rewarding opportunistic and innovative problem solving
HP8: Ensuring healthy problem solving throughout the organization
HP9: Setting tough and realistic performance standards
HP10: Operating an equitable and effective reward system
HP11: Ensuring compatibility of interests
HP12: Encouraging and rewarding ethical behavior for all associates

Note that each of the twelve holonomic processes is a verbal phrase that captures the idea that each is an ongoing process. Each holonomic process has its own technology. Each word in the statement of a holonomic process has its own meaning within the theory. For example, HP3 is ensuring the best decision making. The phrase "decision making" is used in the same sense as it is employed in the literature about decision making. The word *best*, however, has a special meaning here. It is not the same as an optimum; rather, it is defined in terms of a best decision. The *best decision* is one that meets seven criteria:

1. Due diligence indicates that it is workable.
2. The organization benefits.
3. As many other stakeholders benefit as possible.
4. The harm to any stakeholder is minimized.
5. It is the right thing to do.
6. It is congruent with the strategic direction of the organization.
7. It is best overall for the organization.

Note that HP3 implies that all associates should have knowledge of the strategic direction of the organization; otherwise, they would not be able to meet Condition 6. Furthermore, as most decisions involve others, the best decision must consider the stakeholders (Conditions 3 and 4) and try to prevent suboptimization, which might be good for a unit but not best overall for the organization (Condition 7). Note also the ethical component (Condition 5). Sharp practices that are smart but not right are counter to best decision making. The concern for ethics is also the foundation for HP12: encouraging and rewarding ethical behavior for all associates. Ethical behavior not only provides a general guideline for decisions in a dynamically complex milieu, it also prevents many problems in the future created by backlash to unethical behavior and simplifies problems of measurement and control.

Four of the holonomic processes are directly concerned with the strategic direction of the organization. HP1 is the process of establishing and maintaining clear strategic direction. HP3, ensuring the best decision making, has congruence with the strategic direction as a constraint. HP5, ensuring systematic planning that is workable, involved, and understood, is a means for developing the strategic direction and spreading it throughout the organization. HP6, integrating associate selection, development, and flow with the strategic direction, brings the human resources management of associates into the implementation of the strategic direction.

Two of the holonomic processes are involved with updating the formal organization as changes occur. HP2 is defining and maintaining the organization's logic. The organization's logic describes the work processes present in the organization and is the basis for describing positions. HP4, adapting to ensure position clarity, is the process of continually seeking to ensure that associates understand their jobs and those with which they are interdependent and the bonding between the positions and the organization. Over a decade of organizational design consulting has taught me that HP2 and HP4 are poorly performed by most organizations. There are now proven technologies for each. In the theory of the organizational hologram, these two holonomic processes are vital to ensuring that the organization operates as it is designed and that the design changes with the organization.

Three of the holonomic processes concern mechanisms for problem solving. HP3, ensuring the best decision making, specifies the criteria to be met. HP7, nurturing and rewarding opportunistic and innovative problem solving, describes specific mechanisms for finding problems, setting up a task force and one-time rewards for completing the work, and amplifying rewards based on the solution's value to the organization. HP8, ensuring healthy problem solving throughout the organization, is a process to prevent destructive political behavior and encourage cooperation and involvement.

Three of the holonomic processes involve the organization's reward system. HP9, setting tough and realistic performance standards, is the process of goal setting. These performance standards are an integral part of the reward system. HP10 is the holonomic process of operating an equitable and effective reward system. Finally, HP11, ensuring compatibility of interests, is a mechanism to elicit cooperation tied to the organization's reward system.

Desired Organizational Characteristics

The twelve holonomic processes can be employed to derive six desired organizational characteristics (DOCs) of the organizational hologram:

DOC1:   Clarity of direction
DOC2:   Clarity of structures
DOC3:   Clarity of measurement
DOC4:   Successful goal achievement
DOC5:   Results-oriented problem solving
DOC6:   Associates as assets and resources

The first three stress the need for clarity in the strategic direction, the various organizational structures, and the methods of measurement. Clarity fosters adaptation because it is easier to make changes when the thing to be changed is clearly defined, measured, and implemented. DOC4, successful goal achievement, has special meaning in this theory. It means deciding what must be done, determining how to get it done, and then making progress. Successful goal achievement means that the processes for achieving success are a characteristic of the organization. DOC4 means that, throughout the organization, each unit and associate is striving to ensure successful goal achievement. Organizations that are managed by the numbers alone do not have this property. DOC5, results-oriented problem solving, comprises seven conditions for effective participation in problem solving throughout the organization:

- Problem solving occurs at the lowest level at which the problems occur.
- The best available resources are brought to bear on the task.
- These resources are utilized.
- There is clarity concerning the identity of the final decision maker and those in support roles.
- A process is in place to effectively and efficiently deal with conflicts between accountable and support managers when

one or the other believes that the decision to be made is not the best one.

- The criterion of best decision making is met.
- The object of the process is to make something happen that will have a positive impact on the success of the organization.

DOC6 is the characteristic that the associates are assets and resources. The members of an organization facing a dynamically complex milieu are not just costs of operations. Rather, they should be considered both assets and resources. Associates are *assets* if they are a continuing source of results as the organization evolves. Associates are *resources* to an organization when they can continually contribute knowledge, information, and energy to solve its problems and enable it to seize opportunities as it adapts to its environments. Given the reality of rapid change, there will be changes in the needed mix and distribution of essential skills for associates. Associates need to become more involved in problem solving and should be encouraged to develop their skills in order to remain assets and resources. The organization in a dynamically complex milieu needs its associates as its essential renewable resources if it expects to keep up with change. It also requires their commitment to act as assets and resources.

Relationships Among the Holonomic Processes and the Desired Organizational Characteristics

The chief result of the theoretical development of the twelve holonomic processes and six desired organizational characteristics is to show that they are interdependent. More precisely, the theory shows that each of the DOCs depends directly on four holonomic processes. It shows as well that each of the holonomic processes is directly involved in two of the DOCs. The results of these theoretical investigations are summarized in Table 11.1.

The argument for each of the DOCs is contained in the *organizational hologram*. It is instructive to select DOC5, results-

Table 11.1. Relationships Among the Six Desired Organizational Characteristics and the Twelve Holonomic Processes.

Holonomic Process	*Clarity of Direction*	*Clarity of Structures*	*Clarity of Measurement*	*Successful Goal Achievement*	*Results-Oriented Problem Solving*	*Associates Are Assets and Resources*
HP1: Establishing and maintaining clear strategic direction	Yes			Yes		
HP2: Defining and updating the organizational logic	Yes	Yes				
HP3: Ensuring the best decision making	Yes				Yes	
HP4: Adapting to ensure position clarity		Yes			Yes	
HP5: Ensuring systematic planning that is workable, involved, and understood	Yes		Yes			
HP6: Integrating associate selection, development, and flow with the strategic direction		Yes				Yes
HP7: Nurturing and rewarding opportunistic and innovative problem solving				Yes	Yes	
HP8: Ensuring healthy problem solving throughout the organization					Yes	Yes
HP9: Setting tough and realistic performance standards			Yes	Yes		
HP10: Operating equitable and effective reward system		Yes	Yes			
HP11: Ensuring compatibility of interests				Yes		Yes
HP12: Encouraging and rewarding ethical behavior for all associates			Yes			Yes

Note: The entry "yes" refers to the necessity of the holonomic process on the left operating to produce the desired major organizational property of the column. All four must be working in order to produce the desired organizational property.

oriented problem solving, because it is based on seven principles resulting in the holonomic processes HP3, HP4, HP7, and
HP8 (see Table 11.1). This DOC is singled out here because it
provides a glimpse of the types of principles in the theory and
involves interesting sets of holonomic processes. Results-
oriented problem solving rests on seven principles:

> Principle 5:   The Resources Utilization Principle states
> that in making a complex decision, it is necessary to (1)
> bring the best available resources to bear and (2) en-
> sure that the decision utilizes these resources in the
> problem-solving process in order to make the best
> decisions.

> Principle 6:   The Delegation Principle states that deci-
> sions should be made at the lowest possible level at
> which the work or problems occur and, if not resolved
> there, should continue to be brought up successive
> levels of management for review and resolution, as
> required, in order to get the ultimate decision maker in
> conflict resolution.

> Principle 7:   The Best Decision Principle states that or-
> ganizational performance depends on all associates
> striving to make positively implemented best decisions
> at all times.

> Principle 8:   The Decision Responsibility Principle
> means that in making a balanced decision, it is neces-
> sary to ensure clarity about who the final decision
> maker is and who are support associates.

> Principle 12:   The Forums Principle states that an orga-
> nization in a dynamically complex milieu is more
> adaptable and efficiently adaptable if it operates a
> system of parallel problem-solving and information-
> sharing forums.

> Principle 19:   The Rewards Amplification Principle
> states that it is in the organization's interest to seek
> opportunities for rewards amplification in a dynam-
> ically complex milieu.

> Principle 20:   The Opportunistic and Innovative Prob-

lem Solving Principle states that it is in the organization's interest to seek opportunities for innovative problem solving in a dynamically complex milieu.

These seven principles, working together, result in the desired organizational characteristic of results-oriented problem solving.

The Best Decision Principle is used to derive HP3: ensuring the best decision making. HP7, nurturing and rewarding opportunistic and innovative problem solving, is needed to implement the Resources Utilization Principle and the Decision Responsibility Principle and depends on the last three principles listed. These resources will not be properly utilized unless HP8, ensuring healthy problem solving throughout the organization, is operating. Otherwise there will be politics and secrecy, which inhibit bringing the best available resources to bear on the decision and using them in problem solving. Healthy problem solving throughout the organization also encourages delegation and discourages abdication. It provides for the proper review and resolution of the problems at the next higher level when there is a deadlock. Instead of solving the problems by use of personal power and instead of assigning blame and hogging credit, it is far better to employ the Delegation Principle by having HP8 work.

Finally, there is a prerequisite for having results-oriented problem solving. As issues change and as problems are brought up and solved, there will be changes in the organizational positions. HP4, adapting to ensure position clarity, is needed for results-oriented problem solving.

The Holonomic Cube

Figure 11.3 depicts a square in which the four edges represent the four holonomic processes involved in achieving the desired organizational characteristic of involved and responsible problem solving. Similar diagrams can be constructed for the other five DOCs from Table 11.1.

Using the information in Table 11.1, the six figures for

**Figure 11.3. The Results-Oriented Problem-Solving Facet
of the Holonomic Cube.**

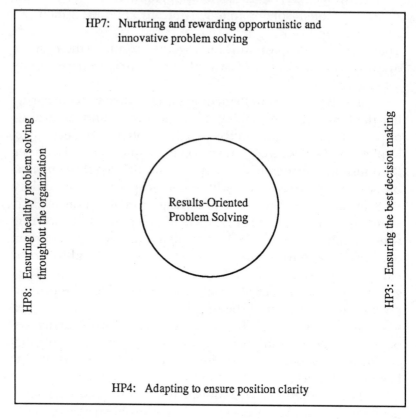

each of the DOCs can be rearranged as shown in Figure 11.4. Folding along the dotted lines and taping together the edges gives one a *holonomic cube.* The holonomic cube is useful in visualizing the interdependencies among the holonomic processes. It is also a valuable device for diagnosing organizational problems. One can, in the context of a specific organization, start with any of the six facets and ask whether or not the organization has the desired organizational characteristic represented by the circle on the face. If the answer is no, then one can be sure that at least one of the four holonomic processes is not working. Find one and then pivot about its edge to the adjacent facet. One can be assured that this DOC is also missing. There may be another holonomic process on this second facet that is not working well. This allows another pivot and so on. Successive examination of each facet and pivoting about the defective holonomic process eventually cover the entire holonomic cube. Shifting attention from the ends (the DOCs) to the means (the HPs) provides a useful means for diagnosing organizational problems. The diagnosis results in a set of conclusions about what DOCs are absent and what holonomic processes are not working. The theory specifies which principles are likely to be in violation. The resulting diagnosis can then be used to improve the organization. In many cases, the organization is in such bad shape that it will take an organizational redesign to get it back on track.

It should be noted that the holonomic cube only exhibits the direct relationships among the holonomic processes and the desired organizational characteristics. All are indirectly interdependent because of the underlying principles, propositions, and definitions. If the Best Decision Principle is violated, for example, none of the six DOCs will be present throughout the organization. It is this property of interdependence that permits one to move freely from a preliminary diagnosis of the organization using the holonomic cube to a deep investigation of the reasons. Once the reasons are understood and the implications are clear, a program to improve the organization can be planned using the full theory. Generally, if any holonomic process is not working there will be problems with the rest.

Four Macro-Organizational Principles

There is a holonomic cube for the entire organization and there are holonomic cubes for each division, department, and subunit. Furthermore, any combination of units working together can be thought of as operating in a holonomic cube for their combined operations. What one searches for is consistency — up and down the organization and laterally among units — in every holonomic process. If HP1 (establishing and maintaining clear strategic direction) is working for the organization as a whole,

Figure 11.4. Constructing a Holonomic Cube.

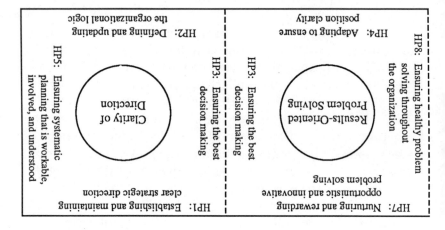

Figure 11.4. Constructing a Holonomic Cube, Cont'd.

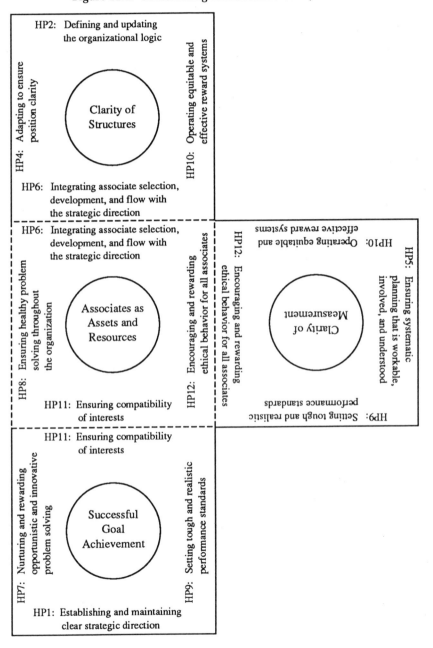

Figure 11.5. Embedded Holonomic Cubes.

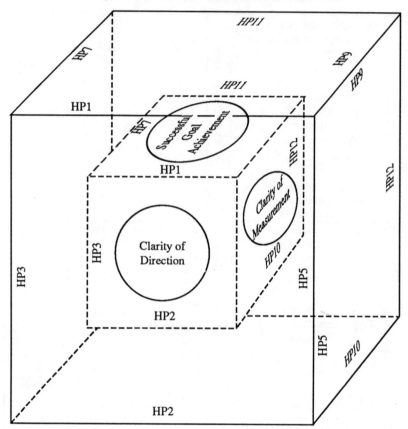

for example, it should also be working and consistent with the subordinate divisions and, in turn, the subunits. This gives rise to the notion of an *embedded* holonomic process to capture the idea that the holonomic cube for a unit is a special case of the same holonomic process of the whole. Figure 11.5 illustrates the concept of embedded holonomic cubes.

This idea of an embedded set of holonomic processes is summarized in Principle 21:

Principle 21:   The Holonomic Cube Principle states that the holonomic cube for each unit should be consistent with the holonomic cube for all units with which it is interdependent for the organization to be efficiently adaptive.

The next macro-organizational principle concerns the organizational hologram:

Principle 22:   The Principle of the Organizational Hologram states that the twelve holonomic processes supporting the holonomic cube must operate at every level, in every unit, and for every associate in the efficiently adaptable organization.

Related to these principles is Principle 23, which is needed to ensure that the holonomic processes are working:

Principle 23:   The New Associate Principle states that it is the right and responsibility of every associate to ensure the operation of the twelve holonomic principles in his or her own actions, those of his or her unit, and the entire organization in order to maintain efficient adaptability.

When the New Associate Principle is alive and well, there is little need for elaborate controls and rules. There is more need for active participation. It also generates an unusual system of sanctions imposed on those violating the holonomic processes. The New Associate Principle has no chance if the senior associates fail to comply. Since violations by senior associates are deemed intentional, the more senior the associate, the swifter the sanctions imposed when the principle is violated.

The last macro-organizational principle is the Congruency Enhancement Principle:

Principle 24:   The Congruency Enhancement Principle states that achievement of combined congruency depends upon the consistent and continual operation of the twelve holonomic processes.

Figure 11.6. Summary of Major Conclusions.

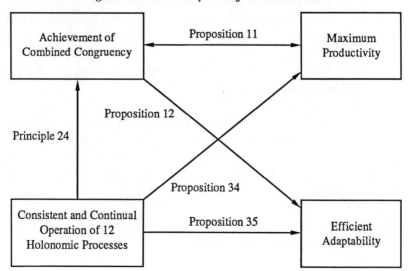

Two other propositions deserve special mention here because they involve the twelve holonomic processes. These are:

Proposition 34: The achievement of the twelve holonomic processes leads to maximum productivity.
Proposition 35: The achievement of the twelve holonomic processes leads to the efficient adaptability of the organization.

Figure 11.6 illustrates the interrelationships among combined congruency, consistent and continual operation of the twelve holonomic processes, the achievement of maximum productivity, and efficient adaptability. The propositions and principles involved in the direction of the arrows are labeled for quick reference. Figure 11.6 unites the means of the twelve holonomic processes and the attainment of combined congruency with the desired properties of maximum productivity and efficient adaptability.

The Competitive Organization

Michael Porter (1980) describes five competitive forces that must be considered in developing a company strategy. The first is the competitive rivalry among existing competitors. The second is the threat of new entrants to the industry. The third is that suppliers can become competitors; the fourth is that customers can become competitors. Lastly, there is the prospect of technological substitutes for one's products and services that can change the conditions of competition. Porter then analyzes how these five forces work in different circumstances in order to define strategies for coping with competition. In today's markets, it is likely that all five forces are present and that these forces are becoming more intense.

There are, of course, other environmental changes with which an organization must contend in order to survive and prosper. One of these is the rate of technological change. Others include government regulations and changes in economic conditions such as shifts in interest rates, effects of new tax legislation, and the value of the U.S. dollar on international markets. Social and political changes can buffet an organization, as well. These changes, along with the competitive forces, have several main effects on organizations.

One of these effects is the reduced length of product and service life cycles. It is not uncommon in some industries to have product life cycles that last less than a year. Another effect of these environmental changes is the reduced stability of the relevant organizational environments, which leads to the requirement that organizations become efficiently adaptive. As well, there are changes in the distribution and mix of the individual skills the organization needs to manage its adaptations. Another effect is the greater uncertainty in goals and in the cause-and-effect relationships in one's strategic thinking.

Given the bewildering pace and variety of organizational change, a new way of thinking is required. Namely, competitive firms must learn to become simultaneously more productive, adaptable, and efficiently adaptable. In essence, the key to becoming more competitive is to operate organizations as if they were organizational holograms. The theory of the organizational hologram is one of managing the change processes throughout the organization in a consistent and continual effort to achieve the twelve holonomic processes. And when one does, the results are combined congruency, efficient adaptability, and maximum productivity.

References

Kilmann, R. H. *Beyond the Quick Fix: Managing Five Tracks to Organizational Success.* San Francisco: Jossey-Bass, 1984.

Kilmann, R. H., Covin, T. J., and Associates. *Corporate Transformation: Revitalizing Organizations for a Competitive World.* San Francisco: Jossey-Bass, 1988.

Kilmann, R. H., Saxton, M. J., Serpa, R., and Associates. *Gaining Control of the Corporate Culture.* San Francisco: Jossey-Bass, 1985.

Kilmann, R. H., and others (eds.). *Producing Useful Knowledge for Organizations.* New York: Praeger, 1983.

Mackenzie, K. D. *Organizational Design: The Organizational Audit and Analysis Technology.* Norwood, N.J.: Ablex, 1986.

Mackenzie, K. D., and Holder, G. W. *The Organizational Hologram: The Effective Management of Organizational Change.* Boston: Kluwer Academic, 1990.

Morgan, G. *Images of Organizations.* Newbury Park, Calif.: Sage, 1986.

Morgan, G., and Ramirez, R. "Action Learning: A Holographic Metaphor for Guiding Social Change." *Human Relations*, 1984, *37*, 1–28.

Porter, M. *Competitive Strategy: Techniques for Analyzing Industries and Competitors.* New York: Free Press, 1980.

Pribram, K. *Languages of the Brain.* Englewood Cliffs, N.J.: Prentice-Hall, 1971.

12

IMPROVING GOAL–SETTING PROCESSES

PETER HESS

A t a meeting of the Eastern Academy of Management several years ago, a group of us heard Hicks Waldron, then president and CEO of Heublein, Inc., tell the story of what he termed one of the most remarkable turnarounds in U.S. business history. He described how Heublein's Kentucky Fried Chicken group, plagued in the late 1970s by discontent among its franchisers, declining sales, old facilities, and falling profits, was transformed into a leader in the fast food industry. The key to the turnaround, according to Waldron, was setting goals and establishing performance standards in each of the areas regarded as critical for success in that industry—from service, quality, cleanliness, and value to facilities, advertising, marketing, and staffing; from inventory and cost control to franchise relations.

Recently we were working with a group of management trainees from a twenty-two-unit regional retail food store chain. At a point in the program where we were introducing the concept of goals as a powerful means for enhancing productivity, we asked this group—all of whom had been assistant store managers and with the chain for ten years or longer—what quality standards the chain had developed to guide the performance of store managers. They looked at each other and then at us: "Standards?"

We told them Waldron's story about the turnaround of Kentucky Fried Chicken. Then we asked them again what goals or standards their chain had developed in the areas of service,

265

for example, or cleanliness. Their basis response was that there were no standards, really, in terms of service or cleanliness or any of the other areas they were responsible for. Basically, they explained, store managers are just expected "to do the best they can." Different stores had different standards—or none—depending on the store manager.

Now it was our turn to look at one another. Maybe we were so familiar with the textbook examples of goal setting in organizations—Kentucky Fried Chicken, for example, or Emery Air Freight—that we just assumed goal setting had become common managerial practice. Or maybe we assumed that the uniform image that even medium-sized corporations develop through their marketing activities would somehow translate into uniform standards of performance in operational areas. Or maybe we had become so convinced of the power of well-defined goals and performance standards that we just could not believe that an apparently well-managed business had not developed any.

For whatever reason, we were surprised. But the more we thought about it, the more we realized that maybe we should not have been.

The Status of Goal Setting

Think about the most visible management strategies of the past few years. The emphasis has been on restructuring, downsizing, merging, and automation, all to cut costs, and on worker participation and employee involvement to enhance quality. There is some goal setting implicit in all of this, especially relative to reducing costs. But in all of these approaches, goals are clearly the ends rather than the means.

This is an important distinction. The goal setting I mean is not of the strategic variety. I am not talking about market share, profit margin, or rate of return. Clearly those goals are there, and have been, and will be for a good long time. The focus of this chapter, rather, is goal setting at the operational level. I am talking about work-unit targets and individual performance standards. These are the goals that seem to have worked so well for KFC and Emery Air Freight, and this is the level of goal setting that, it seems, has not been much discussed in the popular business media.

The Media, MBO, and Human Nature

Take a look at any of the mass-circulation business magazines. The coverage over the past several years has been of restructuring, automation, strategy, and, to a lesser extent, leadership, employee involvement, and culture. *In Search of Excellence*, the most widely read book on management during this period, discusses Caterpillar's commitment to "forty-eight hours parts service to anywhere in the world," Maytag's "ten years of trouble-free operation," and Frito-Lay's pursuit of a "99.5% service level." These are exactly what I mean by goals or performance standards, but Peters and Waterman (1982) call them values and speak of their power, not as goals, but as elements of belief systems that can drive the effective organization.

Blanchard and Johnson's (1982) *One Minute Manager*, the other business mega-best-seller, clearly is about goal setting. But it is also about reprimands and praise and actually has more to do with what might be termed "performance contracting" at the manager-subordinate level than with defining goals and performance standards (à la KFC) at the work-unit level.

Goal setting simply has not been discussed much in the press, at least not since Peter Drucker's management by objectives (MBO) quietly fell into disuse by the mid-1970s. It appears that the goal-based management systems at the work unit and individual employee level that Drucker suggested were just more work than most organizations were willing to put into them, at least below the middle-management level. Negotiating goals with individual subordinates appeared to be more trouble than it was worth. Most managers we talk to are so consumed with "putting out fires" and "crisis management" that the time and psychological energy necessary to work out performance goals with subordinates and work units just do not seem to be available.

As we have also learned from our experience with MBO,

there appears to be another subtle yet persistent source of resistance to developing goals and performance standards for a work unit. S. Bruce Smart, CEO of the Continental Group, offers this insight in the foreword to Locke and Latham's (1984a, p. vi) *Goal Setting: A Motivational Technique That Works!*:

> Some American managers find it subliminally un-
> settling to set performance goals for others. As
> schoolchildren many of us were taught the values of
> self-reliance and encouraged to hitch our wagons
> to a star. Striving to meet personal goals has been a
> recurring theme for American entrepreneurs, folk
> heroes, and sports stars. But we have never been
> particularly comfortable in setting goals for others.
> There is something in our national psyche that
> views goal setting for subordinates and colleagues
> as vaguely dictatorial and stifling to their own sense
> of initiative and direction.

We share Smart's experience: There does appear to be a culture-based resistance to setting goals and performance standards for others.

The more we thought about it, the more it made sense to us that a foodstore chain—a relatively young organization still headed by its entrepreneurial founders, neither of whom had received any formal management training—might not have developed goals and performance standards as a powerful means for enhancing managers' performance: Goals and performance standards have not been much in evidence in the popular management press and media during the past decade or so; the limitations and difficulties of an MBO approach to management have been fairly widely experienced; and there does appear to be a persistent, culture-based resistance to "imposing" goals and standards on others.

The Question

But this did not settle the question for us. Actually, it suggested a larger question. We went from wondering how a young but nevertheless substantial organization could have overlooked the benefits to be derived from developing goals and performance standards to wondering to what extent goals and performance standards have been adopted as an important productivity enhancement strategy by American organizations in general.

To answer this question, we arranged interviews with managers from a variety of major businesses with facilities in New England. We selected the organizations because they are in some limited way representative of several major business sectors: financial services, production/manufacturing, medical/health services, and convenience food/restaurant. In many cases the person we spoke with was one of the highest-ranking managers at that facility. In other instances we spoke with lower-ranking managers whom we knew well. In every instance, we had confidence that the person with whom we were speaking could respond to us both with candor and with some authority. An appendix at the end of the chapter describes the organizations covered in our survey.

While our initial purpose was clearly to gain some sense of just how widely goal setting is being used, we discovered fairly early in the interview phase that these companies had already begun to accumulate extensive experience with setting goals and performance standards—and with the consequences of these processes. As much as anything else, then, this chapter is a report on the level of development of goal setting in a sample of fairly typical American organizations and what one might learn from their experience.

Report from the Field

I must repeat that we were not interested in strategic goals or corporate financial performance standards. As noted earlier, these goals and standards are already in place—primarily because they work (Rue and Holland, 1986). Nor were we interested in the incentive-focused goals traditionally associated with management and sales positions. The focus of our concern was human resources and whether the use of goals and performance standards had spread to the operational levels of the organization as part of the effort to enhance individual and work-unit productivity. Had organizations recognized the potential benefit of generalizing from the strategic to the operational the process of setting specific goals and performance standards? The response from our survey: They had not before, but they certainly do now.

Only one of the companies we spoke with, Company B, reported a long-standing practice of goal setting and performance standards in both the strategic and operational domains, extending from executive management to front-line positions. Each of the other nine organizations, though to varying degrees that we will discuss, report two things: First, before 1980 there was little concern for work-unit and individual goals or performance standards; second, things certainly have changed.

InsurCo A, for example, described how it has always had some sense of strategic plan, financial goals, and performance standards for the corporation, as well as a quota system for its sales activities. But now, for the first time, the company is beginning to formalize its strategic planning process to allow it to link, through "a modified MBO format," its managers' unit and developmental goals to the strategic goals of the corporation.

InsurCo B is even further along in the process. The company has had a long-standing, target-based executive management incentive plan, but that plan touches only perhaps 2 percent of more than 32,000 employees. This year, after three years of development, a standards-based "Performance Management and Appraisal System" has been introduced, extending from the lowest-level job classification to the level just below the position of full director, where an executive performance incentive program is already in place. The focus of this system is on identifying and prioritizing individual responsibilities and objectives and on establishing specific measurement standards to determine results, rather than relying on employee ratings. Obviously the possibility of negotiating objectives and standards increases as you move up in the organization. The significant fact here is that in an organization where 98 percent of the employees previously had been expected basically to "do their best," now there will be agreed-upon objectives and performance standards from the mailroom to the executive offices.

Company A has abandoned the annual-checklist-with-comments approach to rating front-line supervisors and now uses a quarterly review of seven weighted areas of supervisor responsibility: safety, communication, quality, technical competence/progress, production, leadership, and problem solving. Most important under the new system, each area is defined by specific performance standards. Safety, for example, was always one of the rated dimensions of supervisory performance. But the ratings were always global—unacceptable, poor, fair, good, excellent—with room for optional comments by the rater. Under the new system, safety is defined in terms of number of accidents, enforcement of rules and procedures as reflected in disciplinary actions, attitude, communication as reflected in the quality and content of follow-up reports, and housekeeping (both ongoing and special projects).

Bank A, in a effort to shift service into a production mode, has developed, over the past several years, quality-related performance standards such as the number of customer service calls answered within three rings (or the number abandoned), the number of statements mailed within three days of the end of the billing cycle (or the number mailed in error), average time waiting in line, and so on. While the focus of these standards is more problem resolution than direct performance enhancement, it can certainly be argued that the resolution of performance problems is a form of performance enhancement. Nor are service standards the only application of goal setting at Bank A: During the past year alone some $300,000 was paid directly to individual front-line branch personnel for achieving or exceeding target numbers of new accounts and cross-selling additional services to existing accounts.

Bank B's performance planning and appraisal system for its exempt employees is now entirely goal-based: There is nothing on the form but spaces for goal statements and assessments of results. Branches are visited monthly by a "mystery customer" who rates the service provided by the branch on a forty-five-point scale of performance standards, and results are quickly fed back to the branch manager. Account or portfolio managers set goals and report monthly on new business generated, transactions with existing customers, and "activities" for the generation of new business or the expansion of existing accounts. Bank B also awards incentive dollars to branches achieving or exceeding targets in terms of the sale of specific products. Unlike Bank A, however, Bank B awards the bonus to the manager, who then allocates 70 percent of the total to the other branch personnel.

Convenience Stores Inc. has its area supervisors develop ninety-day goals with each store manager or operator and meet twice monthly with the director of operations and the director of human resources. These meetings are not to assess progress, however, but to refine the supervisor's own goal-setting skills. Focus for the goal setting emerges from a twenty-item "store development checklist" of key areas of store performance. Performance standards have so far been carefully articulated only for the most critical areas—for example, shrink control, for which sixteen specific performance standards are listed for review by the supervisor and the manager/operator. For the other areas on the checklist, regional supervisors and store managers are expected to set their own goals.

Coffee Shops has developed extensive performance standards, both for managers-in-training and for waiters and waitresses. Standards for managers-in-training are clustered in three performance areas: technical skills, leadership/interpersonal skills, and management skills. Specific competencies in each are carefully articulated. For waiters and waitresses, for example, standards are grouped at three levels of performance: sixteen specific performance standards defining the completion of training, thirteen defining satisfactory performance, and an additional four standards defining above-average performance. Achievement of each successive level is recognized by a distinctive employee name badge.

Both of the health care institutions we spoke with were until recently insulated by the state's regulatory apparatus from the competitive pressures felt elsewhere in the country by similar institutions. In both institutions the initial response to the newly competitive environment has been to restructure to meet

competitive threats and opportunities. At one of the institutions, this process has now moved to the stage of more carefully
articulating general strategic directions. In the other institution,
strategic goals have already been fully articulated and performance indexes have been established for each of the system's
major businesses: hospital care, long-term care, and human
services. The emphasis there is on the development of a systemwide database to follow the operating results. Only now do both
institutions report an increasing concern with setting corporate
goals and performance standards, and only at the strategic
rather than the operational level. Both institutions recognize
that similar institutions in the rest of the country are well ahead
of them in creating goal-based management systems, but both
are convinced that the steps necessary to create those systems
cannot be skipped or hurried.

Of the ten organizations we interviewed, only Company B
did not report the emphasis on goal setting and the development of performance standards at the operational level as a
recent phenomenon. Indeed, Company B developed customer
service standards more than fifteen years ago. Order fill rates,
for example, are followed and monitored for timeliness and
completeness. Customers are surveyed regularly to ensure that
products and service are rated "better than average." There are
engineered work standards for both quality and quantity for
groups and for individuals. Performance is measured hourly in
many cases, and feedback is immediate.

Are organizations using goals and performance standards to increase the performance of work units and individuals? The answer from the organizations we interviewed was
either an emphatic yes or (in the case of the health systems) "We
aren't there yet, but we certainly intend to be." Our next question
was *Why*. Why this fairly sudden, wide-scale move to goal-based
management systems? The answers we received, either directly
or indirectly, all point in the same direction: the competitive
environment.

Understanding the Move to Goal-Based Systems

In the course of our discussions it became clear that for nine of
the ten organizations we interviewed, the emphasis on setting

goals and developing performance standards has come mostly during the past four or five years. Company B said that its emphasis on goals and standards has been there "forever" because it works. When we talked with the other nine about this new emphasis, we heard different explanations. But they all pointed to the recent emergence of a more highly competitive business environment.

The banks talked about deregulation and the emergence of the superregional banks with the huge resources they now bring to the competitive arena. The insurance companies talked about the unacceptability of the old inefficiencies and the need to focus on results rather than mere survival in the emerging marketplace. Company A pointed to foreign competition as the impetus. Both health care systems spoke about having to respond to market forces rather than "gaming" the regulatory apparatus of state government. For Coffee Shops Company the trigger was a regional labor shortage that required significant increases in the efficiency of available workers if the company was going to remain competitive.

While the increased competitive demands of the 1980s appear to be the major lever lifting goal-based systems onto organizations' agendas, there are other factors as well. One is technology. Defining standards used to mean engineered standards, suspect data collection, and irregular feedback. Computer-based information technology has made it logistically and economically possible to develop performance standards based on cumulative data rather than on time and motion studies and, as well, to monitor individual and group performance to permit timely feedback and recognition of achievement.

The third factor mentioned in explaining the recent emphasis on goals and performance standards seems to be a perception that management based on goals and performance standards is better management. It is not clear where this perception originates, but it seems to come from professional managers who are hired or promoted by owners or executives who were not themselves trained in management. And once management systems in some organizations begin to reflect the perception that goals and standards yield better results, there is a ripple effect to other organizations. For whatever reason, the perception that goal-based management is better management appears to have taken root and to be growing.

Convenience Stores, for example, has been much less concerned with competitiveness than with developing the capability required to manage its explosive growth. Its leaders are as much in the management development business as they are in the convenience store business. So convinced are they that goal setting is the critical managerial skill that, as noted earlier, the focus of the corporate involvement with area supervisors is almost entirely on the development and refinement of their ability to set goals with store managers/operators. Rightly or wrongly, Convenience Stores appears to assume that if goals are effectively set, the quality of management will be improved sufficiently to ensure the desired level of performance.

InsurCo B appears also to be focused more on management issues than on environmental demands. For quite some time now, InsurCo B has had at least a nominal form of performance-based compensation. In reality, managers were not distinguishing among levels of performance that are necessary to make such a system meaningful. It was felt that one of the significant reasons managers were not making such distinctions was that performance standards were either soft or nonexistent. Rather than having to justify significant differences in performance ratings to employees, managers tended to restrict ratings within a narrow range. The obvious consequence was that the high-level performer received little more of a raise than a low-level performer—effectively reducing to near zero the credibility of the "pay for performance" system.

In response to this essentially internal problem, InsurCo B developed and implemented the "performance management and appraisal system" described earlier. Managers and supervisors at every level of the organization are required to identify, with employees, each individual's job responsibilities and work objectives as well as the standards used to measure performance. The system is now in only its first cycle, but initial results indicate broader ranges of performance ratings within work groups. Managers seem able to make sharper distinctions when the system itself provides justification and support for the distinctions. Performance can now be considered not just in the context of the manager's personal perceptions, but in the context of the objectives and performance standards that themselves provide feedback.

The reasons for the fairly sudden move to goal-based management systems? First, the competitive environment is demanding better results and more effective management in every industry. Second, goals and performance standards appear to be viewed as an effective means to both these ends.

Lessons Learned

Once it became clear to us that goal-based management systems were actually happening on a broad scale, we shifted the focus of our interviews to find out what might be learned about goal setting from these organizations' recent experience. What problems, for example, have been encountered in the move to goal-based management? In fact, there have been problems. And along with the problems have come some interesting solutions, or at least attempted solutions. Just as interesting, many of the problems associated with goal setting had to do with the work group manager.

Problems with Managers

Company A very quickly discovered that using the plant manager as rater was the biggest barrier to its standards-based evaluation of front-line supervisor's performance. One concern was that not all of the standards permitted objective verification — the "quality and content" of safety-related written communications. The concern was with both positive and negative rater bias. The organization's solution to this problem was to create a set of performance standards governing the manager's evaluation of supervisors. Managers are now required to document the frequency and types of interaction with each supervisor that are reflected in the particular evaluation and to support their assessments with anecdotes or "critical incidents."

Another concern was that some plant managers view the system as evaluative rather than developmental in its emphasis and therefore tend to avoid it. As a result, supervisors were not receiving the level of feedback intended by the organization. For this reason, as noted earlier, performance reviews at Company A are now conducted quarterly rather than annually. In a similar vein, one of the executives described his experience when he was with a national food store chain. There it was noted that many managers tended to provide a far less complete set of goal statements and performance-related comments for the supervisors they rated critically. The chain's position was that weak supervisors need more goal-driven direction, not less, and told its managers that goal statements for all supervisors should be explicit regardless of the person's performance rating.

It is ironic that the effectiveness of goal-based management systems appears to require goals for managerial performance relative to the goal-setting function itself. But each of these cases reminds us that managerial performance, no less than performance at any other level of the organization, benefits from the clear direction that goals and standards provide.

Problems with Measurability

In goal setting there is often concern that certain areas of performance and certain kinds of tasks do not lend themselves to performance standards. InsurCo A, for example, indicated that it may not be able to identify individual performance standards in its claims processing units because there is so much variation in terms of the degree of activity a given claim might require for processing. When InsurCo B was confronted with this problem, it assigned the work group in question responsibility for developing specific standards measuring individual performance in that area. The results of that assignment are not yet available.

From a slightly different direction, Company A, even though most of its standards relate to observable performance, still has listed under the safety dimension something called "attitude." The feeling is that even though attitude cannot be directly observed, it is so critical to the safety dimension that it should be included anyway. Yet is not attitude usually something attributed to someone based on that person's behavior? Rather than asking for an assessment of a supervisor's "attitude" and leaving the interpretation up to the rater, the InsurCo B model might be used—that is, plant managers and supervisors together establish performance indexes that allow the assessment of attitude based on specific kinds of behavior.

Problems with Equity

A third kind of problem arises when incentive compensation is available to some groups in the organization and not to others performing different tasks but at a comparable level. Banks, as noted earlier, cite the increasing practice of awarding bonuses to branch personnel who meet or exceed targets in terms of new accounts or cross-selling services to existing accounts. No similar program is available to personnel working in the account services or operations areas. One bank reports that there have been no complaints so far regarding equity. People working "in the back room," this bank says, have the opportunity to move to the front end of the business whenever they want. The other bank has created an appreciation program, including rallies at which branch personnel recognize the contributions of the people behind the scenes. Both banks continue to monitor this potential problem, but neither thinks it will reduce the effectiveness of its goal-based incentive programs.

It is a problem worth monitoring. InsurCo B reports that gainsharing programs are being experimented with in several of its claims processing and policy services areas. And the health care systems—who monitor banking, the airlines, and other deregulated industries for hints about the future of their own industry—say, with tongue only slightly in cheek, that if banking is doing it now, health care will be doing it within three years.

Differential systems of compensation are nothing new to organizations. Executive management and sales personnel have operated under different systems from the rank and file for years. But the differences are perhaps easier to justify when there are perceptible differences in terms of responsibility, as with executive management, or in terms of the task, as with outside sales personnel. As these differences begin to diminish, as jobs included in incentive compensation programs begin to look more and more like the kind of jobs not included, the potential for dissatisfaction increases among workers in the excluded jobs. As this pattern of differential systems of compensation expands, so too does the potential for perceived inequity.

The Question of Monetary Incentives

The problem of differential compensation systems would not exist, of course, if the assumption did not also exist that goals, performance standards, and the subsequent feedback are not of themselves sufficient to ensure high-level performance. The tacit assumption is that sufficient performance improvements are possible only when goals and standards are combined with monetary incentives. This is an assumption with which neither Company B nor the Coffee Shops would agree.

Company B's experience has been that when goals and standards are clearly communicated, when performance is continuously monitored and results are rapidly fed back, goals and standards are achieved. There is no payout at Company B other than an occasional round of free coffee or having your name thrown in a lottery for gift certificates for dinner or the movies. Company B's experience has been: "People like to set records, they like to do better than yesterday."

The experience at Coffee Shops apparently is similar. The payoff for a waiter or waitress achieving the next level of performance standards is a name badge reflecting the achievement. No bonus, no raise, just a name badge that reflects your achievement. Does it work? The purpose of the standards-based program was to increase efficiency and reduce turnover in the face of extremely tight labor market conditions. Efficiency and turnover were monitored as the program was brought on line. The turnover reduction targets were met and continue to be met.

There is also the case of Emery Air Freight, which dramatically increased performance in terms of shipping container utilization, response time for customer inquiries, and on-ground delivery with a program consisting of nothing more than identification of a performance standard, continuous monitoring and feedback, and nonmonetary forms of positive reinforcement. These signs of recognition included, among other things, statements of appreciation and involving the worker in task-related decisions.

In fact, in one of the earliest field experiments on goal setting, conducted by Gary Latham in the wood products industry beginning in the late 1960s, logging supervisors were given the task of increasing their crews' productivity by setting production goals with no additional financial resources. The result was a significant increase in productivity compared with crews whose only instructions were "do your best" (Locke and Latham, 1984a). A similar goal-setting experiment, this time with logging truckers, also involving no financial incentive, targeted increasing the percentage of each load's utilization of the truck's capacity. Again the result was a significant increase in performance, this time with a documented nine-month savings of $250,000 — money the company would have had to spend on additional trucks to deliver the same quantity of logs to the mill. Locke and Latham (1984a) note that this figure does not include the cost of additional diesel fuel, registration, insurance, or maintenance or the cost of recruiting, training, and paying additional drivers. They also note that by 1984 this improved level of performance had been sustained for over eight years (p. 124).

In light of all this it is interesting that the financial services organizations seem to have moved so quickly to a system of goals plus monetary incentives. This suggests, at least implicitly, a basic belief that goal-based management cannot pay off without a payout. Actually, Locke and Latham (1984a, p. 116) admit that monetary incentives may be necessary, especially when:

- The employee is being asked to show a substantial increase in performance that necessitates working substantially harder than in the past.
- The job requires an unusual degree of initiative.

- The employees take little pleasure in achievement for its own sake.

They cite research to support their position. Their review of sixty studies of the effect of various motivation techniques on performance has produced the following results (1984a, p. 117):

Motivation	Median Improvement in Performance
Money plus individual incentives	30%
Money plus group incentives	20%
Goal setting	16%
Job enrichment	9%
Participation	0.5%

But the question here is not whether goals and monetary incentives result in greater improvements in performance than goal setting alone. The question is whether organizations are pushing themselves hard enough to understand just what gains are possible when goals are combined with nonmonetary incentives such as recognition and the opportunity for self-management. The question is this: Are we conceding too quickly the need for money in the performance improvement equation, rather than exploring what might be accomplished by some alternative — though admittedly less tested — combination of goals and incentives? The New United Motor Manufacturing, Inc. (NUMMI), a joint effort by General Motors and Toyota, represents one organization's commitment to testing an alternative combination.

Testing the Alternatives

NUMMI produces Chevy Novas at the rate of sixty cars an hour — about the average for American automobile assembly plants. But NUMMI is doing it with one-third fewer workers. At NUMMI workers are being required to "show a substantial increase in performance" and to work "substantially harder than in the past"—two of the conditions that Locke and Latham suggest might necessitate monetary incentives. At NUMMI, there are none. Wages are only average for the industry. The incentives for workers have been increased job security and increased involvement in problem solving and self-management.

Some observers question whether these incentives will be sufficient if jobs in the industry ever become more plentiful again; but in a very real sense, NUMMI is testing the potential of alternative, nonmonetary incentives to effect significant increases in performance. NUMMI is not alone. Tom Peters (1988) reports that NUMMI, along with the WIX Division of $4.75 billion Dana Corporation and Harley-Davidson, is typical of a growing number of companies experimenting with performance improvement programs fueled not by monetary incentives but by the satisfaction of becoming self-managing.

It is reassuring to conclude that the two banks studied here are not typical in their apparently direct move to monetary incentives. It is also interesting to note that these banks have not yet experienced the pressures of international competition. If only for this reason, they might do well to follow the lead of companies, like those just mentioned, who have. Organizations in the government and not-for-profit sectors should be even more concerned. Lacking, in most cases, the kind of resources necessary for monetary incentives, hospitals, schools, and state, local, and federal governments increasingly must rely on their ability to leverage improved performance by means of nonmonetary incentives.

The Stress Factor

There is another question that the experiment at NUMMI raises: At which point do goals become counterproductive? Can goals, rather than serving as a source of improved performance, become instead a source of fatigue or performance-sapping stress that can lead to burnout? The NUMMI experiment carries a significant downside in this regard. Daniel Forbes (1987, p. 36) reports: "The excitement of the early days is gone for many NUMMI workers. Fewer and fewer team members arrive early at the plant to maintain their equipment. . . , and voluntary meetings are not as common as they were. . . . 'Here (comments one NUMMI worker) you come in tired and you go home tired. On weekends, it's all you can do to lie around the house.'"

While it should be pointed out that goals can in fact reduce stress by clarifying roles and performance expectations, the question remains: At what point do goals cause the counterproductive effect of stress? If the trends described here are typical, we can expect that the need to find some answers in this regard will steadily increase in urgency.

Imposed Goals Versus Participation

A final question relates to the relative effectiveness of goal setting "from above" versus participative goal setting. There are obvious advantages to assigning goals or performance standards—both in terms of the efficiency with which they can be developed and in their acceptability to management. There is also research done by Meyer, Kay, and French (1965) at General Electric in the 1960s that suggests that *whether* a goal is set, and whether it is accepted, are more important than how it is set. Locke and Latham (1984b), on the other hand, point out that participative or self-set goals may result in higher goals than the boss might have set—and higher goals tend to result in higher performance. Their overall conclusion, however, is that while participative goals may result in higher performance for this reason, "assigning goals is not ineffectual" (p. 14).

In a general sense, our study tends to confirm Locke and Latham's somewhat ambivalent conclusion. While a range of goal-setting approaches is represented in our sample, each of the organizations surveyed reported improved performance in the areas targeted by the goals. And while a more careful consideration of the relative effectiveness of assigned versus participative goals was clearly not part of our study, just as clearly the tremendous growth in goal-based management systems now

affords an unprecedented opportunity to increase our understanding of assigned versus participative goals.

Conclusion

If the organizations surveyed in our interviews are at all representative of trends elsewhere in the country, then goal setting for
improved performance at the operational level is alive and well
in American organizations. While restructuring, automation,
and employee involvement have been getting most of the press
as the key strategies for increasing competitiveness, goal-based
management systems have been quietly but dramatically altering the way companies manage individual and work-unit
performance.

The dimension of the change is nothing less than remarkable: front-line bank personnel with goal-based incentives, waiters and waitresses with elaborate performance standards, supervisors with standards for their performance reviews, operating
units with goals tied directly to the strategic goals of the organization. The scale of this transition to goal-based systems represents nothing less than a quiet revolution in organizational
management in America.

Yet this quiet revolution provides an opportunity for, even
requires, the continuing expansion of our understanding of the
problems that accompany the process of goal setting and the
conditions under which goal setting can most effectively improve performance. In an environment so sensitive to cost, we
cannot merely assume that monetary incentives represent a
necessary condition for the desired impact of goals on performance. Nor can we ignore the relation of goals and performance
standards to stress or the relative merits of assigned versus
participative goals. Alternative conditions are being tested in
the form of fully implemented systems in organizations all
around us. These systems and their outcomes should be monitored, assessed, and compared. This is not an academic exercise.
It is a task that can make a significant contribution to the ability
of American organizations not only to compete in the world

marketplace but to provide excellent health, education, and government services here at home.

Appendix: Organizations Interviewed

Production Co. A (Company A) is a local division of a *Fortune* 100 company, a manufacturer of art and fine printing papers, with annual sales exceeding $100 million.

Production Co. B (Company B) is a local division of a *Fortune* 100 multinational corporation specializing in personal care and household products and employing 400 workers locally.

Bank A is a $1.8 billion community bank, a regional unit of a superregional banking corporation.

Bank B is a $0.5 billion regional bank, a subsidiary of one of the fifteen largest superregional banks with international operations.

Insurance Co. A (InsurCo A) is a multi-line insurance and financial services company with more than 7,000 employees nationally.

Insurance Co. B (InsurCo B) is a $50 billion, multi-line insurance and financial services company with more than 30,000 employees nationally.

Health Care Systems A is a teaching hospital, one of the three or four largest medical centers in New England.

Health Care Systems B is a multi-institutional, multi-services health care system with facilities in New England and the South.

Coffee Shops Company is a division of a *Fortune* 100 company in the family restaurant/coffee shops segment of the food services industry with several hundred locations, mostly in the eastern United States.

Convenience Stores Inc. is one of the five largest convenience store chains in the nation, having grown from fewer than 100 locations in 1980 to nearly 1,200 in 1988.

References

Blanchard, K., and Johnson, S. *The One Minute Manager*. New York: Berkley Books, 1982.

Forbes, D. "The Lessons of NUMMI." *Business Month*, June 1987, pp. 34–37.

Locke, E. A., and Latham, G. P. *Goal Setting: A Motivational Technique That Works!* Englewood Cliffs, N.J.: Prentice-Hall, 1984a.

Locke, E. A., and Latham, G. P. *Goal Setting for Individuals, Groups, and Organizations*. Chicago: Science Research Associates, 1984b.

Meyer, H. H., Kay, E., and French, J.R.P., Jr. "Split Roles in Performance Appraisal." *Harvard Business Review*, 1965, *43*, 123–129.

Peters, T. J. "Big Bucks Not Enough to Raise Productivity." *Peters on Excellence* (nationally syndicated column), Oct. 17, 1988.

Peters, T. J., and Waterman, R. H., Jr. *In Search of Excellence: Lessons from America's Best-Run Companies*. New York: Harper & Row, 1982.

Rue, L. W., and Holland, P. G. *Strategic Management: Concepts and Experiences*. New York: McGraw-Hill, 1986.

13

IMPROVING DECISION-MAKING PROCESSES

CARL A. RODRIGUES

I mmediately following World War II, a large technology gap opened between the United States and other industrialized countries. This is no longer the situation. Firms from Europe and Japan now compete with U.S. manufacturers in the high-technology industries. In the mature industries, moreover, many U.S. firms now face fierce competition from manufacturers in less-developed countries, such as Taiwan and South Korea. In other words, many of the U.S. companies that were once global leaders have relinquished considerable command of markets to multinational competitors.

There are numerous reasons why intense international competition has evolved. One is that U.S. firms have for economic and other reasons transferred technologies to less-developed countries. The transfer has enabled firms in those nations to progress technologically and eventually to compete with firms from the advanced countries in global markets (see Rodrigues, 1987). Along with the evolution of multinational competition, another factor has contributed to America's declining competitive edge: the management–labor dichotomy existing in many U.S. enterprises. This is one reason why many U.S. managers have not been able to fully mobilize the know-how of their enterprise's work force. In fact, the historical unwillingness of U.S. managers to share power with employees has led to the formation of powerful labor unions. Growing ill will against unions in some U.S. production sectors has caused numerous firms to manufacture low-quality products at high cost—thus putting these firms at a disadvantage in competing with overseas manufacturers who produce high-quality products at low cost. On the other hand, Japanese managers have used participative management techniques to improve product quality and productivity, thus enhancing their firms' competitive edge in the global market. Yet another factor contributing to America's declining competitiveness is the dichotomy existing between the U.S. government and business. Whereas in Japan the role of government is to enhance Japanese business competitiveness in the global market, the role of the U.S. government has been one of control and regulation.

In light of the global changes, an important issue that needs to be addressed is how to improve the U.S. firms' competitive edge. There does not seem to be much doubt that, in order to improve their competitive edge in the global market, many U.S. firms must now transform themselves. Since the transformation may involve changes in the way many U.S. managers make and implement decisions, this chapter presents a conceptual model to assist U.S. managers in this respect. Basically the model—which is developed by describing the actors in organizations who have an impact on decisions—provides a guide that may be useful to managers in making and implementing effective decisions. The conclusion is that managers must in many situations apply the participative approach to decision making. Certainly the case of Japan illustrates how improved decision making has enhanced Japanese firms' competitiveness. Some U.S. companies, such as General Motors, Bank of America, Southern Bell, and Honeywell, are used as examples in developing the framework presented here.

Four Paradigms

Huber and McDaniel (1986) have described three fundamental paradigms that influence organizational decision making: the paternalistic/political paradigm, the accountability/authority paradigm, and the workflow paradigm. The main idea behind the paternalistic/political paradigm is that power-enhancing resources, such as authority and subordinates, are allocated to individuals who are likely to be loyal supporters because of family or political affiliation. This paradigm, which leads to defensive managers, would not be effective in organizations that require participative management for decision-making effectiveness. Participative decision making requires an environment of trust and openness between managers and subordinates.

Applying the accountability/authority paradigm involves designing an organization that specifies who is accountable for fulfilling which responsibilities and then allocates to those figures accountable authority adequate to enable them to meet their responsibilities. The power bases in this model are reward, punishment, and position. This approach often leads to the creation of bureaucratic organizations, which generally make mechanical decisions, develop a culture that resists change, and function mainly in a stable environment. Mechanistic organizations are not usually suited to a dynamic environment because frequent change is required. Organizations operating in a dynamic environment would be more effective if they applied a participative decision-making approach because it generally leads to employees accepting decisions more rapidly.

The workflow paradigm's major thrust is that the organization's structure and administrative processes are matched to its production processes and operations. The design of this type of organization places strong emphasis on the production of goods and services. Organizations operating in a dynamic environment, however, as we will see, need to place strong emphasis on the production of decisions.

As societies progress technologically, economically, politically, and socially, the most suitable decision-making paradigm generally changes. That is, environmental changes create the need for different paradigms. Many changes have taken place in the United States in the past two centuries. In the 1880s, the country shifted from an agrarian to an industrial economy. Now, along with several other societies, such as Japan and some Western European countries, the United States seems to be on the threshold of what has been labeled the postindustrial society. This society is characterized by rapid growth of the service sector, by enormous growth in the knowledge industry, by high levels of affluence, education, and leisure, by instability and uncertainty, by change becoming a way of life, and by the requirement for new organizational, political, and cultural values (Trist, 1970). In this society, traditional organizational forms will remain; traditional organizational politics, however, will diminish (Schick, 1971).

This new society will demand that organizational decision making be more frequent and faster. That is, it will "require consideration of more variables and more complex relationships among these variables" (Huber, 1984, p. 933). Decision making in the postindustrial society is likely to become a great deal more complex than it has been in the past. In light of the changes taking place in the United States, Huber and McDaniel propose a fourth paradigm: the decision-making paradigm. The main thrust of this paradigm is that (1) "organizations should be designed primarily to facilitate the making of organizational decisions and (2) the implied organizational effectiveness criterion is maximation of the quality (broadly defined, e.g., including timeliness) of organizational decisions" (Huber and McDaniel, 1986, p. 576).

This chapter builds on the fourth paradigm; it develops a framework to assist managers in making sound decisions and then implementing them. Fundamentally, I describe three levels of organizational decision making and use these levels to develop the framework. In the concluding section I discuss the conditions that must be present in order for the framework to apply.

Three Decision Models

According to Allison (1971), there are three kinds of decision models in organizations: the rational actor (or classical) model, the government (bureaucratic) politics model, and the organizational process model. The *rational* actor, given specific objectives, calculates the logical thing to do in that situation. In the U.S. automobile industry, for example, innovative production techniques, such as flexible-system or high-tech production, were proposed several years ago as a rational solution to meet rising foreign competition.

Political actors make decisions by bargaining and compromising among the players. The outcome of their decision is thus difficult to predict. There does not seem to be much doubt that political actors in the U.S. automobile industry, government, and unions have compromised rational decisions. Flexible-system production was not implemented immediately by U.S. car manufacturers, for example, and quotas on imports were established in order to protect the old automobile production system.

Organizational actors behave on the basis of organizational procedures and repertoires. The key basis for their decision is their frame of reference and accustomed behavior. A person's frame of reference determines how he or she reacts in a situation. Because they have become accustomed to a certain way of doing things, people normally resist change. The rational and political actors' decisions cannot therefore be implemented until the organizational actors' procedures and repertoires are changed—that is, until their frames of reference are changed. Since people become accustomed to working in a certain way, implementing flexible-system production in the U.S. automobile industry would naturally take a long time. General Motors (GM), for instance, has for several years been attempting to implement such a system to improve production.

Thus implementing change in the United States takes a long time. One reason for the slowness is that there is little harmony among the three organizational decision-making levels in the United States, where competitiveness in the global market has been steadily declining. Many U.S. managers simply make a decision and pass it on down—that is, they do not use a participative approach to decision making. As a result, decisions are often sabotaged or drastically modified by the lower levels.

In Japan, whose competitiveness in the global market has been steadily increasing, the three decision-making levels work in unison. There is close cooperation between government and industry and direct communication between them at all levels. Mutual decisions are reached relative to economic policies and planning. New programs are pursued by the government only after consensus has been reached within industry. Industrial views are represented on many government advisory councils and committees — thus enabling industry to be involved in government planning at the embryonic stages. Moreover, industrial managers and business executives maintain close contacts with government officials (Gee, 1981, p. 143).

Following World War II, Japan's environment changed: Unemployment arose, sources of materials declined, there were rapid changes in markets, and so on. Japan's rational actors recognized the problem and found a solution; they sought to restructure Japan's economy. They believed that the country's science and technology policy would have to be interwoven with its economic and industrial policies. Science and technology policy involves several government agencies, advisory councils, quasi-public corporations, and R & D laboratories. To some degree, every government ministry is involved in science and technology. The overall responsibility for science and technology rests in the Office of the Prime Minister. The Council of Science and Technology (CST) and the Science Council of Japan (SCJ) are located in the Office of the Prime Minister. This is the *rational* policy level. The function of CST is to carry out long-range science and technology planning and to review research projects in coordination with SCJ. The SCJ deals with science, the use of research, scientific education, and relations with industry. Both CST and SCJ make recommendations to the prime minister. Policy decisions are subsequently developed.

Underneath the policy level are the Science Technology Agency, the Ministry for International Trade and Industry, the Ministry of Finance, and other ministries. These are vehicles for the implementation of policy decisions. Within these ministries there are several components. Under the Ministry for International Trade and Industry, for example, there is the Agency of Industrial Science and Technology, the Agency for Small and Medium Enterprises, and the Patent Agency. The Agency of Industrial Science and Technology promotes industrial standardization for the purpose of improving mining and manufacturing products, modernizing production processes, and providing improved commercial services to the consumer (Gee, 1981, pp. 145–149).

To monitor the internal and external technological environment, the Japan Industrial Technology Association was formed. The purpose of this association is to promote the transfer of technology both domestically and internationally. This organization facilitates the exchange of technical information between the Agency of Industrial Science and Technology research laboratories and foreign countries. Normally it attempts to keep abreast of technological developments at home and abroad and facilitates the transfer of technical information and technology between the source and the potential user (Gee, 1981).

At the political level, Japan's private sector has a strong voice in shaping the government's science and technology policy. One of the many organizations representing business and industry is Keidanren, which was established in 1946 through the merger of several economic associations. In 1980, Keidanren had a membership of approximately a thousand firms and associations representing Japan's entire industrial, commercial, and financial sectors. Keidanren is representative of the organizational actor's level. It promotes interaction across industrial sectors. It also keeps a close contact with other trade and economic organizations such as the Japan Federation of Employers' Association and the Japan Chamber of Commerce. Keidanren has representatives on many government committees and advisory bodies. The rational actor's level generally solicits this organization's views in trying to reach a consensus on matters concerning policy planning and implementation (Gee, 1981, p. 151).

At the organizational level, many managers in Japan use a decision-making process known as the *"ringi."* The *ringi* system requires that everyone involved in the execution of a decision must have the opportunity to voice his or her views. During meetings, all issues are considered and everyone involved contributes to the discussion of options, facts, and the philosophy underlying the decision. Thus when a decision is reached, everyone knows what he or she must do. Because everyone has agreed to the decision, its execution can proceed quickly (Johnston, 1981, p. 16). In other words, people will accept change more readily.

In brief, Japan, whose firms are fierce rivals of U.S. firms in the global economy, has (1) an industrious and frugal people, (2) a labor–management relationship founded on consensus and participative management, (3) a framework for close government–industry cooperation, (4) a free-enterprise commitment that allows weak, noncompetitive firms to go out of business, (5) a heavy industrial R & D emphasis self-financed by industry in the main, (6) an unimpeded, bidirectional flow of technology across national borders, (7) the existence of linking organizations to expedite the transfer of technical information and technology, (8) a broad system of fiscal and regulatory incentives to stimulate all stages of innovation, and (9) special attention to small and medium-sized business enterprises (Gee, 1981, p. 159).

Essentially, then, Japanese upper-level, middle-level, and lower-level managers act in unison by linking the various government institutions, industry associations, and so forth to expedite the process of implementing innovation in Japan. By forming this link, change is implemented with less resistance than would be met in an authoritarian system. The next section develops a framework to aid U.S. managers in linking the three organizational decision-making levels so that sound decisions can be made in a participative fashion.

A Framework for Making Effective Decisions

In a broad sense, rational actors equate with what Katz and Kahn (1966, pp. 308–309) have labeled the institutional level of management, whose function is to monitor the internal and external environment and establish policies that align the two. Political actors' roles are similar to the roles Katz and Kahn described as being carried out by the administrative level of management, whose function is to interpolate structure or improvise — that is, to implement the policies and objectives in their respective subunits. And the organizational actors compare with what Katz and Kahn call the operational level of management, the level that uses the structure provided to keep the organization operating effectively.

It should be noted that in a macro perspective the institutional level is represented by the top-level managers in government, the administrative level is represented by top-level managers in the various industries, and the operational level is represented by the top-level managers of each organization within the various industries. In a micro perspective, however, institutional managers are represented by the top-level managers of the individual organization—for example, the board of directors, the president, and a few key executive vice-presidents; the administrative level is represented by middle-level managers—for example, the vice-president of marketing, vice-president of production, and vice-president of finance; the operational level is represented by the lower-level managers—that is, managers and supervisors responsible for carrying out day-to-day activities. Whether the perspective is micro or macro, all levels contain decision makers, and all decision makers are confronted with at least six problems (see Figure 13.1).

First, the rational solution must be determined. To help in this respect, decision makers, whether at the institutional, administrative, or operational level, must make sure that the rational solution has been determined. As Peter Drucker once stated, managers often apply the right solution to the wrong problem. That is, decision makers often treat symptoms as opposed to root causes. This means that effective decision makers must spend a great deal of time in search of the root causes.

Second, those responsible for facilitating the decision must be identified. A serious problem emerges here since organizations have both formal and informal facilitators—that is, those who implement or expedite the decision. The informal facilitators include those with expert power and charismatic power bases. Both the formal and informal facilitators, who often form powerful coalitions, can readily sabotage an organization's rational choices. When "vanguard" union actors resisted changes at GM, for example, many of GM's managers, rather than accept-

Figure 13.1. A Normative Model for Making and Implementing Decisions in Organizations.

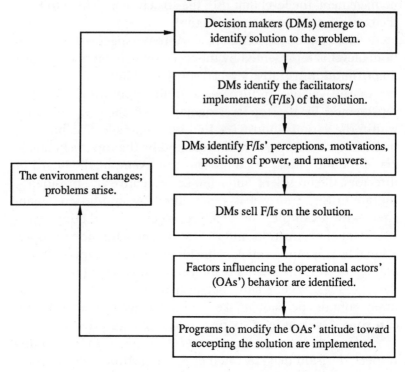

ing a new vision, decided to wait for "the good old days" to return (Hampton and Norman, 1987; Tichy and Ulrich, 1984).

There are several methods decision makers can use to help them identify the organization's informal facilitators (Rogers, 1983). Using the *sociometric* approach, people in the organization are asked who they would consult to get information about a specific idea. Those receiving the greatest number of sociometric choices are the informal leaders. Another approach is the *informants' rating.* Using this technique, key figures in the organization are asked who the leaders are. Another technique is the *self-designating method*—asking people in the system a series of questions to determine the degree to which they perceive themselves to be informal leaders. Yet another approach is *observations.* Using this method, people are observed unobtrusively and their communication behavior is recorded. A fifth technique is *awareness*. Using this approach, decision makers recognize that informal leaders evolve naturally in formal organizations and remain continuously aware of who these leaders are. This technique applies the cybernetic approach to organization. Applying the cybernetic approach to organization, the managers monitor the internal and external environments (Schick, 1971) and apply reactive and proactive solutions as required. The fifth method, because it is ongoing, may be more expensive to administer than the other four, but it enables decision makers to develop and implement changes more rapidly. Cybernetic organization is imperative for organizations operating in a dynamic environment.

Third, the facilitators' perceptions, positions, power, and maneuvers must be established. Some facilitators will readily support the decision, others will oppose it, and many will be middle-of-the-road — that is, they can easily be swayed one way or the other. In other words, the decision maker needs to know what motivates each of the facilitators so that he or she can appeal to individual motivators, the fourth problem.

Fourth, a program aimed at modifying the facilitators' perceptions of the rational choice must be developed and implemented. A problem here is the traditional conflict between the old guard and the new. There is also the problem of what Tichy and Ulrich (1984) label "indictment to change." That is, the facilitators are being asked to indict their own past behavior — the behavior that helped create the problems they are being asked to correct.

The program should provide the facilitators with training to handle technical and social tasks involved in innovation, and it must provide a reward system and career opportunities necessary to attract high-caliber people. The program's activities must also include structuring the production and implementation of specific technological innovations and allocating authority and responsibility for tasks and functions. In addition, the standard management functions of leadership, planning, and staffing are needed (Shrivastava, 1984).

In an effort to mobilize support for GM's new vision, Roger Smith took his top nine hundred executives on a five-day retreat where GM's new vision was explained and discussed. Lee Iacocca relied on his intuitive and directive leadership, philosophy, and style (Tichy and Ulrich, 1984). Bank of America established a program called the Management Forum to link all levels in order to generate support for its new vision. The program's objective was to provide tools to the top hundred executives by which they would link with others to generate support (Beck, 1987). The executives were given a leader's guide on how to administer sessions and how to make them two-way discussions pertaining to the factors that prevented Bank of America from achieving its goals. A major aim of the Management Forum was to build awareness and begin integrating that awareness throughout the enterprise.

In their efforts to obtain support for change, Honeywell launched an executive leadership program (Renier, 1987) and Southwestern Bell linked 55,000 employees and spouses in fifty-seven locations via satellite (Barnes, 1987). Honeywell's program involved holding a series of seven-day workshops at a conference center in southern Minnesota. The program was conducted by Professor Noel Tichy of the University of Michigan. At the workshop each participant was asked to tell two stories from the firm's past—one story illustrating a value worth saving and the other a value worth dropping. Teams were established to analyze current performance of key management tasks and to determine what changes would be required to create the culture Honeywell wanted. Then they were asked to scrutinize Honeywell's current culture and tie it to values and business strategy and then to project those values into the future by writing articles. Subsequently, each participant was asked to negotiate deals with two others to help them achieve their desired goals. The participants left the program "with a greater understanding of their own style, an appreciation of the need for teamwork, and strong commitment to the change process" (Renier, 1987, p. 49).

The objective of Southwestern Bell's program was to develop a viable outlet for AT&T's divestiture-related emotions. This was accomplished with "visible leadership, hard business information, and old fashioned fun through humor, music, and dance" (Barnes, 1987, p. 45).

Fifth, the procedures and repertoires that influence the operational actors' behavior must be identified. This too is a complex task. Basically, statements of organizational goals and fundamental purposes are explicitly described by statements of organizational strategies and policies. Organizational strategies and policies articulate frames of reference for sharing among operational actors. They also describe shared understanding about work procedures, performance evaluation criteria, and the reward structure in all functional areas. Organizational myths, stories, and rituals also help articulate the operational actors' frames of reference. These mechanical aspects tell them what is valued and give a detailed account of accepted interpretations of events (Shrivastava and Schneider, 1984).

Organizational frames of reference explain what occurs inside and outside the organization. Since they also influence the way events are perceived, categorized, and given meaning, they influence the way decisions are made and the way actions are generated. Ideologies, which are implicit frames of reference, tend to enhance the operational actor's commitment to the organization—but they may also become barriers to organizational change by deterring organizations from viewing threats clearly (Shrivastava and Schneider, 1984). In essence, the operational actors are often unaware of the decisions they make—their behavior is programmed.

Sixth, a program aimed at changing these procedures and repertoires in order to develop organizational behavior consistent with the rational choice must be developed and implemented. This means reorganizing to make use of the choice. GM, for example, has in recent years made several reorganization moves. Its Fremont venture is applying participative behavior (Hampton and Norman, 1987), which is a departure from its traditional military-like culture. GM's recent mergers are likely to import new myths, rituals, and ideologies that can help develop new frames of reference. GM's Fremont plant, which applies a measure of Japanese management behavior, is a good example of such a merger. Another example is GM's transfer of 10,000 data processing employees to the newly acquired Electronic Data Systems. These activities should cause changes in GM's culture.

According to Bennis (1969), the only way to change organizations is to change their culture—which is changed by altering the systems within which people live and work. By closing many of its old plants and establishing modernized ones, GM is to some degree changing the way people work. Tichy and Ulrich (1984) have proposed that in order to change their organizations, managers must alter their communication, decision-making, and problem-solving systems, and new visions must be shared throughout the organization.

It should be noted that the sequence outlined in Figure 13.1 may vary according to the situation. For example, decision makers may sometimes have to determine who the facilitators are and obtain their input relative to the rational choice. They may also have to obtain input from operational actors in order to determine the rational choice. In other words, participative management must often be applied. Normally managers should use input from others when the importance of the decision exceeds the cost of the participative process. Managers should bear in mind that when a problem is complex, many people would prefer to have someone else solve it. Thus simply involving them in a decision may suffice for its acceptance.

Cybernetic Organization, MBO, and Proactive Management

The preceding section described a reactive approach to change. It should be mentioned, however, that managers may now need to apply a proactive approach. Cybernetic organization (Schick, 1971) and management by objectives (Raia, 1974) are two techniques they can use in applying the proactive approach. Using cybernetic organization, institutional actors act as the organization's focal point—they monitor the external and internal environments, and when a problem or threat is foreseen they act to correct or avert it. General Electric, for example, uses the scanning approach quite effectively. GM seems to have been somewhat lacking in this respect for many years, as substantiated by its pattern of developing cars first and looking for customers later (Hampton and Norman, 1987).

Fundamentally, management by objectives ensures that

the various levels in the organization have a common direction. Goals at each level are to some extent tentative, subject to their development at the next lower level. The fact that many of GM's workers and managers say they are not listened to is an indication that these tools have not been fully utilized by GM's traditional subsystems. At its Fremont plant, where these tools are being more widely applied, GM has learned "that simply organizing work more efficiently and giving workers more say can produce more impressive results than millions of dollars worth of robots" (Hampton and Norman, 1987, p. 107).

Using these tools develops communication and collaboration among the various subunits. Basically, these are participative approaches to management. People throughout the organization are to some extent involved in the decision-making process — either in the initial decision, if the situation requires it, or in its implementation. If people are involved in making a decision that has an impact on them, they tend to accept the decision more readily — or at least they are less likely to resist it.

Southwestern Bell, Honeywell, and Bank of America have used these tools to bring about change. According to CEO Zane E. Barnes (1987), Southwestern Bell has stressed intrapreneurial behavior and participative management. Honeywell, according to CEO James J. Renier (1987), considers it important to reward desirable changes in behavior by managing participatively, establishing high standards for the quality of everyone's work life, and providing leadership. Lockheed has used quality circles to help it save millions of dollars in production costs (Lawler, 1986, p. 61), and Sears, Westinghouse, and IBM have used attitude surveys to anticipate and prevent employee dissatisfaction (Lawler, 1986, pp. 65–81).

Conclusion

This chapter has outlined a general framework that can help managers in making and implementing the decisions that will make their organizations more competitive in the ever-shifting global economy. The case of Japan illustrates the framework. One must recognize, of course, that the cultures of Japan and the

United States are very different and that what works in one will not readily work in the other. But one must also recognize that societies have always borrowed aspects of culture from each other. Thus it is not unrealistic to accept that what has worked in Japan could, with modifications, work in many U.S. institutions — especially those that must change. For there is no doubt that institutions must periodically change or die.

Many American managers have been reluctant to apply participative management — traditionally decisions have been made by the manager alone. As this study has attempted to demonstrate, participative management can be an important tool for assisting managers in making and implementing sound decisions. Participative management does have certain advantages. First, because of the diversity of input, good decisions can be made. Second, because many people were involved in the decision-making process, resistance to change can be mitigated. Third, an environment of trust, which is vital to an organization's effectiveness, can be developed. And fourth, because of the involvement and trust, an achievement orientation can be developed among the employees.

Participative management can be effective, however, only under the right circumstances (Filley, House, and Kerr, 1976). First, the manager must have the right skills. This means that the manager must be willing to share power with subordinates when the situation calls for it — as suggested earlier, this is imperative for organizational effectiveness in the dynamic global economy. Second, employees must have a favorable attitude toward participation. Some people have a need for dependence on the more powerful, and some do not want to participate — they prefer paternalistic leadership and structure. On the other hand, many people do want to be involved and these individuals, as McGregor (1960) proposed, will be more productive if they are given more responsibility. And third, the task to be performed must be complex, nonroutine, and above all challenging. By sharing power — that is, by transferring more responsibility to subordinates — managers can in many situations create challenging work for employees. The advent of the U.S. service industry and the introduction of robotic labor to perform many of the menial and structured jobs previously performed by humans can aid in this respect.

To improve their global competitiveness, many domestic firms will have to produce in foreign countries where labor and material costs are lower than in the United States and where, as a result of economic development programs, new markets have evolved. Making sound decisions in the dynamic global economy, as this chapter suggests, is a very complex task that will require the input of many minds. Making sound *cross-cultural* decisions will be far more complex. Application of the traditional top-down approach to decision making in cross-cultural settings is extremely difficult. For example, Theobold (1980) has proposed that people are having increasing problems as they come to realize that others have profoundly different visions of reality and there is no way of determining which vision is correct. Simon and Newell (1970) say that managers base their decisions on simplified rather than real situations and that "subjective rationality" narrows and alters the objective facts. The implication is that managers cannot effectively apply the top-down decision-making model and cannot make sound decisions in a global marketplace where different cultures perceive the world differently.

All this suggests that to make sound decisions managers must indeed use the input of others. Lacking the appropriate inputs, many U.S. managers continue to make costly and wrong-headed decisions (see Ricks, 1983) that in fact retard their firms' competitiveness. In conclusion, if U.S. managers want to make their organizations more competitive in the dynamic global economy, they will have to become more innovative — not only in the production of high-quality goods and services but in the application of high-quality decisions as well.

References

Allison, G. T. *The Essence of Decision: Explaining the Cuban Missile Crisis.* Boston: Little, Brown, 1971.

Barnes, Z. E. "Change in the Bell System." *Academy of Management Executive*, 1987, *1* (1), 43–46.

Beck, R. N. "Visions, Values, and Strategies: Changing Attitudes and Culture." *Academy of Management Executive*, 1987, *1* (1), 33–41.

Bennis, W. G. *Organization Development: Its Nature, Origins, and Prospects.* Reading, Mass.: Addison-Wesley, 1969.

Crane, D. F. "The Case for Participative Management." *Business Horizons*, 1976, *19*, 15–21.

Filley, A. C., House, R. J., and Kerr, S. *Managerial Process and Organization Behavior.* (2nd ed.) Glenview, Ill.: Scott, Foresman, 1976.

Gee, S. *Technology Transfer, Innovation and International Competitiveness.* New York: Wiley, 1981.

Hampton, W. J., and Norman, J. R. "General Motors: What Went Wrong." *Business Week*, Mar. 16, 1987, pp. 102–107.

Hofstede, G. "The Cultural Relativity of the Quality of Life Concept." *Academy of Management Review*, 1984, *9* (3), 389–398.

Huber, G. P. "The Nature of Design of Post-Industrial Organizations." *Management Science*, 1984, *30* (8), 928–951.

Huber, G. P., and McDaniel, R. R. "The Decision-Making Paradigm of Organization Design." *Management Science*, 1986, *32* (5), 572–589.

Johnston, J. "Ringi: Decision-Making Japanese Style." *Management Review*, 1981, *70*, 16.

Katz, D., and Kahn, R. L. *The Social Psychology of Organizations.* New York: Wiley, 1966.

Katz, D. "Skills of an Effective Administrator." *Harvard Business Review*, 1974, *52*, 93.

Lawler, E. E., III. *High-Involvement Management: Participative Strategies for Improving Organizational Performance.* San Francisco: Jossey-Bass, 1986.

McGregor, D. *The Human Side of Enterprise.* New York: McGraw-Hill, 1960.

Morley, J. W. *Prologue to the Future: The United States and Japan in the Postindustrial Age.* Lexington, Mass.: Lexington Books, 1974.

Raia, P. A. *Management by Objectives.* Glenview, Ill.: Scott, Foresman, 1974.

Renier, J. J. "Turnaround of Information Systems at Honeywell." *Academy of Management Executive*, 1987, *1* (1), 47–50.

Ricks, D. A. *Big Business Blunders: Mistakes in Multinational Marketing.* Homewood, Ill.: Dow Jones–Irwin, 1983.

Rodrigues, C. A. "Implementing New Technology: A Normative Approach." *Central State Business Review*, 1985a, *4* (1), 25–28.

Rodrigues, C. A. "A Process for Innovators in Developing Countries to Implement New Technology." *Columbia Journal of World Business*, 1985b, *20* (3), 21–28.

Rodrigues, C. A. "Product and Manufacturing Technology Transfer from Advanced to Less-Advanced Countries: Two Conceptual Models." In K. D. Bahn and M. J. Sirgy (eds.), *World Marketing Congress International Conference Series*. Barcelona: Academy of Marketing Sciences, 1987.

Rogers, E. V. *Diffusion of Innovation*. (3rd ed.) New York: Free Press, 1983.

Schick, A. T. "Toward a Cybernetic State." In D. Waldo (ed.), *Public Administration in a Time of Turbulence*. New York: Chandler, 1971.

Shrivastava, P. "Technological Innovation in Developing Countries." *Columbia Journal of World Business*, 1984, *19* (4), 26.

Shrivastava, P., and Schneider, S. "Organizational Frames of Reference." *Human Relations*, 1984, *37*, 795–805.

Simon, H. A. *The New Science of Management*. New York: Harper & Row, 1960.

Simon, H. A. "Applying Information Technology to Organization Design." *Public Administration Review*, 1973, *33* (3), 268–278.

Simon, H. A., and Newell, A. "Human Problem Solving: The State of the Theory in 1970." *American Psychologist*, 1970, *26*, 145–159.

Theobold, R. "Management of Complex Systems: A Growing Society Challenge." In F. Feather (ed.), *Through the 80s: Thinking Globally, Acting Locally*. Washington, D.C.: World Future Society, 1980.

Tichy, N. M., and Ulrich, D. O. "The Leadership Challenge—A Call for the Transformational Leader." *Sloan Management Review*, 1984, *26* (1), 59–68.

Trist, E. "Urban North America: The Challenge of the Next Thirty Years (a Social Psychological Viewpoint)." In W. Schmidt (ed.), *Organization Frontiers and Human Values*. Belmont, Calif.: Wadsworth, 1970.

PART THREE

MANAGING NETWORKS AND RELATIONSHIPS ACROSS BOUNDARIES

14

DESIGNING MULTINATIONAL NETWORKS

RIAD AJAMI

Until the early 1960s, very little was known about one of the most important economic institutions in contemporary global society—namely, the large multinational firm that produces and distributes a significant share of the world's wealth and output with minimal reference to national boundaries and loyalties. During the 1980s, however, the multinational enterprise attracted a good deal of attention and stimulated a significant body of research and writing. While much of the attention of scholars of international business remains focused upon the traditional multinational enterprise, a new kind of enterprise is emerging—an enterprise about which very little is known. This new variation of the multinational enterprise requires organizational structures and management strategies quite different from our present-day concepts of organizing global economic activities.

Traditional transnational corporate linkages must be al-

Note: My use of the term *triad* should not be confused with that of other writers. As introduced in my 1979 book, *Arab Response to the Multinationals* (New York: Praeger), my usage is not geographically limited. Kenneth Ohmae recently defined the triad geopolitically (*Triad Power*, 1985). Essentially he conceptualized his "triad" to be the United States, Japan, and Europe emerging as the most important strategic battlefield for any globally operating company. His narrowly defined use of the term has little to do with my broader usage.

I am indebted to Professor Ned Bowman, director of the Jones Center for Strategy and Policy, for criticism of an earlier draft of this chapter and for partial funding of this study by the Center for Strategy and Policy, Department of Management, Wharton School, University of Pennsylvania.

tered to reflect the preferences of the participants in an international marketplace. More important, they must also reflect major environmental changes. Global entry strategies of the equity type, where ownership and control go hand in hand, must give way to an evolving mode of global networks based on contractual and service-oriented collaborative ventures. While this mode of transnational economic linkages is being taken up by various corporate actors in the global marketplace, little if any academic research has addressed this phenomenon. Once again, theory lags behind practice.

Managers have long known and scholars have long theorized that a company's performance greatly depends on matching an appropriate strategy to the kind of environment it faces. This fit between strategy and environment changes whenever the environment changes. Thus the evolution of global markets has changed the nature of international commerce. The traditional structure of the multinational corporation (MNC) appears to be increasingly a *misfit* with its environment. Although the far-flung traditional MNC may not be centrally controlled at the operational level, ultimate authority still resides in the home country. The legitimacy of that centralized authority rests on equity ownership. That is, the MNC has final authority over the host-country operations because it owns them. Thus the term *multinational corporation* is often a misnomer; it is really a *uninational* firm that just happens to cross national borders. The typical MNC structurally resembles the typical Western multidivisional form. The evolution of that form, as eloquently chronicled by Alfred Chandler (1977), is eminently rational given the existing economic forces.

The changing global economy, however, has given rise to an equally rational approach to organizing transnational enterprise. Showing that theory does indeed lag behind practice, Table 14.1 lists fifteen massive international ventures that do not fit the traditional mold. Instead, they fit a new triadic mold, one more literally *"multi*national," a most intriguing ménage à trois. The new mold is a consequence of a less placid global marketplace and of ventures where the MNC does not provide the lion's share of the managerial, technological, and financial resources.

Table 14.1. Examples of Triadic Trading and Production Systems.

Companies	Project/Product
1. Nissan Motor Co.–Volkswagenwerk AG	Cars in Japan
2. BL Ltd.–Honda	Cars in Japan
3. General Electric–Sadelni (Italian construction firm)	Power plants
4. Ocean Mining Associates–Ocean Management Inc.–Ocean Minerals– Kennecott–Afernod	Undersea mining
5. Toyota–General Motors (ten-year project)	Cars in California
6. MW Kellogg Co. of Houston–China National Technical Import Corp. (CNTIC)	Construction– residential consulting agency
7. MW Kellogg Co. of Houston–China Petrochemical International Corp. (SINOPEC)	Engineering construction
8. McDonnell Douglas–Shanghai Aviation Industrial Corp. of China	Aircraft
9. Mitsubishi Heavy Industries Ltd.–CNTIC Nissho Iwa Corp.	Polyethylene plant
10. LURGI of West Germany–United Coconut Chemicals Corp. (Unichem) of Philippine government	COCO chemical plant
11. Boeing–Saudi Arabia	High-tech industry
12. BBC–TEK in Turkey	Generation equipment
13. Allis-Chalmers–India	Sponge iron manufacturing
14. Union Carbide–India	Chemicals
15. Kawasaki Steel Corp. of Japan–Siderugia Brasiliera of Brazil–Society Finanziara Siderugia of Italy	Steel plant and deep-water harbor facilities

This chapter presents evidence of the phenomenon and outlines the characteristics common to these ventures. A formal analysis of the linkages will follow, along with a discussion of how changes in the global economy promote the viability of these triadic ventures. After noting how one theory of organizations supports the critical role of the environment in shaping organizational structure, I discuss the salient issues of implementation.

Triadic Ventures: Some Evidence

Table 14.1 presents a nonexhaustive list of projects completed between 1970 and 1985 dealing with infrastructure design and manufacturing. These projects, amounting to $500 billion, utilize corporate structures that depart from the traditional hierarchical MNC form yet share key similarities and advantages.

These emerging transnational schemes are characterized, first, by a shift from an equity-based investment, a wholly owned subsidiary, to that of a service-based organization providing technology know-how and other managerial services. Second, these firms represent a variant organizational ownership mode that rests upon contractual arrangements rather than the conventional ownership arrangements. Third, management and ownership in the traditional sense are more diffused; ownership can reside in the hands of the host societies, while managerial services can be provided by multinational firms. Fourth, there is a greater propensity to transfer technology via contracts rather than through the establishment of subsidiaries and foreign direct investment. Fifth, from a firm's life-cycle perspective, triadic firms appear "organizationally young" and partially transient, and thus they have a greater propensity to favor cooperative ventures with multiple participants rather than entering international markets via the establishment of wholly owned organizational units and subsidiaries.

This form of organizing international business activities has several advantages:

- The costs of factor prices for fully owned multinational subsidiaries—internal corporate markets—spread across the globe are becoming, in some cases, prohibitive. Factor prices in external markets—non–fully owned subsidiaries—are likely to be less costly, and so are the risks.
- The ability to respond quickly to changing needs, demands, and market shifts is another advantage. Market contractions become easier to deal with: Divest when necessary; launch new products and services when warranted.

- An effective international production system can rationalize production based upon regional comparative advantage.
- Yet another advantage is better utilization of human resources to fit the profile of various regions' labor forces and managerial talents and human resource endowments. In the past, hosts provided raw resources (including unskilled labor) and MNCs supplied the managerial and technological skills. The triadic venture can employ specific expertise no matter where it is found (including the host). Triads thus have an obvious incentive to develop local expertise.
- A lesser likelihood of political friction and resentment on the part of host societies flows from the increased legitimacy of the venture. The diffusion of ownership and management increases the host's control over the venture.

Union Carbide–India is partially a triadic venture operated and essentially controlled by Indian nationals. Union Carbide's equity ownership, however, left the parent firm vulnerable to legal liabilities for massive damages from the tragedy at Bhopal. If ownership had been diffused (as in a fully triadic system) the responsibility that accrues to ownership would have been diffused as well. The price of equity ownership there was indeed costly. Yet ownership is not necessary for control. Other contractual relationships could provide control while reducing the legal vulnerability imposed by equity ownership.

The factors leading to the creation of triadic trading and production systems are (1) the increasing difficulties many multinational corporations experience in entering and staying in host markets — not only in developing countries and the Eastern bloc but also industrialized countries; (2) the globalization of capital markets and the rise in the private syndicate financing method; and (3) the financial requirement of new projects — on average $500 million each.

While high risk provides a strong motive to share equity, there are strong pressures within most host countries to keep foreign equity to a minimum. Formerly, a participant (multinational corporation) could count on negotiating an equity arrangement that reflected its contribution to the project. More and more, host governments are regulating the allowable share of foreign ownership and use other means to bind participants to the partnership. With the rise in limitations on foreign ownership and the concomitant erosion of equity rights, a variety of contractual mechanisms have been devised to enable the participants to continue to make their contributions to the project and reap their profits from it. The allocation of risks and rewards can be complex even in a traditional MNC-owned venture. The triadic system's contractual nature lends itself to a negotiated sharing of all the various risks (financial, technological, and political) and rewards (financial, technological, and political) among the partners.

Given the current trend of the international economic environment, triadic systems, contract manufacturing, and production sharing are likely to become the fastest-growing modes of conducting international business. Several countries have begun to amend their investment codes and alter their business climate to exploit these new opportunities and attract multinational firms. These growing changes to the competitive environment often allow, even mandate, changes to the structure and strategy of transnational ventures. Let us turn our attention to how managers are already taking advantage of these changes and the kind of enterprises now evolving.

Multinational Corporate Linkages: The Production and Trading Systems

One important direction for multinational organizational development is the emergence of collaborative transnational activities — triadic trading and production systems. Such linkages are characterized by a triad. An international production and trading system is a complex arrangement whereby a project is not undertaken by a single firm but rather by a triadic construct (Figure 14.1). Each participant supplies the necessary factors for which it has a competitive advantage in a value-added chain. These are as follows: (1) local inputs, (2) technology, managerial services, and market access, and (3) transnational capital.

The triadic system refers to functions, not entities; one

Figure 14.1. The Triadic Construct.

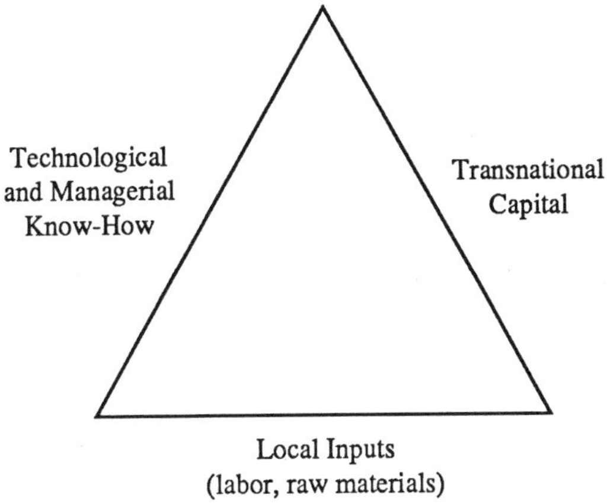

Technological
and Managerial
Know-How

Transnational
Capital

Local Inputs
(labor, raw materials)

entity can provide multiple functions. (Japanese trading companies often provide capital and expertise.) Or one function may be provided by multiple entities. (Host countries may insist on providing managerial expertise while an MNC provides technological expertise.) Similarly, it might be misleading to assume that each function represents an equal and independent partner. Whichever resource is most critical will usually have more leverage, though it may not be obvious which resource that is. Capital may be scarce, for example, but local politics and regulations may still have the upper hand.

Local input in a production and trading system refers to those elements supplied by the host country—the country in which the project is undertaken. The host country may supply labor, natural resources, and capital. The representatives of the host country may be the government itself or local developers or entities. They enter into this type of arrangement for a variety of reasons—perhaps they see the need for development within the country but are not willing to take the risk alone; perhaps they do not have sufficient capital to finance the project, the technological know-how to complete it, the managerial skills to run it, or access to the market once the project is completed.

Host governments are often hamstrung by a lack of influence over ventures (short of draconian measures such as nationalization). The triadic system increases the host's perceived control and, in turn, the venture's perceived legitimacy. In a traditional MNC venture, the host country is most concerned with inputs (labor and materials). Under the triadic system, hosts are strategically more equal partners and therefore must also be more concerned about outputs. That is, the host entity is now less of a vendor and more of a partner. As hosts increasingly accept this new role, more MNCs may find their strategies and structures to be incompatible with their new environment.

Project size is still a major obstacle to many Third World enterprises. Developed countries' multinationals have different but equally compelling reasons for participating in such collaborative ventures—lower economic cost factors and reduction of financial risks as well as cultural accommodations and the minimization of political risks. Moreover, many multinational enterprises believe that this sort of linkage is concomitant with the cost of doing business in an increasingly protectionist environment, both in industrial and nonindustrial countries alike.

Significantly, international banks play a major role in triadic enterprises as financiers of such projects. They may finance a project wholly or partially. The loans are tailored to fit the project and the host country and are written to reduce the banks' risk exposure through a limited recourse or nonrecourse agreement—the repayment being ensured by the project's expected cash flow.

The triadic enterprise project is completed through the involvement of large multinational corporations who participate as project managers/technical consultants. These corporations are not always direct financiers of projects but provide services on a contractual basis, such as design and engineering, procurement, training of management and local personnel, and project coordination and management. They may also provide market access—to sell the output of a specific venture—through either established contacts or direct purchase.

The critical resource has become capital. The critical skill has become "financial engineering." Financiers or their agents may assemble triadic systems to protect their investments and to seize attractive investment opportunities. (See Figure 14.2.) This

Figure 14.2. Financial Engineering in the Triadic Venture.

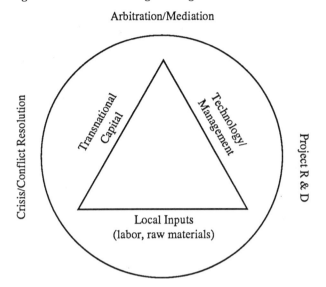

"financial entrepreneurship" has historically been crucial to large-scale development (for example, the U.S. railroad system). The other partners may play this role as well. Governments may directly involve themselves as in newly industrializing countries. The MNCs themselves may arrange for capital rather than supplying it directly. Bechtel is a particularly cogent example. Although it does not finance projects itself, it does provide financial engineering.

Perhaps Japanese trading companies are the truly global multinationals: The trading company banks finance projects, and the other entities within the trading company provide such services as market access and technology. "Manufacturing with no facilities" is a new idea developed by Japanese trading companies, and for years Japanese executives have been willing to market the products of other manufacturers, foreshadowing the newer triadic systems. As noted before, these trading companies are accustomed to a more contractual (less equity-bound) approach. They may have an advantage in this new environment where risks and rewards are negotiated, not bought and sold.

Figure 14.3. International Entry Modes.

		Mode of Entry		
		Licensing	FDI	Triad
Form of Technology and Management Transfer	Bundled	—	—	Triad
	Semibundled	—	FDI	—
	Unbundled	Licensing	—	—

One could make the case that they provide a model for the triadic system, though they often provide both financing and expertise.

The matrix shown in Figure 14.3 visualizes this international entry mode by contrasting the triadic system to the two dominant modes in international operations: licensing and foreign direct investment (FDI). The triadic framework provides the fully bundled package of technology and management and marketing services to the host economy; licensing provides the unbundled element; FDI lies somewhere in between. The bundled technological and managerial services provided under the triadic system have special benefits and appeal for both the recipient and the supplying firm. The fact that there is no single enterprise with a significant level of comparative advantage in all phases of business (design innovation and know-how, production, management, and marketing) clearly supports the contention of superior results possible under a triadic framework. Given the absence of perfect markets for goods and factors of production, this allows for synergy.

Triadic systems should thus arise where the environment is relatively turbulent and no single entity has enough of the required resources to demand a dominant equity ownership position (usually where the size of projects is very large). Conversely, the traditional MNC structure should persist where the environment is relatively placid (that is, controllable) and the MNC can provide much of the managerial and technological resources. Let us now examine how the triadic framework is a consequence of the evolving global economy.

The New Global Economy

The upsurge of interest in multinational firms and in their impact on the global economy has been matched by a plethora of terms, such as *multinational corporation, cosmo corp,* or *transnational corporation,* to describe a particular model. In this model, a typically large firm is principally oligopolistic, having both an integrated production and marketing system of affiliates spread across several countries and a parent headquarters domiciled in a primarily industrial country. The essential point here is that the parent headquarters, where managerial control and decision-making power lie, is located in a single home country. The operation and decisions of this single unit have immense impact upon other countries, however, the so-called host countries.

This traditional structure is extremely well suited for a placid global marketplace where managerial and technological skills are in relatively scarce supply, requiring a more centralized management. Where capital markets are relatively inefficient, firms find it more effective to provide capital themselves. This concentration of managerial, technological, and financial control is sustained by the MNC's equity ownership of ventures in host countries. This equity-based dominance of the MNC over host countries affords enough stability to maintain its organization as a well-ordered hierarchical structure. Changes in the business environment arising from changes in the global economy, however, leave the strategies and structure of the traditional MNC at great risk.

Today, in such a setting, this centralized, equity-based control over global integrated production systems is becoming ever more costly. That is, internal multinational corporate markets — for capital, for skills, for technology, for goods — are becoming, in many cases, less efficient (more costly) than the markets outside the multinational corporate system. Accordingly, the multinational corporations' orientation will focus on cooperative contractual agreements with new partners, often newly industrializing countries, in order to better penetrate global markets. To deal with the multiplicity of international actors, new international financial institutions have evolved; likewise, international services and trading companies, some of enormous size, appear to be growing rapidly. Drucker (1980) has noted another promising form of global network with potential for growth: production sharing.

Production sharing can be defined as a bringing together of resources from one set of economies (abundant and relatively low-cost labor for traditional jobs) with resources of another set of economies (management, technology, skilled people, markets, and purchasing power). The prevalent production-sharing ventures are of two types:

- North–north linkages: firms from highly developed countries linking with others from similarly highly developed economies. U.S.–Japanese and U.S.–European collaboration in the car market exemplifies organizational variants of such ventures.
- North–south triads: production-sharing among highly industrialized countries' firms and newly industrializing Third World entities. A good example is Ford's decision to team up with Toyo Kogyo, Japan's third largest auto company, to head south to take advantage of Mexico's low wage rates.

An equally compelling argument for the production-sharing model lies in the lower cost of labor in the newly industrializing states of the Third World. These newly industrializing countries (NICs) have the labor; the multinationals have the technology, managerial know-how and skills, as well as market access to the world economy. It is natural, therefore, to suggest a symbiotic relationship for production sharing or contract manufacturing. This is where manufacturing and production are performed in the NICs by local and regional production units, while multinational service affiliates provide know-how and market access. Thus a substantial share of international manufactured output in maturing manufacturing industries would be allocated to the newly emerging economies bent upon increasing their share of global manufacturing. Increasingly, the more dynamic NICs of the Third World are spinning out their own multinational corporations.

These Third World multinational corporations seem to be less capital-intensive than those of developed countries. Moreover, their output is more suited to Third World consumers; they use a greater amount of locally made materials and appear to compete more on price than on brand names. Their advertising and marketing concepts are thus more appropriate to less industrialized markets and settings. They also appear more likely to enter into cooperative ventures locally because they have less to protect in terms of products and technology.

The Evolving Strategy Paradigm

One can also find evidence to support the need for multinational corporations to adapt to the new global economy. Organizational researchers generally accept the premise underlying this study. Contingency theories argue that a company's performance is contingent upon the fit between strategy and environment. Population ecology theories go even further, insisting that the very survival of firms depends on this fit. Firms survive because their structure and strategy are appropriate to crucial elements of their environment; firms fail because they do not (Aldrich, 1979).

While population ecology is perhaps an extreme perspective, there is considerable evidence for contingency theories. Stable environments are best served by hierarchical organizations; turbulent environments are best handled by more flexible structures. Lawrence and Lorsch (1967) found that an organization deals best with a turbulent environment by differentiating itself—reducing the centralization and standardization of its bureaucratic structure. A highly stable environment calls for more integration—trying to reap economies of scale and scope by centralizing and standardizing.

The relatively stable environment enjoyed by many MNCs is changing to a turbulent environment. Where once all critical resources (capital, technology, management) were provided in-house and cheap, expendable resources were acquired in host countries, the landscape has grown increasingly more complex. Critical resources derive increasingly from outside the MNC. Where once managerial and technological expertise and capital resources were routinely provided by internal markets, the MNC must increasingly deal with external markets that are increasingly more cost-effective. A more turbulent environment requires a more flexible, less bureaucratic organizational structure and strategies that use external markets to their full advantage. This shift may entail significant changes in the rules of doing business, but those who wish to thrive in the global economy must learn them.

Implementation Issues

Transnational corporate linkages are likely to generate conflicts and stress in the planning and control systems of traditionally organized multinational corporate units. What is changing for managers? Managers must first of all recognize that the landscape has changed far more than many realize. The increasingly contractual (and decreasingly equity-based) nature of transnational ventures requires different skills. At best, ventures are more complex. Negotiation, not market-based exchanges, is the key organizational element. Managers need to recognize that the most effective and efficient sources of a critical resource are often external to the firm. The traditional prescriptions of intelligent boundary spanning and thorough environmental analysis are even more important today. Indeed, the triadic system does not raise drastically different issues of implementation. In a sense, it merely requires better management to handle a more complex environment. ·

It also provides new opportunities for managers who are adroit enough to read the new landscape. It provides opportunities (and threats) to international financial institutions. Different skills (such as negotiating across countries) and increased environmental understanding will test many current institutions. The Japanese banks seem to be farther down the learning curve (through association with trading companies) than their American counterparts. In the United States, we find that financial engineering is provided by firms such as Bechtel, not banks. The laggard American banks were well schooled in financing traditional MNC-type ventures—perhaps too well?

Managers must also be aware that triadic ventures carry with them certain disadvantages, as well, which they must fully consider:

- There is a new set of rules (especially about how and what to control).
- There is less strategic direction because ownership diffusion reduces the strategic control wielded by centralized management.
- The venture may become more important than the partners and take on a life of its own. (An ad hoc project may become entrenched.)
- Two partners could hold the third one hostage.

The planning and control system must function as a problem-solving and decision-making vehicle that can address potential conflicts in a straightforward fashion.

One caveat: The peril of separating ownership and control is a red herring. In most large firms, ownership and control are clearly divorced. The separation here is simply a matter of degree. Different structures and arrangements are controlled by different mechanisms, requiring different managerial skills. Ownership of proprietary technology, for example, must reside more in contractual agreements than in equity ownership. The major control differences in a triadic system include:

- No partner may be dominant in a given situation. Partners may need different ways to influence each of the other partners.
- This approach is tantamount to decentralization. Thus one encounters the traditional opportunities and threats posed by decentralization. Most traditional MNCs retain strategic control while delegating operational control. Under the

triadic system more strategic control is held by the venture itself.

- Increased local strategic control implies increased local adaptation, which may cause too much sensitivity to local circumstances and prevent (for instance) a global marketing strategy.
- Any two partners can override the third. This improves long-run *dynamic* stability but reduces the shorter-run stability that a hierarchical MNC can provide.

It is important to develop a common sense of shared direction: a way of reaching a broad consensus on the venture's strategic direction and a means of implementing such a strategic direction. A participative, interactive, and iterative strategic planning process is necessary in this context. A number of executives must be involved from each of the participating focal organizations. It is vital to have explicit decision-making vehicles within the cooperative venture to initiate changes in response to the early warning signals.

Central to promoting a balance among the participants' interests is the role of the project's management. Effective management should provide an early warning system in the life cycle of the venture and must function as an evolving learning system capable of making compromises and adjustments to minimize the financial and organizational costs and dysfunctions. Moreover, to minimize conflicts, organizational forms must reflect the following:

- Shared goals and objectives: There must be a chosen set of shared goals and objectives among all focal actors and organizations.
- Risk and responsibility: There must be an organizational connection between those who bear the financial risks and those who wield management and operational responsibility.
- Flexibility among focal entities: There must be flexibility among all participants in order to fight the numerous managerial problems that arise, to interpret changed environ-

mental and organizational circumstances, and to identify situations that require timely trade-off decisions among competing and conflicting goals.
*   Shared understanding and acceptance of control mechanisms.

The management process must evolve to reflect the mutual priorities and desired goals of the participants. The participants *explicitly* agree on the key performance measures and the key control mechanisms. Project management "milestones" control will be useful here, but only if the milestones are explicitly agreed upon. Finally, clearly defined ground rules and conflict resolution processes can facilitate such collaborations and resolve conflicts whenever they arise.

Conclusion

The promise of collaborative ventures for the rapidly changing international economy is immense. One is beginning to see the emergence of a symbiotic relationship between highly developed countries' firms and ones from newly industrializing and Third World economies, as well as a movement toward a truly global economy. Moreover, the result of such linkages is a relative decline in the importance of the traditional multinational enterprise—as we know it today—and the coming of age of new international business firms utilizing networking systems on an international and regional scale. The consequences for global economic realignments are substantial: A shift of industrial production to newly industrializing economies will leave to postindustrial economies the jobs more suitable to their endowment of "knowledge workers." The appeal of this production and trading system stems from the economic and human environments facing international business. These environments are manifested by juxtaposing economies endowed with technology, know-how, and managerial resources (such as the United States, Japan, and Western Europe) and newly industrializing economies with surplus labor and a shortage of managerial and financial resources.

In response to these global developments, the multinationals must evolve and adapt to become a service-based trading system. The multinational enterprise will become more of a marketing company and less of a manufacturing unit. It must become adept at marketing goods wherever produced: developed or developing markets, internal or external markets. The enterprises of the future will also become a management system dispensing managerial service and research and development. Moreover, because of the rapid shifts in design, production, and marketing, the multinational firm will scale down its structure to a set of loosely coupled organizational units—small or medium size—capable of responding better to market shifts and opportunities.

Finally, the advantage of this organizational construct lies in the fact that it will allow for more viable organizations capable of reflecting the values and aspirations of the various participants and organizations. This will in turn foster a more entrepreneurial, opportunistic entrepreneurship among a cluster of multinational entities and will hasten the development of flexible global linkages and configurations—modes more suitable for the rapidly changing and turbulent environment of the future.

References

Aldrich, H. *Organizations and Environments*. Englewood Cliffs, N.J.: Prentice-Hall, 1979.

Chandler, A. *The Visible Hand*. Cambridge, Mass.: Belknap Press, 1977.

Drucker, P. *Managing in Turbulent Times*. New York: Harper & Row, 1980.

Lawrence, P., and Lorsch, J. *Organizations and Environment*. Cambridge, Mass.: Harvard University Press, 1967.

Pfeffer, J., and Salancik, G. R. *The External Control of Organizations: A Resource-Dependence Perspective*. New York: Harper & Row, 1978.

15

FORGING NEW LABOR–MANAGEMENT RELATIONSHIPS

ROY B. HELFGOTT

T he unhealthy state of many basic manufacturing industries in the 1980s has had a profound effect on labor–management relations. Buffeted by competition, both domestic and foreign, companies needed to replace old, less efficient equipment with the latest technology, but they seemed incapable of responding sufficiently and rapidly enough to make a comeback. With declining product markets and falling company profits, old-time collective bargaining had simply become a game in which both parties lost. Every union "victory" in winning higher wages and benefits detracted from the employers' ability to modernize and regain lost sales. The net result was the disappearance of still more jobs for union members.

In the last few years, however, companies have been moving boldly to improve their competitive abilities by modernizing their production facilities. In a study by Industrial Relations Counselors, Inc., of the human resource and employee relations impact of computer-based technology (Helfgott, 1988), we found that companies are using the advent of new technology as an opportunity to reverse the traditional adversarial nature of labor–management relations and achieve employee involvement in pursuit of enterprise goals. (The examples cited in this chapter are drawn from that study.)

Before we examine that experience, however, we must place it in perspective. In order to understand current labor–management developments, one must see them operating in an environment of deep malaise in the basic manufacturing industries, the heartland of American unionism. The manufacturing sector's problems transcend labor relations, but they have contributed. To see why this is so, it is necessary to review the past half century's labor history.

Labor History in Review

Five and one-half decades ago, the basic industries were almost entirely nonunion, but in the depths of the Great Depression a combination of government encouragement and a rise of unions in factories, often spontaneously, changed the picture. The fledgling industrial unions went forth to do battle with the giant corporations. The Supreme Court's 1937 decision upholding the constitutionality of the National Labor Relations Act (NLRA), which required employers to recognize and bargain with unions chosen by a majority of employees, paved the way for the triumph of unionism. Between 1933 and 1939, unions gained more than 3.5 million members; by the latter year, total union membership stood at 6.5 million.

During World War II, under the pressure of a labor shortage and the benign influence of the NLRA and the War Labor Board, unions were able to consolidate their gains and to enjoy further expansion of membership. Between 1939 and 1945, they added another 6 million members and collective bargaining was institutionalized in most of basic industry. Union membership continued to grow after the war, reaching about 17.5 million, one-third of the nonagricultural labor force, in 1953.

The two decades 1933 to 1953 saw a decided reduction in corporate power over workers, since so many of them had some say, through their unions' bargaining with management, over the terms and conditions of their employment and they were protected from arbitrary treatment through union-won grievance procedures. (Although unionism has declined to one-sixth of the nonagricultural labor force, arbitrary treatment of workers has not been reasserted. In fact, many nonunion plants provide employees with means of adjudicating disputes through appeals procedures akin to the grievance procedures of unionized plants.)

The first postwar decade was a period of great economic achievement. Reconversion to peacetime production was easily accomplished and, in response to the pent-up demand for goods, production surged. With Europe and Japan prostrate, there was no problem of foreign competition; on the contrary, they provided markets for American goods. In the interests of developing those markets while forging an alliance against Soviet expansionism, the United States transferred some of its largesse to Europe and Japan in order to aid their rebuilding. It could do so and, at the same time, see its own living standards rise, because national productivity was growing at a fairly rapid rate.

It was in this favorable economic environment that American labor–management relations evolved. The economic pie was expanding and industry was quite willing to share the gains with labor. To reduce the chance of production stoppages, the long-term agreement, typically of three years, replaced annual negotiations. Unions went along with management's desire for long-term agreements because deferred annual wage increases were built into them. To protect workers against changes in the price level, cost-of-living escalator clauses were added. An elaborate panoply of "fringe" benefits — retirement, medical, unemployment — also became commonplace.

Following an interruption in the late 1950s, good times resumed in the 1960s. So did the bargaining pattern of ever-greater gains, now including pay for more time not worked. Collective bargaining appeared to be fulfilling the philosophy of American unionism as enunciated by long-time AFL president Samuel Gompers: "More, more, and more."

Management too benefited from the industrial relations system. Continuity of production was an overriding management goal. Strikes might occur over the terms of contract renewal, but they were barred during an agreement's life, since the grievance procedure provided the means of resolving conflict. (When unauthorized work stoppages did occur, companies often would call upon the national union to get the workers back on the job.) The union aim of taking labor out of competition, achieved through standardization of wage rates within an industry, also protected companies from competitors' being able to pay less. The claim has been made (Freeman and Medoff, 1984) that although unions exact a hefty wage differential for their members over nonunion workers, by providing workers with a collective voice they also reduce labor turnover and encourage informal training, which results in increased productivity.

Corporate Market Power

Unionism, however, was not an independent force in winning these gains for workers in manufacturing. The basic source was rising productivity, but market structure also played a role. Large-scale, highly capitalized, mass production industries, as, for example, automobiles, rubber, and steel, tended to have oligopolistic structures. Firms in such industries exercised a degree of market control that enabled them, when the costs of union gains surpassed productivity improvements, to shift those costs to the consumers of their products.

Although other factors have impinged on labor-management relations, such as deregulation in transportation, in manufacturing the key factor has been the rise of a global economy, which has curtailed company pricing power. With imports taking large shares of American markets, settlement costs can no longer be passed on in product prices. The resurgence of competition, for which neither companies nor unions were prepared, lies at the heart of the need to forge new labor–management relationships to restore American manufacturing competitiveness.

A number of factors, ranging from product design and inferior quality to poor marketing, help to explain why American goods have become less competitive, but their prices have also played a role. Even before the escalation in the value of the U.S. dollar, American production costs were well above those of other industrial nations, particularly Japan. Usually the blame is placed on the high wages of American workers, but more important was insufficient growth in productivity—that is, output per unit of input.

From 1973 to 1979, output per employee hour in U.S.

manufacturing rose at the paltry rate of 1.4 percent per year compared with 3.2 percent per year from 1960 to 1973 (Neef, 1986). In the motor vehicle and equipment industry, for example, the Bureau of Labor Statistics (1983, p. 247) reports that output per employee hour more than doubled from 1957 to 1977 but then declined 3.5 percent to 1981. Other industrial nations, moreover, were achieving considerably higher rates of productivity growth. In fact, during that quarter century, U.S. manufacturing productivity grew just half as fast as that of eleven other industrial nations. Wages and benefits meanwhile were mounting rapidly, particularly as rising rates of inflation triggered cost-of-living increases. As a result, U.S. labor costs climbed well above those of competing nations.

New Technology and Union Response

Although the economic problems of American industry were growing during the 1970s, neither companies nor unions reacted quickly. Unions remained loath to change existing practices. By 1981, however, dramatic events had taken place to shake their resistance. The new Reagan administration had broken the strike of the air traffic controllers and the United States was sinking into its eighth postwar recession with unemployment climbing to its highest level in more than four decades. The Teamsters (IBT) and the United Automobile Workers (UAW) each had some quarter of a million members without jobs, the United Rubber Workers (URW) had suffered a one-third decline in membership, and other unions were experiencing similar difficulties. Organized labor had to face reality. When hard-pressed employers sought relief, unions no longer turned a deaf ear; instead they negotiated concessions in wages, benefits, and hours.

Continually lowering wages, however, is no means for regaining competitiveness, for there is no way that American wages could be brought down to levels prevailing in Taiwan, Korea, and other newly industrializing countries. Instead, we have to work smarter by introducing new technology, better utilizing the human input to the production process, and developing and implementing new ways of managing and structuring organizations. We also must move to a more cooperative labor-management relationship at the plant level, increased flexibility in work rules, and employee involvement in decision making with respect to their jobs.

While concessionary bargaining helped companies get back on the competitive track, changes in work rules could be much more important and of greater long-run significance in improving manufacturing efficiency. The outstanding finding with respect to labor–management relations that emerged from our study of the human resource effects of computerized manufacturing was the absence of union resistance to technological change. In fact, we could find no difference between union and nonunion establishments in management's ability to introduce new technology. Nonunion plants, however, could more easily effect the organizational changes necessary to utilize programmable automation. Although unions have accepted new technology, they have been much less amenable to altering work rules to facilitate more flexible use of the work force.

All such changes, which must be negotiated at the plant level, impinge on existing labor–management agreements. Some of them have profound effects that actually challenge the historic means by which unions have sought to protect workers—the definition and rigid control of jobs. As we will see, however, this old Tayloristic way of organizing work is no longer compatible with the requirements of the new computer-based technology. Union agreement to the adoption of new approaches to work involves such significant change as to literally require the forging of new labor–management relationships.

The new computer-based technology includes computer-aided design, which permits the drafter or design engineer to generate lines and shapes on a video screen by typing at a computer keyboard; robots, reprogrammable multifunctional manipulators that can move material, parts, or specialized devices through variable motions to perform a variety of tasks; computer numerically controlled (CNC) machine tools that shape or cut metal according to programmed instructions; automated material handling systems, which link work stations in a computerized manufacturing environment; automated

storage and retrieval systems, which are computerized ware-
houses; vision systems that combine optical instruments and
computers to perform such tasks as quality control and machine
guidance; and various forms of computer-controlled systems, as,
for example, automated continuous casting processes. In a few
instances, work stations were combined into flexible manufacturing systems, but no one has achieved true computer-
integrated manufacturing whereby design, manufacturing, and
management are tied together in an integrated system.

The key to the new technology is its versatility — the ability
to perform different operations without costly retooling. Thus,
in addition to increased productivity, reduced production costs,
improved product reliability, and lower inventory on hand,
computer-based technology provides the flexibility with which
to respond quickly to market shifts. Through reprogramming, it
can be applied to the production of a diverse mix of products. At
a plant we visited, for example, CNC machines with robot arms
for feeding had replaced automatic screw machines and the
setup time for machining a different size part had been reduced
from thirty hours to thirty minutes of reprogramming. This
greater flexibility is of immense importance because, as Vernon
(1986, p. 99) points out, "it is plausible to assume that the rapid
rate of industrial change in the world will continue, requiring
frequent changes in product lines."

Increasing Emphasis on Plant-Level Relations

Among the changes in collective bargaining in the 1980s has
been a shift in its structure, away from industry-wide or even
company-wide relations, to the local level. Moving the emphasis
to the plant level can focus attention on work rule issues that
emerge from the introduction of new technology. The nature of
jobs changes as workers have to do less but think more. Kochan
and Barocci (1985, p. 396) have described the present way of
organizing work as one in which jobs are arranged in a hierarchy of distinct, often multiple, classifications, each of which is
assigned its own wage rate. Programmable automation has
made such a system outmoded. Given the technology's flexibility

in production, there also has to be greater flexibility in work-force utilization, which can lead to improved productivity and thus lower labor costs. Narrow demarcations must give way to more multiskilled jobs.

The typical collective bargaining agreement, however, specifies narrow job classifications that restrict the tasks that workers may perform. Narrowly defined jobs hamper the achievement of optimal manning levels. Thus management would like to modify classification systems by broadening jobs. Such changes must be negotiated at the plant level, but local unions generally resist efforts to widen jobs because they believe this diminishes their members' job security.

There are differences between national and local unions that help to explain the problems in negotiating work rule revisions. Workers and local leaders, familiar only with their plant, do not have the national union officers' broad view of the industry, and hence they fail to perceive the need for changing present policies. Plant labor–management relations, moreover, often are acrimonious. Although plant management is becoming less directive, local leaders are suspicious that the change may be only temporary and so they remain leery of altering current practices.

Sometimes local leaders who do recognize the need for adjustment remain reluctant to act because they fear stirring up rank-and-file opposition. Managements seeking better plant-level labor relations, therefore, should be sensitive to the problems of local leaders. In some cases, union leaders cognizant of the need for contract changes have requested that the work rule agreements be concluded either well before or after the local elections. Managements were wise enough to accede to such requests. (One company even postponed introduction of a new process, at the union's request, until after local elections were completed.)

Forging a More Cooperative Relationship

More cooperative plant-level labor–management relations in pursuit of greater competitiveness can be achieved. Management must take the lead, however, and experience shows that planning and communications are crucial. Human resource planning must be an integral part of overall strategic planning, and the employee relations function must be involved in the formulation of policies and plans.

Communications are especially vital where labor and management have had an antagonistic relationship. Management must not only seek to assuage employee fears concerning changing technology; it must also attempt to foster a better labor–management climate with reduced employee–management conflict. One case shows how this can be done. A division of an electrical company faced such a challenge when it undertook a $40 million modernization program to make it the lowest-cost, highest-quality manufacturer of a particular product. The program's success — especially enhanced product quality — required greater worker cooperation. Management recognized, however, that in light of the parties' antagonistic relationship, it would not be easy to secure the desired cooperation. In order to change the industrial relations climate, management fully informed the union about the proposed product and process changes and solicited its involvement in the project. There were no threats designed to frighten the local into cooperation. On the contrary, management worked diligently to obtain cooperation voluntarily.

Impressed with management's openness and aware of the need to increase competitiveness in order to preserve jobs, the local agreed to participate. It became part of the project with union representatives, that is, stewards, serving on the planning committees. Management, for its part, kept the union fully informed on the progress of the change and meetings with employees were held regularly. Labor–management relations have changed significantly at the plant. Once adversarial, with frequent work stoppages and lost production, they are now cooperative. Attesting to the new industrial relations climate is the fact that hours lost due to work stoppages dropped a dramatic 75 percent. The new relationship has benefited the local union, too: There is no internal dissension, it is represented on plant committees, and the changes did lead to improved competitiveness, a gain in product market share, and thus a recall of its members who had been laid off.

This experience of converting a hostile relationship to a cooperative one leads to a number of conclusions. First, it is possible to forge new labor–management relationships, but this requires special management efforts—particularly advance and full communications. Second, involving employees in a project is a key to its successful implementation. Finally, a union will cooperate with employee involvement efforts only if it too has a role; otherwise, the leadership will view involvement as a management scheme to undermine the union. Other experience indicates that changes are taking place, albeit slowly, in labor–management relations at the plant level. Union stewards are learning to take steps to avoid problems instead of waiting for them to crop up and then trying to solve them. Thus the number of grievances has declined in almost every plant we visited. At the same time, plant management is acting in a less authoritarian manner and is more willing to consult with local union officers.

Resolving Disputes

Labor relations managers disagree on the proper approach to changing work practices. Some, usually those dealing with recalcitrant local leaders, advocate unilateral action—institute change and let the union grieve if it does not like it. While such a strategy sometimes accomplishes its immediate objectives, it tends to create greater union intransigence on the next issue. Managements seeking to forge more cooperative relations, therefore, pursue the opposite course—reaching agreement with the union before proceeding. This strategy sometimes means that management may have to grant quid pro quos for union acquiescence to work rule changes. At one plant, the union agreed to testing of applicants for jobs on new processes, and management, in return, sweetened the retirement formula. The two issues were not directly related, but the union took advantage of the situation to obtain something it had long sought.

Rigid seniority systems can be another impediment to efficient operations. Bumping rights, whereby a senior worker losing a job can take that of a junior worker, can prevent management from keeping qualified workers on advanced processes and they can undermine maintenance of a stable skills bank. Unions are loath to alter seniority regulations, but some are convinced of the need and negotiate changes. At one plant that had introduced CNC machines for enhanced production flexibility, the local, at the urging of the chief steward, agreed to work rule changes to ensure their effective utilization, including taking the CNC operator job out of the bumping procedure. At another company, after fierce contention, the parties negotiated a series of provisions to facilitate the operating efficiency of new CNC machines. One created a new position, numerical control machinist (NCM), responsible for operating the machines. Worried that bumping rights would prevent it from maintaining a cadre of trained NCMs, management was able to obtain the local's agreement to a further stipulation that only workers skilled in all the operations performed by the equipment could bump into the NCM job. This wording was designed to protect the company's training investment and to eliminate the need for redundant training of CNC operators.

Rigid seniority systems not only jeopardize management's ability to keep trained workers in jobs that require special skills; they can also lead to the placement of less qualified workers in jobs. This historic problem reaches new heights under computerized manufacturing, for the equipment is very expensive and the cost of downtime is extremely high. The typical solution to this problem was to require job bidders to demonstrate their abilities via qualification testing—written examinations, hands-on operation of equipment, or both. Not all companies, however, could get unions to agree to testing, since some unions believe that tests do not capture potential and hence do not accurately predict future job performance.

At a plant in which new technology led to job upgrading, the senior qualified worker seeking the position always received it. Management never sought to advance a less senior worker, even when it thought the person could perform the job better. In return, the local has been more receptive of new technology. Furthermore, since there is testing of ability to perform the work, no unqualified worker has ever been placed on a job. There was a contrasting experience at another plant. The fact that the senior employees always got the jobs in new technology caused problems because some, even with training, turned out to be poor operators. Seniority even determines who is to be trained, but management believes that the major selection criteria should be ability and willingness to learn. The union was unrelenting on seniority, and the management did not press the issue since the local had recently agreed to a sharp reduction in the number of job classifications. Management recognized the union's political nature—and thus the limits to the changes a leadership could negotiate in any period without provoking opposition within the ranks.

Management at a steel mill, convinced that qualification testing was essential for jobs in its new continuous casting operation, undertook an intensive campaign to educate union leaders on testing's value and validity. The union was ultimately persuaded that only the most qualified workers could efficiently operate the new system, and it cooperated in developing an effective program. The workers themselves participated in the process of determining the skill requirements for the new jobs. An important feature of the program is that someone who fails to qualify receives counseling and has an opportunity to retake the test when a new opening occurs.

Contention also arises when management seeks to have operators perform maintenance tasks, because this often leads to jurisdictional disputes with maintenance employees seeking to preserve their work opportunities and the integrity of their crafts. The problem is especially acute when production and maintenance workers belong to different unions. Nevertheless, many companies believe that the benefits from broadened operator responsibilities are much greater than any resulting labor relations problems. The steel mill's management wanted to staff the new casting operation as efficiently as feasible. One way to accomplish that goal was to have operators perform preventive maintenance. In management's opinion, the labor contract permitted this. But instead of unilaterally instituting the new job duties and forcing the union to grieve, management chose to work it out with the local. The negotiation process was not easy, but agreement was eventually reached.

Having built much of their job protection on existing classifications, unions are reluctant to abandon them. Yet some unions, seeing the anachronism of the old system and recognizing that their members want more meaningful work, have agreed to consolidation of narrow jobs into ones that encompass a greater variety of tasks. Negotiations at an electronics plant compressed 160 classifications into 40 jobs that now entail more responsibility and higher pay. Job consolidation has given management greater flexibility in assigning work. Thus, in the face of higher wage rates for expanded jobs, total labor costs have gone down. At an automotive plant, after long and arduous negotiations, 125 separate classifications, including more than 20 for the skilled trades, were telescoped into 25 for production workers and 8 for skilled workers. According to corporate headquarters, less union resistance to such work rule changes was encountered at plants that had suffered layoffs during the severe 1981–1982 recession. Consolidation of jobs at this plant, therefore, represented a significant achievement, since its product was not cyclically sensitive and there had been no layoffs.

Union resistance to broader classifications can sometimes be overcome by adding work to expanded jobs that was not previously in the bargaining unit; typically, this means including setup work. Workers like the expanded jobs, so unions are more amenable to the change. There is an added advantage: changed attitudes. Since the worker has set the job up, he or she gets a feeling of ownership unlike the former attitude, "I only run the machine." In one case the production process was reorganized so that people worked in teams that were responsible for setting up their own work. Management found that the setup was performed much better than when it had been done by industrial engineering.

Expanded jobs are upgraded and their pay levels are raised accordingly. When a plant institutes a team approach, a growing practice is to adopt a skill-based compensation structure so that workers are paid higher rates as they acquire additional skills. At one plant, for example, all thirty workers in a plastic molding operation that had been automated were retrained so they could operate the system and keep it functioning by making minor repairs. They were divided into autonomous work teams and all differences in job titles, duties, and pay were eliminated and one new higher grade was established.

A new compensation issue has arisen in a number of plants: what to pay workers who are being trained for broadened and upgraded jobs. One union claimed that the training was so rigorous that the new rates should be put into effect immediately. Since the workers were not yet performing the new jobs, management demurred, but it did concede that the existing wages were inappropriate, so interim rates, between the old and the new, were established for the training period.

Workers and their unions would be more amenable to changes in work practices if they believed that jobs would not be jeopardized. Job security, therefore, has become a major union objective. Some nonunion companies, such as IBM, have had full-employment policies and never lay off regular employees. Such policies, also known as the Japanese model, are spreading to companies with organized employees. One company even guaranteed not to lay off workers with at least one year of seniority who are displaced as a result of new technology. An office machine manufacturer, wishing to further the existing union–management cooperation, agreed to a unique form of job security. All employees on payroll at the date of contract signing were guaranteed their jobs for its duration; the guarantee was extended when the agreement was renewed three years later. (This type of job security agreement is no longer unique, since in October 1988, it was included in the new collective agreement between John Deere and the UAW.) The company's potential economic burden diminishes over time as attrition trims the work force.

The 1987 automobile contracts, whereby each company agreed to maintain a certain level of employment, were a further step toward job security. Jobs were guaranteed against loss due to technological change and other factors under management's control, but not against market declines. Since workers can be laid off when there is a drop in product demand, the companies can afford the employment guarantee. They will use human resource planning—normal and speeded-up attrition basically—to prevent technological change from leading to job loss. Management, moreover, will be in a better position to redeploy redundant workers since, in exchange for the guarantees, the UAW has agreed to establish plant-level labor–management committees to seek ways of increasing productivity and quality through work teams and relaxed work rules.

Employee Involvement

American industry is facing competitive problems so severe as to call into question such long-held concepts as mass production and the benefits of economies of scale. Similarly, authoritarian management is no longer viable, for the new technology requires greater cooperation among all members of the work force. Companies recognize that while technology can increase productivity, product reliability, and flexibility, people are needed to operate it—and that, indeed, people are equally important for realization of these goals. Consequently, changes in labor–management relations have not been all one way, with unions merely giving and employers taking. Companies, for their part, have granted greater union and employee participation in decision making, have adopted more open communication programs, and have consulted with unions before undertaking major changes.

Employee involvement facilitates the introduction of change, creates a climate of trust and credibility between labor and management, and provides a means to educate workers about a company's economic situation. It also allows management to obtain workers' ideas on the proper design and operation of new technology. Workers' years of experience with actual operations on the plant floor mean that, if given the opportunity, they can be of assistance in developing new production systems.

At the electrical plant where the union was involved in the

introduction of new technology, management asked it to evaluate the planning process. The local responded that everybody
was committed to quality, that informative meetings had been
held, and that the workers and management were working together. It was pleased that when problems arose management
listened more freely than in the past and that work areas were
improved. The union, however, criticized management for not
having solicited the workers' ideas about how to design the
equipment. When questioned on this, management agreed with
the union. For had the workers been involved, their ideas could
have helped the engineers avoid problems that did arise later in
the operational stage.

    Employee involvement is based on the claims of behav-
ioral scientists (McGregor, 1960; Maslow, 1954) that workers want
to share responsibility. Unlike European concepts of "industrial
democracy," it is not assumed that workers want a say in the
company's overall management. What workers want are meaningful jobs on which they exercise autonomy and intellectual as
well as manual skills.

    There is a burgeoning movement in industry, unionized
or not, toward employee involvement. Workers are being given
more decision making with respect to their jobs, and work
groups meet regularly with their supervisors to review problems
and fashion solutions to them. In unionized situations, these are
generally known as quality of work life (QWL) programs. Although attitudes toward involvement vary among companies
and unions and even within a given company or union, management has always taken the initiative and the unions have responded—favorably, unfavorably, or halfheartedly, but usually
favorably.

    It must be recognized that an employee involvement
program carries risks for a union. For if things go wrong, it is
the local leaders that the members blame. There is ideologi-
cal opposition, as well. Some people in the labor movement
see employee involvement merely as a management technique
to get workers to view production from a managerial perspective and thereby coopt the unions into acceding to management's aims. They continue to advocate an adversarial labor–

management relationship, denying a connection between employer efficiency and employee welfare.

Such an attitude was exhibited by the local at an automotive plant. Management sought to conduct work group meetings where it could provide information about the new computerized equipment and respond to workers' anxieties. The local union, however, forbade membership participation. Management appealed to the national union, but its leaders said that while the national endorsed the company's QWL efforts, it could not force local compliance. Since many workers ignored their leadership's admonition and attended work group meetings voluntarily, even this local had to modify its position to that of merely discouraging participation.

Philosophical differences about granting workers more decision-making authority exist within management's ranks, as well. Some companies cling to the idea that since production is a line management responsibility, decision making cannot extend beyond first-line supervision. In other companies, even when top management favors it, those further down the hierarchy can block implementation of an involvement program. Such opposition may be overcome by ensuring that middle- and lower-level managers are themselves included in the program.

Union–management programs for employee involvement carry risks for management, too, for they can complicate labor relations. Quality of work life is supposed to be separate from collective bargaining, but negotiation matters can creep into it. One company that has had such problems still wants to extend QWL to all of its plants, since it has found QWL to be a change agent — particularly for transforming labor-management relations from adversarial to cooperative.

At an office equipment manufacturer, employee involvement permeates nearly every aspect of business activity. Through participation in QWL circles, employees learn about market competition and thus recognize the need for more efficient production. Being knowledgeable about the business, union leaders and workers are more agreeable to contract changes for staffing the technology more efficiently — as, for example, permitting machine operators to perform maintenance duties. Workers also participate on teams that study how products can be designed for more efficient assembly. (The employment security provision obviously makes them more willing to contribute ideas, even if they may lead to the elimination of some jobs.)

Facilitating sociotechnical approaches by means of autonomous work teams confronts local leaders with having to negotiate changes in the agreement, many of which may be unpopular with some members, such as condensed job classifications and blurred distinctions between production and maintenance categories. One local agreed to such changes only under pressure from the international representative. If the new system did not work out, the leadership could escape the wrath of the membership by pointing the finger of blame at the national union.

Making the union a partner is one way of strengthening plants. This is the strategy adopted by a diversified products manufacturer that bargains with a number of different unions. In this case headquarters advocates the formation of plant labor–management committees to resolve issues of shared interest that fall outside the contract. The committees have co-chairmen, one from each party, who alternate chairing the group. Management recognizes that such a labor–management relationship requires it to share business information with the union, seek union ideas for improvement, and acknowledge union contributions to accomplishments. The union, in turn, must be willing to explore new means for strengthening the labor–management relationship, become familiar with productivity and QWL issues, not be overly protective of its role in communicating with workers, and be dependable in implementing agreed-upon actions. The program, in an early stage of implementation, is a significantly different approach to labor–management relations.

Future Trend or Temporary Expedient?

The 1980s experience in labor–management relations is not entirely unexpected. American unions always have been pragmatic, seeking to advance the immediate interests of their members, rather than dedicated to long-term goals such as the achievement of socialism. American unions are job-conscious, not class-conscious.

The concept of job-conscious unionism was formulated by John R. Commons and extended by his student and colleague at the University of Wisconsin, Selig Perlman. According to the theory, the function of unionism is to prevent workers from competing among themselves for available jobs. Thus unions have devised job allocation mechanisms and ensured their members greater security in their jobs and better standards on those jobs. Their concern with jobs means that unions take into account the employment effects of their collective bargaining practices. The reaction of the unions to the adversities besetting the companies that employ their members, therefore, is understandable. In the interest of saving jobs, unions have been willing to work with management to achieve greater operating efficiency and thus promote greater company competitiveness.

These developments have resulted in a more cooperative approach. Many students of labor relations, however, are skeptical of any long-range alteration in the adversarial nature of the labor–management relationship. John Dunlop (1988), for one, sees the present situation as merely accommodation to temporary economic malaise and expects that, as conditions improve, unions and managements will revert to their traditional types of behavior. I, however, believe that cooperation may be a long-run trend in many industries. The present atmosphere of joint problem solving will continue, because the difficulties confronting those industries will not disappear. Foreign competition will not evaporate, and companies will be under constant pressure to become more efficient. The longer labor and management must work together to solve problems, the greater the likelihood that these behavior patterns will become institutionalized.

American manufacturers, through their introduction of computer-based technology, new approaches to work organization, and less adversarial labor relations, have been making a comeback. In contrast to the previous quarter-century, manufacturing output per employee hour has risen at an annual average rate of more than 4 percent in the past five years. Thus the gap is closing in rates of productivity growth between the United States and other industrial nations. Due in good part to union awareness of the problem of competition, compensation in the United States has been rising only moderately—and less than in nine other industrial nations. As a result, U.S. manufacturing has been enjoying a drop in labor costs while those of its competitors have increased.

If leading companies remain serious in trying to adopt less directive workplace management and more worker involvement, their actions could go a long way toward blunting the rank-and-file union member's deep distrust of "the bosses." Then, as the new approaches continue to lead to healthier, more competitive firms, ensuring greater economic opportunity and security for workers, both labor and management will recognize the long-run advantages of a cooperative over an adversarial relationship.

References

Bureau of Labor Statistics, U.S. Department of Labor. *Handbook of Labor Statistics*. Washington, D.C.: U.S. Government Printing Office, 1983.

Dunlop, J. T. "Have the 1980's Changed U.S. Industrial Relations?" *Monthly Labor Review*, 1988, *111* (5), 29–34.

Freeman, R. B., and Medoff, J. L. *What Do Unions Do?* New York: Basic Books, 1984.

Helfgott, R. B. *Computerized Manufacturing and Human Resources: Innovation Through Employee Involvement*. Lexington, Mass.: Lexington Books, 1988.

Kochan, T. A., and Barocci, T. A. *Human Resource Management and Industrial Relations*. Boston: Little, Brown, 1985.

McGregor, D. *The Human Side of Enterprise*. New York: McGraw-Hill, 1960.

Maslow, A. H. *Motivation and Personality*. New York: Harper & Row, 1954.

Neef, A. "International Trends in Productivity and Unit Labor

Costs in Manufacturing." *Monthly Labor Review*, 1986, *109* (4), 98–106.

Perlman, S. *A Theory of the Labor Movement*. New York: Augustus M. Kelley, 1970. (Originally published 1928.)

Vernon, R. "Can U.S. Manufacturing Come Back?" *Harvard Business Review*, 1986, *64* (4), 98–106.

16

FOSTERING NEW UNIVERSITY—INDUSTRY RELATIONSHIPS

MARIA L. NATHAN
THOMAS G. CUMMINGS

In the global recession of the late 1970s and early 1980s, companies that made technological breakthroughs experienced growth while those that did not either stagnated or declined. This historical event reinforces the lesson that today's competitive environment requires technological leadership for economic prosperity. Technological innovation and market competitiveness can mutually reinforce each other. Competition can drive investment in research and development; failure to make such investments can result in loss of business to rivals who introduce better or cheaper products. Reciprocally, innovation can increase competition: Successful innovators can gain competitive advantage through increasing market share and sales. Thus, in an increasingly competitive global economy, an essential strategic goal for U.S. companies is technological innovation.

Among the major attempts to promote technological innovation, one strategy is to identify leaders of innovation in organizations such as the intrapreneur, the product champion, and the organizational gatekeeper (Roberts, 1987). Attention has also been directed at techniques and structures that promote innovation such as matrix designs, participative management programs, quality circles, task forces, and pay-for-performance systems. Increasingly, the demand for technological sophistication has forced organizations to look beyond their boundaries for new ideas, products, and processes. How can organizations relate to their environment to maximize organizational innovations? Strategists have recommended such measures as internal development, acquisition, licensing, minority venture-capital investments, and internal corporate joint ventures.

Another source of innovation that complements in-house research and development (R & D) efforts is the collective strategy. Here organizations work cooperatively with each other to achieve common goals such as research and development. Joint ventures and university–industry R & D consortia are examples of such collective efforts. This chapter addresses a particular collective strategy for technological innovation—the university–industry R & D consortium—which has been growing in popularity and has been shown to lead to technological innovation (Gray, Solomon, and Hetzner, 1986; Brodsky, Kaufman, and Tooker, 1980). The Institute for Manufacturing and Automation Research (IMAR) and R & D consortia will serve as examples of how such collective activity operates and is developed.

We begin with a conceptual scheme for explaining how collective R & D efforts develop and then consider a case study of a specific university–industry R & D consortium to provide a concrete example of the concept. Finally, we discuss the implications of creating and managing such systems.

Conceptual Overview

In today's increasingly complex and changing environment, organizations are extensively interdependent. They seek to manage this interdependence through internal mechanisms such as the adaptation of processes and products to fit market needs—for example, adjustment of the organization's structure, information system, technology, and management practices (Salancik and Pfeffer, 1978). But organizations cannot afford to ignore the complex workings of their environment, so they also manage interdependence through collective efforts such as mergers, joint ventures, trade associations, coalitions, and consortia.

Cummings (1984) has described collectives of two or more organizations engaged in joint efforts to attain goals they could not achieve alone as "transorganizational systems" (TS). The TS might be temporary or permanent. It might occur among private businesses, within the public sector, or involve a public–private partnership. The purposes served may also vary: common social good, enhanced U.S. competitiveness, regional, state, or local economic development, technology transfer, or compliance with government mandate. The transorganizational systems described here are collaborative R & D efforts of organizations intent on technological innovation. Members' reasons for participating may be many and varied, but a common denominator is resource dependence. Organizations seek to collaborate with other organizations because they cannot individually accomplish desired R & D goals.

R & D consortia can take a variety of forms including joint industry, industry–university, and industry–university–government. Our main concern here is the university–industry R & D consortium. Given the goal of sharing in the yield of breakthroughs in basic research, member organizations (university and industry) contribute their time, money, ideas, and facilities. Each R & D consortium must choose an appropriate structure and form of leadership, address issues of antitrust and patent rights, and ease the transfer of technology from university to industry.

Examples of such efforts include the Industry–University Cooperative Research Centers Program (Tornatzky and others, 1982), which is university-based, typically interdisciplinary, and engaged in basic research. Research projects receive joint support from a number of companies and the National Science Foundation (NSF). Joint industry–university efforts aided by NSF have spanned such diverse areas as polymers, telecommunications, hazardous and toxic waste management, manufacturing innovation research, medical research, and agriculture (Swartzel and Gray, 1987). The Manufacturing Engineering Applications Center (MEAC), a university–industry consortium housed at Worcester Polytechnic Institute, has four corporate sponsors and conducts applied research. Each of these ventures promotes innovation and competition by conducting research that would not (or could not) ordinarily be undertaken by individual firms.

As in all transorganizational systems, resource dependence underlies these collaborative research efforts. The university lacks the resources; research progress is frequently slow and laborious and may be irrelevant to immediate industry interests. On the other hand, industry research driven by short-term objectives seldom makes true technological advances because basic knowledge is neglected (Swartzel and Gray, 1987). The principal stimulus to cooperation is the growing inability of private industry to produce profits from R & D spending (Krosin, 1971). Membership in a university–industry R & D consortium allows costs associated with many projects to be distributed among participating firms. Cooperation can also avoid unnecessary and costly duplication.

Research done by such consortia is typically generic and can potentially benefit all members. Individual firms may be unable or unwilling to assume speculative risks associated with long-term, basic research projects. Basic research is more unpredictable and riskier than applied research, but it is necessary for the technological advancement of an industry. Organizations can undertake the necessary expense by sharing in these risks. Cooperation among competitors is facilitated because no organization yields the secrets constituting its competitive advantage. Technology transfer is aided, as well. Since university and industry are working in cooperation, they take special measures to facilitate an innovation's adoption by industry.

Thus collaboration among universities and businesses enables members to share expenses and risks in basic research and facilitates a smooth transition of innovations from university to industry. Underlying this cooperation is the assumption that it will be more efficient than individual efforts—both in significant innovation for the dollars spent and in the time it takes to transfer innovations to practice.

Though the R & D consortium has great potential to enhance organizational competitiveness and innovation, there are numerous obstacles to its success. Rosenzweig and Tarlington (1982) complain that the lack of cooperation between university and industry is to blame for the recent decline in U.S. innovation, productivity, and competitiveness in the global marketplace. These obstacles, discussed next, are no doubt among the causes of this failure of organizations to cooperate with one another.

Member organizations may be reluctant, for example, to relinquish sufficient autonomy to join with others. They may not believe that the benefits of forming a consortium outweigh the costs. Even when motivated to join, members may have problems organizing their joint efforts and managing lateral relations. Exhibit 16.1 outlines the practical issues these consortia must address at different stages of their development. The framework is based on earlier work (Cummings, 1984; Nathan and Cummings, 1987) and describes four stages for developing consortia into effective collectives: identification, convention, organization, and evaluation. For each stage there are fundamental issues that must be resolved if the consortium is to continue to develop. We turn now to these basic developmental issues.

Identification Stage

The first stage is concerned with defining the R & D task and deciding whether a consortium is appropriate for accomplishing it. R & D tasks for which consortia may be an ideal solution include basic research, facilitation of technology transfer, and advanced technological innovation that requires pooling of risks and resources. This stage identifies potential members of the consortium who have sufficient knowledge, skills, and resources to contribute to joint R & D efforts. This requires specifying the relevant stakeholders who should be represented in the consortium if it is to succeed. Do potential members have complementary resources, share needs, and show a willingness to contribute?

Convention Stage

Once potential members are identified, the group must meet to determine whether there is sufficient motivation to form a con-

Exhibit 16.1. Phases of Consortium Development.

Stage 1: Identification
- What is the task/problem?
- What skills, knowledge, and resources are needed?
- Which organizations possess the necessary skills, knowledge, and resources?
- Who should select these organizations?

Stage 2: Convention
- Who should convene the group? Where?
- What is the motivational basis for the group's existence?
- Is there enough common interest to support a consortium?
- What are potential obstacles to the consortium's success?

Stage 3: Organization
- Who should the leaders be?
- How should the consortium be structured?
- How can members' commitment to the consortium be sustained?

Stage 4: Evaluation
- What are the criteria for the consortium's success?
- Who should evaluate the consortium's efforts?
- How should evaluative information be communicated to members?

---

sortium. What does each member stand to gain and lose from the association? Benefits must be seen to outweigh costs. Members must also reach consensus about the goals of the collective. After consensus has been reached, members must next assess potential obstacles to joint R & D efforts—antitrust restrictions, patent rights, freedom of academics to disseminate findings in their research journals, availability of funding sources, potential conflicts over choice of research projects, and technology transfer procedures.

Organization Stage

Once members have dealt with these barriers, they must decide how to organize themselves for the joint R & D task. Key issues concern the leadership of the consortium. Should a single, strong leader be chosen, or should leadership be shared among members? If it is shared, the consortium may have problems coordinating efforts as individual agendas pull it in different directions (Dimancescu and Botkin, 1986). Should the leader be appointed or be allowed to emerge as the consortium develops? Can a full-time leader be appointed? Since part-time leaders have another source of employment, they frequently have to wrestle with other time and energy commitments to promote the interests of the consortium. Even when highly motivated, consortium leaders may lack the necessary managerial skills: how to motivate continued contributions by the membership; how to empower the membership; how to resolve conflicts.

This stage also involves choosing an appropriate structure for the joint R & D task. The consortium's structure depends on the degree to which it is decentralized and the degree to which rules and regulations are formalized. Communication channels must be regularized to facilitate the flow of information among members. Informal channels can be designed in order to complement formal communication links.

Since individuals participate in the consortium on a voluntary basis, inducements for them to exert effort must be made salient. Are representatives from member organizations rewarded by their employers for contributions to the consortium? The membership will be largely professional people (industry engineers, research professors, and the like) who are committed first to their profession over and above their loyalty to their primary employer, let alone the consortium.

Since most commitments of membership last for a limited time, the consortium must continually reckon with the possible loss of major corporate sponsors. It must continually work, therefore, to replenish sources of sponsorship. Since membership in the R & D consortium can be fluid, its leadership must strive to engage more than one organizational representative in the consortium's operations. Otherwise the promotion or relocation of a vital organizational link could mean that the consortium loses a sponsor. Many of these mechanisms will be continually refined as the consortium encounters the inevitable communication failures and lack of progress.

Evaluation Stage

Few collectives subject themselves to ongoing evaluation of their efforts, yet feedback from an objective source is invaluable. In order to evaluate, members must agree on criteria for measuring the consortium's success. Size of sponsorship, number of innovations successfully brought to practice, number of research publications, member reports of satisfaction with the consortium — these are but a few of the possible criteria. It must be determined who will do the evaluating and how frequently. Moreover, it must be decided how the information will be relayed to members: formal written reports, formal meetings, informal discussions, and so forth.

The conceptual underpinnings of consortium development have now been described: identification of potential members, their convention to determine if a consortium is viable, organization of the consortium, and ongoing evaluation of the members' efforts. Now that these stages in the development of a consortium have been considered, we turn to a specific case that applies these concepts.

A Case Example: IMAR

The Institute for Manufacturing and Automation Research (IMAR) was founded in 1987 in Los Angeles by a group of manufacturing industry members. In its earliest stages of development, one person who had a clear picture of the obstacles to manufacturing excellence was Dale Hartman, IMAR's executive director and former director for manufacturing at Hughes Aircraft Company. He and several other industry associates pinpointed the predominant reasons for flagging competitiveness: needless duplication of effort among manufacturing innovators; difficulties in transferring technological breakthroughs from university to industry; frequent irrelevance of university research to the needs of industry; and the inability of individual industry members to commit the time and funds to research projects needed for continued technological advances.

Hartman and his colleagues determined that a pooling of funds among organizations was necessary and concluded that the research would most efficiently be carried out in existing university facilities. They worked through at least several plans before they arrived at the idea of the IMAR consortium. The navy had been interested in joint efforts for innovations in artificial intelligence, but the navy's constraints and interests were judged to be too narrow to address the problems this group identified.

Networking with other industry members—TRW, Hughes, Northrup, and Rockwell—and two universities with which Hughes had been engaged in ongoing research—University of Southern California (USC) and University of California, Los Angeles (UCLA)—this original group formed a steering committee to investigate the viability of a joint R & D consortium. Each of the six early planners contributed $5,000 as seed money for basic expenses. The steering committee, based on past experience in cooperative research, determined that a full-time person was needed to assume leadership of the consortium. Members of the committee persuaded Dale Hartman to retire early from Hughes and take on IMAR's leadership full time. Hartman brought with him a wealth of knowledge about barriers to innovation and technology transfer. He had a solid reputation in both industry and academia—crucial for the success of multiple-sector partnerships. As a former Hughes networker, he knew how to lobby state and federal government sources for funds and legislation that promoted industry innovation. He also knew a host of talented people in Southern California whom he would persuade to become IMAR members.

In his thirty years in manufacturing, Hartman found that university-driven research had not produced a respectable yield of usable information. University research was frequently irrelevant to industry needs and seldom provided for transfer of usable innovation to the plant floor. Industry was only tangentially involved in what the university was doing and saw little opportunity for the two sectors to benefit from a partnership. Therefore, it was determined that IMAR would be user-driven.

Industry would set the agenda by choosing projects from among university proposals that promised to be of generic use to industry members. Industry would benefit by being able to influence the direction of research and would also receive early information on research results.

In the next several months, the steering committee and Hartman met regularly to define common research needs and locate funding sources. They sought industry sponsors from high-technology companies with an understanding of the problems in manufacturing research and a desire to more than merely supply a check. They wanted members who would be willing to get involved in IMAR's programs. Furthermore, they wanted all members to be able to use the results of IMAR's generic research while not competing directly with each other. Finally, they decided that they wanted a relatively small membership. If the membership grew too large, it might become unwieldy and thus obstruct efforts to get things done.

IMAR's industrial advisory board was formed with six industrial organizations represented—Xerox, Hughes, TRW, Northrup, IBM, and Rockwell—in addition to USC and UCLA. Members were to pay $100,000 each and make a three-year commitment to IMAR. With initial objectives in place and a committed membership, Hartman was already searching for additional funding sources. He was successful in getting a bill introduced into California's state legislature, later signed by the governor, which authorized the Department of Commerce to fund IMAR $200,000. Moreover, IMAR was able to tie into the NSF's Industry–University Cooperative Research Center Program (IUCRCP) by further forming a university–industry consortium called the Center for Manufacturing and Automation Research (CMAR). NSF funded CMAR with a $2 million grant and a five-year commitment. NSF funding in particular was sought because of the instant credibility that NSF sponsorship gives to such an institute.

NSF requested that several more universities be added to the consortium. In addition, an NSF evaluator was to be present at all IMAR meetings and conduct ongoing evaluation of CMAR's progress. IMAR already had UCLA and USC among its members and now added four university affiliates to work on research projects: University of California, Irvine; University of California, Santa Barbara; Caltech; and Arizona State University. The IMAR Steering Committee then voted to fund research projects at an affiliated university only if it involved cooperation with either USC or UCLA. Each of the four university affiliates was paired with either USC or UCLA. Each affiliate university was selected because it provided expertise in an area that had been targeted as of interest to IMAR's industrial membership. Arizona State, for example, had expertise in knowledge-based simulation systems in industrial engineering, a field of special concern to IMAR's membership.

At this time, IMAR has funded nine projects: Four are joint with the affiliated universities, one is joint between investigators at USC and UCLA, and two each are conducted separately at USC and UCLA. Figure 16.1 shows IMAR's structure.

CMAR operates under the auspices of IMAR with the same board of directors serving both IMAR and CMAR. There are two codirectors of CMAR: Dr. George Bekey, chairman of the Computer Science Department at USC, and Dr. Michel Melkanoff, director of UCLA's Center for Integrated Manufacturing. As codirectors they have an indirect reporting relationship to Dale Hartman. Their responsibilities are to distribute the research funds and to serve as the focal point on their respective campuses. Questions from project team members are directed to one or the other codirector depending on the project. Each of the codirectors takes on responsibility for management of project team members, providing rewards such as reduced courseloads to research professors wherever possible.

The codirectors further work to encourage informal ties with industry members. For example, Dr. Bekey has initiated efforts to have IMAR representatives regularly visit others' facilities to encourage cooperation and sharing of ideas among members. This practice further deepens each industrial member's commitment to IMAR, for not only are the representatives associating with one another but colleagues in the workplace are often brought to these meetings. In the event that an industry or university representative leaves, an associate is more likely

Figure 16.1. Transorganizational Structure of IMAR.

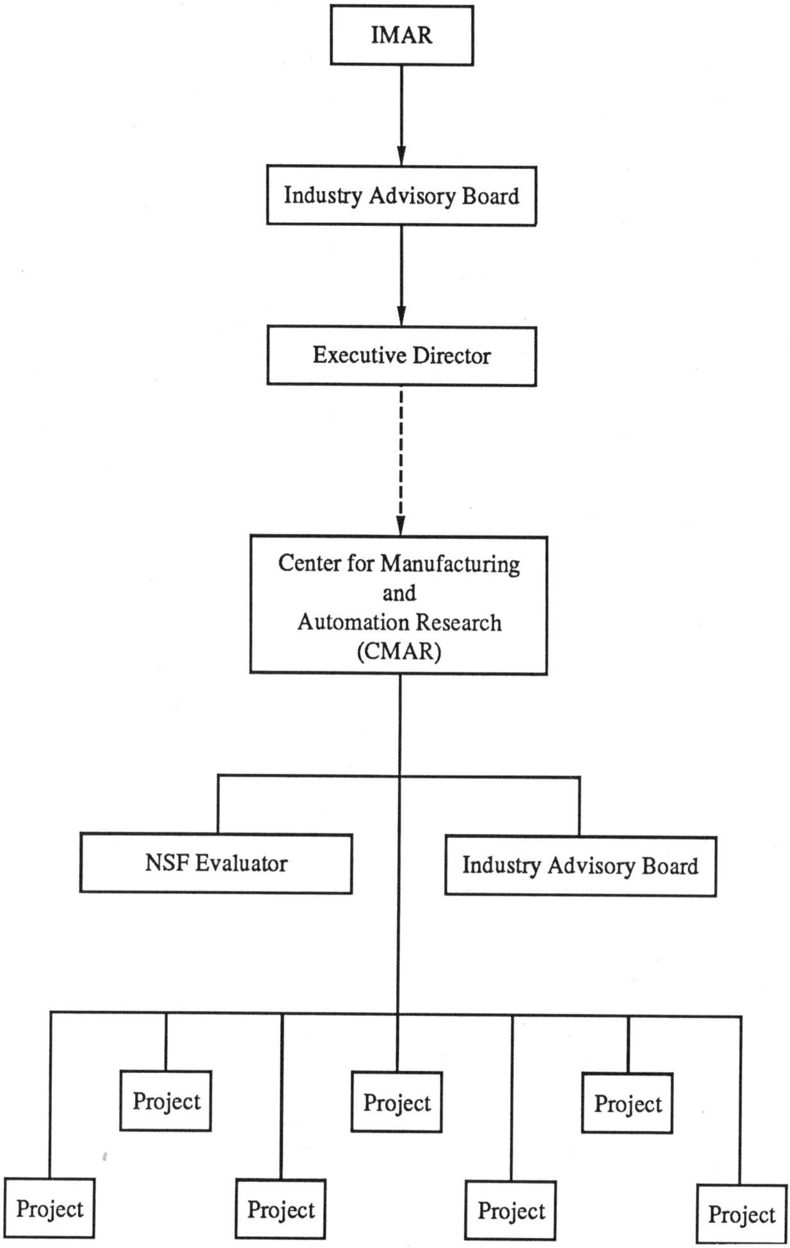

to be there to take his or her place. Further, Bekey notes that the association between industry and university helps industry to overcome its short-term orientation and helps university people to appreciate applied problems and manufacturing needs.

IMAR's board of directors sets the research agenda at annual reviews in which they make recommendations for topics to be funded. IMAR takes these recommendations and then translates them into "requests for proposals" to be circulated among the participating university members. CMAR's codirectors then solicit proposals from the university membership. Researchers' proposals are evaluated and ranked by industry representatives and then passed back to the industry advisory board, which finally determines which projects should be funded.

Not only is IMAR engaged in nine research projects in such technologies as microelectronics, digital computers, lasers, and fiber optics, it is further working to resolve critical problems for manufacturing innovation research. One is technology transfer. IMAR is trying to establish a pilot production facility that Hartman has called a "halfway house for manufacturing." This facility would permit basic research to be brought to maturity and would be capable of producing deliverable parts. The facility would also engage in systems-level research in such areas as management and systems software. Such a facility would also provide an excellent training ground for students.

Yet another function that Hartman believes IMAR must take on is education: continuing education and graduate education. Graduate education is fostered through the various projects; continuing education for industrial members is provided through affiliation with state-of-the-art research being done by university researchers. Furthermore, USC and UCLA faculty are available to assist IMAR in presenting seminars.

Another strength of IMAR is its affiliation with an NSF evaluator who is appointed to follow the progress of the industry–university cooperative research centers. Dr. Ann Marczak is IMAR's NSF evaluator. Since NSF conducts a regular audit of the thirty-nine IUCRCs it sponsors, it makes information available about survey results, others' reports of what works, and so forth. Dr. Marczak serves a valuable function to IMAR as an objective source of feedback. After her first evaluation, for example, Marczak recommended that a project team be formed to conduct ongoing progress assessment for each of the nine research projects IMAR is sponsoring. The evaluator's findings also serve as NSF's means of determining how well each of the funded centers is performing. A center is judged successful if after five years it can exist without NSF funds. NSF also looks at how much industry money was generated, how much additional money was generated in research projects, the number of patents, products produced, and the satisfaction of faculty and industry participants.

    IMAR must grapple with the problem of insufficient numbers of U.S. students choosing manufacturing engineering as a field of study. This suggests problems for the country's future competitive position in manufacturing technology. There is also the practical problem of educating great numbers of foreign students from countries competing with the United States. Indeed, the United States is educating competitors' future technologists in larger proportions than its own.

    Although it is too soon to assess IMAR's success in meeting its objectives, it is well positioned to take advantage of the full range of benefits offered by joint university–industry research. After only one year of operation, IMAR has dealt with many of the problems that so frequently plague collaborative R & D efforts among organizations: It has a well-defined purpose about which its members have formed a strong consensus. It is well structured and has a good balance of resources and needs among its membership. Formal and informal communication networks have been established. It has strong leadership. Members of IMAR respect Hartman for his technological expertise and skills as a networker. He has a strong sense of IMAR's mission. After a discussion with him, one gets the sense that there is not an obstacle he will not overcome. His vision further instills commitment among the IMAR membership. As one member put it: "You end up wanting to see what you can do for the cause."

    Not only does IMAR have the commitment of a full-time

leader and strong feedback from its NSF evaluator, but it involves user-driven research. Though the research is basic, it is
chosen by the users themselves to benefit all members of the
consortium. If the research had been applied, it would have
been more difficult for members to find projects yielding information that all of them could use. The involvement of multiple
universities further provides the talent of top researchers in
diverse areas of technological expertise. Finally, NSF furnishes a
large proportion of the funding for the first five years as well as
regular evaluations.

Practical Implications

Despite serious barriers to the effective operation of R & D
consortia, they are a promising solution to flagging U.S. innovation and global competitiveness. Having considered the conceptual model and the case of a specific R & D consortium, we
turn now to practical advice for creating effective university–
industry consortia.

In the early stages of consortium development, potential
members must have a clear understanding of the joint R & D
task they want to address. Only then can they decide which
parties have the knowledge, skills, and resources needed to
perform the task. Geographical constraints should also be considered. A consortium whose membership is spread across the
country will find it difficult to maintain both formal and informal communications and should anticipate serious obstacles to
performing the R & D task. The size of the consortium is another
issue. IMAR's Hartman described a disagreement with an advisory board member about IMAR's ultimate size. Hartman
thought six industry members and six university affiliates was a
workable size, but the board member had envisioned as many as
thirty future industry members. Increasing the consortium's size
will also increase the complexity of its operations and the difficulty of creating cohesion among its members.

Members should have a balance of talents and other resources. Participation of direct competitors can lead to redundancy of knowledge, skills, and resources and increase the threat

of competition and secrecy among members, thus impeding the flow of ideas among them. Furthermore, if the consortium comprises competitors working on applied research problems, it should anticipate possible charges of antitrust violation. Basic research, however, is not problematic, since it seldom threatens the competitive structure of the marketplace (U.S. Department of Justice, 1981). Furthermore, in recent years at least two federal acts have encouraged joint research efforts: the Patent and Trademarks Act of 1980, which permits universities to own patents resulting from federally sponsored research, and the Stevenson-Wydler Innovation Act of 1980, which permits joint research efforts.

Once the relevant members have been identified, they must meet to discuss the viability of a consortium and its potential to address joint R & D interests. The consortium could be susceptible to a host of problems if it fails to ensure a reasonable level of consensus among members about goals and means to achieve them. The debate about whether R & D projects should be user-driven or university-driven, for example, is never ending. Without industry's advice about which projects to undertake, it would be hard to get industry involved in the consortium. Industry's involvement also ensures that research results will be relevant and usable to the membership. If obstacles are not openly discussed at this point, members may have unreasonable expectations about what a joint effort can accomplish and how soon. Energy may be continually drained by disagreements over the research agenda, patent rights, publication rights, and the like. And if the R & D consortium suffers from the common problem of being "underorganized," it may not be cohesive enough to survive these disputes.

After the organizations that share common goals and a commitment to collective efforts decide to join ranks, they are faced with the task of structuring the consortium and developing processes to promote the flow of information among members. Even in their earliest stages, R & D consortia need strong, competent leaders. Members would do well to seek out leaders having the energy, commitment, and resources to champion the cause of the consortium. These persons should be networkers, boundary spanners from either industry or academia who are known and respected in both sectors, people with a wealth of personal contacts and knowledge of sources of talent. With these leaders' networks already in place, the consortium is in a strong position even in the early stages of its existence.

Experts (Dimancescu and Botkin, 1986; Gray, Hetzner, Eveland, and Gidley, 1986) generally recommend that given the consortium's complexity, fluid membership, and under-organized structure, it should seek the leadership of a single, strong individual. One "champion of the cause" can focus the consortium members' efforts on the task at hand while at the same time pulling the group through those times of flagging commitment.

Among the many functions the leader serves is managing the consortium—an organization of organizations. Once qualified members are on board, the leader must work to sustain their commitment to the goals of the consortium, coordinate its functioning, resolve conflicts, encourage communication and trust among members, and replenish membership and research sources. The leadership's goal should be to involve industry as much as possible, not only to ensure continuing sponsorship but to ensure the smooth transfer of technological innovation from university to industry.

If leadership is central to consortium success, then a committed membership comes in a strong second. Industry members must be willing to contribute more than just funding; university researchers must be willing to share information with industry. The consortium's potential for technological innovation is realized when members are working together both formally and informally, trading ideas, encouraging one another, and availing the consortium of each member's sources for additional funding, sponsorship, and research areas.

Collective research and development needs ongoing evaluation. The purpose of evaluation is to ensure that the consortium is progressing as planned and having the desired effect. Because consortia must compete for time and resources with all the other projects the members are involved in, evaluation can serve the valuable function of imposing added structure to the consortium. For example, Thomas Cummings (1981) has described a tailoring process in which data feedback is used to evaluate the progress of a consortium. Regular feedback can remind members of their original goals if members become scattered in their interests. Positive feedback can also spark their commitment to the consortium. Furthermore, a well-chosen evaluator may be knowledgeable about the efforts of other such collectives and be a source of new ideas about effective methods for organizing, seeking government funding, and so forth.

Conclusions

R & D consortia have been proliferating in recent years. For many it is too soon to assess the success of their efforts, but there is no doubt that they are a promising means of enhancing organizational competitiveness and innovation. They complement the single organization's research lab and the individual inventor, but they are especially promising for permitting high-risk, high-expense basic research of generic use to many competitors. Though competitors work in cooperation, they need not fear charges of antitrust violation. No collaborative basic research project has ever been challenged because they do not threaten the competitive structure of the marketplace.

The university–industry R & D consortium is unique in its capacity to enhance the United States' competitive position because it provides a wealth of academic research talent and promotes the transfer of research findings to practice. It educates and trains the next generation of technologists as well.

References

Brodsky, N. H., Kaufman, H. G., and Tooker, J. D. *University-Industry Cooperation: A Preliminary Analysis of Existing Mechanisms and Their Relationship to the Innovation Processes.* New York: Center for Science and Technology Policy, Graduate School of Public Administration, New York University, 1980.
Cummings, T. "Designing Effective Work Groups." In P. Nystrom

and W. H. Starbuck (eds.), *Handbook of Organizational Design.* Vol. 2. London: Oxford University Press, 1981.

Cummings, T. "Transorganizational Development." In B. Staw and L. L. Cummings (eds.), *Research in Organizational Behavior.* Vol. 6. Greenwich, Conn.: JAI Press, 1984.

Dimancescu, D., and Botkin, J. *The New Alliance: America's R and D Consortia.* Cambridge, Mass.: Ballinger, 1986.

Ewing, K. P., Jr. "Joint Research, Anti-Trust, and Innovation." *Research Management,* 1981, *24* (2), 25–29.

Gobeli, D. H., and Rudelius, W. "Managing Innovation: Lessons from the Cardiac-Pacing Industry." In E. B. Roberts (ed.), *Generating Technological Innovation.* Oxford, England: Oxford University Press, 1986.

Government-University-Industry Research Roundtable. *New Alliances and Partnerships in American Science and Engineering.* Washington, D.C.: National Academy Press, 1986.

Gray, D. O., Hetzner, W., Eveland, J. D., and Gidley, T. "NSF's Industry-University Cooperative Research Centers Program and the Innovation Process: Evaluation Based Lessons." In D. O. Gray, T. Solomon, and W. Hetzner (eds.), *Technological Innovations: Strategies for a New Partnership.* New York: Elsevier, 1986.

Gray, D. O., Solomon, T., and Hetzner, W. *Technological Innovation: Strategies for a New Partnership.* New York: Elsevier, 1986.

Krosin, K. E. "Joint Research Ventures Under the Anti-Trust Laws." *George Washington Law Review,* 1971, *39* (5), 1112–1140.

Nathan, M. L., and Cummings, T. G. "Transorganization Systems: Definitions, Operationalizations, Measurement, and Future Directions." Working paper, Department of Management and Organization, University of Southern California, 1987.

Roberts, E. B. (ed.).*Generating Technological Innovation.* New York: Oxford University Press, 1987.

Roberts, E. B., and Berry, C. A. "Entering New Businesses: Selecting Strategies for Success." In E. B. Roberts (ed.), *Generating Technological Innovation.* New York: Oxford University Press, 1987.

Rosenzweig, R. M., and Tarlington, B. "The Research University and Its Patrons." In R. M. Rosenzweig and B. Tarlington (eds.),

Industry-University Collaboration: The New Partnership. Berkeley: University of California Press, 1982.

Salancik, G., and Pfeffer, J. *The External Control of Organizations: A Resource Dependence Perspective.* New York: Harper & Row, 1978.

Shortell, S. M., and Zajac, E. J. "Internal Corporate Joint Ventures: Development Processes and Performance Outcomes." *Strategic Management Journal,* 1988, *9,* 527–542.

Swartzel, K. R., and Gray, D. O. "Industry-University Cooperative Research in Agriculture and Food Science: North Carolina State University's Center for Aseptic Processing and Packaging Studies." *Food Technology,* Dec. 1987, *41* (12), 96–98.

Tornatzky, L. G., and others. *University-Industry Cooperative Research Centers: A Practice Manual.* Washington, D.C.: Innovation Processes Research Section, Division of Industrial Science and Technological Innovation, National Science Foundation, 1982.

U.S. Department of Justice, Anti-Trust Division. "Anti-Trust Guidelines for Joint Research Programs." *Research Management,* 1981, *24* (2), 30–37.

17

ENHANCING R & D ACROSS FUNCTIONAL AREAS

WILLIAM A. PASMORE
KATHLEEN GURLEY

Interest in enhancing the effectiveness of R & D units is as old as R & D itself. The pharaohs of ancient Egypt put considerable pressure on the designers of the pyramids to hasten their planning and construction; Socrates endeavored to heighten the critical thinking of his best students; the Romans supported a class of citizens whose only work was to assist in the advancement of what today would be referred to as engineering know-how. More recently, we can trace some of our most advanced thinking about organizational design and management to work begun in R & D units. TRW's Space Park in Redondo Beach, California, for example, served as a test bed for the application of T-groups to business and was among the first organizations to adopt a matrix structure.

The reasons for focusing attention on R & D effectiveness are straightforward: First, to the extent that appropriate new products can be developed more quickly and at lower cost, companies stand to gain tremendous competitive advantages; second, organizations continue to risk major expenditures in R & D with no guarantee of recouping their investment (Ranftl, 1978; Packer, 1983). R & D continues to be both vital and unpredictable in competitive markets; even to those involved directly, R & D sometimes seems to be two-thirds magic and one-third science.

Despite decades of management research, the question of how best to design and manage R & D units is still open to debate. Researchers have examined the characteristics of successful scientists and engineers (Pelz and Andrews, 1966; Badawy, 1971; Thompson and Dalton, 1976; Griggs and Manring, 1987), communication patterns and roles within laboratories (Allen and Cohen, 1969; Katz and Tushman, 1979; Tushman and Nadler, 1980), organizational design (Burns and Stalker, 1961; Galbraith, 1982; Quinn, 1985), the dynamics of project groups and teams (Cohen, 1985; Katz, 1982), reward systems and career ladders (Louis, 1985; Lawler, 1981; Sanders, 1980; Souder, 1987), and management styles (Litwin, 1968) — all with the intention of adding clarity to the confused state of our knowledge regarding what goes on inside the R & D "black box." Clarity remains elusive, however, and this function, absolutely vital to many organizational futures, continues to operate cloaked in mystery.

This chapter examines the application of sociotechnical systems theory and intervention methods in R & D organizations. Sociotechnical systems thinking, which was developed in the context of manufacturing operations (Trist and Bamforth, 1951; Trist, Higgin, Murray, and Pollock, 1963; Pasmore, 1988), has been arguably the most powerful lever yet discovered for improving an organization's performance through intervention into human processes (Friedlander and Brown, 1974; Srivastva and others, 1975). Yet sociotechnical systems thinking has been applied only sparingly to nonmanufacturing operations. Although this application was foreseen by early theorists (Emery and Trist, 1978), the publication of Calvin Pava's (1983) *Managing New Office Technology* provided the first workable theory and method for analyzing what he referred to as "nonroutine systems."

Basically Pava calls for a shift from examining variances in a repetitive workflow to key decisions or "deliberations" in nonroutine work. He reasons that since work in nonroutine systems is by definition always in the process of being planned, catching people in the planning process is more important than observing the results of their planning. The quality of inputs to the planning process has a profound influence on the objectives that are pursued and the methods used to accomplish those objectives. By examining who is involved in making key decisions, what information they draw upon, what roles they play, and how relationships affect decisions, Pava argues that systems can be designed to integrate social and technical realities, thereby producing more effective performance.

In our efforts to enhance R & D effectiveness, we have expanded Pava's contribution to sociotechnical systems thinking in nonroutine systems. This chapter outlines our views on R & D organizations as knowledge-based sociotechnical systems and describes a successful attempt to apply these ideas.

R & D Organizations as Sociotechnical Systems

In traditional sociotechnical systems theory, it is held that organizations should be designed around their core production process; in R & D organizations, the core process is clearly that of producing ideas about products or processes. This work is knowledge-based; the availability and utilization of knowledge determine to a large extent the quality and viability of the ideas that are eventually conceived. Thus to improve R & D organizations we must understand the ways in which social and technical systems influence the development and utilization of knowledge. This emphasis on knowledge in R & D systems is made clearer when one contrasts the nature of work in routine (manufacturing) versus nonroutine (R & D) units. Table 17.1 shows some of the major differences between routine and nonroutine work.

Nonroutine work is, by definition, partially undefined at its commencement. How the work will be performed and even by whom the work will be carried out is determined along the way as new information influences thinking about the task. Given the lack of prior experience regarding the current task, many decisions are made intuitively rather than on the basis of complete data and logic. Moreover, many methods can be employed to work toward objectives, which themselves are often in conflict: Consumers desire products that are relatively inexpensive, but they demand high quality as well; trade-offs are made between such things as product durability and weight as different materials are considered; working toward a major break-

Table 17.1. Differences Between Routine and Nonroutine Systems.

	Routine	Nonroutine
Nature of work	• Defined • Repetitive • One right way • Clear, shared goals • Information readily available • Forecasting helpful	• Undefined • Nonrepetitive • Many right ways • Multiple, competing goals • Information hard to obtain • Forecasting difficult
Nature of success	• Efficiency • Technical perfection • Productivity measurable • Physical technology • Standard information • Detail-oriented	• Effectiveness • Human perfection • Productivity unmeasurable • Knowledge technology • Nonstandard information • Completion-oriented
Nature of decision making	• Rules applicable • Experience counts • Authority-based • Complete operational specs • Authority by position	• Rules inhibiting • Experience may be irrelevant • Consensus-based • Incomplete operational specs • Authority by virtue of expertise
Nature of context	• Short time horizon • Stable environment • Predefined outcomes	• Long time horizon • Unstable environment • Emergent outcomes
Nature of variances	• Obvious	• Hidden

through is played against utilizing familiar development techniques. Finding the correct solutions to such trade-offs is complicated by the fact that information regarding consumer tastes, competitors' plans, and many other crucial inputs may be lacking and difficult to obtain. Even if such information is available, forecasting how long it will take to complete the development task or how much the product will ultimately cost to manufacture is often more like reading entrails than running a railroad. Thus, in nonroutine environments like R & D, the inputs that would allow logic, data, and science to guide plans for the use of resources in task completion are often missing. In the absence of this information, choosing the right path to the desired outcome is necessarily an intuitive and political process.

Partly because of this uncertain information and partly because of the nature of R & D itself, success is defined differently in R & D than in traditional manufacturing operations. In manufacturing, repetitive performance of the same tasks allows micromeasurement of routinely observable manufacturing parameters. Often these measures are referred to as indicators of manufacturing "efficiencies." The emphasis in manufacturing is on doing the same thing better and faster with less waste and higher quality—efficiency. In R & D, managers are more concerned with results than in-process measures. Achieving the goal is of paramount importance, not how efficiently material or labor is utilized. Productivity is difficult to measure in the R & D environment. How does one calculate the productivity of an engineer who makes only one major breakthrough in his career, but with it ensures the company's future?

Because of these difficulties in measuring R & D performance, surrogate measures are often applied. Project reports are written and submitted regularly as an indication that "we're working on it"; budgets are measured against what other companies are spending or what we spent last year; headcount is changed in the vain hope that the number of people in the lab somehow relates to the number of new ideas produced there. More appropriately, efforts are made to recruit and develop high-caliber people who have the right education or a good track record. In manufacturing, the emphasis is on finding the best machine for the job; in R & D, the focus is on getting the best people. It follows that decisions about personnel are a key to the evolution of knowledge in R & D systems.

The way decisions are made in R & D organizations also differs from the approach in manufacturing organizations. In manufacturing, technical understanding of the process is nearly complete, leading to tight specifications that dictate how the system is to be operated. Past experience is directly applicable to future operations, so that those with experience are accorded greater authority in decision making. As these people rise in the system, the combination of their expertise and the tight operating specifications for the system lends strength to the hierarchy. Many decisions are made in a top-down fashion; little input is required from those below in order to reach decisions of acceptable quality. In R & D organizations, expertise is widely distributed throughout the organization. Past experience may not be applicable to the development of new products and in fact may inhibit creative thinking. There are few rules to govern the creative process, yet the pieces of complex products must somehow fit together before they are handed to manufacturing. This leads to consensus-based decision making in R & D, as specialists who often understand more about their work than their supervisors meet together over coffee and doughnuts to work out the bugs in promising designs.

Time is measured differently, as well. In manufacturing, timeclocks are punched and minutes of downtime are recorded. In R & D, quarters or years are the appropriate unit of time for most discussions. As Jaques (1986) so eloquently pointed out, the time span of discretion is typically longer for tasks requiring greater cognitive complexity. R & D specialists can go for months without receiving feedback on their performance and even longer before they know whether the product they have designed is a success.

By the time products reach manufacturing and facilities have been constructed for their fabrication, someone has already determined that there is at least a semistable consumer demand for the product. This means that the environment of the manufacturing organization is relatively stable compared to that of the R & D unit. In R & D, projects are started (and stopped) on the basis of incomplete information about consumer demand for the product, projections of manufacturing costs, evidence of unintended environmental impacts, the departure of key scientists, or the whims of the R & D manager. Hence R & D units tend to be more subject to their environments than are routine operations. They are also more sensitive to the loss of knowledge that accompanies the departure of even a few individuals, if those figures have played key roles in the development of important products.

Finally, there is an important difference between manufacturing and R & D operations regarding the variances or problems that affect the quality or quantity of outputs from the system. In manufacturing, variances tend to be visible and repetitive. With some detective work, they can be tracked down and identified. This in turn makes them relatively easy to control. In R & D, variances are often hidden and sometimes go undetected until the product is in manufacturing or even later. The variances are hidden because they tend to occur in people's heads when they are thinking about how to design the product. Incorrect assumptions, mistakes, guesses, misinformation, misunderstandings, and trade-offs are an integral part of virtually every complex product development process. Often it is difficult to trace these variances to their source or to catalogue them for future reference. It is even difficult to recognize variances after they have occurred, for they gradually become an accepted part of organizational life. Since delays, misunderstandings, and miscommunications are taken to be par for the course, they are consequently ignored when people discuss what can be done to improve the system. Understanding what variances look like in nonroutine environments and how they can be controlled requires new sociotechnical systems thinking.

Typical Variances in R & D Operations

Since the core product of R & D organizations is knowledge, it follows that variances in R & D systems will be knowledge-related. Some of the typical variances encountered in R & D units are considered here and examples are given in the appendix at the end of this chapter.

Lack of Knowledge

Perhaps the most obvious variance consists of a lack of knowledge needed to complete a task appropriately. Galbraith (1977) has pointed out that we need not concern ourselves with a general lack of knowledge but only the knowledge that is directly related to the effective performance of tasks. The lack of such knowledge, according to Galbraith, creates "relevant uncertainty" and attendant performance problems in organizations. Typically the lack of relevant knowledge is demonstrated in wrong decisions or in decisions being delayed or avoided altogether. When R & D professionals lack relevant knowledge, they are usually quite aware of it—making this one of the simpler variances to detect in nonroutine systems. Controlling this variance, however, may be difficult or even impossible. Sometimes the knowledge is too costly to develop or simply beyond our capacity to create; under these circumstances, risks are assessed, guesses are made, and consequences are measured somewhere down the road. But often this variance can be corrected by exposing the area of relevant uncertainty and involving people with appropriate expertise to answer the questions being posed.

Failure to Use Knowledge

More difficult to detect is the failure to utilize knowledge that already exists within the system. In common parlance, we generally refer to the results of this variance as "mistakes." In contrast to the preceding variance—lack of knowledge, which is viewed as beyond a person's control—the failure to use existing knowledge to make a proper decision is clearly attributable to human error. People sometimes "forget" to check with the appropriate authority on an issue or forget what they themselves know. Alternatively, they may fail to communicate what they know to others who need it because they assume that the others either would not understand it or "wouldn't value their input." Detecting this variance usually requires an analysis of past project performance, including interviews to discover why existing knowledge was not utilized when it should have been.

Lack of Cooperation

When parties who possess knowledge relevant to the tasks of others deliberately withhold it, incorrect decisions often result.

People may withhold knowledge if they view their relationships with others as fundamentally competitive rather than cooper- ative, if they feel wronged by the other party in the past, if they are working toward opposing objectives, if they stand to lose political power by making the other look good, or if they feel that their help is not desired. Lack of cooperation is also appar- ent when one group shows reluctance to adopt or evaluate fairly the ideas generated by another group. People tend to work on their own ideas and to resist input from others. This tendency is so common in R & D that it has become known as the "Not Invented Here Syndrome." Its occurrence frequently results in delays or even barriers to innovation.

Many organizations are designed in ways that heighten the chances that competition and politics will overshadow coop- eration and mutual support. Raises and promotions are limited in number; tall pyramidal hierarchies and clear functional boundaries interfere with natural tendencies by those at lower levels to help others in need; those who play political games are often the most highly rewarded; cooperation is given little recog- nition. All too often, those who cooperate feel as if they do so at their own peril and almost in violation of the wishes of their superiors.

Missing Parties in Key Discussions

One of the beliefs underlying hierarchical forms of organiza- tion is that the most qualified decision makers rise to the top. When this belief is not challenged during key discussions, those in positions of authority may trust themselves to make the choices without soliciting the opinion of others. A notorious example of this type of variance occurred at Morton Thiokol, where lower-level engineers tried to stop the launch of the *Chal- lenger* but were excluded from key discussions by their superiors. This variance also occurs when colleagues in other functions are excluded from discussions in which their ideas would be crucial. The old "toss it over the transom" relationship between R & D and production units is a classic expression of this variance. Production people are explicitly excluded from R & D discussions that will affect production because R & D people tend to view production people as inflexible, anti-innovation, and too narrowly focused on efficiencies rather than the "pull" of the product in the marketplace.

Wrong Parties in Key Discussions

This variance is the obverse of the previous one. Just as excluding certain people can bias decisions, so can including others. Some people are invited to important meetings because they always have been invited, not because they possess technical information or experience relevant to the choices at hand. Nevertheless, because of their status or verbal dexterity, they are allowed to influence decisions in disastrous ways. Many organizations will never know the missed potential of ideas shot down by those who did not know what they were talking about. Instead, we have only reminders of a persistent few who risked their careers to prove that what others thought was impossible was indeed feasible.

No Key Discussions at All

These days, everyone hates meetings. Scientists and engineers may hate them more than most people. Given the choice of attending a meeting to have her ideas ripped apart by others or trusting her own professional judgment, a scientist may not hesitate to press on alone. The same is true of managers; if there is a chance that an idea may be shot down, many would prefer to make the decision on their own and live with the consequences rather than take the time to have it reviewed.

Some time ago, we were advising a data processing organization that had tried to institute structured programming techniques. These techniques consisted basically of two things: having software programmers use similar methods in order to minimize the complexity of the program and having them meet on a regular basis so that other programmers could help to correct each person's work. The process did not take. It seems that the programmers objected that the new methods were not as elegant as the old way of programming; the old way might take longer, they said, but it would result in better programs for the users. The new approach offended the programmers' sense of professional dignity because it reduced the process to one that almost anyone could perform. The group reviews were seen as simultaneously threatening and a waste of time. Some people clearly needed them because their work was always poor; the better programmers felt that the organization should simply get rid of these people rather than wasting time in meetings correcting their work. The better programmers were rarely challenged by their peers, although their superiors often used the meetings as an opportunity to admonish them for not following the structured programming methods. As this example shows, there are powerful reasons for avoiding discussions of one's work with others. But when discussions are not held, knowledge cannot be transferred or developed among decision makers.

Lack of Goal Clarity

Even in single projects, efforts often proceed in multiple directions because goals are unclear. Should the product be elegant or cheap? Should it be developed quickly or incorporate all the latest discoveries? Should it be considered high priority or low priority? In many projects, the answers to such questions are unclear. Even when goals are clearly stated at the beginning of a project, they may change as the project proceeds. Add to this the fact that most R & D organizations need to juggle multiple projects simultaneously, and the goals of the individual engineer or scientist become even more confused. In the face of this confusion, knowledge crucial to the project's success may not be developed at all, while knowledge that is in reality much less important is developed fully.

Another variance in this genre is goal displacement. In the search for certainty in an uncertain world, some managers of R & D organizations place more emphasis on paperwork being completed properly than on actual project results. When secondary tasks occupy the time needed to work on knowledge development, knowledge output suffers.

Time Frame Too Short or Too Long

The most common form of this variance occurs when insufficient time is allotted to develop critical knowledge on a project. Under the pressure of arbitrary deadlines, knowledge development is sacrificed for the sake of expediency, thereby precluding the expected level of success. At times, however, time frames can be too long. When project deadlines are set too far into the future, they may be regarded as nonexistent. When those trying to develop knowledge for the project approach others for assistance, they may find that attention is riveted on projects with tighter deadlines. In a world where there is never enough time to do everything one would like, short deadlines are used to focus attention on certain projects and away from others.

Procedures Unclear or Nonexistent

When procedures are not clearly stated for such things as project review sessions, the allocation of resources, or project selection, the informal system is allowed to drive decision making. Often this works out well because the informal system may utilize knowledge more effectively than the formal system does. But the informal system also has a way of making decisions that optimize local benefits and short-term gains. Procedures help to specify who should be involved in making key decisions and what knowledge they should use. In the fight against all things bureaucratic, some R & D organizations neglect opportunities to ensure that sound decisions are made more consistently.

Inadequate Attention to External Environment

By now, the joke about what the customer requested versus what the engineer designed has become trite. Nevertheless, it remains true far too often. Contact with the customer, or with other relevant segments of the external environment, is frequently less than it should be. As a result, critical information never enters the design process or is overlooked once the process has begun.

Too Much Bureaucratic Structure

Earlier we noted that a lack of procedures may prevent the utilization of knowledge in allocating resources. At the same time, we recognize that adding too much structure to an R & D organization can kill it. Numerous levels of hierarchy, an over-abundance of rules and regulations, a flood of trivial paper-work — such things sap energy that would otherwise be available for the creation and application of knowledge. Peters has noted repeatedly that skunk works outperform major research labs (Peters and Waterman, 1982; Peters and Austin, 1985; Peters, 1987) — ostensibly because the research bureaucracy gets in the way of people doing what they would naturally do. But if one reads accounts of how highly successful skunk work groups actually function (such as the Data General Eagle computer group described by Kidder, 1981), it becomes clear that a very definite structure is in place. The difference is that the structure is largely self-generated and appropriate to the challenge at hand. Structure is a liability when it interferes with knowledge generation and utilization. It adds little or no value to the outcome and serves mainly to calm the nerves of frightened administrators.

Summary

Since nonroutine systems vary from routine systems in signifi-cant ways, our theories of organizational design and effective-ness must take these differences into account. The following propositions capture our thinking about the effective design of nonroutine systems:

> Proposition 1: The most important technology in non-routine systems is knowledge. Therefore, organiza-tional effectiveness is directly related to the capacity of the organization to develop and utilize knowledge. The availability of knowledge at key choice points sets an upper limit on organizational effectiveness; the organi-

zation will be no more effective than allowed by knowledge that is used to guide decisions.

Proposition 2:   The generation and utilization of knowledge are influenced by the knowledge level of human resources entering the system, by the attention paid to the development of knowledge by human resources in the system, and by organizational arrangements that influence the character and operation of the emergent sociotechnical system.

Proposition 3:   The concepts of organizational choice and joint optimization apply in nonroutine systems; that is, managers of nonroutine systems can make conscious choices to influence the production and utilization of knowledge through deliberate attention to organizational design. Some designs will be superior to others in terms of both knowledge effectiveness and human satisfaction. These designs will emphasize the control of variances that hinder knowledge generation and utilization via methods that meet the emotional needs of members of the system.

These ideas are captured in Figure 17.1, which depicts a theory of organizational effectiveness in nonroutine systems. As indicated in the figure, organizational effectiveness in nonroutine systems is tied to effective knowledge utilization, which is a function of both the availability of knowledge and the organizational arrangements that influence the processes by which available knowledge is applied to key choices. Knowledge availability, in turn, is a function of incoming knowledge levels (analogous to the raw material inputs into routine systems) and the knowledge development processes and organizational arrangements that influence the rate and quality of knowledge development.

Finally, we note again that variances in nonroutine systems like R & D units tend to be associated with the development and utilization of knowledge. This makes them difficult to detect and control. Because we cannot always see them or their immediate effects, we must search for variances where they exist—in

Figure 17.1. A Model of Nonroutine Organizational Effectiveness.

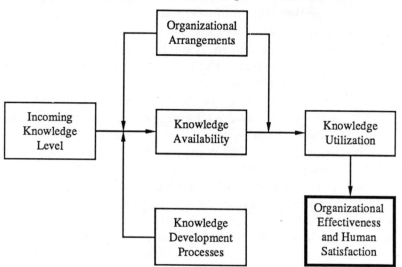

the minds of those who are involved in the R & D process. To improve the effectiveness of R & D systems, we must help these people to become aware of what variances consist of, how they affect the system and its outcomes, and what can be done to detect and control them. The methodology outlined in the following case study is one approach to this challenge.

A Case Study

A sociotechnical change process including both routine and nonroutine work was undertaken by the R & D division of a *Fortune* 100 company. The specific workflow process under study was the prototype tire development and submission process for the major automotive original equipment manufacturers (OEMs). The original equipment segment of the passenger tire business continues to increase in importance because of the volume of the OEM market and the prestige associated with the introduction of new car models.

The major reason behind the need for change was the acceleration in customer demands being made on the system.

The Detroit OEMs were expecting a product developed and fine-tuned to meet their diverse vehicle performance criteria. No longer could a generic tire design meet the requirements of the major OEMs. Moreover, the company was increasing its involvement with the Japanese automotive manufacturers, a move that considerably increased the complexity of the business. Overall the OEMs were demanding more new products in shorter time frames.

Internally, the organization was experiencing an increase in the number of crisis programs going through the system. These programs were leading to hasty decisions on initial trials that often led to a reiteration through the development cycle. Considerable time was being spent negotiating resource priorities and expediting projects through the system. This mode of operation not only caused problems at the original equipment (OE) level but also made it difficult to maintain a cohesive development program ensuring future innovations.

Because of the importance and complexity of the OE tire submission process, technical management saw the need for an in-depth analysis of the process aimed at an unbiased look at the root causes of the problems and not just the symptoms. Since experience with previous task forces often had failed to gain the support needed for implementation, management looked for a process that would build ownership for the change throughout the organization.

The sociotechnical change process was adopted because of its systems perspective, recognizing the close interaction between the environmental, technical, and social subsystems, and the emphasis on data gathering by a cross-functional team. The detailed analysis of every phase in the process helped expand each team member's understanding of the overall system. Attitudes changed from "it's someone else's problem" to "we have a problem, let's solve it together."

The change process began with the formation of a steering committee composed of the department heads of the four major functional areas included in the OE submission process. The steering committee met several times to define the purpose and scope of the change process prior to forming a project team

Figure 17.2. The OE Submission Process.

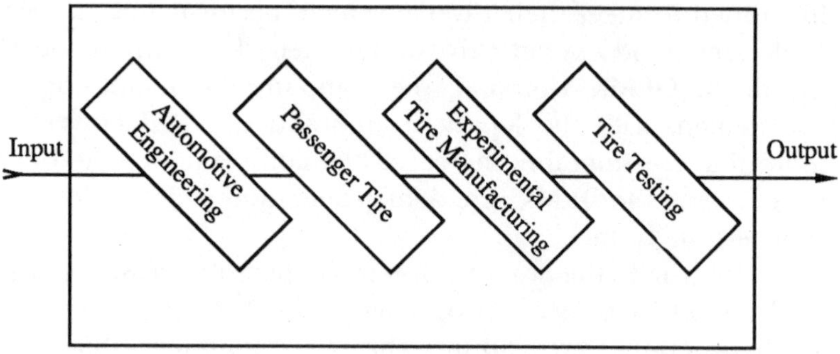

to do the analysis and redesign work. The role of the steering committee during the analysis phase was to provide direction and support for the time commitment of the team members. Later in the project, the steering committee took a more active role in reviewing the recommendations and moving them forward to implementation.

Figure 17.2 illustrates the traditional tire submission process and the four major departments involved in the Original Equipment Process Improvement Project (OEPIP). The traditional process was sequential with the OE requirements submitted through automotive engineering. These requirements were transmitted to the passenger tire program group, which developed specifications for tires to be produced in the experimental tire manufacturing shop. Once the tires were produced, the tire program engineer specified the test procedures to be conducted by tire testing.

The study team conducted the environmental, technical, and social analysis simultaneously by dividing up into subcommittees. The environmental analysis was aimed at clarifying the demands on the tire submission system and determining the success in meeting these demands. The analysis also looked at the technological, economic, and competitive trends that significantly affect these demands. Specific information was gathered on the expectations of each OEM—time frames, test data required, quality standards, additional service requested.

Through interviews with the account managers for each OEM, an assessment was made of the current level of response to these demands and the OEM's degree of satisfaction with the service. The first major result of the environmental analysis was that the system generally met the OEM's deadline for tire submissions but the tires were being submitted without test data. A trend noted by the team was that the OEMs were beginning to rely more on the supplier's test data. All of the OEMs were putting more pressure on suppliers by starting to refuse tire submissions without data. This fact led the OEPIP team to redefine the product for the system to "tires and data" and subsequently to develop a tire/data logo to reinforce this message throughout the organization. The second major result of the environmental analysis was the finding that the company required many submissions before approval. In other words, to obtain approval from the OEM the program group had to develop and submit a larger number of different constructions for testing. This shotgun approach caused a burden on the internal resources as well as the OEM's testing resources.

The social analysis involved a written survey covering both job design factors (Hackman and Oldham, 1980) and organization climate (Taylor and Bowers, 1972). The survey was completed by approximately 80 percent of the employees in the four departments involved in OE submissions. The results of the survey were discussed in small groups to gain a thorough understanding of the significant themes. From the survey data and the group discussions, a culture statement was written describing the major strengths and weaknesses of the current organization. The overall ratings of the job characteristics were below the national average for autonomy, feedback (from the job and agents), meaningfulness of work, and responsibility for work. Moreover, general satisfaction was significantly lower than the national average, suggesting a general frustration not solely related to job design. The major findings from the social analysis were the following:

- Very strong loyalty to the company
- High satisfaction and trust in co-workers

- Inadequate planning and coordination between departments
- Decisions not being made at the level where the most information is available
- Expertise within the organization not being fully utilized by decision makers

The technical analysis included both routine and nonroutine work. The routine work was analyzed through an in-depth study of the sequential steps in the submission process. It determined the variances in each step and finally analyzed the impact of each variance on the total process. The technical analysis identified more than two hundred steps in the process and several hundred variances. These variances were reduced to a manageable number prior to using a variance matrix to determine the key twenty-five variances. The technical analysis confirmed the high degree of interdependency of departments and functions in the overall tire submission system. The analysis further found that 35 percent of the variances were caused by information gaps—not surprising in a traditional sequential process where information can get lost or confused in translation. Besides the key variances it also became apparent that the engineers were spending considerable time expediting paperwork necessary to authorize work procedures—tire building, testing, shipping, and so on. Moreover, the team recognized that the resource allocation priorities facilitated getting tires built but not tested. Only after the tires were built, screened, and put in inventory could a test request be written.

The nonroutine work analysis looked at eight major choice points in the submission process. For each choice point, the parties involved were identified and the information they exchanged was determined. A responsibility chart was put together to clarify the role of each person in the decision-making process. Of the eight choice points, four dealt with establishing priorities among multiple projects for limited resources at different points in the submission process. It became obvious that a great deal of time was being spent negotiating priorities because there was no overall scheduling system to coordinate the flow of projects through the system. Two of the choice points related to the interface with the OEMs. The analysis indicated that commitments were being made to the OEMs without adequate information on resource availability. The system responded to the unrealistic deadlines by creating crisis situations to preempt resource priorities. The analysis also indicated that the communication on new OEM programs and broad program priorities was not widespread, especially in the support or service groups.

Once the data collection and analysis were complete, the team began to integrate the findings from the environmental, technical, and social subcommittees. To guide the redesign of the OE submission process, mission and philosophy statements were written. These statements incorporated the values and goals the team wanted to create. The team focused its effort on developing systemwide recommendations to address the major variances. In addition they compiled the local variances into a report for each of the four major departments and suggested that each department take steps to correct its internal variances. As the team began developing its recommendations, it became obvious that the process itself had been a catalyst for change — especially in the way departments worked together.

The six major recommendations were: a program plan, an efficient process flow, a window concept, improvements in experimental data reporting, a continuous process flow, and the formation of OE teams. The program plan was seen as a computerized project management tool accessible to all team members. It would provide a way of tracking the status of a project all the way through the process. Through a resources-leveling feature, the software was expected to help establish and coordinate priorities at the different phases of the submission process. Both the efficient process flow and the continuous process flow were directed at streamlining the process by reducing the paperwork and eliminating unnecessary bureaucratic procedures. The objective was to integrate the different phases into a continuous process of building and testing a prototype tire. The improved data reporting and window concept related to the experimental tire manufacturing procedures. The window concept proposed a new approach to scheduling the building of tires for top-priority projects. The data reporting recommendation called for better information and quality control systems.

The last recommendation, the OE teams, was a structural change introducing a permanent team overlay on the functional departments. The objective of the matrix team structure was to improve lateral integration across a functional organization. The teams were organized around the major OEM accounts: GM, Ford, Chrysler, and others. Each team was composed of technical experts from the four major departments. The teams were given responsibility for planning, coordinating, and implementing the programs for their account. The team overlay concept was recommended to overcome variances in both the technical and social systems. The advantages of the team were given as follows:

• Increased communications and information sharing
• Increased cooperation toward a common goal
• Improved up-front planning
• Greater task identity (sense of ownership for outcome)
• Increased autonomy and decision-making responsibility

Together these advantages were aimed at enhancing knowledge availability and utilization at key choice points. It should be noted that structural changes in organizational design (such as the formation of teams) may be required to raise the level of performance in knowledge-based systems. Controlling hidden variances calls for those responsible for the development of knowledge to be in continuous contact with those who utilize it, so that knowledge gaps and unanticipated interaction effects may be identified.

All of the preceding recommendations were still at the conceptual stage when presented to the steering committee for review. The steering committee agreed in principle with the major recommendations but expressed concern about the time and resources required for their implementation. When the recommendations received approval and support from senior management, the team was asked to propose an implementation plan. The team suggested that implementation teams be formed to develop the major recommendations further. Several of the OEPIP members agreed to participate and the OEPIP team as a whole requested a role in guiding the implementation process. The OEPIP team also suggested that a measurement system be established to track improvements in the OE submission process.

Significant progress has been made in implementing all of the recommendations. Most of them have required considerable planning and work. The OE teams have brought about the most significant change and continue to drive ongoing improvement in the system. The first noticeable improvement was increased communication and cooperation across departments. Each team member assumed responsibility for ensuring that projects flowed smoothly through his or her department and keeping others in the department informed of different OEM requests. This change came only after a great deal of discussion on the role of the team members and the support required from functional management.

At this point the teams tended to plateau. Work was still being carried out in much the same way as before, and the teams saw their main responsibility as coordinating the functional activities. Management wanted the teams to assume more responsibility, however, so several of the teams began to redefine their mission. In an off-site workshop they began to take ownership of a more strategic mission. The team members learned more about each other's functional roles and began to adopt greater flexibility in their task assignments. Each person's contribution was seen as important to the team's success, and a sense of shared responsibility for service to the account became a norm. As the teams grew more cohesive, they also began to exert greater influence.

Execution of projects has improved as the teams work together on problem solving to better their service to the OEM. Measurable results included an estimated 25 percent increase in the workload or number of OEM requests successfully met with no increase in personnel. Moreover, one of the teams contributed a significant improvement in the supplier rating, which is determined by the OEM. Another team has seen a fourfold increase in the number of Japanese firms to which they supply tires. As these teams matured, they have become more involved in the decision-making process, pushing to ensure quality service and products for their accounts.

Conclusion

As the case study indicates, sociotechnical systems thinking can be applied to nonroutine systems to bring about an increase in their effectiveness. The case blended traditional and nontraditional methods of sociotechnical systems analysis in order to address both the routine and nonroutine aspects of work performed in the R & D lab. The routine analysis identified a large number of variances that could be addressed through traditional means of variance control: training people to recognize variances, teaching them how to prevent or correct them, and granting them the autonomy to do so. The nontraditional analysis of key choice points highlighted the need to create additional knowledge in the system and use it more effectively. Nonroutine variances, often hidden from direct observation, were discovered through the process of investigation set out by the nonroutine methodology for sociotechnical systems analysis.

While one case is insufficient to prove the widespread viability of this approach to thinking and intervention in nonroutine systems, it is nevertheless encouraging. Nonroutine systems have been shrouded in mystery for too long; it is clear to us now that one of the reasons for this is that we have tried to understand them by utilizing inappropriate theories befitting routine environments. Nonroutine organizations are, more than other organizations, *human* systems. It makes more sense to analyze them using models based on human emotions, human psychology, and human learning and change than it does to think of them as machines or extensions of machines. By conceiving of nonroutine systems as knowledge-based and examining the organizational arrangements that affect the availability and utilization of knowledge within them, we begin to gain a clearer sense of the necessary steps for enhancing their effectiveness.

At the same time that we recognize the need for new theories to guide our thinking about nonroutine systems, we should not overlook some of the key similarities between nonroutine and traditional sociotechnical systems design. In general, sociotechnical systems theory appears to hold in nonroutine organizations. Human emotions continue to play a major if not central role in determining the effectiveness of nonroutine systems. The technical system still consists of methods for transforming inputs (ideas and information) into outputs (products, new ideas, or additional information). The only difference is that the technical system operates invisibly for the most part and is more completely under the control of those who operate it.

Just as industrialists were surprised to learn that simply acquiring the latest technology was not enough to maximize output, managers of R & D labs may be surprised to learn that spending large sums of money, adding additional people, and setting up new information systems may have no effect on overall R & D success or the company's competitive position. Instead, they should recognize that the degree of *joint* optimization of social and technical systems—through organizational design, the amount of attention paid to variance control, and the level of environmental responsiveness built into the organization—continues to set the limits of organizational performance.

Appendix: Examples of Variances at Key Choice Points

Lack of Knowledge

Example: inadequate information provided in marketing's request. When marketing or other liaison groups define customers' needs, the request frequently has to be translated into technical requirements. At times critical pieces of information are missing. Without this information the product development group starts work based on their best guess of the customer's needs. Early development work, as well as time, is often lost due to misdirection.

Failure to Use Knowledge

Example: building and testing too many designs. Because of the increased pressure for faster product introductions, R & D groups are finding themselves building and testing a broad range of product concepts and selecting the best option from the test results. Time is not taken at the start of the project to incorporate knowledge from previous projects. Databases that are hard to access or difficult to use contribute to this mode of operating.

Lack of Cooperation

Example: limitations of standard procedures. Since R & D interfaces with a constantly changing environment — technology, customers' needs, new knowledge, and so on — the approach to product development is continually being modified. Support groups such as testing facilities are often seen as a barrier to getting the job done because of their standardized procedures. Without sufficient cooperation and information sharing between functions, time and resources can be wasted in running inaccurate or inappropriate procedures.

Missing Parties in Key Discussions

Example: final product design decision. One of the key choice points in the product development cycle is the selection of the final features of the product design. When the decision is made by the product development group, the choice is based predominantly on the product's technical performance. The ease of manufacturing the product is not taken into consideration. Later, when the product is transferred to the plant, problems may occur when the product cannot be manufactured within quality or cost standards.

Wrong Parties in Key Discussions

Example: allocation of resources. A critical balance for most R & D organizations is the amount of resources invested in long-term technology development versus short-term product improvement. In an environment of scarce resources, negotiations over priorities can occur weekly and even daily. These negotiations are affected by the parties present and the strength of their positions. The urgency of short-term projects involving potential loss of business can unduly influence key decisions.

No Key Discussions at All

Example: inadequate process not detected. In almost all nonroutine work, progress on a project is difficult to judge. When a breakthrough is just around the corner is impossible to determine. Sometimes projects are allowed to continue because those involved are too optimistic about the outcomes. Difficult project reviews with critical input and help from people outside the project are often postponed, resulting in project overruns and missed deadlines.

Lack of Goal Clarity

Example: changing targets due to new information. Customers' needs change over time. Marketing or customer service groups are very aware of the need to stay in tune with these changes. A desire to anticipate the customer's needs can be risky and create confusion for the product development group, especially when predictions are later proved wrong.

Time Frame Too Short or Too Long

Example: unrealistic timing. Because customer service groups interface with the customer frequently, they often find themselves agreeing to time schedules or other commitments without consulting the product development organization. Commitments and deadlines are often unrealistic given the resources available, resulting in dissatisfied customers when commitments are only partially met.

Procedures Unclear or Nonexistent

Example: quality standards. In organizations where projects flow from one department to another, procedures that monitor quality at these handoff points are frequently lacking. Thus it is left to the next department to catch and correct what are perceived as minor errors. Little attention is paid to complaints from departments downstream because there are no formal channels to legitimatize the feedback.

Inadequate Attention to External Environment

Example: prolonged product life cycles. Radically new product innovations are rare in well-established R & D organizations. The work of engineers is focused to a large extent on improving the basic product design. Sheltered within the technical community, engineers assume they know what is best for the customer. Because of this focus on the technical performance of the product, major shifts in consumers' wants can be overlooked — shift to radial tires, downsizing in cars, and so on.

Too Much Bureaucratic Structure

Example: inefficient process. An analysis done in one R & D organization showed that most engineers were spending 35 to 40 percent of their time expediting paperwork. Time-consuming procedures such as multiple approvals, duplicate and triplicate copies, follow-up phone calls, looking for information, and checking the status of projects can become a significant burden on these professionals' time.

References

Allen, T., and Cohen, S. "Information Flow in R&D Labs," *Administrative Science Quarterly*, 1969, *14*, 12–19.
Badawy, M. "Industrial Scientists and Engineers: Motivational Style Differences." *California Management Review*, 1971, *14* (1), 11–16.

Burns, T., and Stalker, G. *The Management of Innovation.* London: Tavistock, 1961.

Cohen, B. *Organization and Productivity in R&D Teams: A Report of Research Findings.* Stanford, Calif.: Center for Sociological Research, Stanford University, 1985.

Emery, F., and Trist, E. "Analytical Model for Sociotechnical Systems." In W. Pasmore and J. Sherwood (eds.), *Sociotechnical Systems: A Sourcebook.* San Diego, Calif.: University Associates, 1978.

Friedlander, F., and Brown, L. "Organization Development." *Annual Review of Psychology*, 1974, *25*, 313–341.

Galbraith, J. R. *Organization Design.* Reading, Mass.: Addison-Wesley, 1977.

Galbraith, J. R. "Designing the Innovating Organization." *Organizational Dynamics*, Winter 1982, pp. 5–25.

Griggs, W., and Manring, S. "What Motivates Technical Professionals to Contribute Their Best Effort and Maintain Commitment to Their Organization?" In R. Niehaus (ed.), *Strategic Human Resource Planning Approaches.* New York: Plenum Press, 1987.

Hackman, J., and Oldham, G. *Work Redesign.* Reading, Mass.: Addison-Wesley, 1980.

Hackman, J., and Walton, R. "Leading Groups in Organizations." In P. S. Goodman and Associates (eds.), *Designing Effective Work Groups.* San Francisco: Jossey-Bass, 1986.

Jaques, E. "The Development of Intellectual Capacity: A Discussion of Stratified Systems Theory." *Journal of Applied Behavior Science*, 1986, *22* (4), 361–384.

Katz, R. "The Effects of Group Longevity on Project Communication and Performance." *Administrative Science Quarterly*, 1982, *27*, 81–104.

Katz, R., and Tushman, M. "Communication Patterns, Project Performance, and Task Characteristics." *Organizational Behavior and Human Performance*, 1979, *23*, 139–162.

Kidder, T. *Soul of a New Machine.* Boston: Little, Brown, 1981.

Lawler, E. E., III. *Pay and Organization Development.* Reading, Mass.: Addison-Wesley, 1981.

Litwin, C. "Leadership and Organization Climate." In R. Tagiuri and G. Litwin (eds.), *Organization Climate: Explorations of a Concept*. Cambridge, Mass.: Harvard University Press, 1968.

Louis, M. "Organization Culture." In R. H. Kilmann, M. J. Saxton, R. Serpa, and Associates, *Gaining Control of the Corporate Culture*. San Francisco: Jossey-Bass, 1985.

Packer, M. "Analyzing Productivity in R&D Organizations." *Research Management*, Jan.–Feb. 1983, pp. 13–20.

Pasmore, W. *Designing Effective Organizations: The Sociotechnical Systems Perspective*. New York: Wiley, 1988.

Pava, C. *Managing New Office Technology: An Organizational Strategy*. New York: Free Press, 1983.

Pelz, D., and Andrews, F. *Scientists in Organizations*. New York: Wiley, 1966.

Peters, T. J. *Thriving on Chaos*. New York: Knopf, 1987.

Peters, T. J., and Austin, N. *A Passion for Excellence*. New York: Random House, 1985.

Peters, T. J., and Waterman, R. H., Jr. *In Search of Excellence*. New York: Harper & Row, 1982.

Quinn, J. "Managing Innovation: Controlled Chaos." *Harvard Business Review*, May–June 1985, pp. 73–84.

Ranftl, R. *R&D Productivity*. (2nd ed.) Culver City, Calif.: Hughes Aircraft, 1978.

Sanders, H. "Recognition for Employed Inventors." *C&E News*, May 26, 1980, pp. 33–40.

Souder, W. "Stimulating and Managing Ideas." *Research Management*, May–June, 1987, pp. 13–17.

Srivasta, S., and others. *Job Satisfaction and Productivity*. Cleveland, Ohio: Case Western Reserve University, 1975.

Taylor, J., and Bowers, D. *Survey of Organizations*. Ann Arbor: Institute for Social Research, University of Michigan, 1972.

Thompson, P., and Dalton, G. "Are R&D Organizations Obsolete?" *Harvard Business Review*, Nov.–Dec. 1976, pp. 105–116.

Trist, E., and Bamforth, K. "Some Social and Psychological Consequences of the Longwall Method of Coal-Getting." *Human Relations*, 1951, *1*, 3–38.

Trist, E., Higgin, C., Murray, H., and Pollock, A. *Organizational Choice*. London: Tavistock, 1963.

Tushman, M., and Nadler, D. "Communication and Technical Roles in R&D Laboratories: An Information Processing Approach." In B. Dean and J. Goldhar (eds.), *Management of Research and Innovation*. New York: North-Holland, 1980.

18

DEVELOPING SERVICE-ORIENTED MANUFACTURING

DAVID E. BOWEN
CAREN SIEHL
BENJAMIN SCHNEIDER

Any U.S. executive who seeks a competitive edge must be prepared for volatility and unpredictability. This imperative is particularly troublesome for U.S. manufacturers who, in order to meet the challenge of enhancing competitiveness in international markets, must change their way of organizing production. To do this, manufacturers will need an abundance of information, as well as organizational arrangements, that will allow them to compress the time it takes to design and manufacture competitive products.

One proposal to achieve enhanced competitiveness is the "factory of the future." This idea is based on advanced technology such as computer-aided design, manufacturing, and engineering (CAD, CAM, and CAE) and computer-integrated manufacturing (CIM). These techniques aim at restoring a balance in the trade-off between increased efficiency (lower per unit cost, greater precision, and higher production volume) and flexibility (Jelinek and Goldhar, 1983). Unfortunately, U.S. industry has tended to emphasize increased efficiency while neglecting flexibility. As a result, we have also ignored such avenues to competitiveness as innovativeness, customized products, and responsiveness to the consumer.

In this chapter we propose that efforts to revitalize American industry, such as the factory of the future, can be usefully conceptualized as efforts to better serve customers. That is, while advocates of the factory of the future claim flexibility as a major outcome, Peters and Waterman (1982) claim that responsiveness and flexibility also accrue to excellent manufacturing firms that offer "customer service" and stay "close to the customer." We propose here that such tactics as flexible manufacturing and increased contact with customers are different means to the same end: an increased ability to compete through the provision of quality service to consumers.

After describing the *meaning* of service, we show how this meaning can translate into an overall corporate vision that guides and integrates the tactics used by manufacturing firms to achieve increased information flow and timely market responsiveness—the keys to corporate competitiveness. The need for this integration of service principles in manufacturing firms is being noted with increased frequency because "service goods" are seen as the key products of the U.S. economy in the future. Indeed, the intangibles associated with service quality that firms provide will be a critical factor in every competitive strategy. In 1987, for example, the Gallup organization polled senior executives at 615 companies on the importance of eight different factors in gaining global competitive advantage. The winner by a significant margin was service quality. Even manufacturing executives whose companies are in the business of producing goods said that offering their customers better service will be nearly as important as making higher-quality products ("Companies That Serve You Best," 1987). According to Stanley M. Davis (1987, p. 108): "In the same way that service businesses were managed and organized around manufacturing models during the industrial economy, we can expect that manufacturing businesses will be managed and organized around service models in this new economy."

This idea—that a service orientation can inform manufacturing organizations—is the motivation for presenting our model of how the meaning of service can be operationalized in a manufacturing firm. This model, which includes implementation of activities affecting the firm's strategy, structure, culture, and individual roles, is supported by case examples. Central to our argument is the premise that for a manufacturing firm to adopt a service orientation, the meaning of service should permeate all organizational subsystems, rather than being confined to only one department such as marketing.

The Meaning of Service

The meaning of service has historically been ignored in a U.S. economy dominated by manufacturing. Managers and theorists have focused instead on refining management models for the industrial era. In the last decade, however, the service sector has come to dominate both U.S. employment and the GNP. As this has occurred, the meaning of service—what a service is and how to provide it—has captured considerable attention. In academia, the meaning of service has been described from the perspectives of organizational behavior (Bowen and Schneider, 1988; Mills, 1986), marketing (Lovelock, 1984), and operations management (Chase, 1981). In the business world, excellent descriptions of the meaning of service are found in Albrecht and Zemke's (1985) *Service America* and Desatnick's (1987) *Managing to Keep the Customer*, and descriptions of how a host of excellent service deliverers do it are provided in Zemke's (1989) *The Service Edge: 101 Companies That Profit from Customer Care.*

These recent works share the common focus of describing the unique attributes of services and service organizations. They have begun to clarify the meaning of service as it is provided by quality health care institutions, hotels, and so on. Two summary characteristics of these services have been cited most frequently, and we review them next to set the stage for suggesting what service can mean in manufacturing.

Relative Intangibility

Services are less tangible than goods. Services are acts or experiences directed toward consumers; products are objects that are possessed. Moreover, services tend to be more nonstandardized, heterogeneous, and customized at the point of sale than products. Service businesses, because they deal with these intangibles, have generally been more externally and customer-benefit oriented than manufacturing firms (Heskett, 1987). U.S. manufacturing firms, by contrast, have tended to evaluate the quality of their products from an internal perspective: Does it conform to predetermined specifications, is it produced efficiently, can it be shipped without damage? Domestic manufacturers have tended to emphasize efficiency while compromising on flexibility (Jelinek and Goldhar, 1983).

Customer Contact and Inclusion

Service organizations tend to be organized differently from manufacturing organizations due largely to a greater degree of interaction between the organization and the customer. This interaction derives from the fact that production and consumption occur more simultaneously with services than with goods. Consequently, services cannot be inventoried as readily as goods. Customer contact also occurs because service operations typically depend on the customer to make a contribution in the form of behavior or information — the raw material to be transformed to service output. The consumer is required to take action when depositing a check at the bank (a form of behavior), for example, and a physician requires information in order to treat the patient. For these reasons, service customers have been called "partial employees" of the firm (Bowen, 1986). The customer's participation in the production of the service, then, adds to the already greater labor intensity of service firms as compared to the capital intensiveness of manufacturing firms.

In sum, services can be described as relatively intangible offerings whose production typically involves a close interaction between provider and customer. Services differ from products in *what* is exchanged and in the roles played by *both* parties to the exchange. Despite these differences between services and goods, many companies, such as IBM and McDonald's, exhibit both service and manufacturing characteristics. In line with this, several writers have described how to apply manufacturing concepts to service organizations. Most notable, here, is Levitt's (1976) work on the "industrialization of service" in which a standardized line of tangibles is produced, the core technology is buffered from customers, and so forth. In stark contrast to the industrialization of service, almost no attention has been paid to the application of the two basic service concepts (intangibility and customer contact and inclusion) to manufacturing organizations.

In the following pages we will develop two significant applications of service concepts to manufacturing: the incorporation of service-related goals in the organizational mission and the implementation of the service concept through the adoption of organizational arrangements and resource allocations. We will argue that service, as defined here, offers a way of conceptualizing a powerful force that can shape how manufacturing firms define their mission and organize to execute it.

Implementing Service in Manufacturing

Implementation of the meaning of service in manufacturing requires a systemwide effort. This proposition is supported by Gronroos and Gummesson (1986), who argue that industrial firms may be technically sophisticated yet fail to be effective precisely because they fail to recognize the service-like elements of their business as a whole: "If these service-like elements, including not only technical service but deliveries and distribution and warehousing systems, claims handling procedures, customer training, R & D systems, invoicing routines, quality control procedures, telephone receptionist behavior, etc., are not handled properly and customer-oriented, or if they are altogether left without consideration, the customer will perceive a less perfect total quality, although the more technical quality may be quite acceptable" (p. 23). In other words, Gronroos and Gummesson argue that unless all parts of an organization are functioning with a goal of customer service, no amount of technical expertise can compensate.

Nadler and Tushman's (1982) general diagnostic model of organizational components can be used to describe the systemwide implementation of service. In this model, shown in Figure 18.1, an organization's transformation processes are segmented into four subsystems: task, individual, formal organization, and informal arrangements. For each of these components, we explain how it can be designed to reflect the key service concepts of intangibility and customer contact and inclusion. Through this total systems approach, the meaning of service becomes an integral part of the organization's strategic mission and such techniques as flexible manufacturing, improved after-sales service, and others become tactics in support of that strategy.

The Task Component

A Mission Based on Dual Cores

Implementing the meaning of service in manufacturing requires the definition of the organization's mission in terms of the *dual* cores of production and service, not a single core technology. Core technology is the central activity of the firm or, more forcefully, its raison d'être. To implement service in manufacturing, the organization's raison d'être can no longer be defined in terms of a single core technology that efficiently transforms tangible input to tangible output while being sealed off from customers.

Instead, the organization must define its mission as being both product-focused and service-focused. Campbell Soup is an excellent example of a company that has enjoyed the benefits of such a dual-focused mission. Campbell's five-year sales growth rate is 14 percent, compared to the industry rate of 4 percent. These impressive numbers have been attributed to the explicit focus on service. Carl Stinnett, a vice-president, left Nestle for Campbell and says, "I'm impressed with the breadth of concern for customer service here. You obviously hear it in sales, but you also hear it in marketing, in the plants, even in finance" ("Companies That Serve You Best," 1987).

Service-Oriented Process Technologies

One strategy by which a firm can organize around the dual mission of both production and service is to design new manufacturing technologies consistent with the meaning of service.

**Figure 18.1. Implementation of the Meaning of Service
in a Manufacturing Organization.**

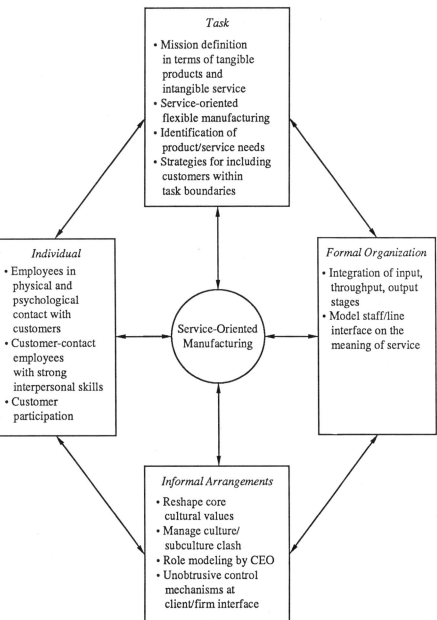

Source: Adapted from Nadler and Tushman (1982).

Figure 18.2. Alternative Orientations to Manufacturing Technology.

Old-Style Technology		*CAD/CAM Environment*
• Flexibility and variety are expensive		• Flexibility and variety create profits
• Standard product design	versus	• Many custom products
• Low rate of change, responsiveness, high stability		• Innovation and responsiveness
• Inventory as a decoupler		• Production tied to demand
• Batch systems		• Flow systems

Source: Adapted from Jelinek and Goldhar (1983).

The relevance of viewing efforts to revitalize manufacturing operations from a service perspective can be seen in the contrast between old-style manufacturing technology and the emerging CAD/CAM environment as depicted in Figure 18.2. In particular, note the parallels in the contrast between products and services discussed earlier and the contrast between old-style manufacturing technology and the emerging environment of CAD/CAM.

In the new manufacturing environment, flexibility is viewed as a source of value added. Products are now tailored to individual customer preferences — indeed, customers may participate in product design and change. Tony O'Reilly of Heinz points proudly to new products developed by integrating customers into the organization. He cites his company's expanded line of pet foods, which is attributable to the input of older customers who lavish attention on their pets ("Corporate Strategies for the 1990s," 1988). Overall, marketing and product design are more closely integrated in the new manufacturing organization. Today the ability to customize, rather than simply lower costs via standardized products, can become a competitive advantage (Jelinek and Goldhar, 1983).

Identification of Product and Service Needs

A second strategy for implementing a dual mission involves the identification of necessary service support for products. The customer's service needs can be divided into three sets (Lele, 1986). The first set is product-related and thus focuses on enhancing the product's reliability, making the product more modular in construction (so it is more easily repaired), and building in redundancy (to reduce the probability of failure). The second set consists of system-related strategies that focus on reducing the response time to the customer's service needs and involves the number and location of service technicians. The third set consists of those support systems that reduce the customer's risk, including warranties and service contracts. These services have been termed the "augmented product" (Levitt, 1969) or the "product bundle" (Albrecht and Zemke, 1985) and are a potential source of product differentiation and, therefore, competitive advantage.

Customer Inclusion

Another set of tactics for implementing a service strategy focuses on including customers within the task boundaries of the organization. To do this manufacturing firms must develop techniques to recruit customers as "partial employees." Once they are recruited, the firm must make use of their associated roles and resources in the pursuit of organizational goals while simultaneously avoiding the danger of becoming captive to the customer's external interests or personal agenda. Bridging strategies, which are effective at linking the organization with other stakeholders such as suppliers, may be equally effective with customers. These strategies involve the formation of partnerships in which both parties contribute and both benefit. IBM is an example of a corporation that has long advocated the use of partnerships with its customers. As reported in its 1985 annual report, IBM works in partnership with customers in new product development, distribution, and research in order to achieve improved productivity at an affordable cost.

The Individual Component

Employees in Contact with Customers

The degree to which service permeates the entire organization can be enhanced by having employees in all functions maintain customer contact either physically or psychologically. Creating physical contact between employees and customers is similar to establishing client feedback—a strategy for enriching jobs and stimulating motivation and higher-quality performance (Locke, 1977). For example, Campbell Soup sends experienced manufacturing people into the field to talk with customers and then act as their advocates back at the plant. These "roving inspectors" discover new ways of improving service.

Essentially, customer contact can lead to employees defining their roles in terms of serving someone rather than producing something. This extends their motivation and involvement beyond the calculative (a paycheck) to a personal identification with the company's mission of quality service and how customers are affected by it. At GM's Fiero plant in Pontiac, Michigan, volunteer assembly-line workers are involved in a program to obtain direct feedback from customers. Frank L. Slaughter, assistant director of personnel, reports what production employees want their reputation to be: "We are concerned, we have ownership of what we do, and we are proud of it." Under the program, fifty workers each follow five Fiero buyers for a year, surveying them with phone calls every three months. The information they learn is passed on to the plant and also to service experts who work with dealers. The costs have been minimal and the benefits have been high—for both the employees and the company ("Making Service . . . ," 1984).

An important postscript to this Fiero example is called for, since GM recently announced it is discontinuing the line. The Fiero did not fail because of this service orientation; it failed because senior management did not act on the information obtained from the customer contact. Customers reported that the Fiero was underpowered, for example, but GM would not commit the dollars necessary for a new powertrain. The moral of the story is that as manufacturers attempt to take service seriously, they should heed what Bowen and Schneider (1988) have found to be true in service organizations: Management may not be able to identify customer needs and attitudes, but customer-contact employees can. These employees should be *listened* to if management is to incorporate customer information into the production process.

Interpersonal Skills in Customer Contacts

On a different level, employees in explicit customer-contact roles — such as product service and joint customer/employee product design teams — need strong interpersonal skills as well as technical skills or product knowledge. Consequently, there is a need to develop within a manufacturing setting human resource management processes that develop interpersonal competencies in customer-contact employees. It would be wrong to assume that these employees already have them, since these skills may not have been essential in doing their jobs.

We have learned that incompetent people cannot provide good service, so companies known for high-quality service tend to recruit meticulously. Singapore Airlines, for example, hires less than 2 percent of the thousands of women who want to become "Singapore girls." Delta Air Lines hires even fewer, accepting fewer than 50 of more than 20,000 applicants for flight attendant jobs each month. Interpersonal aspects of different jobs can be assessed through the use of job simulations and should be used in the selection of customer-contact employees in all organizational functions and levels.

There has been some confusion regarding the relative contribution of recruitment and selection compared to training and development in enhancing employees' effectiveness. Some argue that a training program can be no better than the persons selected for it; thus, they reason, a comprehensive selection program invalidates the necessity for training. This thinking may be especially characteristic of managers of customer-contact jobs who think that people are either service-oriented or not. Even if this is true, there is a difference between service-oriented and service-skilled.

The point is that effective selection systems yield people who have the inclinations and talent to learn the job. Without formal training, however, whether in the classroom or on the job, inclinations and talent will not be realized. Companies such as Merck Pharmaceuticals, Xerox Canada, and Goodyear Tire & Rubber have learned that training pays off. "Training is our obsession," says Jerry Killer, a vice-president at Merck's U.S. drug division. "People who come to us from other companies can't believe we have this kind of program" ("Companies That Serve You Best," 1987).

Xerox Canada has recently finished putting its 5,000 employees across Canada through a six-day service training program. This process was an effort to help employees change the focus of their jobs. There is an example of a staff employee who was involved in redesigning the invoicing system, but had never actually had contact with a customer. After the training program, he went out and talked with customers to determine how they thought an invoicing system should be designed to serve them better. Another example is Goodyear, which is rated as being excellent at identifying customer needs. This excellence is attributed to extensive training for Goodyear employees, including technicians and mechanics. "We have hands-on training for all our consumer affairs personnel in all modes of product failure. Everyone on our staff can answer even the most difficult questions" (American Management Association, 1987).

To implement the meaning of service, manufacturing organizations will also need to create reward systems to account for the service skills demonstrated by employees. Clearly organizations obtain the kind of behavior they reward, and service-oriented behavior will not be sustained if it is not rewarded—

particularly if the behavior (such as collaboration with the customer) is contrary to the values of the production core. Desatnick (1987) describes a number of examples of rewarding customer service, including tying local managers' bonus programs to the volume of customer complaints received and placing complimentary letters from customers in employees' personnel files.

In sum, as customer contact is implemented, increasing numbers of employees will assume boundary-spanning responsibilities and begin to execute the critical roles of external representation and information transmission for the company. To perform these roles effectively, these employees require service-related skills in addition to production-related competencies. Indeed, it has been suggested that the ability to work shoulder-to-shoulder with customers, an intangible, may be the principal source of competitive advantage for U.S. manufacturers trying to reclaim domestic markets from imports (Meredith, 1987). The point is this: Although domestic and foreign manufacturers may possess similar technologies, domestic manufacturers are in a better position to establish contact and relationships with U.S. customers. But this opportunity can only be capitalized upon if the domestic customer-contact employees have both technical *and* interpersonal skills.

Customers as Partial Employees

When customers become partial employees, it is necessary to manage their performance. Performance is viewed as a function of a person's motivation, role clarity, and ability; these determinants hold for both employees *and* customers. That is, customers can be expected to perform in their roles as partial employees to the extent that they obtain rewards through their efforts (motivation), they understand the nature of the task (role clarity), and they have the necessary competencies (ability). If customers are involved in the product-design stage, for example, the firm needs to demonstrate that customers obtain higher quality or lower cost from exerting this effort (motivation), clarify the terms and conditions defining the customers' inclusion in the design process (role clarity), and select or train customers to participate effectively in product design (ability).

The Informal Arrangements Component

Cultural Values

Service-oriented firms rely on cultural mechanisms, such as shared norms and values, in developing and maintaining service quality. Manufacturing firms that have never included service-related goals, such as flexibility, as objectives may require cultural changes to support these goals. Whereas manufacturing values often focus on efficiency, economies of scale, and the belief that variety and flexibility are costly, service-oriented values center on innovation, customization, and the belief that flexibility and variety create profits. This contrast between efficiency and flexibility can be viewed as a clash between a dominant culture and a subculture (Martin and Siehl, 1983). Management's challenge is to maintain the uneasy relationship that exists between them. In effect, this is a means of diffusing resistance to change by managing the *balance* between efficiency and flexibility, rather than the total substitution of one value set for the other.

A side benefit of a focus on service concerns the issue of quality. Indeed, the phrase *service quality* has taken on an almost subliminal unity such that the two words are heard as one. Perhaps people believe that service implies quality. Regardless of the reason, when an organization implements a service strategy it also promotes a quality strategy because, for many, to do service means to do *quality* service.

The CEO as Role Model

The subculture of the firm's top managers should stress the importance of service as a central value. Management's commitment to service must be reflected in the context of the company's other goals and priorities. The intense commitment of the CEO cannot be understated. At companies with exemplary service records such as L. L. Bean, Mary Kay Cosmetics, and Service Supply Corporation, the CEO acts as a central role model of what service means. Leon Gorman, president of L. L. Bean (1986 sales of $369 million), measures his company's order fulfillment in half-days. Mary Kay Ash, founder and CEO of Mary Kay Cosmetics, has said that many CEOs pledge allegiance to service without setting specific targets to which they, themselves, are subject. Without these objectives, she warns, good service will not happen ("Service: A CEO's Perspective," 1987). Mel Seitz, Jr., president of Service Supply Corporation (1986 sales of $55 million), returned home one night to find a message from a customer who needed some two-inch nuts, but when Seitz called back it was too late. The customer had called Seitz's father, Service Supply's retired chairman, and he had taken care of the matter.

Unobtrusive Control Mechanisms

We believe that the control mechanisms appropriate for customer-contact employees should be primarily cultural and unobtrusive rather than formal and obtrusive. Control systems based on direct and formal means are particularly troublesome when three conditions are present: lack of goal clarity, excessive task complexity and interdependence, and high uncertainty (Ouchi and Maguire, 1975). These conditions are almost inevitably present when service is being provided because service quality is hard to define and measure, it is difficult to specify means–ends relationships governing the production and delivery of many services, the customer's involvement creates uncertainty and the need to control the customer's behavior, and it is hard to specify a priori how customer-contact employees are to behave in the unpredictable range of circumstances that may arise in their dealings with customers.

Since the cost of monitoring highly uncertain and interdependent work by means of formal rules and structures is prohibitive, an alternative system must be based on common values. Thus employees encountering idiosyncratic customer demands in product design, sales, or after-sales service may be more appropriately controlled through shared values rather than rules and procedures. Successful service organizations empower employees to offer the best service possible without restrictive rules that attempt to control the uncontrollable. At SAS airlines, for example, CEO Jan Carlzon has created a culture in which front-line service employees, such as flight attendants, are both encouraged and expected to solve customer problems as they arise without first consulting the policy manual or checking with a supervisor. But at the same time he encourages this form of autonomy, Carlzon, in his own words, "dictates" to employees that core objectives such as "managing relationships based on respect rather than fear" cannot be ignored by any employee in any situation. Carlzon's approach to controlling customer-contact employees sounds very similar to Peters and Waterman's (1982) description of how excellent companies simultaneously utilize "loose/tight" controls.

In sum, then, we have learned that although formal means may satisfy the control requirements of producing a tangible product, culture and shared values are needed to control the customer-contact activities that implement service in manufacturing. Organizations require "portfolios of coordination mechanisms" to satisfy diverse interdependence patterns; in the present context, both formal *and* cultural mechanisms are necessary to satisfy the coordination requirements imposed by a dual set of core activities.

The Formal Organization Component

Integrated Production Stages

A strategy advocated for improving product quality has been to integrate sales/service more tightly with the three other stages of product development: product design, process design, and manufacturing operations. This approach expands responsibility for quality control beyond an exclusive focus on the manufacturing operations stage and recognizes the importance of upstream design decisions and downstream sales/service decisions in establishing product quality. It incorporates the role of product intangibles and customer contact as integral components of the transformation process.

The competitive advantage of integrating the input, throughput, and output stages of the transformation process was demonstrated in a study by Delbecq and Mills (1985) of 150 manufacturing firms and hospitals. In their study of the key differences between effective and ineffective innovators, they defined an effective innovator as a company that designed, produced, and sold or implemented a new product or service. Delbecq and Mills discovered that successful innovators were companies in which products were neither designed nor produced until the degree to which the new innovation would be acceptable was assessed. This assessment was accomplished through an integrated production and marketing function.

Internal Role Models

We suggest that the degree to which internal staff units (human resource management, finance, marketing) are effective in serving *internal* clients of the organization (such as line managers) will be positively associated with how effectively the organization serves its *external* clients. This proposition is built on research demonstrating that when front-line employees describe their treatment by the company in positive terms, customers have positive perceptions of service quality (Schneider and Bowen, 1985).

Organizational staff units are frequently criticized for conflicting with line management and being a source of costly overhead. One explanation for these critiques is that staff units execute their mission with a production orientation rather than a service orientation. Although the staff's original raison d'être was to act as a *service* function, many staff units have adopted a production orientation in which tangible products such as software programs, information systems, and training manuals dominate their offerings to line managers and other clients.

Bowen and Greiner (1986) argue that human resources management (HRM) has assumed a production orientation for a number of reasons—primarily because the management principles developed in the 1930s for the manufacturing sector guide the culture of all corporate functions, including HRM. Thus HRM adheres to such principles as protecting the core technology from outside disturbance, standardization of the product line, and short-term return on investment. Bowen and Greiner advocate a service orientation for HRM in which performance is viewed as a group of intangible processes like motivation and counseling, rather than a tangible rating form. They go on to say that training programs should be modified during the course of delivery, if necessary, consistent with simultaneous production and consumption and that line managers should become involved in designing and delivering the training, acting in the role of "customers as partial employees." HRM "products" are not absent in this service approach, but they are driven by the meaning of service to specific markets (consumers).

Extending this argument, one can ask whether other staff activities are organized with a production or a service orientation. In this vein, management information systems (MIS) design has been examined from a service perspective. El Sawy and Walls (1986) observe that there have been a few limited efforts to incorporate service principles in end-user support and information centers. The meaning of service has been ignored in most areas of MIS, however, particularly systems analysis and design. El Sawy and Walls describe the attributes of information systems design with a service orientation in contrast to systems design from a product orientation (Figure 18.3). This comparison of the differences between *internal* products and services neatly parallels the differences between *external* products and services described earlier, as well as the differences between old- and new-style manufacturing environments.

In sum, then, we believe that the service-oriented management of the interface between units *within* the organization can improve its competitiveness in external markets. Enacting such a service orientation underscores the need for collaboration among internal service providers and users to better serve the organization's customers. Jan Carlzon (1987) sends the following message to internal staff: "If you're not serving the customer, you'd better be serving someone who is." Stanley Davis (1987,

Figure 18.3. Alternative Orientations to Information Systems Design.

Product Orientation		*Service Orientation*
• Minimal analyst involvement except at certain points in the life cycle		• Continued analyst involvement throughout the life cycle
• Evaluation based on meeting specifications		• Evaluation based on customer satisfaction
• Little user involvement in design	versus	• Much customer involvement in design
• Orientation toward technology		• Orientation toward customer needs
• Identification with professional community		• Identification with customer
• Formal requirements specification		• Prototyping
• Standardization		• Customization

Source: Adapted from El Sawy and Walls (1986).

p. 107) takes this message a step further in saying that staff groups should ask, "How can I assist you in serving our (real) customers?" Davis asks us all to consider, "Can you imagine how much more powerful a company would be if every employee, no matter what their job, asked, 'How does my job fulfill our customers' needs in the market?'"

Conclusion

We have offered a conceptualization of the meaning of service that can be translated into a significant part of the overall mission of a manufacturing firm. We have also described some of the service-oriented tactics that manufacturing firms should implement in order to achieve increased information flow and timely market responsiveness and, thus, an increased ability to compete in dynamic, global markets.

We have argued that the meaning of service should be implemented within all organizational subsystems: tasks, individuals, informal and formal arrangements. Furthermore, there must be congruence *across* subsystems if the organization is to be effective. Attention to the intangible dimension of tasks must be congruent with cultural values of flexibility, for example, and service-oriented MIS employees must have the interpersonal skills necessary to listen to the tangible and intangible requirements of line units. This perspective supplants the traditional view of manufacturing organizations that service is merely a postproduction supportive and buffering subsystem. Instead, the meaning of service permeates the entire organization. This shift in focus to a strategic service orientation can be an important force for revitalizing the competitiveness of U.S. manufacturing.

References

Albrecht, K., and Zemke, R. *Service America: Doing Business in the New Economy*. Homewood, Ill.: Dow Jones–Irwin, 1985.

American Management Association. "Close to the Customer." Research report, American Management Association, 1987.

Bowen, D. E. "Managing Customers as Human Resources in Service Organizations." *Human Resource Management*, Fall 1986, pp. 371–383.

Bowen, D. E., and Greiner, L. E. "Moving from Production to Service in Human Resources Management." *Organizational Dynamics*, Summer 1986, pp. 34–53.

Bowen, D. E., and Schneider, B. "Services Marketing and Management: Implications for Organizational Behavior." In B. Staw and L. L. Cummings (eds.), *Research in Organizational Behavior*. Vol. 10. Greenwich, Conn.: JAI Press, 1988.

Carlzon, J. *Moments of Truth: New Strategies for Today's Customer Driven Economy.* Cambridge, Mass.: Ballinger, 1987.

Chase, R. B. "The Customer Contact Approach to Services: Theoretical Bases and Practical Extensions." *Operations Research*, 1981, *29*, 698–706.

"Companies That Serve You Best." *Fortune*, Dec. 7, 1987, pp. 98–116.

"Corporate Strategies for the 1990s." *Fortune*, Feb. 29, 1988, pp. 34–42.

Davis, S. M. *Future Perfect.* Reading, Mass.: Addison-Wesley, 1987.

Delbecq, A. L., and Mills, P. K. "Managerial Practices That Enhance Innovation." *Organizational Dynamics*, Summer 1985, pp. 24–34.

Desatnick, R. L. *Managing to Keep the Customer: How to Achieve and Maintain Superior Customer Service Throughout the Organization.* San Francisco: Jossey-Bass, 1987.

El Sawy, O., and Walls, C. "A Service Perspective on Information Systems Design." Paper presented at Decision Sciences Institute, Atlanta, Ga., 1986.

Gronroos, C., and Gummesson, E. "Service Orientation in Industrial Marketing." In M. Venkatesan, D. M. Schmalensee, and C. M. Marshall (eds.), *Creativity in Services Marketing.* Chicago: American Marketing Association, 1986.

Heskett, J. L. "Lessons in the Services Sector." *Harvard Business Review*, Mar. 1987, pp. 118–126.

Jelinek, M., and Goldhar, J. D. "The Interface Between Strategy and Manufacturing Technology." *Columbia Journal of World Business*, Spring 1983, pp. 26–36.

Lele, M. "How Service Needs Influence Product Strategy." *Sloan Management Review*, Fall 1986, pp. 63–70.

Levitt, T. *The Marketing Mode.* New York: McGraw-Hill, 1969.

Levitt, T. "The Industrialization of Service." *Harvard Business Review*, Sept.–Oct. 1976, pp. 63–74.

Locke, E. A. "The Myths of Behavior Mod in Organizations." *Academy of Management Review*, 1977, *2*, 543–553.

Lovelock, C. H. *Services Marketing.* Englewood Cliffs, N.J.: Prentice-Hall, 1984.

"Making Service a Potent Marketing Tool." *Business Week,* June 11, 1984, pp. 74–77.

Martin, J., and Siehl, C. J. "Culture and Counter-Culture: An Uneasy Symbiosis." *Organizational Dynamics,* Fall 1983, pp. 52–64.

Meredith, J. R. "The Strategic Advantages of the Factory of the Future." *California Management Review,* 1987, *29,* 27–41.

Mills, P. K. *Managing Service Industries: Organizational Practices in a Post-Industrial Economy.* Cambridge, Mass.: Ballinger, 1986.

Nadler, D. A., and Tushman, M. "A Model for Diagnosing Organizational Behavior." In M. Tushman and W. L. Moore (eds.), *Readings in the Management of Innovation.* Boston: Pittman, 1982.

Ouchi, W. G., and Maguire, M. A. "Organizational Control: Two Functions." *Administrative Science Quarterly,* 1975, *20,* 559–569.

Peters, T. J. *Thriving on Chaos.* New York: J. Knopf, 1987.

Peters, T. J., and Waterman, R. H., Jr. *In Search of Excellence: Lessons from America's Best-Run Companies.* New York: Harper & Row, 1982.

Schneider, B., and Bowen, D. E. "Employee and Customer Perceptions of Service in Banks: Replication and Extension." *Journal of Applied Psychology,* 1985, *70,* 423–433.

"Service: A CEO's Perspective." *Management Review,* Oct. 1987, pp. 41–45.

Zemke, R. *The Service Edge: 101 Companies That Profit from Customer Care.* New York: New American Library, 1989.

19

INTEGRATING AND AUTOMATING SALES AND MARKETING

HARRIETTE L. CHANDLER
CHARLES A. KHUEN

Maintaining profit margins and growth are key components to being more competitive today in corporate America. Technological advances, increased domestic and foreign competition, and shifts in buying patterns have caused unit prices to either flatten or decline. The average cost of a field sales call, however, continues to increase annually. The result of the narrowing gap between rising selling costs and declining prices is eroding profit margins—with no indication that the trend will abate.

No vertical market is exempt from these problems. The corporate response is to try to increase sales volume while controlling selling costs. This remedy puts yet another burden on the field sales force who have seen their jobs increase in scope and complexity throughout the last decade. As Shapiro and Wyman (1981) have noted, it also drives companies to introduce lower-cost alternative sales channels. The new channels, however, can increase the risk of marketplace confusion, expense, and cross-channel conflict. In sum, the pursuit of greater unit sales volume leads to greater costs—unless something new is brought to the sales situation.

Optimizing selling productivity in the contemporary business environment requires a new approach and new tools. The goal must be to achieve the maximum return from all sales and marketing resources and expenditures. Accomplishing this objective means finding productivity improvements in both direct and indirect selling channels, as well as optimizing each

419

advertising and promotion effort, each product line, and the customer and prospect base. Moreover, it means gaining the acceptance and active support of those employees in the company who will be affected by it.

These improvements demand an integrated approach to the sales and marketing process. They require the ability to collect, screen, collate, analyze, store, retrieve, and disseminate detailed information for the entire sales and marketing process. Companies need to be able to move data between specific operations and functions in order to make the parts as well as the whole more efficient and effective. Moreover, the larger the company, the greater the probability that informational needs will exceed the capacity of traditional systems.

Based on its relationship to the essential elements of a company's operations, the automation of sales and marketing qualifies as a "mission critical system." According to Alex. Brown & Sons, Inc. (1986), who coined the term in a widely read research study, *Computer Services Industry Overview: The Move to Mission Critical Systems — Up from the Slump*, this newest wave of automation holds the promise of providing "significant competitive advantages through increased product or service differentiation, improved customer service, reduced costs, and more streamlined operations" (p. 1).

Studies of automation's impact are sparse in the sales and marketing area. In an effort to contribute to this newly emerging field of interest, the following pages outline how substantial selling productivity can be achieved by using the benefits of information technology to create a sales and marketing mission critical system. The discussion is based on our practical experience working with *Fortune* 500 companies.

The Need for Integration

Sales and marketing should be an integrated process. Like a manufacturing facility that turns raw materials into subassemblies and final products, the sales and marketing unit must move its own raw materials in the form of leads through the qualification cycle, transform them into customers, and then continue to

Figure 19.1. The Sales Process.

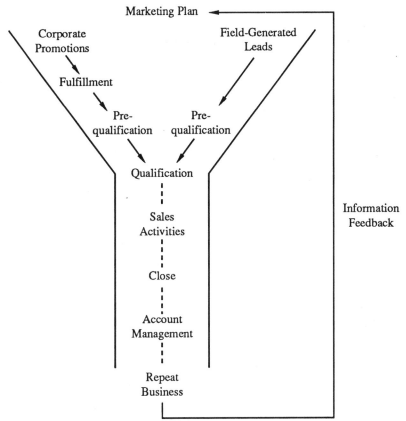

manage them for additional business. Ideally the process provides feedback for analysis and planning (Figure 19.1). In practice, however, the operational components within sales and marketing frequently differ from one another in goals, responsibilities, concerns, and operating styles. Whether it is advertising, fulfillment, national accounts, inbound telemarketing, outbound telemarketing, direct marketing, dealers, agents, or distributors—each goes its own way much of the time, usually resulting in fragmentation, conflict, and waste.

Advertising managers, for example, measure the performance of advertising and direct mail programs by counting the responses. Sales people in the field, however, customarily discard 90 percent or more of these leads claiming lack of quality. Although the advertising or direct mail department may meet its goals by generating more leads at a lower cost, there is no assurance that more sales will result. As a director of marketing communications of a division of Honeywell complained in a company newsletter: "We provide copies of all inquiries to our salesmen. . . . But our salesmen follow and report back. . . on only. . . 2.4% of the total. Of these, they class. . . only 1% 'sold.'"

Within the sales force itself, the branches, divisions, and channels operate independently and there is no easy way for leads uncovered in one sales program or territory to be transferred to another. In some cases, multiple sales channels may even be offering different products or prices to the same account, resulting in confusion and even loss of sales.

Lack of communication between service and sales also kills many good leads. Customer service representatives may learn key information about an account but, lacking any efficient means to provide the information to sales, will proceed with their next call. At the same time, other customer service representatives taking calls may have no idea that the account on the phone is involved in an important sales situation.

While order entry, customer service, and billing information may exist at the corporate level, the sales and marketing unit either cannot extract the data or finds the data format of little value for its purposes. For example, the name listed in the order entry system is more likely to be a purchasing agent than a sales and marketing decision maker.

Because most of these shortcomings of the sales and marketing process involve the transfer of information, it might seem that automation would provide a quick solution. Yet many attempts at automation in sales and marketing have actually encouraged fragmentation by focusing on the productivity of individual sales and marketing elements. If they have proved difficult to implement or have not had the company's full support, they have frequently left a negative impression of automation that lingers in the corporate culture.

A company's call activity measurement or expense reporting might actually detract from field sales' selling time, for example. Or the marketing communications group may have selected an outside service bureau to handle its inquiry fulfillment needs and moved its prospect and customer list off-site. Or the telemarketing center may have automated its calling but have no effective way to transfer leads to field sales. Separate databases may be in use for forecasting, direct mail, customer service, telemarketing, order entry, billing, leasing, and shipping with no interface apparently possible among them. Or a lap-top computer program may have been initiated for the sales force only to be abandoned due to lack of acceptance.

Some of these separate, specialized, automated support programs can be beneficial in meeting specific, short-term needs. Yet they fall short of the major productivity gains that can be captured by integrating the operations of the sales and marketing business unit through automation. Fragmentation in the sales and marketing unit means that the company spends more money and everyone works harder in the pursuit of localized, functional objectives. Any useful information gathered serves only the needs of a specific group. Indeed, without a centralized mechanism capable of capturing and integrating information from activities involving prospects, customers, and products, it is not possible to improve the overall return on the assets or expenses of the sales and marketing unit.

Key Features of an Integrated Solution

Sales and marketing is a complex and intangible process. It should also be an integrated process, although it operates in a dis-integrated environment. Therefore, automating this function is no simple task — it calls for the vision and commitment of senior corporate leadership, as well as a whole new set of tools.

An integrated solution has vital requirements that frequently are dichotomies:

- Centralized control and local ownership
- Structure and flexibility
- Departmental-level support

- Capability for complete integration
- Corporate support

Now let us consider these features one by one.

The system must offer both maximum centralized control and maximum local ownership. From the perspective of the Information Systems Department, a centrally controlled and operated system is essential to meet corporate standards for customer and prospect data security, for information transfer both inside and outside sales and marketing, and for operational discipline and data backup and recovery. On the other hand, the independent and skeptical attitudes that are characteristic of the end users in field sales and other external selling channels, plus their "ease of use" needs, call for a distributed, locally owned approach. If the solution is not integrated, as one large chemical manufacturer discovered to its chagrin, local user-group applications will spring up. These will not be supported by the systems people, will not be able to benefit from access to external data or other corporate databases, and will not be capable of sharing essential information with other parts of the company.

Moreover, the system must offer both maximum structure and maximum flexibility. Structure enables the orderly storage and transfer of information and ensures that reports will have a consistency over time. Yet flexibility is needed by sales and marketing to provide a quick response to changes in programs, territories, and promotions and to support the addition of application enhancements that nontechnical users may require.

As well, the system must support the separate operational goals of each sales and marketing component, allowing each functional group to carry out its own charter while simultaneously ensuring there are a common language and definition structure for integration and change. People will use the system only if they believe it will improve their productivity and achievement. Operational integration occurs as each department begins to rely on the system to meet its own goals.

It is critical, too, that the system have the potential to be integrated across all of the sales and marketing operations. Too many companies today lack that ability and are plagued by "islands of automation." The system must not only integrate the operations of the separate selling channels and other sales and marketing operations. It must also be able to offer optional interfaces to functions outside sales and marketing, such as order entry, credit, and customer service. Bringing valuable information from other corporate sources and systems can increase productivity by reducing nonselling time and enabling better targeting of accounts. The system's architecture — languages, structure, communication provisions, and so on — must interact with the corporate architecture so that data gathered in the sales and marketing process can flow back to the corporation to aid in planning, forecasting, and other activities.

Finally, mission critical systems cannot succeed without ongoing support from the very top of the corporation. While acceptance by the users is essential from an operational perspective, achievement of the strategic benefits of automating sales and marketing requires the consistent vision and commitment of the most senior managers. Otherwise, the system is at risk whenever a problem arises or a reorganization occurs.

Model of an Effective System

Many of these apparent dichotomies affecting sales and marketing productivity can now be resolved by combining the best of currently accepted personal computer, mini, mainframe, and communication technologies. The resulting system must:

- Be structured around a central marketing database
- Have integrated, operation-specific support software
- Offer networked, remote processing that can meet the data storage and distribution needs of the company

Central Sales and Marketing Database

The central sales and marketing database provides the integration, structure, and central control outlined above. It is the repository for account and operational data that can be shared and analyzed in strategic planning. It is also the means of interfacing with existing systems for order entry, customer service, credit, and the like. Furthermore, it is the means to organize and manage a company's customer and prospect base — its single most valuable information asset. After all, the company cannot maximize return on an asset if it knows the location of only part of the asset.

The central database must contain, at a minimum, all the elements shown in Figure 19.2, as well as the structure to link them together properly. The database may be established by selectively merging data from existing corporate databases such as order entry, customer service, and billing, from externally purchased lists available in electronic form, or from both sources. In operation, the database will be refined and updated constantly by its users in various departments.

Integrated, Operation-Specific, Support Software

Whereas the central database provides the integration, storage, and control, the software modules support the direct operational needs of each department. Each module, in turn, uses and enhances the central database. Each module is integrated through the database to maximize the return of each department, as well as to provide the closed-loop system necessary to optimize the productivity of the entire process.

When all modules rely on the same central database, there is no loss of data through individual department ownership and no duplication of valuable time and resources to track down information on any aspect of the sales and marketing operation. Rather, the application software ensures a continual exchange of data from one discipline to another — all relating to a consistent set of sales and marketing terminology, processes, and standards. Figure 19.3 shows a working model of integrated software modules.

Networking and Remote-Processing Capabilities

In addition to a central sales and marketing database and closed-loop software modules, an effective sales and marketing

Figure 19.2. The Central Marketing Database.

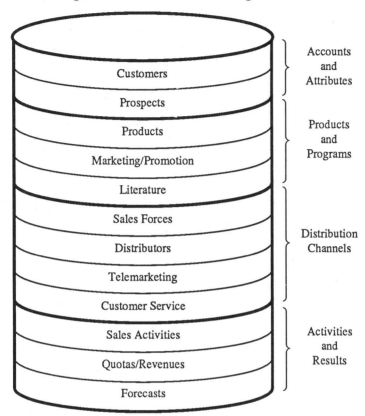

system must offer the option of operating on satellite processors in a network. This option provides local ownership and ease of use, as well as implementation flexibility, without sacrificing central control and integration. The database structure in the remote processors must be the same as in the central office. While the central database has all the data, each remote processor has only the portion that is relevant to its area and task. Data backup, lead distribution, and updates are managed through the central database. The central database is also able to replace any data lost at field locations.

With standard network technology as the mechanism, the integrated software modules enable information relevant to

Figure 19.3. The Closed-Loop Sales and Marketing System.

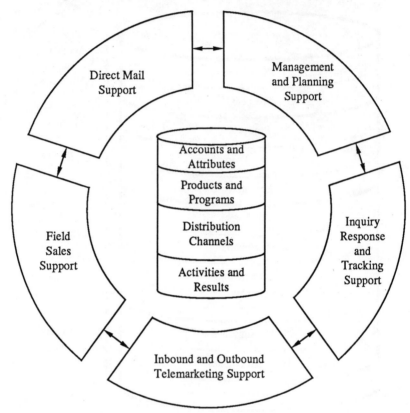

each user department to move intelligently through the network. For example, the telemarketing group might want to know when a sale is closed in the field so that they can follow up and sell training, maintenance, and other add-ons (which are often more profitable than the original sale). Figure 19.4 illustrates the opportunities for networking with an integrated sales and marketing system.

   The resulting technical system is not just a hypothetical concept to be realized someday. Integrated systems have been tested and proven and are beginning to be found in some of America's leading corporations. Porter and Millar (1985), Zuboff (1988), and other leading observers of the strategic sig-

Figure 19.4. The Sales and Marketing Information Network.

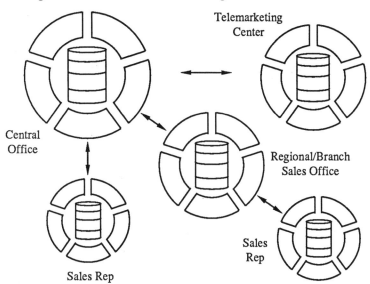

nificance of information technology predict that it is becoming a requirement for companies who seek a competitive edge. Mere automation of data is no longer sufficient; nor are the use and exploitation of data limited to data processing and communications departments. Data must now, and in the future, be used and generated by nearly everyone in the corporation—particularly those with customer contact. Manufacturing operations have already addressed this problem. It is now being addressed for sales and marketing and, indeed, for the entire corporation.

To that end, continuing efforts to improve the technology base are under way. Technology platforms are being released that allow for greater user friendliness. We can expect more use of "windows" in applications to work with multiple data sets simultaneously, as well as more intuitive front-end systems and more focus on relational database technology to meet the need for flexibility and ease of use.

Other Issues

While the technology modeled above is absolutely necessary for a company to move ahead, it alone is not sufficient to ensure the success of sales and marketing productivity. The remaining concerns that must be addressed are the embedded psychosocial-cultural issues of the sales and marketing environment.

This model system will change the way that work is accomplished, measured, and shared. The human element becomes a critical and difficult factor in the implementation. Virtually all aspects of the sales and marketing function will be affected. Thus department goals, performance measurement, compensation, job descriptions, workflow, and organizational relationships are just a few of the nontechnology items that must be carefully evaluated in designing and implementing a sales and marketing system. This requires top-level corporate commitment.

The sales and marketing process is like a moving train with relentless timetables and quotas. The challenge of implementing a total sales and marketing productivity system is the equivalent of upgrading from an old steam engine to a new diesel locomotive while the train is not only moving but accelerating.

It is a process that does not happen overnight, nor without considerable investment of human and financial resources. It demands the assistance of experts who understand the corporate objectives, information systems technology, and sales and marketing, and who know how to bring about cultural change. Ideally, a company should select a phased-in approach that will deliver interim benefits at each step.

A component solution beginning to be seen in many companies is the use of teams to remove traditional barriers between their key functions and develop a corporate-wide perspective. Pioneered originally in the manufacturing environment to bring new products more quickly to market, the team approach is being used in the sales and marketing arena to bring together representatives of all potential system end users as well as people representing finance and information systems. The most successful teams include a senior line manager or representative. The project team is involved in everything from planning and design to the final stages of implementation and reports to senior management. Some teams also include a knowledgeable human resource participant.

How the System Can Increase Productivity

The success of a fully integrated and computerized sales and marketing system can be measured by its ability to increase productivity. To understand how this would work, consider:

1. How much more revenue would be generated from the customer base by identifying who the customers are, knowing at a glance their history, sharing all relevant contact data between sales channels, determining the decision makers, knowing which product they use, and selecting high-potential targets for mailings, telemarketing, and timely calls?

2. How much more new business would be generated from the prospect base by keeping track of all prospects, monitoring the sources of their inquiries, classifying their interests, ensuring coordinated follow-up, ranking their potential for mailing and calls, and recycling them when appropriate for future contact?

3. How much value would be added by identifying which products are selling, where, by whom, at what cost, and why and to whom sales were lost?

4. How many more opportunities would be recognized by identifying which markets are successful or unsuccessful, where, why, and how?

5. How much more return would be generated from the advertising and promotion budget by knowing the exact sales impact of each ad, promotion, or article and by completely testing and monitoring the sales impact of new promotional programs?

6. With McGraw-Hill Research reporting that the average salesperson spends only 25 percent of his or her workday in face-to-face selling (Laboratory of Advertising Performance/McGraw-Hill Research, 1986), how much would the sales volume per field salesperson increase if the company provided high-quality leads, support tools to manage accounts, time, territory, prospecting, and lead generation, a complete sales history for each account with personal notes on each sales situation, and personalized letters and on-call telemarketing support?

7. How much would the total sales volume increase by expanding the use and effectiveness of alternative sales channels:
    - By allowing telemarketing (in addition to accepting orders) to provide lead qualification and support for field sales, as well as targeted, proactive, new-account selling and add-on business to the customer base?
    - By providing direct marketing with a high-quality database, and the mechanisms to select high-potential targets, to offer follow-through by telemarketing and field sales for interest generated by mail, and to ensure that direct mail activities use the same pricing, product, and account information as other channels?
    - By providing distributors with qualified leads, coordinated joint promotional programs, telemarketing follow-through where appropriate, as well as reducing cross-channel conflict with field sales?

8. How much more accurate and complete would planning and control become by quantifying the results of all selling and promotional programs, measuring the strengths and weaknesses of each market and product, and determining why sales are being won and lost?

As each of these eight operations becomes more effective, incremental productivity gains accumulate and build on each other.

The companies today who are bringing information technology to their sales and marketing functions are beginning to eliminate much of the waste and inefficiency that catapult selling costs. By using technology to create the tools and showing sensitivity to the human issues that surround their acceptance, these companies are finding that increased efficiency can also encourage more effective sales and marketing efforts—with bottom-line results and market share increases that are critical for them.

References

Alex. Brown & Sons, Computer Services Group. *Computer Services Industry Overview: The Move to Mission Critical Systems—Up from the Slump.* Baltimore: Alex. Brown & Sons, 1986.

Buzzell, R. D. (ed.). *Marketing in an Electronic Age*. Boston: Harvard Business School Press, 1985.

Laboratory of Advertising Performance/McGraw-Hill Research. *Daily Activities of Industrial Salespeople—#1 of a Series*. No. 7023.2. New York: McGraw-Hill Research, 1986.

Marketing Communications Department. *Newsletter*. Minneapolis: Honeywell Corporation, 1985.

Porter, M. E., and Millar, V. E. "How Information Gives You Competitive Advantage." *Harvard Business Review*, 1985, *63* (4), 149–160.

Shapiro, B. P., and Wyman, J. "New Ways to Reach Your Customers." *Harvard Business Review*, 1981, *59* (4), 103–110.

"Survey of Selling Costs." *Sales and Marketing Management*, 1988, *140* (3) (entire issue).

Zuboff, S. *In the Age of the Smart Machine*. New York: Harper & Row, 1988.

20

CONCLUSION: CREATING THE PERFECTLY COMPETITIVE ORGANIZATION

RALPH H. KILMANN
INES KILMANN

In the introductory chapter of this book, we summarized the contents according to five key themes: creating new models of organizations and institutions, developing new linkages out of old categories, redefining the role of top management, developing global mindsets and competitive skills, and redefining organizational goals and performance assessments. At the close of that chapter, we suggested that one major challenge emerged that would be addressed here: how to design the "perfectly competitive organization" for the twenty-first century.

Network is a term used repeatedly throughout the book to describe the new form of organization for global competitiveness. It represents a highly elaborate but flexible system of interrelationships among organizational members and their associates around the world—held together by personal and electronic connections. These associates represent any external individual, group, organization, institution, or nation that can contribute to the company's value-added goals. In sharp contrast to the traditional company that focuses most of its attention on itself, the network organization highlights and explicitly develops cross-boundary relationships with its shifting environment. In a sense, the network organization integrates all the basic themes that have been presented in this book by designing an interrelated system of cooperation that will make any company more competitive.

In this concluding chapter we attempt to shed more light on the functioning of the network organization. First, we sum-

434

marize some of the work that has already been done on this topic. Many researchers, in fact, have examined how networks operate within small groups, within a formal organization, and across organizational boundaries. Second, we will suggest how the network organization differs from the traditional organization and why only a network organization can succeed in our increasingly dynamic, global economy. Third, we present our vision of the "perfectly competitive organization" as a way of integrating the key ingredients of the network organization. And fourth, given the traditional attributes of most organizations today, we offer one approach by which any organization can be transformed into a well-functioning network system.

The Nature of Networks

Moreno (1934) was one of the first researchers to study small groups as informal interrelationships among group members. By using the *sociometric* method — assessing who likes or dislikes whom or who wants to work with whom — a diagram can be developed that depicts the reported friendship circles or the work relationships among the members of the group. Several years later, Bavelas (1951) made use of the sociometric method to examine communication nets in small work groups. His research demonstrated that different networks (such as the circle or the star) have different effects on a group's performance of problem-solving tasks — independent of the persons in the group. Mackenzie (1966, 1976) developed one of the most elaborate models of small-group networks, based on the processes and structures that enable group members to complete various tasks.

The network approach was easily extended from small groups to informal organizations and then to formal organizational structures. McKelvey and Kilmann (1975) developed a sociometric assessment of members' task and people preferences (gathered via survey questionnaires) to form homogeneous clusters of autonomous groups (derived via factor analysis). This methodology, referred to as multivariate analysis, participation, and structure (MAPS), was then developed into a computer-based methodology for redesigning organizational structures and mobilizing problem-solving efforts (Kilmann, 1977).

In the 1980s, additional methods were developed to study the informal and formal networks inside large organizations. Brass (1984), for example, used questionnaire data to assess three types of organizational networks: workflow networks, communication networks, and friendship networks. Nelson (1988) further developed the "blockmodel" approach first proposed by White, Boorman, and Breiger (1976). Organizational members are grouped into "blocks" based on the similarities they share regarding various attributes of the network. Shrader, Lincoln, and Hoffman (1989), for example, analyzed an organization according to such network attributes as density of ties (the ratio of actual to potential relations among organizational members), connectivity (linkages among members through direct and indirect ties), clustering (the grouping of ties into subsets), and hierarchy (the degree of reciprocity and symmetry of power and control among member ties). Blockmodeling also allows for the examination of *multiple* networks within the same organization—for the purposes of diagnosing structure, identifying coalitions, and analyzing intergroup relationships (Nelson, 1988).

Regarding networks that span organizational boundaries, the literature on interorganizational relationships was molded by the studies of Levine and White (1961), Litwak and Hylton (1962), and Evan (1966), as further elaborated by Thompson (1967). Mandell (1984) examined interorganizational networks by drawing upon two additional sources: the population-ecology model (Aldrich and Whetten, 1981) and the resource-dependency model (Pfeffer and Salancik, 1978). Network analysis via open-ended interviews was used to track the interorganizational processes involved in completing a complex project—by examining various adaptive processes used by organizations that are interdependent with one another with respect to the acquisition and use of valued resources. Nelson (1986) applied a similar approach by collecting data through a mail survey to assess the decision-making network among the leaders of different organizations and institutions considering various programs of planned change. Johannisson (1987b) concluded that such cross-boundary networks are precisely what enables an entrepreneur to flourish—by creating disorder in the environment through circumventing formal structures so that new products, services, and technologies can be developed. Such is the case, for example, of a former employee—the entrepreneur—who leaves his job with a large organization to establish a separate firm that either complements or competes with his former employer through a new network with previous customers (Johnsson and Hagg, 1987).

Since all the approaches to understanding networks (within small groups, within organizations, and across organizational boundaries) focus on the *exchange* that occurs among network members, several researchers have sought to define the different dimensions and dynamics of the exchange process. Dunn and Ginsberg (1986) considered the different interpretations that network members place on their interactions, based on their frames of reference. They suggest a "sociocognitive" approach to understand the subjective meaning of networks before addressing the issue of formal measurement. McGuire (1988) also notes that many views of networks are incomplete, since they fail to consider the different interpretive systems that are operating in network exchanges. He suggests a dialectical approach for examining how different frames of reference produce conflicts, a strategy that eventually requires a synthesis (or acceptance) of contradictory views (and fundamental differences) among network members. Such a sociocognitive approach, emphasizing the social construction of reality, seems particularly useful when considering the many different frames of reference that are likely to be operating in interorganizational, let alone transnational, networks.

The constructs of power, influence, authority, and control are frequently considered in trying to understand the nature of organizational networks. While certainly subject to different interpretive schemes, as noted above, Astley and Sachdeva (1984) examine the power construct through both formal structures and social relationships. They suggest that power is endowed by hierarchical position, the capacity to obtain resources, and the centrality of an individual's (or group's) network position. Regarding the latter characteristic, it seems that a member's ability to integrate the different *workflows* in a complex organization is the key to power in network relationships. Further examining such "task-oriented" networks, Walker (1985) suggests five types of relationships that characterize network exchanges: reporting, information dependence, performance feedback, problem referral, and resource dependence. He finds that individual positions in the network (determined by clusters of similarity in members' experiencing the five types of relationships) have an important impact on cognition—whether members could see and, therefore, distinguish short-term versus long-term goals and product-developer versus product-user goals.

Hellgren and Stjernberg (1987) extend the study of influence and power to the realm of interorganizational networks. The position of an *organization* in a network is determined by its control over material resources (money, land), immaterial resources (time, knowledge, contacts), and authority (formal rules and regulations). The power and influence of an organization in the decision-making process (parallel to an individual's source of power) are determined by the extent to which the focal organization provides those things that are essential for the functioning of the whole network. Johanson and Mattsson (1987), while examining the "division of labor" within an interorganizational network, also suggest how bonds among member organizations (including decision-making influence) develop. They consider how technical, planning, knowledge, socioeconomic, and legal bonds form as a result of social, business, and information exchanges among member organizations. Oliver (1988) has examined interorganizational relations according to similar network exchanges: personal meetings, exchange of resources, common boards, joint programs, and written contracts. Similarly, Wiewel and Hunter (1985) have summarized the different types of resources that are exchanged in interorganizational networks: personnel, training, money, facilities, and information. Thorelli (1986) proposes that power, influence, money, and utilities flow along the links in a network, although he indicates that the flows of power and information may be more important than money and utilities.

In sum, then, even if various writers use somewhat different terms, concepts, and categories to research the kinds of things that are exchanged in a network of organizations, there do seem to be more similarities than differences in what they have learned thus far. Essentially, different members apply different frames of reference — mindsets — for making sense of their position, role, and function in the network organization. Furthermore, it seems that the power and *value* of an individual or organizational member are determined by a dynamic analysis of what that member adds to the network's current functioning and performance. By providing the necessary information, expertise, or resources (material or immaterial), the member — either an individual or organization — can apparently influence the outcome of key network decisions and actions. And this basis of influence and power is fundamentally different from decision making based on formal authority.

But Why Networks Now?

Several writers address the fundamental questions of why network organizations are being discussed so frequently and how these forms of organization approach the challenges of a competitive environment better than the traditional — bureaucratic — organization. Jarillo (1988) provides the most compelling explanation of why network organizations form and the conditions under which they are likely to survive. Starting from the economic theory of the firm as augmented by Williamson's (1975) examination of transaction costs, Jarillo considers the *internal* cost to perform a business function versus the *external* cost of having that work done outside. Only if the external cost is lower than the internal cost should a firm even consider developing a dependency relationship with another organization. But there is also a transaction cost incurred in the process of securing and maintaining that outside relationship. And this cost could drive the firm to retain the activity inside its own traditional boundaries — even if the external cost is less than the internal cost. Thus all three costs must be considered simultaneously: Only if the internal cost *plus* the transaction cost are less than the external cost would it be worthwhile for the firm to subcontract business functions outside its traditional borders.

Jarillo then points out that the existence of so many network arrangements in today's world seems to indicate that entrepreneurs are somehow able to *reduce* transaction costs by their past reputation and track record with such endeavors, their present trust-building activities, and their future commitments to network exchanges (versus being opportunistic at a given moment for their own personal gain at the expense of other network members). So long as the possibility of being permanently cut off from the network for opportunistic behavior (violations of trust) remains a credible outcome, an interorganizational network can become an ongoing, win/win scenario for all concerned—by distributing risks and rewards among all network members over an extended period of time.

Miles and Snow (1986) conclude that new interorganizational forms are arising in direct response to the challenges and opportunities in the external environment. They draw attention to the increasing evidence of joint ventures, subcontracting, and offshore operations. They define the emerging "dynamic" network as characterized by vertical disaggregation, the use of brokers, control through market mechanisms, and the advent of sophisticated information systems. They suggest that cross-organizational cooperation generates a *synergy* for the network that is greater than the efforts of the separate organizations constituting it. Such synergistic outcomes are virtually impossible to obtain if traditional, hierarchical organizations all compete with one another through separate strategies.

Likewise, Drake (1986) makes similar comparisons between the sluggish hierarchical firm and the dynamic network organization; Dow (1988) contrasts the old and new types of organization according to the configurational (hierarchy and administrative mechanisms) versus the coactivational view (dynamically processing resources and information); Dailey (1984) suggests that bureaucratic structures are analogous to a pedagogical education (teaching passive children) while interorganizational structures parallel an andragogical education (teaching mature adults).

It is interesting to note that most discussions today, as outlined here, describe the network organization in very positive terms while the traditional organization is depicted in disparaging ways. But putting aside the differences in tone and connotation as observers compare the characteristics and functioning of both types of organization, there does seem to be widespread agreement regarding certain attributes of the traditional organization: a well-defined management hierarchy — with the higher positions having more authority, information, and influence than the lower positions; a well-accepted way of dividing and assigning the work — manufacturing, finance, marketing, human resources, R & D (or whatever the standard organizing principles for the industry happen to be); and a well-ingrained mindset that views the ownership of assets as the boundary of the organization. It has been demonstrated repeatedly that such an organization is most efficient only when the environment is stable, predictable, protected, regulated, segmented, uniform, domestic, and familiar.

But circa 1980, as we now know, the nature of the world fundamentally changed — resulting from a conjoint technological and political revolution along the lines of "future shock" (Toffler, 1970). On the technological side of the revolution, the world became instantaneously accessible: With a personal computer (PC), modem, telephone, and facsimile (fax) nearby, the world is at one's fingertips. On the political side, the world became increasingly interconnected — due to the deregulation of many industries and the global competition for world markets. Forming *one* European economy in 1992 out of many diverse nations and peoples, for example, vividly demonstrates how all the traditional barriers, boundaries, and borders between organizations and nations are being transformed into one intertwined social reality. As this fragmentation of traditional institutions and nations continues, only a new social order — the network — can provide the necessary social structure (of linkages and nodes) for collective action in a dynamically interconnected world.

A Vision of the Network Organization

Now that we have surveyed the history of the network organization and explained why this form of organization can better
adapt to today's world, we can offer our vision of the "perfectly
competitive organization." This vision integrates many of the
ingredients of a well-functioning network that have been widely
observed and researched. We do not claim to have the final word
on the topic, only a modest extrapolation of how the network
organization might function in the twenty-first century.

In the new global environment, the perfectly competitive
organization consists of an interpersonal and electronic network of people, information, and influence. The nucleus, or
hub, of the organization is connected primarily (but not exclusively) through face-to-face relations among team members,
while interorganizational and international relations are connected electronically via PC-to-PC communications, fax trans-
missions, and the like.

The hub of the network organization represents the management of assets and a distinct competency: what the organization can do particularly well relative to its global competitors.
The outside links represent negotiated arrangements that extend the influence of the organization to other relevant business
functions: what others, referred to as associates, can do better
than the organization itself. Joint ventures, partnerships, associations, informal modes of cooperation, temporary deals
across traditional "walls" — all will become commonplace. Every
organization will have access to the entire world.

The hub is relatively small. It is centralized, local, based on
ownership of assets, and self-managed. Interaction takes place
in person. It focuses on a single function of excellence, which
provides the organization's *comparative* advantage. The extended
network is relatively large. It is decentralized, global, based on
control of resources, and negotiated. Interaction takes place
primarily on screen. It is designed for the multiple functions
that others can perform better than the hub itself, which provides the organization's *competitive* advantage.

The new challenge of organizational success is to simultaneously manage the face-to-face hub and the PC-to-PC links to form a holistic system of coordinated action. Making those two opposing — dialectical — elements work together places increasing demands on interpersonal skills such as trust building, collaborating, communicating, deal making, and negotiating, as well as on information management skills such as using new technology, searching out, processing, and analyzing information, and integrating data files.

Network organizations will replace traditional management hierarchies and typical functional areas with power distributed according to who at any time, in any place, has the relevant information to contribute to the task at hand. Influence in decision making, whether by full-time members in the hub or by their associates, is based on expertise and information power, not on formal authority, job description, or other irrelevant traditions.

To ensure such widespread reciprocal influence in decision making, the hub of the network organization has a rotating membership so that a larger set of persons (representing customers, governments, suppliers, manufacturers, banks, and other key stakeholders) internalize the strategic focus, cultural spirit, and global mindset needed to compete in the changing technological and political scene. The traditional division of *labor*, therefore, is replaced by the contemporary division of *knowledge* organized according to new categories: setting goals and benchmarking results, collecting strategic information, identifying customer needs, attracting resources, delivering new services, and keeping the paradoxical network together through whatever broker function seems appropriate.

A typical day in the life of a hub member might include a series of group meetings to address complex business problems with diverse experts. Although each specialist may have only a limited view of the whole situation, all the necessary wisdom to resolve any such problem is available to the group as a whole. To supplement these formal hub meetings, hub members turn to information technology. High-powered, portable PCs equipped with fax and teleconferencing capabilities connect with additional resources around the world — from centralized databases to people in other organizations and nations who have the needed expertise and information. (When contractual arrangements — instead of informal exchanges — are deemed necessary to reduce uncertainty or to satisfy legal requirements, multi-language software packages would facilitate the development of formal agreements across organizational and national boundaries.)

Lap-top PCs equipped with network connections add a new element of freedom to hub members. Other than the in-person hub meetings, the remaining tasks of each hub member's workday can be performed anytime, anywhere. Indeed, in some network organizations hub members might spend as little as one day a week in the office while the remainder of their time is spent on the road or at home. Instead of a physical place, the "office" becomes any convenient time when hub members convene a teleconferenced meeting. PC communications allow these meetings to draw on the same information resources available at the headquarters location, no matter where the members are.

Between formal meetings, all members of the hub would keep one another informed about various opportunities to improve the value of their organization through on-screen exchanges. But any time a problem becomes greater than the expertise of any one person, a group meeting is called to discuss — in person — the various viewpoints, opinions, and expert judgments that would be necessary to address the complex problem in question. Again, it is through an effective interpersonal process that synergy among diverse experts provides the basis for decision making and action taking. In effect, information technology is used to address focused search and specialized agreements, whereas interpersonal skills are used to resolve complex problems that transcend current technological limitations — that is, those cases in which people have the comparative advantage over technology. Thus to gain a competitive advantage for the network organization in managing its relations with the world, the network itself has to live according to its own principles: Do those things you can do best (a unique brand of complexity management) and network the rest (what can best be managed by existing channels, technologies, and other organizations).

Creating the Network Organization

While many organizations already possess some aspects of a network organization, the key ingredients are usually hidden, informal, and deemphasized in relation to traditional hierarchy, rigid functions, and narrow mindsets. In most cases, the challenge is to take what is already being done piecemeal — through the informal organization and various boundary-spanning efforts — and begin doing these same things more formally, regularly, visibly, and thoroughly throughout the organization and its environment.

Transforming a traditional organization into a network organization, moreover, requires a "completely integrated program." Since the world has become so interconnected, only an interconnected program of planned change can hope to bring a true network orientation to life. Isolated efforts at management training or restructuring may have been sufficient for fine-tuning autonomous organizations in a relatively stable world. Now, however, coordinated efforts are essential for improving interconnected organizations in a constantly changing world.

An extensive field has developed around the topics of planned change, organizational development, large-scale systems change, and corporate transformation. Since it would be impossible to review here all the work that has been done on changing and improving organizations, the reader is referred to Mohrman and others (1989), Quinn and Cameron (1988), and Kilmann, Covin, and Associates (1988) for descriptions of the numerous approaches to systems change and transformation. But in order to present at least one such approach to the topic, we will take the liberty of summarizing the methodology with which we are most familiar — our own. This is not to suggest that our approach is better or more deserving of attention than any other approach; it is simply more convenient to discuss at this time.

Our completely integrated program for transforming traditional organizations into network organizations is composed of five tracks: the culture track, the management skills track, the team-building track, the strategy-structure track, and the reward system track. (See Kilmann, 1989, for a detailed presentation of the theory and methodology behind this program.)

The first three tracks adjust the people side of the organization—the informal organization, how people interact with one another on the job. These tracks are designed to foster an effective, synergistic interchange among all hub members in their face-to-face discussions and to develop informal guidelines for PC-to-PC exchanges. The last two tracks adjust the formal side of the organization—the systems, resources, technologies, and documents that guide what hub members and their associates are supposed to do. The strategy-structure track determines where the organization is headed and how it will be organized into a network to get there. The reward system track sets the monetary and psychological compensation that participants will receive for their contributions. The sequential nature of the five tracks is critical to their useful implementation. Without first developing an effective hub via the first three tracks, any adjustments to the extended network in the last two tracks will be merely cosmetic, not fundamental, sustained, or successful.

The culture track is designed to enhance among all current members trust, communication, information sharing, and a willingness to change—all conditions that must exist before any long-term improvement effort can be sustained. It is interesting to note that Johannisson (1987a) places major emphasis on the symbolic and personal aspects of network exchanges in addition to the production—task-oriented—aspects. He suggests that the symbolic network is controlled by social norms that sanction conformity, which in turn fosters a "shared reality" among network members. Mutual trust, he argues, is the foundation of the personal network, which fosters not only affective bonds but productive exchanges as well. Wintrobe and Breton (1986) view the network of any organization as primarily rooted in trust. In fact, they conclude that the "black box" of organizational relationships may best be explained through the analysis of vertical and horizontal networks of *trust* — a key topic of discussion throughout the culture track.

The management skills track aims to give members new ways to cope with complex problems and hidden assumptions, including the development of interpersonal and information-management skills. Dailey (1984) explicitly considers the kind of educational experience — andragogy as opposed to pedagogy — that is essential for learning skills for a network organization (as compared with learning to survive in a traditional organization). Just as the network itself must foster flexible, responsive, trusting, adaptive, collaborative, and responsible behavior, the learning experience to *acquire* these skills must similarly be relaxed, trusting, mutually respectful, informal, warm, collaborative, supportive, and flexible.

The team-building track is intended to instill the new culture and updated skills in everyday practice — both within the hub itself and between the hub and the extended network — so that crucial problems will be addressed with all the wisdom and expertise available. Thus whatever is learned in a relaxed workshop setting must ultimately be transferred back to the workplace so that everyone *behaves* according to the principles and practices of the program. Virtually every observer stresses the role of cooperation, teamwork, and joint problem-solving efforts as essential to the success of the network — especially when formal authority, rules and procedures, and market mechanisms are not sufficient to dictate interorganizational decisions and actions.

In the strategy-structure track, the organization develops either a new or a revised strategic plan for the future and then aligns current members, present associates, and potential future associates into an effective network of cooperation. This structure — including information technology, plans, procedures, and the allocation of resources — is designed to keep the talent and energy of the informal organization on course. Venkatraman and Camillus (1984), building on the work of Fombrun and Astley (1983), recognize a new area for strategic management: developing a collective strategy for a network of interorganizational relationships. Forming strategic networks across organizational boundaries and then designing new structural arrangements that fit the new collective strategy add an extra dimension to traditional strategy-structure (within-firm) alignments. Thorelli (1986) suggests that the position of an organization in a network represents "structure" while the links or interpositional relationships among organizations resemble "strategy." He notes that such a perspective on organizational interdependence, which he terms "network thinking," significantly alters the strategy–structure–performance model of the autonomous organization that has been postulated by the classic—traditional—theory of the firm.

The strategic plan, when aligned with a well-conceived structure, also facilitates measures of performance that capture the true and complete contribution of each *individual* in the network organization and each *organization* in the interorganizational network. Essentially, the reward system track calls for members to establish a performance-based incentive system that also sanctions the network's new culture, updated skills, and cooperative orientation. Companies must be sure to assess and reward both short-term performance results and long-term behavioral contributions (for example, to encourage trust building and collaboration among all members of the network).

It is somewhat surprising to note, however, that virtually no attention has been given to the design and development of a collective reward system that would increase the likelihood of sustaining the success of a well-functioning network. While some of the customary reward practices in the traditional organization may no longer apply, it seems important to consider new ways of assessing interorganizational performance and then distributing rewards to members who have contributed to that end. Certainly this would be a more proactive approach to providing network incentives than simply allowing external market mechanisms and short-term opportunism to run their course, often at the expense of long-term, systemwide benefits (Jarillo and Ricart, 1987).

Scheduling the five tracks requires careful use of personnel and time. Companies must decide who will be involved in each track, how often their participation will be required, and for how long. Whether a focal organization should begin with transformation itself — before attempting to involve other organizations in the purposeful design of an interorganizational network — is another matter to consider at the outset. For convenience we now summarize some of the logistical aspects of the five tracks applied to a single organizational unit. Expanding the effort across organizational boundaries makes the logistics more complex but, conceptually at least, the process remains the same.

Ensuring every member's extensive involvement in the whole program of transformation is the only way to change an ingrained — traditional — corporate culture. Therefore, the culture track typically includes all current members at all levels and areas in the organization or designated business unit. Members attend off-site workshop discussions one day a month for three to six months. In these monthly workshops, the members gradually extinguish outdated cultural norms such as "Don't share information with other groups" while they continually reinforce new cultural norms like "Provide timely and accurate information to all members and associates."

Because it takes months to create an open and trusting culture — at least until the team-building track is initiated — companies should subdivide work groups into peer groups for each workshop in the culture track. To provide the best opportunity for a candid and forthright conversation, these peer groups should be formed by separating superiors from their subordinates. A bit later (in the team-building track), former superiors and subordinates will become partners or associates — based on the information, expertise, and mutual influence needed to solve complex problems rather than formal authority, rules, and regulations.

The management skills track involves everyone in the organization or network who plays a significant role in the decision-making process. Traditionally this meant only supervisory personnel from first-line supervisors to the chief executive officer. Now, however, virtually everyone — whether a person has direct reports or not — is a manager of information and decision making. Everyone attends additional off-site workshop sessions conducted one day a month for three to six months. In these sessions, they use cases, exercises, and instruments to develop the critical skills needed to define and solve complex problems through face-to-face meetings and electronic exchanges. Just as in the culture track, however, all group discussions take place in peer groups to foster open communication and information sharing before the culture has changed.

The team-building track reunites "superiors" with the "subordinates" for on-site work group meetings in their formal organizational units. To ensure that the new knowledge gained from the off-site sessions is transferred directly and completely into the everyday life of the new organization, the on-site meetings should be held at least once a month until the network organization is fully operational. In these team-building sessions, the participants use process observers and constructive feedback to learn how to apply the lessons of the first two tracks to their business and technical problems. Gradually, a partnership develops that makes it difficult for any stranger to detect who is the boss and who are the subordinates. Influence at group meetings is based on knowledge, not authority.

The company must be careful not to initiate the team-building track too soon. If it brings together superiors and subordinates before fully internalizing the new culture and skills, almost everyone will fall back on the norms and practices of the traditional organization: working to support old fiefdoms, involving only similarly minded members in the decision-making process, and withholding the vital information needed to produce the best solution to a complex problem. It takes time in a relatively safe environment for people to learn the new mindsets, behavior, and skills they need for approaching network decisions in new ways.

The last two tracks involve the formation of two separate task forces (networks of people, information, and influence) with about twenty-five members each. One task force addresses strategy-structure while the other handles the reward system. The people chosen for these special missions must represent all former levels and areas of the traditional organization. More than that, they must include the associates of the newly forming network organization, such as representatives of consumer groups, suppliers, universities, government agencies, community organizations, and so on. These task force meetings should continue for several hours each week over several months (through both face-to-face meetings and PC-to-PC exchanges), making use of the informal organization established in the first three tracks.

Following their deliberations, the task force members present to the key decision-making group (a representative board of organizational members) their recommendations for designing the organization's strategy-structure and reward system into a well-functioning network organization. Once these plans for refocus and redesign are approved, these groups will play a key role in implementing the changes they have recommended.

The Challenge

Making the transition from a traditional organization to a network organization requires a well-orchestrated approach with sufficient time and effort devoted to each track. The first three tracks provide the foundation for the full utilization of the organization's human resources. The last two tracks serve a dual purpose: They make an ideal forum for designing the new organization, and they offer the first taste of how the network organization will work in practice.

The twenty-first century will be full of organizational surprises. But the essential process for arranging cooperative efforts to achieve a strategic mission is already emerging: equal opportunity to link with anyone in the world, to connect people and information for comparative and competitive advantage, to add value by creating products and services with new associations, and to influence the definition and experience of human relationships. Because this instantaneously accessible world makes it easy to acquire capital and copy new products, services, and technologies, the perfectly competitive organization must nurture its unique culture and the quality of its human resources above all else — they are its only renewable assets. The particular way a network organization makes decisions and acts (what gets done face-to-face and how, what gets done electronically and how) cannot easily be copied or implanted within another organization. Ultimately, what makes each network organization a sustained value-added partnership is analogous to what makes each individual in the universe unique—its essential character, mindset, and manner of coping with changed circumstances.

References

Aldrich, H., and Whetten, D. A. "Organization Sets, Action Sets, and Networks: Making the Most of Simplicity." In P. Nystrum and W. H. Starbuck (eds.), *Handbook of Organizational Design*. Vol. 1. London: Oxford University Press, 1981.

Astley, W. G., and Sachdeva, P. S. "Structural Sources of Intraorganizational Power: A Theoretical Synthesis." *Academy of Management Review*, 1984, *9* (1), 104–113.

Bavelas, A. "Communication Patterns in Task Oriented Groups." In H. Lasswell and D. Lerner (eds.), *The Policy Sciences*. Stanford, Calif.: Stanford University Press, 1951.

Brass, D. J. "Being in the Right Place: A Structural Analysis of Individual Influence in an Organization." *Administrative Science Quarterly*, 1984, *29* (4), 518–539.

Carroll, G. R., Goodstein, J., and Gyenes, A. "Organizations and the State: Effects of the Institutional Environment on Agricultural Cooperatives in Hungary." *Administrative Science Quarterly*, 1988, *33* (2), 233–256.

Dailey, N. "Adult Learning and Organizations." *Training and Development Journal*, 1984, *38* (12), 64–68.

Dow, G. K. "Configurational and Coactivational Views of Organizational Structure." *Academy of Management Review*, 1988, *13* (1), 53–64.

Drake, R. L. "Innovative Structures for Managing Change." *Planning Review*, 1986, *14* (6), 18–22.

Dunn, W. N., and Ginsberg, A. "A Sociocognitive Network Approach to Organizational Analysis." *Human Relations*, 1986, *40* (11), 955–976.

Evan, W. M. "The Organization-Set: Toward a Theory of Interorganizational Relations." In J. D. Thompson (ed.), *Approaches to Organization Design*. Pittsburgh, Pa.: University of Pittsburgh Press, 1966.

Fombrun, C., and Astley, W. G. "Beyond Corporate Strategy." *Journal of Business Strategy*, 1983, *3* (4), 47–54.

Hellgren, B., and Stjernberg, T. "Networks: An Analytical Tool for Understanding Complex Decision Processes." *International Studies of Management and Organization*, 1987, *17* (1), 88–102.

Jarillo, J. C. "On Strategic Networks." *Strategic Management Journal*, 1988, *9* (1), 31–41.

Jarillo, J. C., and Ricart, J. E. "Sustaining Networks." *Interfaces*, 1987, *17* (5), 82–91.

Johannisson, B. "Beyond Process and Structure: Social Exchange Networks." *International Studies of Management and Organization*, 1987a, *17* (1), 3–23.

Johannisson, B. "Anarchists and Organizers: Entrepreneurs in a Network Perspective." *International Studies of Management and Organization*, 1987b, *17* (1), 49–63.

Johanson, J., and Mattsson, L. "Interorganizational Relations in Industrial Systems: A Network Approach Compared with the Transaction-Cost Approach." *International Studies of Management and Organization*, 1987, *17* (1), 34–48.

Johnsson, T., and Hagg, I. "Extrapreneurs Between Markets and Hierarchies." *International Studies of Management and Organization*, 1987, *17* (1), 64–74.

Kilmann, R. H. *Social Systems Design: Normative Theory and the MAPS Design Technology*. New York: Elsevier North-Holland, 1977.

Kilmann, R. H. *Managing Beyond the Quick Fix: A Completely Integrated Program for Creating and Maintaining Organizational Success*. San Francisco: Jossey-Bass, 1989.

Kilmann, R. H., Covin, T. J., and Associates. *Corporate Transformation: Revitalizing Organizations for a Competitive World*. San Francisco: Jossey-Bass, 1988.

Kilmann, R. H., Pondy, L. R., and Slevin, D. P. (eds.). *The Management of Organization Design*. 2 vols. New York: Elsevier North-Holland, 1976.

Levine, S., and White, P. F. "Exchange as a Conceptual Framework for the Study of Interorganizational Relations." *Administrative Science Quarterly*, 1961, *5*, 583–601.

Litwak, E., and Hylton, L. F. "Interorganizational Analysis: A Hypothesis on Coordinating Agencies." *Administrative Science Quarterly*, 1962, *6*, 395–420.

McGuire, J. B. "A Dialectical Analysis of Interorganizational Networks." *Journal of Management*, 1988, *14* (1), 109–124.

McKelvey, B., and Kilmann, R. H. "Organization Design: A Participative Multivariate Approach." *Administrative Science Quarterly*, 1975, *20* (1), 24–36.

Mackenzie, K. D. "Structural Centrality in Communication Networks." *Psychometrika*, 1966, *31* (1), 17–25.

Mackenzie, K. D. *A Theory of Group Structures*. 2 vols. New York: Gordon and Breach, 1976.

Mandell, M. "Application of Network Analysis to the Implementation of a Complex Project." *Human Relations*, 1984, *37* (8), 659–679.

Miles, R. E. "Adapting to Technology and Competition: A New Industrial Relations System for the Twenty-First Century." *California Management Review*, 1989, *31* (2), 9–28.

Miles, R. E., and Snow, C. C. "Organizations: New Concepts for New Forms." *California Management Review*, 1986, *28* (3), 62–73.

Mohrman, A. M., Jr., and others. *Large-Scale Organizational Change*. San Francisco: Jossey-Bass, 1989.

Moreno, J. L. *Who Shall Survive?* Washington, D.C.: Nervous and Mental Disease Publishing, 1934.

Nelson, R. E. "Social Networks and Organizational Interventions: Insights from an Area-Wide Labor-Management Committee." *Journal of Applied Behavioral Science*, 1986, *22* (1), 65–76.

Nelson, R. E. "Social Network Analysis as Intervention Tool." *Group and Organization Studies*, 1988, *13* (1), 39–58.

Oliver, C. "The Collective Strategy Framework: An Application to Competing Predictions of Isomorphism." *Administrative Science Quarterly*, 1988, *33* (4), 543–561.

Pfeffer, J., and Salancik, G. R. *The External Control of Organizations:*

A Resource-Dependence Perspective. New York: Harper & Row, 1978.

Quinn, R. E., and Cameron, K. S. (eds.). *Paradox and Transformation: Toward a Theory of Change in Organization and Management.* Cambridge, Mass.: Ballinger, 1988.

Shrader, C. B., Lincoln, J. R., and Hoffman, A. N. "The Network Structures of Organizations: Effects of Task Contingencies and Distributional Form." *Human Relations,* 1989, *42* (1), 43–66.

Thompson, J. D. *Organizations in Action.* New York: McGraw-Hill, 1967.

Thorelli, H. B. "Networks: Between Markets and Hierarchies." *Strategic Management Journal,* 1986, *7* (1), 37–51.

Toffler, A. *Future Shock.* New York: Bantam Books, 1970.

Venkatraman, N., and Camillus, J. C. "Exploring the Concept of 'Fit' in Strategic Management." *Academy of Management Review,* 1984, *9* (3), 513–525.

Walker, G. "Network Position and Cognition in a Computer Software Firm." *Administrative Science Quarterly,* 1985, *30* (1), 103–130.

White, H., Boorman, S., and Breiger, R. L. "Social Structure from Multiple Networks: 1. Blockmodels of Roles and Positions." *American Journal of Psychology,* 1976, *81*, 730–780.

Wiewel, W., and Hunter, A. "The Interorganizational Network as a Resource: A Comparative Case Study on Organizational Genesis." *Administrative Science Quarterly,* 1985, *30* (4), 482–496.

Williamson, O. *Markets and Hierarchies: Analysis and Antitrust Implications.* New York: Free Press, 1975.

Wintrobe, R., and Breton, A. "Organizational Structure and Productivity." *American Economic Review,* 1986, *76* (3), 530–538.

NAME INDEX

457

SUBJECT INDEX

A

Acquisition, and development strategy, 66–67

Advantage. *See* Competitive advantage

AEG (Germany), and acquisitions, 66

Afernod, in triadic system, 311

Agency of Industrial Science and Technology (Japan), 292–293

Alex. Brown & Sons, 420, 433

Algeria, strategic success in, 45–46, 48

Alliances: and network organizations, 71; for recovery, 59–60

Allis-Chalmers, in triadic system, 311

American Airlines: people costs at, 134; and quality, 165–166

American Federation of Labor (AFL), 329

American Hospital Supply, and human resources, 143

American Management Association, 408, 416

Anheuser-Busch, and quality, 166–167

Apollo Moon Project, macroleadership for, 209

Apple Computer: and macroleadership, 208; and prices, 21; and strategic responsiveness, 29

Appraisal, in human resources, 138–139, 141, 144, 147

Arizona State University, in consortium, 358

Artificial intelligence (AI): and information technology, 86; impact of, 113

AT&T, divestiture of, 159, 298

Automation, for integrated sales and marketing, 419–433

B

Bank of America, decision making at, 288, 298, 301

Banks A and B, goal setting at, 271–272, 274, 278, 282, 285

Banks, international, and multinational corporations, 316

Baxter Travenol, and human resources, 143

BBC, in triadic system, 311

Beatrice, people costs at, 133

Bechtel, financial engineering from, 317, 323

BL Ltd., in triadic system, 311

Black & Decker, market area for, 98–99

Blockmodeling, and networks, 436

Board of directors, structure of, 179–181

Boeing: and education, 223; in triadic system, 311